As a mother of five and a respected pediatrician, Dr. Marianne Neifert understands the needs and concerns of new mothers. Now she shares her knowledge in an authoritative new guide that answers all your questions and tells you what to expect:

- Why breastfeed?
- What are the advantages of breastfeeding over formula feeding?
- How can I prepare for breastfeeding before the baby arrives?
- Does breast size or appearance affect my ability to nurse?
- What can I expect during the first weeks of breastfeeding?
- What are the most common breastfeeding problems and their solutions?
- What effect will breastfeeding have on my partner and our sex life?
- How can I continue to breastfeed after returning to work?
- What's involved in breastfeeding a premature or high-risk infant?
- How common is insufficient milk and what can I do about it?

MARIANNE NEIFERT, M.D., is a pediatrician and lactation specialist, and the author of *Dr. Mom* and *Dr. Mom's Parenting Guide*. In addition to writing for *Parenting* and *Baby Talk* magazines, and lecturing to health professionals nationwide, she is Medical Consultant to the HealthONE Lactation Program at Rose Medical Center in Denver. She has over 20 years experience as a lactation specialist, has conducted breastfeeding research and published articles in the medical literature, serves on the Health Advisory Council of La Leche League International, and started one of the first breastfeeding referral centers in the United States. She lives in Denver, Colorado.

Also by Marianne Neifert, M.D.

Dr. Mom: A Guide to Baby and Child Care

Dr. Mom's Parenting Guide:
Commonsense Guidance for the Life of Your Child

DR. MOM'S

 Guide to

Breastfeeding

MARIANNE NEIFERT, M.D.

A PLUME BOOK

PLUME
Published by the Penguin Group
Penguin Putnam Inc., 375 Hudson Street, New York, New York 10014, U.S.A.
Penguin Books Ltd, 27 Wrights Lane, London W8 5TZ, England
Penguin Books Australia Ltd, Ringwood, Victoria, Australia
Penguin Books Canada Ltd, 10 Alcorn Avenue, Toronto, Ontario, Canada M4V 3B2
Penguin Books (N.Z.) Ltd, 182–190 Wairau Road, Auckland 10, New Zealand

Penguin Books Ltd, Registered Offices: Harmondsworth, Middlesex, England

First published by Plume, an imprint of Dutton NAL, a member of Penguin Putnam Inc.

First Printing, November, 1998
10 9 8 7 6 5 4 3 2 1

A NOTE TO THE READER
The ideas, procedures, and suggestions contained in this book are not intended as a substitute for medical treatment by a physician. The reader should regularly consult a physician in matters relating to health.

 REGISTERED TRADEMARK—MARCA REGISTRADA

LIBRARY OF CONGRESS CATALOGING-IN-PUBLICATION DATA

Neifert, Marianne R.
   Dr. mom's guide to breastfeeding / Marianne Neifert.
     p.   cm.
   ISBN 0-452-27990-9
   1. Breast feeding—Popular works. I. Title.
  RJ216.N43   1998
649'.33—dc21
                    98-19125
                    CIP

Printed in the United States of America
Set in Sabon
Designed by Leonard Telesca

BOOKS ARE AVAILABLE AT QUANTITY DISCOUNTS WHEN USED TO PROMOTE PRODUCTS OR SERVICES. FOR INFORMATION PLEASE WRITE TO PREMIUM MARKETING DIVISION, PENGUIN PUTNAM INC., 375 HUDSON STREET, NEW YORK, NEW YORK 10014.

*This book is dedicated to the
cherished memory of my mother—
Mary Annabel Egeland—
and her enduring love.*

ACKNOWLEDGMENTS

I gratefully acknowledge the many individuals, breastfeeding pairs, and families who contributed to this work, either directly or by their significant influence on me:

My beloved husband, Larry; our extraordinary five grown children (Peter, Paige, Tricie, Heather, and Mark); and our precious daughters-in-law (Courtney and Becky), for being my primary circle of love and sustenance;

My devoted father (Andrew Egeland); esteemed siblings (Andy Egeland, Marcy Poncelow, Aleta Boylan, and Tom Egeland); and my wonderful extended family, for encouraging and uplifting me;

Joy M. Seacat, Ph.D., P.A., R.N., my longtime friend and colleague, for cofounding the Lactation Program in Denver and for discerning with me the art and the science of breastfeeding;

The numerous support staff and clinicians who have worked at the Lactation Program since its inception in 1985, for their important contribution;

Amy Lutz, R.N., I.B.C.L.C., Anne Merrill, R.N., I.B.C.L.C., and Stacey Levin, R.N., I.B.C.L.C., the most recent Lactation Program clinical staff, for their competent and compassionate care and exceptional dedication;

Presbyterian/St. Luke's Medical Center in Denver, for their longtime support of the Lactation Program;

HealthONE Foundation, which now sponsors the Lactation Program, and Rose Medical Center, which provides office space, for their commitment to breastfeeding;

Lisbeth Gabrielski, R.N., B.S.N., I.B.C.L.C., Betty Heerman, R.N., C.L.E., Martha Illige-Saucier, M.D., Nancy Krebs, M.D., R.D., Debbie Montgomery, R.D., M.P.H., and other key members of the Colorado Breastfeeding Task Force, who challenge and inspire me to keep breastfeeding promotion a high priority;

Betty Crase, I.B.C.L.C., Amy Lutz, R.N., I.B.C.L.C., Anne Merrill, R.N., I.B.C.L.C., Sherry Lyons, M.A., Debbie Montgomery, R.D., M.P.H., and Amy Spangler, B.S.N., M.N., I.B.C.L.C., for graciously reviewing the manuscript and providing valuable feedback.

The knowledgeable and committed colleagues representing the American Academy of Pediatrics Work Group on Breastfeeding and the Academy of Breastfeeding Medicine, for their collective expertise and enlightened efforts on behalf of breastfeeding;

La Leche League International, for indelibly influencing both my mothering and my professional career;

The thousands of health professionals who have attended my breastfeeding lectures nationwide, for keeping me energized by their enthusiasm and feedback;

Faith Hamlin, my capable literary agent, for unwavering support and faith in me;

Deborah Brody, Senior Editor at Dutton Plume, for supreme patience and expert guidance;

Tim Burkhardt, for his superb illustrations that greatly enhance the book, and Kim Fiedler, for her graphic artwork;

The countless breastfeeding mothers who have influenced this book, for sharing their personal stories that spurred me to pursue the causes, treatment, and prevention of breastfeeding problems;

My heartfelt thanks is extended to the many others who have collectively taught me about the art and the heart of breastfeeding.

Contents

Introduction

The content of this book is based on the firsthand joys of nursing my own five babies and the knowledge and experience gained in more than twenty years of helping new mothers reach their breast-feeding goals. I first began dealing with the concerns of breast-feeding women as a young pediatric intern and resident who was having and nursing my own babies while completing my medical training. The birth of my fifth child on the final day of my pediatric residency represented both the completion of my family and the culmination of my long preparation for a medical career. As I weighed the several attractive professional offers that immediately awaited me, I intuitively knew that each option under considera-tion would mean another abbreviated course of breastfeeding, another babyhood laid at the altar of medicine. "Not this time," I vowed. "This time must be different. This final babyhood must be savored, not sacrificed. This breastfeeding experience must be unhurried, not hassled." And so this time, I made the decision to place my baby's needs and my heart's desire first by changing my priorities and my lifestyle to accommodate unrestricted breast-feeding. This time, I took an adequate maternity leave, returned to work part-time, and joined La Leche League (LLL) to bolster my chances of success. That decision not only changed my mothering experience, it profoundly impacted my career.

Some months later, I launched my medical career as a faculty member in the Department of Pediatrics at University of Colorado School of Medicine while fully breastfeeding my last baby. National breastfeeding rates were starting to soar after several decades of predominant bottle-feeding practices. Perhaps because I was a female pediatrician and an experienced nursing mother, breastfeeding women increasingly sought my help to overcome common and unique lactation difficulties. My interest in breastfeeding mounted as I continued to nurse my own baby, attend LLL meetings, and voraciously read everything I could find about the advantages of human milk, the physiology of lactation, and the management of breastfeeding.

The number of breastfeeding women seeking my advice steadily grew, and before long inquiries were arising from out of state. I began lecturing on breastfeeding nationwide, eventually speaking in forty-five states and several foreign countries. I became involved in breastfeeding research and published in the medical literature some findings concerning insufficient milk and other breastfeeding management issues. I coedited a medical textbook on lactation and became a Medical Associate, and eventually a member of the Health Advisory Council, of LLL. In 1985, my colleague Joy Seacat, Ph.D., P.A., R.N., and I cofounded the Lactation Program at St. Luke's Hospital in Denver to serve as a model of comprehensive breastfeeding clinical services, education, and research.

The motivated women who sought consultation at the Lactation Program often lamented that breastfeeding was supposed to be natural, yet it hadn't proceeded naturally for them. A wide discrepancy was apparent between women's stated breastfeeding goals and the duration of breastfeeding they actually achieved. I encountered a variety of maternal and infant breastfeeding difficulties, including mother-baby separation due to premature birth and infant illness, infant latch-on and sucking problems, sore nipples and breast engorgement, inadequate infant weight gain, low milk supply, breast infections, breast surgery, and more. Typically, women reported receiving little help for breastfeeding problems from their own or their baby's doctor. Worse yet, they had received little validation for the loss of their anticipated breastfeeding experience, and many women wept as they voiced their deep disappointment.

While seeking effective interventions for specific clinical problems, I remained keenly interested in the origin of women's difficulties and in learning how they might have been avoided altogether or recognized and remedied sooner. Every problem to be solved for a particular breastfeeding pair became a problem to be prevented in all those who followed. Learning how things could go wrong actually helped me refine a prescription for success. The journey has been characterized by learning many new truths, unlearning some mistaken beliefs, and periodically relearning a few valuable principles that I had forgotten or taken for granted. My constant challenge has been to balance the message that breastfeeding is natural and convenient with the reality that mother-baby pairs sometimes encounter difficulties that jeopardize breastfeeding success. Fortunately, such difficulties often can be anticipated and avoided.

In December 1997, just as I was putting the finishing touches on this manuscript, the American Academy of Pediatrics (AAP) released a new, updated breastfeeding policy statement—"Breastfeeding and the Use of Human Milk." I had had the privilege and honor of serving on the AAP Work Group that crafted this document, with its powerful conclusion that breastfeeding is primary to achieving the best possible health, development, and psychosocial outcomes for the infant. The strongly worded policy cited recent convincing research to document the nutritional, immunologic, health, developmental, economic, and environmental advantages of breastfeeding over other feeding options. It also offered recommended practices to promote breastfeeding success and endorsed breastfeeding for the first year of life and longer.

A flurry of media coverage ensued, with breastfeeding being featured on the *Today Show*, *ABC World News Tonight*, CNN, *Morning Edition* of National Public Radio, the front page of *USA Today*, the Associated Press, United Press International, Reuters, the *Los Angeles Times*, *Washington Post*, *Chicago Tribune*, and *Time* magazine. This long overdue national attention paid to the importance of breastfeeding was indeed gratifying. But the news coverage was marred at times when the media distorted the spirit and content of the policy statement. For example, the recommendation that newborns should be nursed approximately eight to twelve times in twenty-four hours for ten to fifteen minutes per breast was twisted into a defeating headline: "Pediatricians Advise Up to 6 Hours a Day of Breastfeeding For a Year."

Among the many media inquiries I received were a number of

calls from reporters who opened their interview with disparaging remarks like, "Get real." "This document actually made me laugh." "Who can possibly achieve these recommendations in today's society?" It seems that some reporters, upon reading the new policy statement, chose to view breastfeeding as a maternal sentence to be served rather than as a precious and selfless gift to be offered to one's baby and as a reverent rite of motherhood. They were convinced that contemporary new mothers, the majority of whom return to work during their baby's first year, are logistically unable to achieve these ideal infant-feeding recommendations and are doomed to feel guilty and inadequate. A representative for the National Organization for Women stated that the guidelines will present a problem for new mothers who must return to work.

As I reflected on how to answer these challenges, I recalled my own breastfeeding experiences and the countless stories I have been privileged to hear from nursing mothers who have sought help to breastfeed successfully. I personally resented the negative advice of well-meaning, but uninformed, individuals who counseled me against trying to breastfeed under my difficult circumstances as medical student, intern, and resident. On the other hand, I will always be grateful to those who not only acknowledged that breastfeeding was best but also provided me with specific information about how to overcome the barriers I faced and how to modify my lifestyle to achieve the success I sought.

This book will assure you that meeting ideal breastfeeding recommendations is both possible and realistic. To suggest that contemporary women are uniquely unable to do what women have accomplished throughout history is to rob them of the opportunity to experience the intimacy, fulfillment, and esteem that comes from successful breastfeeding. *Dr. Mom's Guide to Breastfeeding* is a blueprint for attaining your breastfeeding goals, a practical guide to help you achieve the success you desire and deserve so you can one day look back on your breastfeeding experience with infinite pride and satisfaction.

Let me make a few suggestions about how to read this book. Because your baby will never be easier to care for than during your pregnancy, I urge you to read at least the first six chapters before you give birth. You will want to refer to chapters 4 and 5 again when you begin breastfeeding. They are chock full of advice about proper breastfeeding technique and expected norms. Next, I encourage you to review chapter 6 once you get settled into your breastfeeding routines. You'll find that reading is relatively easy while nursing. You can refer to chapter 7 for solutions to specific breastfeeding problems as they arise. If you anticipate working outside the home, read chapter 8 during your pregnancy or shortly after delivery. You'll want to review it at least a month before going back to work. An in-depth discussion of the complex and frustrating problem of insufficient milk can be found in chapter 9. Chapter 10 is directed to women who give birth to sick or premature infants who must remain hospitalized. If you have a high-risk pregnancy, you will want to check out this information before you deliver. Chapter 11 is devoted to special circumstances, including breastfeeding twins, breastfeeding through a pregnancy, adoptive nursing, the impact of breast surgery on breastfeeding, and illness in the breastfeeding mother or infant. Chapter 12 covers continued breastfeeding into the toddler period and the unique process of weaning.

Because breastfeeding involves both art and science, and because every mother-baby pair is unique, breastfeeding advice sometimes varies among well-meaning lactation experts. I have shared in this book the knowledge and experience I have gained and the management strategies that I have found effective for other women. In some instances, you may hear different approaches from the lactation consultants and breastfeeding counselors whose help you seek. I acknowledge that there is often more than one approach to a problem, and I trust you to tailor differing advice to your unique circumstances.

Few memories bring me as much joy as the recollection of breastfeeding my five babies. While the circumstances were far from ideal, each breastfeeding experience was enormously rewarding. I can never sufficiently thank those who made this exquisite privilege possible: the army nurse I can't name who got my firstborn latched on after four days of exclusive bottle-feeding in the nursery due to his severe jaundice; the individual who taught me to hand express my milk when I had to go home without my second baby who remained hospitalized due to jaundice; the administrator in the registrar's office who allowed me to rearrange my medical school clinical rotations to allow me a glorious maternity leave after my third child was born; the revered faculty mentor who convinced me that the two-week maternity leave I was to receive during my internship was sheer insanity and who gave me the courage to ask for more time; and finally, the La Leche League mothers and leaders who not only taught me an enormous amount of factual knowledge about breastfeeding but also gave me the modeling and support I needed to finally enjoy the full, natural course of unrestricted breastfeeding with my fifth and last child. It is in partial repayment of that debt of gratitude that I wrote this book to help a new generation of mothers and babies experience the timeless and matchless gift of a mother's love—breastfeeding.

Chapter 1

Why Breastfeed?

Every expectant or new mother thinks about providing the material necessities for her baby that we have come to associate with modern infant care, including furniture, clothes, and convenience items. But the truth is, babies have been raised for thousands of years without benefit of luxuries like changing tables, deluxe strollers, hooded baby towels, or colorful sleepers. No material gift that can be purchased for your baby will ever be as significant as the gift of yourself. As you prepare for parenthood, remember that only a mother can give her baby the priceless gift of superior nutrition, improved health, optimal development, and unique intimacy that comes from the decision to breastfeed. Is it worth it? The answer is a resounding "yes!"

The advantages of breastfeeding compared to formula-feeding are numerous, diverse, and convincing. These advantages extend not only to babies but to their mothers, families, and society. One might assume that the merits of breastfeeding would be widely recognized and enthusiastically promoted within families, the health care system, and the greater community. The truth is that the advantages of breastfeeding must be rediscovered by each new generation of parents. While the marketing of infant formulas represents a lucrative industry, human milk attracts little commercial interest. Expectant parents get bombarded with advertising from infant formula companies, while the promotion of breastfeeding depends largely on testimonials from other mothers and the endorsement of enlightened health professionals. Breastfeeding proponents may not have any slick ads or a big advertising budget, but nothing has yet been manufactured by man that can compete with the natural benefits breastfeeding can provide your baby, yourself, and your family.

Infant Advantages of Breastfeeding

In my experience, the numerous health benefits to infants are the chief reasons parents give for choosing to breastfeed. Prospective parents who are informed about the compelling arguments in favor of breastfeeding usually are motivated to give nursing a try. After all, what parent doesn't want the very best for his or her baby? An in-depth discussion of the advantages of breastfeeding and human milk easily could fill an entire text. Every year, scientists discover new ways that human milk enhances an infant's health and development. The most commonly cited infant benefits of breastfeeding are reviewed below.

Breastfeeding benefits mothers, babies, and families.

Human milk is the ideal food for infants.

All infant feeding experts agree that human milk is nature's perfect design for feeding babies and that it is uniquely suited to promote optimal infant growth and development. Human milk contains more than two hundred constituents—proteins, fats, carbohydrates, vitamins, minerals, trace metals, growth factors, hormones, enzymes, antibodies, white blood cells, and more—each in ideal proportion to one another. This precise biochemical balance—virtually a "symphony of ingredients"—cannot possibly be duplicated artificially. The components in human milk represent more than necessary nutrients, and many play multiple roles in promoting the health and development of babies.

The *proteins* in human milk not only provide essential building blocks for growth but also perform other vital functions including helping to protect babies from illness. The proteins in human milk include disease-fighting antibodies and many other important immune properties. Human milk has less protein than the amount added to formulas because breast milk protein is utilized more efficiently by babies. It forms a softer curd that is more easily digestible than cow's milk or formula curd. Breastfed babies feed more often than formula-fed infants because their stomachs empty sooner. Proteins break down into amino acids, the composition of which is ideally suited to meet the unique requirements of infants.

The *fats* in human milk provide its major source of energy and are essential for the optimal development of the infant brain and nervous system. Breast milk conveniently contains a fat-digesting enzyme, lipase, that aids an infant's fat digestion. Human milk is rich in long-chained polyunsaturated fatty acids, including docosahexaenoic acid (DHA), an essential omega-3 fatty acid. DHA is present in large amounts in human milk, and at the current time, is absent in U.S. formulas. DHA is found in the infant's rapidly developing brain and eye tissue and is necessary for proper brain and eye development. It is not yet known whether an infant diet lacking the fatty acid composition of human milk has permanent adverse effects. However, a recent study found poorer visual ability in formula-fed premature babies than in those fed breast milk. Human milk is also rich in cholesterol, while formulas have little or none. Although the significance of this is unknown, research in rats suggests that animals who consume high levels of cholesterol in infancy may be better able to cope with dietary cholesterol and maintain a lower cholesterol level in later life.

The predominant *carbohydrate* found in milk is lactose, also known as milk sugar because it is found only in milk. In addition to being an important source of calories, lactose improves the absorption of certain minerals, including calcium. Lactose also promotes the growth of harmless intestinal bacteria in the breastfed baby's gut. These benign bowel germs create an acid environment that helps protect against the proliferation of harmful bacteria that cause infant diarrhea.

Human milk is a dynamic fluid, varying in composition depending on the stage of lactation, the maternal diet, the time of day, and other factors. The first milk your breasts produce, known as *colostrum*, is scant in volume, but high in protein, rich in immunities, and easily digested by your baby. Over the first ten days, colostrum gradually changes to *mature milk*, which is lower in protein and higher in lactose and fat. Although thinner in appearance, mature milk remains unmatched in nutritional quality. The fat content of milk is low at the beginning of a feeding and increases throughout the feeding. Breast milk is easily digested and produces loose bowel movements that are passed easily and that are not unpleasant smelling.

Species Specific. One of the strongest arguments for the superiority of human milk in infant feeding is the way the milk of each species of mammal is specifically tailored to the unique growth needs of its young. So specialized is the process of lactation that the composition of the milk, the location and number of nipples, and the frequency of feedings all are designed to optimize the survival and development of the offspring. In general, the nutrient content of a particular mammal's milk is directly related to the rate at which the newborn doubles its birth weight. Mammals with more dilute milks typically feed their young at close intervals, while those with more nutrient-dense milks feed less frequently. Aquatic and cold-weather mammals, like whales and polar bears, produce milk with an extremely high fat content to ensure sufficient calories to maintain an insulating layer of blubber. Human babies are among the most immature mammalian newborns, completely dependent on adults for care and survival. Human babies also have one of the slowest rates of growth, taking about four and a half months to double their birth weight. As expected, human milk is among the most dilute of all mammalian milks, and our feeding pattern is a frequent one–every couple of hours around the clock. This frequent feeding schedule provides an additional benefit. Each time the baby is positioned to nurse, the distance between his eyes and his mother's face is ideal for allowing him to focus well. An intimate bond is forged during the feeding process, ensuring the close, attentive parental care necessary for survival and growth.

Inadequacies of Infant Formulas. While mother's milk is the gold standard upon which all infant formulas are modeled, it is impossible to create an infant formula that exactly mimics your own milk. For one thing, all the ingredients in human milk have not been fully identified. Scientists are constantly discovering new properties in human milk that are absent in formulas, or are gaining new understandings about the function of a previously known component of human milk. Whenever it is possible to add an essential ingredient to formulas, manufacturers scramble to modify their product to more closely resemble human milk. While I am grateful that infant formulas are available for those instances when they are needed, we must never lose sight of the fact that human milk is uniquely superior to any breast milk substitute and it is impossible to precisely match—no matter how many times a product is "improved."

We also must remember that many components of breast milk simply cannot be incorporated into formulas. Although manufacturers are able to produce formulas containing approximately the same *percentage* of protein, fat, and carbohydrate found in human milk, the *quality* of each of these nutrients differs significantly from the composition of breast milk. Even minor differences between human milk and formula could have important consequences since a newborn is totally dependent on a single food during a critical period of growth and development.

Finally, remember that formulas are based on cow's milk, and it is virtually impossible to change the milk from one mammal into that of another. Thus, no formula will ever be able to exactly duplicate your own milk. Even if clever advertising messages try to convince you that a particular formula is "closest to mothers' milk," infant formulas actually represent a *distant* second choice.

When a mother decides to breastfeed, she doesn't have to worry whether her baby will tolerate her milk, whereas many formula-feeding mothers have discovered too late that their babies can't tolerate human milk substitutes. Few things are more discouraging to new parents than having a baby with a formula intolerance and being unable to find a formula that agrees with him.

> *Breastfeeding confers valuable protection against infant illnesses, including diarrhea and respiratory infections.*

Breast milk contains many substances that benefit your baby's immune system, including antibodies, enzymes, white blood cells, and other factors. Antibodies against germs to which the mother recently has been exposed appear in her milk a short time later to protect her baby against the same infecting organisms. Breastfeeding provides the greatest protection against illness in developing countries. However, even in the United States and other developed nations, the protective effect of breastfeeding is significant against diarrhea, ear infections, pneumonia, and other illness.

For a middle-class baby in America, childhood infections cause discomfort and inconvenience and only rarely produce life-threatening consequences. In developing countries, however, formula-fed infants face a dramatic increased risk of suffering malnutrition, infection, and death when formula is prepared using contaminated water and diluted excessively. Women in the United States serve as influential role models for disadvantaged women worldwide. I strongly believe that American women are obligated to strengthen the global message that breastfeeding is highly desirable in every culture and is something to be cherished by women the world over.

Diarrhea. Infant diarrhea is a major cause of childhood illness in the United States, resulting in more than a million office visits, two hundred thousand hospitalizations, and about three hundred deaths each year. It has long been recognized that breastfed infants have far fewer bouts of diarrhea and vomiting than formula-fed babies. If a breastfed infant does develop an intestinal illness, continued nursing usually is well tolerated and the duration of illness is shortened. The protective effect of human milk against diarrhea is greatest while a baby is exclusively breastfed.

Premature infants are particularly susceptible to a serious, potentially life-threatening bowel infection known as necrotizing enterocolitis (NEC). Several studies, including a large, multicentered study of nearly one thousand infants, have found that NEC occurred more commonly in premature infants who were solely formula-fed compared to those who were fed breast milk alone.

Respiratory Illness. Breastfeeding helps protect against serious lower respiratory illnesses, such as pneumonia and bronchiolitis, as well as upper respiratory infections, including ear infections. Respiratory syncytial virus (RSV)—the most common cause of serious respiratory illness in infants and young children—is responsible for ninety thousand infant hospitalizations and about forty-five hundred deaths each year in the United States. Breastfed infants have fewer RSV infections, and when they do get sick with RSV, they have less severe cases and fewer hospitalizations.

Ear infections are the most common childhood illness, accounting for nearly thirty million pediatric office visits each year. Nearly half of all infants get at least one ear infection in their first year of life, and close to 20 percent of babies suffer from recurrent ear infections (three or more bouts in six months). Breastfed infants, especially those who nurse exclusively for four to six months, experience only half as many ear infections as formula-fed infants.

Other Illnesses. Recent studies suggest that breastfeeding provides substantial protection against urinary tract infections in infancy and early childhood. Breastfed infants have a lower risk of blood-borne infections and spinal meningitis compared to bottle-fed babies. Breastfed infants also appear to be protected from the most severe form of infant botulism, a rare illness that results when *Clostridia botulinum* spores, present on agricultural products, including honey, are consumed by infants. (Honey should not be fed to infants under one year.)

Breastfeeding protects against allergies in infancy and later childhood.

A number of studies link breastfeeding with a lower incidence of food allergies, asthma, eczema, hayfever, and other allergic disease. As many as 15 percent of Americans and Europeans display one or more allergy symptoms in the first two decades of life. Infants who have a parent or sibling with known allergic disease are at greatest risk. Exclusive breastfeeding of such infants, especially when the mother eliminates certain allergenic foods from her diet during lactation (See Common Problems Encountered by Breastfeeding Women, page 222), has been shown to have a protective effect against the baby developing allergic symptoms.

A recent long-term, follow-up study from infancy until early adulthood examined the link between infant-feeding method and subsequent allergic disease (food allergy, respiratory allergy, asthma, and eczema). The results showed that breastfeeding (preferably for six months or longer) provided significant protection from allergic disease throughout childhood and adolescence. Another study that followed more than four hundred children who had a close relative with allergic disease found that wheezing occurred twice as frequently in the first year of life in youngsters who were never breastfed compared to those who had received some breast milk.

Breastfed infants have a lower risk of chronic immune system disorders, such as juvenile-onset diabetes mellitus, childhood cancers (especially lymphoma), and Crohn's disease.

☙

Several studies comparing possible causative factors associated with childhood cancers have found the duration of breastfeeding to have been significantly greater among healthy children than children with cancer. The findings are most prominent for cases of childhood lymphoma.

Other studies suggest that breastfeeding may help protect against the development of insulin-dependent diabetes mellitus (IDDM). The destruction of the insulin-secreting cells of the pancreas in individuals with IDDM is known to be an autoimmune process. Cow's milk has been implicated as a possible trigger of this autoimmune reaction in genetically susceptible persons. Some studies have shown a reduced risk of diabetes in breastfed children, especially those with a longer duration of exclusive breastfeeding.

Evidence is also accumulating to suggest that breastfeeding provides significant protection against inflammatory bowel disease

(Crohn's disease, ulcerative colitis). These disorders can cause chronic diarrhea, fever, poor growth, and other symptoms.

Breastfeeding offers some protection against sudden infant death syndrome (SIDS).

❧

Recently, much national attention has been given to the relationship between the prone (tummy-down) sleeping position in infants and the incidence of SIDS. The American Academy of Pediatrics has recommended that the prone position be avoided for sleeping infants and that babies be placed to sleep on their backs. Several other factors have been shown to reduce the risk of SIDS but have received far less publicity, including not smoking, breastfeeding, and not overheating infants. Parents deserve to know *all* the factors that potentially can reduce their child's risk of SIDS.

Breast milk contains growth factors believed to impact development and maturation, plus a whole host of factors that may shape a baby's brain and behavior.

❧

Many of the hormones and growth factors in human milk have only recently been identified, and their importance to babies is not yet fully understood. Some hormones appear only in the colostrum, others are present only in later milk, while still others are present in variable amounts throughout the course of lactation. These precisely regulated hormones may influence the timing of certain developmental events in the baby. So little is known about the various hormones and growth factors in human milk that it is impossible to try to replicate them in formulas. Meanwhile, no one knows whether what a baby eats in early life will later affect his well-being as a senior citizen.

Whether nutrition in early life has a long-term impact on brain development remains controversial. However, several studies involving both full-term and preterm infants have found a link between later cognitive performance and method of infant feeding. Children who were breastfed as infants achieved significantly higher scores on a variety of intelligence tests compared to those who had been artificially fed. The differences attributed to breastfeeding were distinct from other factors known to influence intelligence, such as education and socioeconomic status of the parents.

Nursing provides a valuable source of security and comfort for your infant.

The breastfeeding relationship involves unique giving and receiving between mother and baby. A baby has a regular and vital need for her mother's milk and physical closeness, while a mother's full breasts regularly need to be relieved and drained. Thus, breastfeeding assures that mothers and babies remain intimately connected through the making and taking of milk. This reciprocal interaction can deepen the bond between a mother and baby and continue long after breast milk has been the sole source of a baby's nutrition. The breastfeeding relationship can extend into the second and third year, or even beyond, as a means of intermittently soothing and emotionally satisfying a toddler as he or she becomes more independent.

A breastfed baby gets the privilege of being held for every nursing, with the opportunity for extensive social interaction during feedings. The formula-fed baby who learns to hold his bottle, or worse yet has it propped for him, may be required to take his feeding alone, without the presence of an attentive caretaker with whom to socialize. Recently, I witnessed a small baby in an infant carrier who was trying in vain to feed from a precariously propped bottle, while his mother was preoccupied nearby. Whenever the position of the bottle shifted, no milk filled the nipple and he was left sucking air while facing the side wall of the carrier without any human interaction. How I wished this little one were able to enjoy being breastfed in his mother's loving arms, receiving her undivided attention. I also ached for the mother's own loss. In not being fully attuned to her infant's cues, she remained unaware of the ways in which she herself could be fulfilled by meeting his needs.

Maternal Advantages of Breastfeeding

In addition to the many infant health benefits just cited, breast-feeding clearly is advantageous to a mother's well-being. Consider the following:

Breastfeeding causes release of the hormone oxytocin, which helps shrink your uterus back to its normal size after delivery.

When this hormone is at work during the first few days of breastfeeding, you might notice some contractions of your uterus while nursing. These afterpains, as they are called, are more pronounced among women who have delivered more than one baby. While oxytocin's effect on the uterus can produce temporary discomfort, it also can be lifesaving for some women in settings where access to medical care is limited. By putting the baby to the breast immediately after birth, postpartum bleeding can be reduced. In the United States, it is customary to give an intravenous injection of synthetic oxytocin after delivery to help control uterine bleeding. Before the advent of modern technology, routine breastfeeding after birth offered the best protection against postpartum hemorrhage.

Breastfeeding utilizes additional calories, which helps mothers lose some of the extra fat they accumulated during pregnancy.

It is nature's plan for pregnant women to store fat reserves to be used to subsidize lactation. That's why the combined weight of the baby, placenta, amniotic fluid, and blood lost at delivery doesn't add up to the total weight gained during pregnancy. After the first month, many breastfeeding women find they lose about two pounds a month while lactating, and they can expect to return to their prepregnancy weight sooner than bottle-feeding women. A recent study showed significantly greater weight loss in breastfeeding than formula-feeding women, primarily between three and six months postpartum.

Breastfeeding provides maternal protection against osteoporosis and hip fracture in later life.

Osteoporosis is an age-related bone loss that leads to brittle bones and fractures of the hip, wrist, spine, and elsewhere. This crippling bone disease affects approximately one in three women over sixty years of age. Studies of postmenopausal women have shown higher bone mineral densities in those who have breastfed. A recent study of Australian women over sixty-five years found that having breastfed offered a protective effect on the risk of hip fracture in old age.

Women who have breastfed have a slightly reduced risk of premenopausal breast cancer and ovarian cancer.

Approximately one in nine women will be diagnosed with breast cancer in her lifetime. Many of the established risk factors for breast cancer are beyond our control, such as age at first menstruation, age at menopause, family history of breast cancer, and age at birth of first child. However, breastfeeding is one factor within a woman's control that can reduce her breast cancer risk. A number of studies have shown a significant protective effect of breastfeeding against premenopausal breast cancer. In general, the effect increases with the cumulative months of lifetime breastfeeding. It is estimated that if all women who gave birth were to achieve a combined breastfeeding duration among their children totaling twenty-four months or longer, the national incidence of premenopausal breast cancer might be reduced by nearly 25 percent. A recent study suggests that being breastfed herself is a possible factor that lowers a woman's risk of breast cancer.

Several studies also have shown a protective effect of lactation against ovarian cancer. One of the most important of these studies found a 20 to 25 percent reduction in risk of ovarian cancer for women who breastfed at least two months.

Breastfeeding is very convenient because no matter where you are, you always have the perfect food ready for your infant, at the right temperature, and in the correct amount.

🙟

When you breastfeed, you can conveniently take your infant with you anywhere, knowing your milk will be ready for her whenever she is hungry. Despite power outages, snow storms, or natural disasters, the breastfeeding mother can feed her hungry baby, in the absence of electricity or potable water. I often enjoyed the freedom of traveling and camping with a nursing baby, without being bogged down by formula preparation.

Breastfeeding in the middle of the night is much more convenient than going to the kitchen to mix and warm a bottle of formula. With your newborn in a bassinet at your bedside, you can scoop up your baby when she gets hungry and nurse her without leaving your bed. Some women choose to sleep with their nursing infants in the same bed and scarcely have to disrupt their sleep for feedings.

Before I'm accused of overselling the convenience of breastfeeding, let me acknowledge that the first few weeks with a new baby are a particularly exhausting time. When breastfeeding is just getting launched and feedings seem to preoccupy a great deal of time and everyone is overwhelmed with the demands of a new baby, "convenience" in relation to any aspect of baby care might seem a remote concept. In chapter 5, Off to a Great Beginning— The First Weeks of Breastfeeding, I offer advice to help you survive the early weeks and get off to a successful start so that you really can enjoy the remarkable convenience of long-term breastfeeding.

During exclusive breastfeeding, a woman's menstrual periods are usually suppressed.

🙟

Women who breastfeed fully, without supplementing their baby with formula, may go months or a year or more without menstruating. Not only does amenorrhea (lack of periods) provide limited birth control as discussed below, but it conserves iron stores and helps the body replenish the iron lost during fetal development, childbirth, and postpartum bleeding.

The suppression of the menstrual cycle during exclusive breast-feeding also offers a contraceptive effect during the early postpartum period, although this effect declines over time. The Lactational Amenorrhea Method, or LAM, is a postpartum introductory method of contraception that uses three criteria to define the period of lowest pregnancy risk (see Lactational Amenorrhea Method, pages 190–191). Studies confirm that breastfeeding provides 98 percent protection against pregnancy, as long as a woman can answer yes to all three of the following questions:

Are you less than six months postpartum?
Are you breastfeeding exclusively, without the use of formula supplement or solids?
Have you been amenorrheic (no periods) since delivery?

Alternate methods of birth control should be used if a woman's periods have returned, if routine supplements have been introduced, or if a breastfeeding woman is more than six months postpartum. Alternate methods of birth control also should be used if a breastfeeding woman is unwilling to accept even a remote risk of pregnancy.

Breastfeeding is highly cost effective.

That's not to say you won't spend any money by breastfeeding, but you'll spend a lot less than the cost of formula. Feeding a baby is an expensive proposition; ready-to-feed formula costs more than three dollars a day. It takes only a fraction of that to feed a nursing mother the additional five hundred calories required daily to produce sufficient milk. However, I believe most sources that promote the advantages of breastfeeding err on the side of overstating how inexpensive it is. When the anticipated cost savings of breast-feeding are overemphasized, many parents, expecting to breastfeed for free, may be reluctant to spend any additional money to assure their success.

Despite the anticipated cost savings of breastfeeding, I strongly encourage expectant parents to budget some funds to help them achieve their breastfeeding goals. It is unrealistic to assume that you will have no expenses associated with breastfeeding. The fact is that feeding a baby costs money, and you might as well spend your dollars providing the very best nutrition. Some women may want to purchase nursing clothing or a sling that allows them to breastfeed discreetly in public. Others may need to rent an electric breast pump to maintain lactation while they are employed outside the home. Still others may encounter breastfeeding difficulties requiring professional consultation or the purchase of breastfeeding aids. By budgeting for the likelihood of such expenses, parents will be better prepared to spend a little extra, should the need arise (see Budgeting Money for Breastfeeding, page 50).

By giving breastfeeding a try, you keep your options open.

You can always stop nursing and switch to bottle-feeding later if you prefer. If you begin bottle-feeding, however, you might wonder whether you would have enjoyed the chance to breastfeed. Whenever a woman has any ambivalence about how to feed her baby, I urge her to at least begin breastfeeding. Why close the door too soon on something you might really enjoy if you would just give it a try? Besides, there are only a couple of times in a woman's life when she can nurse a baby, but anyone can feed a bottle anytime.

Breastfeeding is far more than a method of infant feeding.

Breastfeeding is a style of mothering and nurturing, as much as the act of nourishing your infant at your breast. Nursing serves not only as the source of life-sustaining food, but also as a way to provide warmth, succor, and the consolation of a mother's touch. Whether the newborn cries out for food or human contact, once suckled at the breast, his every need is met. Whether the fretful toddler searches for the nipple to return to sleep, calm a fear, or soothe an ache, she finds peace nestling at the breast. "Token," or occasional breastfeeding cannot be equated with "unrestricted" breastfeeding where a baby nurses at will. The mothering and nurturing aspects of breastfeeding prompt some adoptive mothers and others who may not produce a full milk supply to endeavor to nurse their babies even partially in order to experience the interactions unique to breastfeeding. While nutritional superiority and immune benefits can be quantitated and appreciated by virtually anyone, the nurturing and interactive aspects of breastfeeding may be hugely undervalued unless one has experienced firsthand what it means to view breastfeeding as a form of mothering. Employed women and other mothers who must be separated from their babies, can attest that feeding expressed breast milk by bottle is not the same as breastfeeding.

Breastfeeding requires a mother to regularly stop what she is doing, get off her feet, sit down, and relax.

The hormones prolactin and oxytocin, which are released during breastfeeding, have been called "mothering" hormones because they produce a peaceful, nurturing sensation. Having to take a break and nurse your baby actually has a calming effect on a busy mother. Breastfeeding breaks can pull a hectic mother away from the distractions of her other duties to force her full attention on her infant, thereby renewing her perspective. The whole time I was raising five infants, I maintained a near-frenetic pace as a medical student, intern, resident, and junior faculty member. "Needing" to nurse my baby was a breath of fresh air, forcing me to sit down, become fully engaged with my infant, and refocus my energies. I would have considered it a great loss had I not experienced the intimate giving and receiving that characterized my own personal breastfeeding relationships.

Advantages of Breastfeeding to the Father

You might not have considered the many ways your baby's father can benefit from being part of a breastfeeding family. Although fathers often worry that they will feel left out of the breastfeeding experience, the truth is that fathers are positively impacted when their babies are breastfed.

The father of a breastfed baby will reap the benefits of a healthier partner and healthier infant.

Traditionally, fathers view themselves as providers and protectors of their families. Naturally, a father wants to assure the welfare of his partner and his baby. His support, encouragement, and direct help can be the decisive factor in a woman's breastfeeding success. When his infant is breastfed, a father experiences pride and confidence, knowing he has contributed to the healthiest outcome for his baby and his partner. Fewer infant illnesses mean less disruption of family life and less expense, while the long-term health benefits to his partner can have a powerful impact on their quality of life.

Fathers appreciate the convenience of breastfeeding in the middle of the night and the increased flexibility that breastfeeding affords.

Many fathers choose to share responsibility for night feedings by bringing the baby to the mother and burping and changing the infant after nursing. Other men choose to sleep through some night feedings, especially at times when their sleep is critical to work-related activities. When the mother is breastfeeding, middle-of-the-night nursings are minimally disruptive to the parents' sleep, since no one has to shuffle to the kitchen to prepare a bottle.

The baby can be fed anywhere without any preparation or fuss, and a breastfed infant can be consoled and quieted in virtually any setting, simply by nursing. When our first son was born, my sailor husband had just returned from being stationed overseas during the Vietnam conflict. We still were getting reacquainted ourselves after enduring a six-month separation when we were suddenly thrust into our new, unfamiliar roles as parents. We had no one with whom we could leave our baby, so Larry was delighted to discover that we easily could take Peter with us and still enjoy an outing together. When our middle child, Tricie, was only a month old, we drove from Denver to California to visit Larry's family. Although Peter and Paige were only three and two, I found the trip to be thoroughly manageable because of the convenience of breastfeeding. I can't imagine trying to travel while having to deal with formula, bottles, a cooler, warmer, and other paraphernalia required for a formula-fed baby.

Fathers welcome the reduced cost of breastfeeding over bottle-feeding.

Despite contemporary changes in traditional sex role stereotypes, most fathers still bear greater responsibility for family financial commitments. With all the additional costs of caring for a new baby, they appreciate not having to spend money on infant formula. Some fathers have calculated the projected savings that breastfeeding will achieve and then suggested ways to use the unspent money—perhaps a vacation together since breastfed babies are so portable!

The father of a breastfed baby can make an important contribution to the success of breastfeeding.

One often hears expectant parents express their desire that fathers share more involvement in their babies' care than in the past generation. Certainly, feeding is one of the most gratifying and visible ways adults give care to newborns. I have even met a few parents who chose to bottle-feed specifically to allow the father to play an equal role in child rearing.

While I believe that babies ideally need and deserve both a mother and a father, I am convinced that the dual parental roles are meant to complement one another, not to compete with one another. The enlightened father doesn't lament, "I feel so left out when she's nursing my son; there's nothing for me to do." Instead, he recognizes his unique role as the principal supporter of the mother, the one who enables her to nurture the baby in an optimal fashion. He views supporting his partner through lactation as a logical continuation of his support role during pregnancy and his coaching role during labor. The enlightened father encourages and compliments his breastfeeding partner every chance he gets, brings a glass of juice to the nursing mother, gives her a back rub, changes the baby's diaper, and helps with household chores. Fathers of breastfed infants soon learn that there are many ways, apart from feeding, that they can bond with their babies, e.g., bathing, mas-

Advantages of Breastfeeding to Society

Breastfeeding is more than a personal or family matter, and the decision to breastfeed affects more than an individual mother-baby pair or a single family. Breastfeeding rates have a powerful impact on the whole society by affecting the health of mothers and babies, the economy, and the environment.

Our entire society benefits when babies are given the best possible start in life.

The babies being born today will be our country's leaders tomorrow, and the nutrition they receive in infancy will serve as the cornerstone of their optimal growth and development. When our nation's children are given every chance to reach their full potential, all of us stand to benefit. Conversely, when babies face health disadvantages because of their early diet, we all pay the price.

Human milk uses no natural resources and generates no industrial waste.

On the other hand, the production of formula, cans, bottles, nipples, labels, packaging, and advertising uses trees, metal, glass, plastics, paper, and fuel. Artificial feeding of infants creates an enormous volume of waste materials. In hospital nurseries, formula-fed babies are offered a single-use glass or plastic bottle up to eight times a day. Often, little more than an ounce is consumed from a three- or four-ounce bottle and the rest is discarded.

Breastfeeding saves Americans millions of dollars that would otherwise be spent on formula.

The average family of a bottle-fed baby spends $750 to $1,000 each year on formula. The U.S. government spends hundreds of millions of dollars each year purchasing formula for the Special Supplemental Nutrition Program for Women, Infants, and Children (WIC).

Breastfeeding reduces infant health care costs because breastfed babies have fewer hospitalizations and fewer infections.

The additional number of illnesses needlessly suffered by formula-fed babies translates into staggering medical costs. The medical and surgical treatment for childhood ear infections alone has been estimated to cost $3 to $4 billion per year. The annual cost of hospitalizations due to RSV infections is over $300 million, while diarrhea illness in childhood costs almost $1 billion. Increasing breastfeeding rates could drastically decrease societal health care costs by greatly reducing the number of infections and resulting hospitalizations during infancy. Recent studies confirm that insurance payers spend more health care dollars on the medical costs of formula-fed infants than breastfed infants.

Current Infant-Feeding Recommendations

With all the advantages just cited, it should come as no surprise that the American Academy of Pediatrics (AAP), together with numerous other health professional organizations, recognizes breastfeeding as the ideal method of feeding and nurturing infants. In December 1997, the AAP released an updated breastfeeding policy statement that strongly recommends human milk as the preferred feeding for infants and acknowledges breastfeeding as primary in achieving optimal infant and child health, growth, and development.

The AAP recommends a diet of exclusive breast milk as ideal nutrition for about the first six months of life, during which babies more than double their birth weight. Iron-enriched solid foods should be added to the infant's diet, beginning around six months, with breastfeeding continuing for at least twelve months, and longer if mother and baby desire. If breastfeeding is discontinued before a year of age, infants should drink iron-fortified infant formula and not receive cow's milk until after twelve months of age.

A Generation of Bottle-Feeding Grandmothers. In societies where breastfeeding is traditional, the art is passed from mother to daughter. Girls frequently observe breastfeeding, beginning in childhood, and grandmothers routinely offer guidance about nursing technique and expected norms. In the United States today, the majority of grandmothers lack firsthand experience with breastfeeding since they bottle-fed their own children. This makes it difficult for them to give their daughters and daughters-in-law practical advice or direct assistance when it comes to nursing babies. At best, they can provide encouragement and support, but little practical help. At worst, unfamiliarity with breastfeeding may cause a grandmother to sabotage its success by making disparaging comments, doubting the adequacy of the mother's milk, or giving the baby unnecessary supplemental formula. The sight of her daughter or daughter-in-law nursing her grandchild may cause a bottle-feeding grandmother to feel remorse about not having breastfed her children. To help resolve such issues, I like to explain that, at the time these grandmothers were having their families, breastfeeding was not strongly encouraged and hospital practices did little to promote its success. One way to make up for not having breastfed oneself is to play a support role in helping one's daughter or daughter-in-law succeed at breastfeeding.

Early Return to Employment. The new breastfeeding policy statement of the American Academy of Pediatrics encourages women to breastfeed for at least a year. Yet, the majority of new mothers in the United States rejoin the workforce before their baby is a year old. Some return to work only six to eight weeks after giving birth. The separation of mothers and babies during the workday poses a logistical obstacle to continued breastfeeding. Although many options exist for employed mothers to maintain lactation, ranging from on-site child care to expressing breast milk at the workplace, there's no doubt that employment represents a societal barrier to successful breastfeeding. If you anticipate returning to work while still nursing your baby, the information in chapter 8 will give you practical strategies for successfully combining breastfeeding and employment.

Lack of Insurance Reimbursement for Lactation Services. As more women choose to breastfeed, more lactation concerns surface that require specialized counseling and management. Most physicians acknowledge that time constraints in a busy office and unfamiliarity with practical aspects of breastfeeding combine to limit their effectiveness in handling lactation problems. Lactation consultants are relatively new members of the health care team who provide breastfeeding education and consultation for breastfeeding problems. A lactation consultant may recommend that you rent a hospital-grade electric breast pump or purchase some breastfeeding supplies to help overcome specific problems. While the need for lactation counseling continues to grow, medical insurance companies often view specialized breastfeeding services as an elective expense that is not reimbursed. However, recent research showing that breastfeeding reduces health care costs may prompt insurance companies to start paying for lactation consultation services. Meanwhile, plan to budget money for necessary breastfeeding counseling or equipment to help you achieve success.

Lifestyle Issues. Successful breastfeeding is best fostered when mothers and babies are kept in close proximity and when infants are allowed to nurse in an unrestricted fashion. However, in our fast-paced, highly mobile society, many new mothers expect their nursing babies to conveniently fit into a structured routine. They may be unprepared for the normal frequency and unpredictability of nursings and the fact that breastfeeding can't be delegated to anyone else. Mother-to-mother support groups are one of the best ways for women to observe other breastfeeding mothers and learn how they accommodate a nursing baby in tow (see La Leche League International, pages 41–44).

Our society's emphasis on the breast as a sensual organ rather than a source of infant nutrition causes many nursing mothers to feel self-conscious when they need to breastfeed in public and makes others feel uncomfortable in the presence of a breastfeeding woman. Breastfeeding mothers need to know how to nurse discreetly in public and they require frequent reassurance that "breastfed babies are welcome here" (see Nursing in Public, pages 193–194).

A Brief History of Infant-Feeding and Breastfeeding Trends

Successful lactation is required for the survival of mammalian species. The main exception to this rule is human infants in this century. The feeding of breast milk substitutes to human infants has occurred on a large scale for only about seventy years. This radical departure in infant-feeding practices has been of relatively short duration in terms of the history of mankind. The truth is that the long-term consequences of this biological experiment are still unknown.

Although the widespread decline of breastfeeding has been a twentieth-century phenomenon, the fact is that throughout history, some women have chosen to opt out of breastfeeding. The lengthy search for an alternative to breastfeeding can be traced by numerous historical accounts: reports of women who sold their extra milk to other women at the market; the finding of ancient feeding vessels at infant burial sites; elaborate descriptions of the ideal wet nurse; and records of nonmilk feedings of "pap" or "panada" made by mixing flour, rice, and barley or biscuits with water and butter. Nonhuman milk feeding of newborns was almost always fatal, while wet-nursing also carried a high mortality rate due to corrupt practices, such as taking on too many babies and sedating them so they wouldn't demand to feed. Generally, it was the more privileged women who, through the ages, sought alternatives to breastfeeding, while less affluent women traditionally have breastfed. What is so shocking in the history of infant feeding is that many women have declined to breastfeed even when their decision was sure to seal the death of their baby.

With this historical background, you may find it less surprising that breastfeeding declined so dramatically once artificial feeding became reasonably safe and economically feasible. By 1920, numerous scientific advances contributed to the promotion of artificial feeding, including the appearance of glass bottles and rubber nipples; the availability of evaporated milk that could be stored on the shelf; sanitary water supplies and pasteurization; ice box refrigeration; and vitamin supplementation (e.g., cod liver oil to prevent rickets). Breastfeeding was dealt another blow as a result of the widespread employment of women in industry during World War II. National statistics document the drastic decline in breastfeeding rates as artificial feeding emerged as a new normative behavior. For example, in 1911, 58 percent of American infants were still being breastfed at one year of age. By 1946, only 38 percent of newborns left the hospital being solely breastfed. By 1966, fewer than one in five newborns (18 percent) were exclusively breastfed at hospital discharge. Typically, it was the higher-income, better-educated women who led the departure from breastfeeding. Ironically, this turned out to be the same population of women who, decades later, were the first to return to breastfeeding.

In the 1970s, breastfeeding rates again began to climb in the United States. The return to breastfeeding was part of a broader movement to "normalize" the childbirth experience. Breastfeeding was promoted along with more family-centered maternity care practices, including less medication during childbirth; the presence of partners during labor and delivery; rooming-in of infants and mothers; informed consent for circumcision; and other more natural approaches to maternal-child care. From 1971 to 1982, in-hospital breastfeeding rates increased dramatically from 24.7 percent to 61.9 percent. By the mid-1980s, breastfeeding of newborns was again the "community norm" for the first time in more than four decades.

But the good news didn't last. Between 1982 and 1990, in-hospital breastfeeding declined to 51.5 percent. Possible reasons for the unexpected decline in breastfeeding were shorter hospital stays, decreased promotion of breastfeeding, increased numbers of employed mothers, and lack of practical help for women with breastfeeding problems.

Happily, in the 1990s, in-hospital breastfeeding rates again have increased steadily. The 1997 rate of 62.4 percent matched the 1982 peak. Women most likely to breast-feed are over thirty years, college-educated, with higher incomes and living in the western states. However, breastfeeding rates are climbing rapidly among mothers who traditionally have been less likely to breastfeed, including black mothers, younger moms, and those with lower incomes and less education. The recent increase probably is due to many factors, including sustained promotional efforts, especially by the Special Supplemental Nutrition Program for Women, Infants, and Children (WIC); increased availability of lactation services, lactation consultants, and electric breast pumps; more work-site support for employed breastfeeding women; more specialized help for women with high-risk infants; increased education of health professionals; and increased documentation of the benefits of breastfeeding.

Unfortunately, the rates of women who continue breastfeeding haven't kept pace with those who begin breastfeeding. While most women now start out breastfeeding, the number still nursing at five to six months has hovered around 25 percent for twenty years. The peak six-month continuation rate was 27.1 percent in 1982, and the figure for 1997 was 26 percent of all new mothers (or 41.7 percent of women who begin breastfeeding). The fact is that many women who desire to nurse their babies have trouble keeping breastfeeding going as long as they would like. In 1997, only 14.5 percent of women who began breastfeeding were still nursing their babies at 12 months, as recommended by the AAP.

This book is aimed at helping you make an informed choice about breastfeeding, acquire the basic skills and knowledge that will promote success, overcome any difficulties that arise, and achieve your personal breastfeeding goal. I sincerely hope that you will be among those fortunate women who are able to give their babies the best possible start in life and who are able to enjoy the full natural course of breastfeeding. Despite the challenges that remain, the truth is that, in terms of improved hospital policies, new lactation services, and increasing professional and community support, there hasn't been a better time to breastfeed in the United States in more than fifty years!

Chapter 2

Preparation for Breastfeeding— Before the Baby Arrives

If you're wondering, "Who needs to prepare for breastfeeding?" you're certainly not alone. Many expectant parents, friends, and relatives—even the health professionals who care for families—subscribe to the myth that breastfeeding is completely natural and easy. After all, women have been doing it for millennia. Even women who admit they don't know the first thing about breastfeeding are easily convinced that their baby automatically will know what to do. However, breastfeeding is not performed by sheer instinct; it is a learned art. Generally, the more knowledgeable and prepared you are, the more successful and satisfying your breastfeeding experience will be.

More than twenty years ago, when I first began lecturing to health professionals about breastfeeding, I mentioned to my aunt that I was giving a two-hour talk on the topic. She was incredulous. "Two hours! What could you possibly say that could fill two whole hours?" she wondered. Since then, I have lectured on breastfeeding in nearly every state and in several foreign countries. When my first book, *Dr. Mom: A Guide to Baby and Child Care,* was published, the breastfeeding content made up only a portion of one chapter. Now, I have written an entire book on the topic! In recent years, the new health care role of lactation consultant has emerged to help handle the growing volume of breastfeeding management issues that have arisen. The more knowledgeable we become about breastfeeding, the more we realize there is much for us to learn.

Prenatal Breastfeeding Classes

Childbirth educators will attest that attendance at childbirth preparation classes exceeds attendance at prenatal breastfeeding classes, even in areas where breastfeeding rates are extremely high. Admittedly, the amazing changes your body is experiencing during pregnancy and the anticipation of discomfort during labor and delivery can easily eclipse any concerns about breastfeeding after the baby arrives. Imagining a baby in your life, especially one who needs to be fed and cared for, can seem rather remote during pregnancy, when the placenta conveniently meets all the infant's nutritional and waste removal needs. Still, I find it baffling that most pregnant women and their partners are eager to attend a whole series of classes to prepare for *twelve hours* or so of labor, while far fewer couples are motivated to show up for even one class to prepare for breastfeeding, which might well continue for *twelve months* or longer. My own explanation for this is simple: *pain is a great motivator*! Learning how to handle the discomfort of labor all too often takes precedent over learning how to succeed at breastfeeding. Even though both processes are considered "natural," women flock to classes about giving birth while many assume that breastfeeding requires no preparation.

With the present trend toward shorter postpartum hospital stays, it is totally unrealistic to expect to learn everything you need to know about breastfeeding before you are discharged. The postpartum stay has become so abbreviated that newly delivered mothers find themselves virtually bombarded with critical information during the brief time they are hospitalized. You can expect to hear explanations about your own care and recovery, as well as instructions about every aspect of infant care from bathing to signs of illness. Those women lucky enough to have acquired some knowledge about breastfeeding prior to giving birth will be much better equipped for success. They will be able to ask more pertinent questions of the nursing staff and to readily grasp the explanations given to them. In short, arriving at the hospital with a good base of knowledge about breastfeeding will increase your chances of getting off to a good start.

Many women falsely believe they will have ample time at home with their new baby to leisurely read about breastfeeding in case they don't learn everything they need to in the hospital. Or, parents may imagine that any early breastfeeding glitches will work themselves out once their baby gets settled in her own nursery. Instead, those precious first days of becoming a family may be marred by sleep deprivation, physical discomfort, unfamiliar infant care requirements, lack of confidence, curious guests, and an unhappy baby whose parents feel unprepared to meet her needs. The truth is that there is no better time than the prenatal period to become as informed as possible about breastfeeding. A little investment of effort now can save you immeasurable anxiety and distress after your baby arrives.

Prenatal class time devoted to breastfeeding can range from less than an hour to multiple sessions lasting several hours each. Often, a basic two-hour class is offered to all parents, while an additional session is available for those wanting to learn how to combine breastfeeding and employment. Whatever the length, a prenatal infant-feeding class provides an excellent opportunity to become informed about the advantages of breastfeeding, to strengthen a couple's commitment to nurse, and to learn specific breastfeeding techniques and routines.

When a nurse colleague of mine was pregnant with her first child nearly thirty years go, her obstetrician insisted she attend a breastfeeding class. "What do you mean I need to go?" my friend objected. "After all, I'm a nurse and I've already learned about infant feeding during my training." "Well," the physician explained, "I ask all my patients to attend this class because I believe it's very worthwhile. I'd like you to go, and I want you to tell me if you don't learn anything useful." Not only did my friend attend, but she learned so much new and valuable information about breastfeeding that she couldn't wait to thank her doctor. "I was too uninformed to appreciate how much there was to know about breastfeeding," she exclaimed with renewed enthusiasm. After a thoroughly satisfying experience breastfeeding her two children, she went on to devote much of her professional career to the management of lactation problems and the breastfeeding education of health professionals. I hope your own obstetrical care provider will strongly encourage you to attend a prenatal breastfeeding class and that you will take the time to give them feedback about its value to you.

"Infant-Feeding Classes" vs. "Breastfeeding Classes." One day, while contemplating how to increase attendance at prenatal breastfeeding classes, it dawned on me that the title of these classes excluded intended bottle-feeders—the very group of expectant parents who most need to hear about breastfeeding. Obstetrical practitioners often ask pregnant women how they plan to feed their babies *before* they've acquired enough information to make such a decision. Then, expectant parents are divided into those who will learn more about breastfeeding and those who probably won't. Intended breastfeeders are directed to the breastfeeding class to strengthen their resolve and provide them with practical how-tos, while intended bottle-feeders may gain no such exposure to the benefits and basics of breastfeeding. Meanwhile, we know that women who are uninformed about breastfeeding are unlikely to choose it. Can you appreciate the irony? Women least knowledgeable about breastfeeding in the first place are least likely to attend an informative class that could influence their infant-feeding decision. The truth is that couples really aren't equipped to make an informed infant-feeding decision until *after* they've heard all about breastfeeding—its advantages and how it's done.

Instead of scheduling "breastfeeding classes" as an option for selected women, I believe we should be holding "infant-feeding classes" for *all* expectant parents. Breastfeeding needs to make up a large portion of the content of infant-feeding classes if parents are to make a truly informed decision about feeding their baby. Whether to breastfeed is such an important child health issue that *every* parent needs to be thoroughly familiar with it *before* they weigh their own decision.

Bring Partners to Prenatal Feeding Classes. Every pregnant woman who attends prenatal classes knows to bring along her support person or "coach." Even though the woman's body will go through labor and delivery, women acknowledge their vital need for an informed, supportive, encouraging advocate to help them birth their child. But often the same women who wouldn't think of leaving their partner at home on Lamaze night will arrive unaccompanied to their prenatal feeding class. Just as you expect to need support through pregnancy and labor, you should surround yourself with effective support people who will physically help you and cheer you on while you breastfeed. Fathers, grandparents, baby-sitters, and friends can all benefit tremendously by accompanying you to your breastfeeding classes and becoming knowledgeable about lactation. Since many contemporary grandmothers bottle-fed their own babies, they may not know how to play an effective support role for their breastfeeding daughters and daughters-in-law unless they remedy their knowledge-gap about breastfeeding norms.

Visual Aids and Other Resources. In addition to the content covered in classes, prenatal teaching sessions offer informative resource materials. Instructors may have a lending library or recommended reading list covering pregnancy, breastfeeding, and infant care. They also may have a variety of patient education materials addressing issues of particular relevance to you, such as working and breastfeeding or nursing twins. Most instructors use visual aids to enhance their presentation, including flip charts, slides, overheads, dolls, and breast models. Some classes also display or sell an array of useful breastfeeding aids such as nursing pillows, baby carriers and slings, breast pumps, breast shells, nursing pads, and USP modified lanolin for sore nipples (see Breastfeeding Supplies, pages 46–50).

Many expectant parents, especially those who have not witnessed breastfeeding firsthand, appreciate the opportunity to view an instructional videotape that depicts actual breastfeeding. Such tapes represent an ideal way to teach essential techniques, including correct infant latch-on, how to arouse a sleepy baby, discreet nursing, how to relieve breast engorgement or use a breast pump.

I am delighted that you are reading this book, and I trust it will help you prepare for an enjoyable and successful breastfeeding experience. I strongly recommend that you read at least through chapter 6 *before* the birth of your baby. After your baby arrives, you can review pertinent sections and read additional chapters as they apply to your situation. Your infant will never be easier to care for than during your pregnancy. Even if you are employed outside the home right now, you still probably have more time for reading during your pregnancy than you will have in the early weeks with a newborn. The leisurely reading you thought you would accomplish after giving birth may not prove realistic after all. Once breastfeeding is well established, you can expect to read and nurse for many relaxing hours each day. But in the first weeks when you need answers the most, you will have the least time to read and track them down. Instead, you'll wish you had acquired some basic information in advance.

I recall a highly educated, motivated woman who diligently read throughout her pregnancy about prenatal changes and preparation for delivery. She savored every morsel of new information and particularly enjoyed learning about the stages of pregnancy and childbirth in chronological order as she was experiencing them. While still pregnant, she placed a bookmark in her book, beginning with the section on the baby's arrival. "I'll read about the baby's care and breastfeeding after he gets here," she figured. Unfortunately, the woman encountered unexpected breastfeeding problems that prevented her infant from obtaining adequate milk and made feeding her baby an exhausting and frustrating experience. She had little time to shower, eat, wash, or finish the nursery preparations, let alone send birth announcements. Reading the book that might have held the answers to her problems now loomed as a virtual impossibility, as her situation seemed to spiral downward. New parenthood was being marred by lack of information, lack of confidence, and mounting exhaustion. How she wished she could go back and read all about breastfeeding *before* her baby arrived. Doing so might have averted her problems and certainly would have left her better equipped to deal with them.

La Leche League International

In 1956, at the height of the U.S. bottle-feeding era, seven young mothers in a Chicago suburb were brought together by their mutual belief in the importance of breastfeeding and their common perception that physicians and society provided inadequate support for their breastfeeding efforts. These dedicated women began meeting together regularly for mutual support and to provide information and encouragement for other breastfeeding women. Out of these early informal gatherings grew an enduring, international mother-to-mother breastfeeding group, known all over the world as La Leche League International. This grassroots, nonprofit organization is active in sixty-six countries, with more than three thousand groups meeting every month, led by seven thousand fully trained and accredited Leader volunteers who have themselves successfully breastfed. More than two hundred thousand breastfeeding women are helped every month by their contact with La Leche League, whether through meetings, telephone counseling, publications, or the internet. A series of four monthly meetings represent the cornerstone of La Leche League's activities. These meetings are informative, interactive group discussions based on the following topical series:

1. **The Advantages of Breastfeeding.** Maternal, infant, and global advantages of breastfeeding and human milk are reviewed and backed by scientific evidence. This knowledge strengthens women's commitment to prepare for and succeed at breastfeeding.

2. **The Baby Arrives: The Family and the Breastfed Baby.** This topic focuses on the baby's birth, getting started breastfeeding, and the early weeks with a new baby. Knowing what to expect smooths the integration of a new baby into the family and helps assure the successful initiation of breastfeeding.

3. **The Art of Breastfeeding and Overcoming Difficulties.** The normal course of breastfeeding is presented, including a discussion of common problems and their successful resolution. Mothers gain an appreciation of the full course of breastfeeding and confidence in their ability to reach their breastfeeding goals.

4. **Nutrition and Weaning: Baby's Changing Needs.** Information about sound nutrition during lactation and starting a baby on solid foods is tied to healthful nutrition principles for the whole family. The philosophy of baby-led, natural weaning is explained.

La Leche League Meetings. In addition to the topical content and informal discussion that occurs at La Leche League (LLL) meetings, expectant and new mothers learn invaluable parenting skills by observing the nurturing styles of member mothers. Meetings are held in members' homes or convenient public locations and might be attended by ten or more breastfeeding mothers and their nursing babies, ranging in age from newborns to preschoolers. Mothers interact and visit with one another before and after the content portion of the meetings, babies tentatively explore and play together, and nursing occurs spontaneously, without social inhibition. To me, La Leche League meetings depict a breastfeeding subculture within our society. To walk into a league meeting is to be immersed and engrossed in a breastfeeding society. There's just no substitute for witnessing firsthand what is meant by the La Leche League motto, "good mothering through breastfeeding." Newcomers casually observe breastfeeding at all ages and stages amid a group of mothers for whom it is truly the norm. On top of all this, a nutritious snack is served, and a resource table piled with reference materials provides the opportunity for lots of stimulating reading until the next meeting.

My Own La Leche League Experience. I first became involved with La Leche League in the final month of my pediatric residency training, as I was about to give birth to my fifth child. In the course of helping a new mother, Kathy, establish a milk supply for her tiny premature infant, I had mentioned La Leche League (LLL) to her. At that time, I had no direct exposure to LLL but was aware of their existence and their widely recognized expertise. Kathy immediately contacted an LLL Leader from whom she obtained valuable help. Shortly thereafter, Kathy attended an LLL meeting and returned brimming with excitement about all that she had learned. She shared with me some of the reference materials she had borrowed, and as I reviewed these scientific documents, I was riveted by their content. "Why hadn't I learned any of this in medical school and residency?" I wondered.

By the time my own baby was born, Kathy was hosting LLL meetings in her home and began urging me to attend a meeting with my infant, Mark. "All right," I conceded, "I'll go as a health professional to observe. That way I'll be more knowledgeable about referring other mothers." I was totally unprepared for what awaited me that evening. When I entered Kathy's home with my newborn, I walked into a nurturing, supportive community where women celebrated their family life and extolled motherhood. Immediately someone brought me something to drink, while others welcomed me and complimented my baby. I had never experienced such affirmation for being a mother. Although I already had four other babies, my pregnancies were never cause for community celebration. Instead, they always represented a crisis in the on-call schedule, an inconvenience to others that would have to be accommodated. Until this point, my principal identity had been that of a doctor-in-the-making who happened to have children. This night I was first and foremost a mother—a nursing mother—who happened to be a physician. In the past, I had felt tremendous pressure to resume a full course load or on-call rotation shortly after delivery, even if it would lead to my relinquishing breastfeeding before I had wanted. Amid my new LLL friends, I was being validated in my role as a mother, and for the first time, I felt I had permission—indeed responsibility—to place my own baby's needs over the demands of others.

I faithfully attended LLL meetings for two years as I continued to nurse my baby. It was the information and support I received from LLL that empowered me to remain available to my baby and to turn down attractive professional opportunities that would have meant the loss of breastfeeding. Instead, I accepted a flexible academic position that allowed me to nurse Mark uninterrupted. I kept attending meetings because I continued to need a regular infusion of factual information, peer support, and inspiration.

Not only did LLL provide me the opportunity to breastfeed my last child the full course, but it taught me invaluable lessons about parenting, family life, nutrition, discipline, and wellness. In the year after Mark was born, I read everything LLL published for parents and professionals, and before long, I became an LLL Medical Associate. Within a few years, I was being invited to speak at the LLL Annual Physicians' Seminar and I had met the founding mothers I once read about with such admiration. Eventually, I became a member of LLL's Health Advisory Council—all because I had been invited to an LLL meeting with my fifth child. I think it's safe to say that my whole career was indelibly influenced by La Leche League, for which I am most grateful. I will always be indebted to Kathy for introducing me to this wonderful organization. I am confident that LLL can do as much for you as it has for me.

In addition to monthly meetings, LLL offers telephone advice, numerous publications, conferences, breastfeeding products, professional education, and more. Look for a local group in the white pages or see Resource List, page 446, to locate a group or to contact La Leche League International headquarters.

Nursing Mothers Counsel

Nursing Mothers Counsel (NMC) is another nonprofit, volunteer, peer support group for breastfeeding mothers available in many U.S. communities. Trained counselors provide telephone advice for mothers with breastfeeding inquiries. In special cases, home visits are available to resolve persistent or difficult problems. NMC counselors are mothers who have nursed a baby and who have received training on breastfeeding and counseling techniques. They also complete additional reading on breastfeeding and related topics. Many NMC chapters rent electric breast pumps and carry a selection of breastfeeding products. Although not as widespread as LLL, several states have local NMC chapters. Check the white pages or contact the national office (see Resource List, page 446).

The WIC Program

The WIC Program (Special Supplemental Nutrition Program for Women, Infants, and Children) is a federal program, operated by the U.S. Department of Agriculture in partnership with state and local health departments. WIC provides nutrition education, extra foods, and health care referrals for eligible women, infants, and children up to age five. Eligibility is based on income guidelines and a nutritional need for WIC foods. Many working families qualify for WIC benefits, and 45 percent of U.S. infants participate in the WIC program. WIC strongly promotes breastfeeding and offers a variety of breastfeeding support services. WIC clients receive one-on-one prenatal breastfeeding education, breastfeeding classes, and routine postpartum follow-up and counseling. Many WIC clinics have peer support programs for breastfeeding women and some offer pump loan programs for nursing mothers who require the use of an electric breast pump. Call your state health department or local WIC program to find out if you are eligible for WIC services (see Resource List, page 447).

In-Home Support

Support groups alone cannot provide the in-home practical help you will need in the early weeks of breastfeeding. Unfortunately, few couples receive enough help from the right helpers. Often, no one is able to come and stay with the new family, due to distance and work schedules. (Perhaps because no one was able to help me after I gave birth, I resolved to be present when my sisters and sisters-in-law brought new babies home.) In other instances, well-intentioned relatives descend upon the new family and, without meaning to, may deplete their dwindling energies. We've all been warned about the insensitive guests who insist on holding and feeding the baby while the new mother waits on them. How often I have heard in the clinic comments like, "Things should get better on Saturday after we take my mother and stepfather to the airport." Indeed, no help might be better than the wrong "help." Since many contemporary grandmothers did not breastfeed their own babies, they may not be able to provide practical assistance with nursing despite their good intentions. Finally, some dedicated bottle-feeders have been known to overtly or covertly sabotage the breastfeeding attempts of their daughters and daughters-in-law.

Think long and hard about whether you want anyone to stay in your home after delivery, and, if so, who that person should be. A close relative with whom you have a good relationship and who successfully breastfed her own children would be an excellent choice. If the person lives nearby but can't stay, maybe she can come for a few hours each day. Fathers definitely should plan to take paternity leave. My navy husband (who had just returned home from overseas) got two weeks off after our first child was born. Living in Hawaii, we were thousands of miles from our nearest relative, making Larry's help and encouragement indispensable to me. In addition to family members, friends, neighbors, church groups, and other sources of volunteer help, professional *doula* (one who mothers the mother) services for new mothers are available in many cities (see Resource List, page 449).

Breastfeeding Supplies

While it is certainly possible to breastfeed successfully without any special equipment or supplies, a wide array of breast-feeding aids can facilitate the nursing experience. Like myriad other baby care articles, breastfeeding supplies can make your life easier. I recommend you acquire some of the following items before or shortly after your baby's birth, based on your budget and personal preferences.

• **Nursing bras.** You will need several comfortable maternity bras to support your enlarging breasts during pregnancy. Also purchase at least two nursing bras, although it is difficult to predict the proper size correctly, since your breasts will enlarge more when your milk comes in. Toward the end of the first postpartum week when breast engorgement is subsiding, you can get several more nursing bras. The bra should fit comfortably both in the cup area and around the rib cage. Nursing bras have a release mechanism to allow the cup flaps to be pulled down to expose the breasts for

some women arrange multiple bed pillows to help position their infant at the breast, others find that a custom-made nursing pillow greatly facilitates breastfeeding. The main benefit of a nursing pillow is to decrease the distance from your lap to your breast and make you more comfortable nursing. Others provide support for the mother's arm at the elbow. Nursing pillows come in various shapes, sizes, and attractive designs. Check out several to find the style that works best for you. Many can be used for other purposes as the baby gets older.

• **Footstool.** A breastfeeding mother spends many hours a day nursing her baby. If she is hunched over or awkwardly positioned, backaches can result. A nursing footstool is a sloped footrest that raises the mother's upper legs and brings her baby closer to the breast during nursing. As a result, the mother's back is kept straighter and she is more comfortable feeding. After weaning, these stools make ideal footrests, especially for shorter women. I have one under my desk.

• **Nursing clothing.** It doesn't take special clothes to breastfeed successfully. Skirts or pants and blouses are convenient for lactating women. By unbuttoning your blouse from the bottom, you can nurse without your breast being visible. Some women like to own a nursing nightgown, with inapparent slits where the breasts can be exposed for feeding. Nursing clothes, ranging from simple blouses to evening gowns, allow for discreet nursing on any occasion. Special nursing clothing can be purchased at maternity shops or through specialty catalogs and cottage industries. These nursing fashions can make it easier to breastfeed in public. The Association for Breastfeeding Fashions (AFBF) is a trade organization whose member companies (most of which are owned by former or current nursing mothers) sell maternity and nursing apparel. You can contact AFBF to obtain a copy of their directory of member companies and their newsletter (see Resource List, page 450).

• **Rocker.** Many expectant mothers relish the thought of nursing and rocking their baby and will select a special chair for that purpose. Make sure it is comfortable, with adequate back and arm support, and that it is the right height for you. The rocker motion may not be ideal for learning to nurse, but once things are going smoothly, a comfortable rocker can be a blessing.

• **Bassinet.** No matter how elaborate a nursery you have prepared or how fancy the crib, you will probably find it most convenient to keep your baby in a bassinet at your bedside at night during the early weeks. When she is ready to nurse, you just lean over, scoop her up, and voilà! Many parents are more comfortable with their newborns in bed with them (not a waterbed, however). What's least desirable with breastfeeding is having your new baby down the hall in a nursery where you trudge in a half-sleep state several times each night. If this is the case, a twin bed in the nursery may allow you to get some extra shut eye.

Budgeting Money for Breastfeeding

In my opinion, too much emphasis has been given to the cost savings of breastfeeding. Certainly breastfeeding is cheaper than buying formula, but you shouldn't expect to feed your baby for free. Just as you are spending money on your baby's nursery and layette, plan to budget some funds to help you succeed at breastfeeding. Whether you purchase some of the supplies just mentioned or rent an electric breast pump or pay to see a lactation consultant, you should consider it money well spent. Ask your friends and relatives who want to give you a baby shower gift to consider contributing to your breastfeeding fund so your baby can receive ideal nutrition.

Prenatal Nipple Preparation

Whether and how to prepare your nipples for nursing is a controversial topic. Recommendations range from regularly expressing some colostrum, rolling the nipples, and applying lubricants to leaving the nipples alone. About the only thing everyone agrees on is: "First do no harm." This is particularly sound advice because, in the past, many of the recommended nipple preparation techniques thought to prevent sore nipples actually damaged the nipples and created problems. Many of the earlier nipple creams contained alcohol and other irritating ingredients. Overly harsh techniques, like rubbing the nipples with a rough towel, previously were advised to "toughen" the nipples and prepare them for nursing. But nipple skin is not callus-forming tissue that can be toughened. All too often, these inappropriate manipulations and topical applications resulted in damaged, painful nipple skin that was prone to cracks and fissures once breastfeeding commenced.

Conventional thinking among lactation specialists is that

Mother Nature doesn't need any help with nipple preparation. During pregnancy, numerous small, raised areas on the areola, known as Montgomery's glands, enlarge and secrete a substance that naturally lubricates and cleanses the nipples. In primitive societies where women's breasts are uncovered, sore nipples are rare, suggesting that exposure of the nipples to air and sunlight helps condition them for nursing. Some experts advise women to lower the cup flaps on their maternity bra for an hour or so each day to expose their nipples to air and allow them to gently rub against outer clothing. Because soap can cause excessive drying, many counselors advise women to bathe without using soap on the nipples during the latter months of pregnancy, especially in low-humidity climates. Properly designed studies have not been conducted to answer the simple question of whether various prenatal preparation techniques reduce sore nipples when breastfeeding is initiated.

In areas where humidity is low and dry skin is a common problem, USP Modified Lanolin (medical grade) makes an excellent emollient or moisturizer for the nipples, both prenatally and after delivery. I find that, beginning in the last trimester, a daily application of a thin coating of lanolin serves to make nipples supple and elastic. Moisturizing the nipples offers the added benefit of helping women become comfortable handling their breasts. A woman who is reluctant to touch her breasts and nipples may find it difficult to position her baby correctly to nurse.

While numerous nipple creams are marketed, many of them contain multiple, unnecessary, irritating, and potentially sensitizing ingredients. The common effective agent in almost all nipple preparations is lanolin. I prefer to use this single ingredient in its ultra-purified, anhydrous form (Lansinoh for Breastfeeding Mothers, PureLan). A popular myth claims that anyone allergic to wool cannot use lanolin. Actually, allergy to topical lanolin is extremely rare, and I have seldom encountered women who have reacted adversely to it.

Some breastfeeding counselors advocate prenatal nipple manipulation, such as pulling or rolling exercises, or attempts to express colostrum. However, these maneuvers have not been shown to improve breastfeeding success, and I do not routinely recommend them. Furthermore, prenatal nipple stimulation can trigger uterine contractions and initiate labor. *You should always get your obstetrician's approval before performing any prenatal nipple exercises.*

Prenatal Breast Exam

For some inexplicable reason, both physicians and parents tend to assume that "every breast is just perfect for breastfeeding." We readily accept the fact that some couples have trouble conceiving, that many women require cesarean delivery, that millions of people wear eyeglasses, or that some individuals don't make enough insulin. But when it comes to lactation, convention has it that "every woman can breastfeed" and that every breast makes sufficient milk for as long as required. Fortunately, most women's breasts do work well most of the time. Nevertheless, a few women have lactation risk factors that can be detected by a prenatal breast exam. Early identification of inverted nipples, potential problems due to breast surgery, or other breast variations allows a woman to take steps to improve her chances for success. Prenatal care providers routinely examine women's breasts and check for suspicious lumps as part of their initial pregnancy evaluation. However, I believe the breasts should be examined again at the beginning of the last trimester, and the exam should include an assessment of possible breastfeeding risk factors. Women with normal breasts ought to be given appropriate reassurance, while those with any apparent variations that could impact breastfeeding should be offered an individualized feeding plan and close follow-up after delivery.

Breast Enlargement During Pregnancy. The breasts normally undergo considerable enlargement under the influence of the pregnancy hormones estrogen and progesterone. These hormones cause tremendous growth in the number and size of the milk-producing glands and the system of ducts that carry milk to the nipple openings. The amount of breast enlargement women experience is highly variable, but generally the breast changes of pregnancy are quite obvious. In a study we conducted at the Lactation Program in Denver on 319 women, those who reported little or no prenatal breast enlargement had an increased risk of producing insufficient milk after delivery. While the risk certainly isn't an absolute one (some women with little or no breast enlargement breastfeed just fine), I think such women should be followed more closely after delivery to be sure that they establish an adequate milk supply and their babies gain appropriate weight.

Breast Size, Contour, and Symmetry. Conventional wisdom says that breast size has nothing to do with breastfeeding ability. I agree that *prepregnant* breast size is a poor predictor of breast-feeding success, since even small breasts can undergo remarkable development of the glands and ducts during the prenatal period. In my experience, a woman whose breasts remain very small at the end of her pregnancy should be considered at increased risk for producing insufficient milk. (Admittedly, some women with minimal prenatal breast enlargement will go on to experience remarkable breast changes when their milk comes in after delivery and to produce an abundant supply.)

Bigger isn't always better, as extremely large breasts also can represent a potential lactation risk factor. Large breasts don't necessarily have more functioning glands than average-size breasts, and may, in fact, have fewer. Very large, pendulous breasts can make it awkward to position the baby to nurse. In addition, the weight of excessively large breasts may stretch and flatten the nipples, making them more difficult for an infant to grasp correctly.

Breast contour can represent another clue to a potential breast-feeding problem. Tubular-shaped breasts, which are somewhat elongated and narrow and lack typical fullness, may have a limited number of milk glands (see Tubular Hypoplastic Breasts, chapter 11, pages 411–412.) The milk glands are concentrated under the areola, making it appear disproportionately large in comparison to the breast and giving it a bulbous appearance. While some women with this type of underdeveloped breast produce insufficient milk, good breastfeeding management after delivery can help such women maximize their milk production.

Nearly half of women have slightly asymmetrical breasts, and such minor differences are considered normal. However, moderate or marked differences in breast size can point to potential problems with milk production. Sometimes one breast (usually the larger) produces a normal volume of milk, while the other side may produce little. Variations in breast appearance don't necessarily mean that a woman will encounter problems with breastfeeding, but they shouldn't be ignored or dismissed lightly.

While the variations I have described don't mean that a woman can't breastfeed, I believe it is only prudent for women with potential breast risk factors to seek close medical supervision after delivery until they are certain that breastfeeding is going well. The

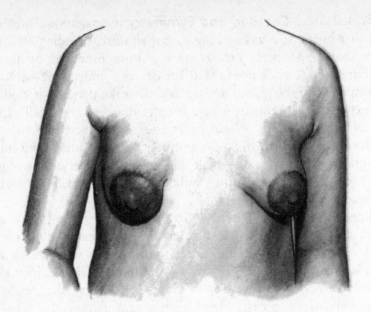

Tubular-shaped breasts lack typical fullness.

purpose of identifying possible risk factors is not to be *pessimistic*, but rather to be *realistic*, and optimally prepared.

Previous Breast Surgery. In the past, it didn't occur to most women or to their physicians that diagnostic or cosmetic breast surgery might affect subsequent lactation. We now have sufficient experience evaluating breastfeeding women to appreciate that an operation on the breast sometimes impacts the success of breast-feeding. As more older women bear children, the number who have had at least one breast biopsy has increased greatly. Cosmetic breast surgery, including augmentation, reduction, and breast lift, is a relatively common occurrence in our society among women of childbearing age. The influence of breast surgery on breastfeeding is discussed in detail in chapter 11. I believe the principal lactation risk comes from surgical incisions in the vicinity of the nipple margin. Incisions in this area may cut milk ducts, which can inter-fere with proper milk drainage. In general, breastfeeding after aug-mentation surgery often is successful, while reduction procedures usually result in a diminished milk supply. If you have had surgery on one or both breasts, don't jump to conclusions. Instead, review the material on pages 407–413, and inform both your obstetrical

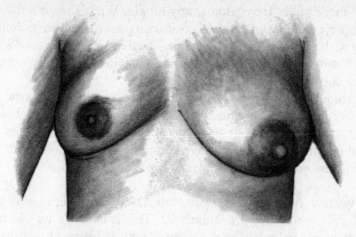

Differences in breast size may predict
differences in milk production.

and pediatric health care providers about your operation. If possible, contact your surgeon and obtain your medical records explaining the procedure. Your surgeon may be able to predict the probable effects of your particular surgery on breastfeeding, although little information is available in the medical literature about this issue. What's most important is that you and your baby are followed very closely after hospital discharge to evaluate the success of breastfeeding and to tailor a feeding plan that assures your baby receives adequate nutrition.

Nipple Protuberance. A wide range of normal appearance exists in the size and shape of a woman's nipple and areola, the dark circular area around the nipple. Most nipples are somewhat protuberant and become even more erect when they are stimulated or compressed. Thus, when a newborn nuzzles and licks her mother's nipple as she is learning to nurse, her exploratory motions cause the nipple to become more protuberant and easier to grasp correctly. Some women's nipples are slightly flattened, and others have almost no definition from the surrounding areola. An infant can have more difficulty learning to nurse when the mother has flat nipples that do not protrude with stimulation. (I also have seen nipples so long that they caused the baby to gag at first.) Nipples also range widely in diameter, from tiny to extremely large and wide. While some nipple shapes pose a greater challenge to successful breastfeeding than others, in general, a baby can learn to nurse successfully from almost any nipple. What's most important is proper guidance in correct positioning and latch-on technique, along with patience and perseverance (see chapter 4, pages 88–99). Even flat nipples can be drawn far back into the baby's mouth during correct breastfeeding.

Fortunately, most women's nipples become more elastic and protuberant during pregnancy as a result of hormonal changes. Sometimes, however, one or more of the prenatal techniques suggested for inverted nipples are recommended for women with very flat nipples (see below and chapter 7, pages 222–225).

Inverted Nipples. As stated above, normal nipples become more erect when they are stimulated. This is nature's way to make nipples easier to grasp by a newborn who is learning to nurse. A small percentage of women (2 to 3 percent in our study of 319 women) have inverted nipples that pull inward when they are compressed, instead of protruding outward. Inverted nipples can range from those that appear normal unless compressed or those that are

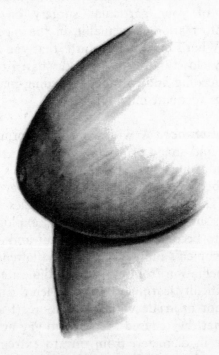

Some nipples are very flat, with little definition from
the surrounding areola.

loosely dimpled to nipples with a readily apparent deep central indentation.

Since nipple protractility tends to increase as your pregnancy progresses, an inverted nipple may improve somewhat without any specific treatment. A nipple that remains inverted can pose several obstacles to successful breastfeeding. An infant can have difficulty latching on correctly to an inverted nipple, which tends to retract inward as the baby tries to grasp it. Attempts to nurse can be extremely frustrating to both mother and baby, and the infant may have difficulty obtaining enough milk. In addition, inverted nipples are very prone to skin injury with breastfeeding. Whereas normal nipples are pliable, supple, and capable of elongating to a marked degree, the skin of inverted nipples can be tight and nonelastic. Finally, a few inverted nipples are so deeply retracted that they pose a mechanical obstruction to milk flow.

Detecting an inverted nipple. To test for an inverted nipple, use your thumb and index finger to gently compress the areola (the dark circle around your nipple) about an inch behind the base of your nipple. A normal nipple will protrude with this maneuver. If your nipple pulls inward, it is inverted. Also ask your obstetrical care provider to examine your nipples. When inverted nipples are recognized prenatally, one or more therapies may be recommended in the last month or two of pregnancy to help pull the nipples out.

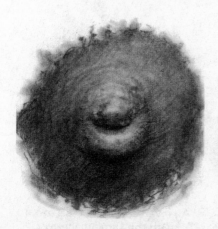 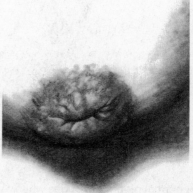

Loosely dimpled inverted nipples can be readily everted.

Some inverted nipples are pulled deeply inward.

Breast shells. The most popular treatment for inverted nipples is to wear breast shells, which are also known as breast shields or milk cups, to draw the nipples out. A breast shell is a dome-shaped, hard plastic device made up of two parts—an inner ring and an attached overlying dome. The breast shell is worn over an inverted nipple and held in position by the maternity bra. A bra with a larger cup size is needed to accommodate the device. The central opening in the inner ring is placed over the inverted nipple, causing gentle, steady pressure around the base of the nipple that tends to direct it into the central opening. The overlying dome keeps the bra from touching the nipple. The devices usually are prescribed during the last month or so of pregnancy. A mother begins wearing them a few hours each day and progressively increases her time, based on her comfort level. In many cases, after weeks of use, an inverted nipple will protrude normally. If treatment is delayed until after birth or is not completed by the time of delivery, breast shells can continue to be worn between feedings after the baby is born (see chapter 7, page 224). *Before using breast shells, make sure you get permission from your obstetrical care provider to wear the devices.*

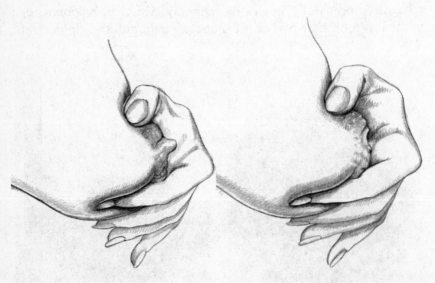

A normal nipple protrudes when the areola is compressed with the thumb and index finger behind the base of the nipple.

An inverted nipple pulls inward with the same maneuver.

Because any type of nipple stimulation can provoke contractions of the uterus, the shells are not recommended for high-risk pregnancies or cases of threatened premature labor. Breast shells are available from Ameda/Egnell, Medela, La Leche League, lactation consultants, hospitals, and other sources of breastfeeding supplies (see Resource List, page 449).

Hoffman's exercises. Some breastfeeding specialists also recommend manual nipple manipulation, known as Hoffman's exercises, to improve the protractility of inverted nipples. These maneuvers are performed by placing the thumbs or forefingers at opposite points at the base of the nipple. Then, by pressing inward and pulling away, the nipple is stretched, and tightness at the base is loosened. The exercise, which should be demonstrated by a health professional, is performed several times each day during the last month of pregnancy, with the mother working her fingers around the base of the nipple. Again, you should clarify with your obstetrical care provider whether such nipple stimulation poses a risk of premature labor in your situation.

You should know that, while breastfeeding counselors have long recommended the use of breast shells and Hoffman's exercises

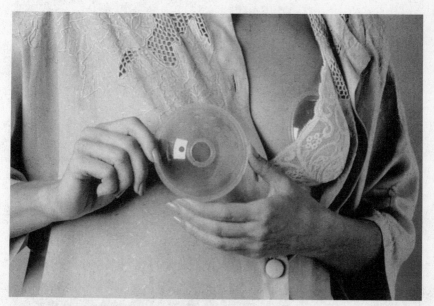

A breast shell worn over an inverted nipple is held in position by the maternity bra.

for the prenatal treatment of flat or inverted nipples, their effectiveness in improving breastfeeding outcome has not been proved. Two studies have failed to show that recommending the use of breast shells and Hoffman's exercises actually increased the percentage of mothers still breastfeeding at six weeks postpartum. Some mothers in the studies actually felt the breast shells were a disincentive to breastfeeding and found them to be conspicuous, embarrassing, uncomfortable, and the cause of skin rashes. Nevertheless, many breastfeeding experts, myself included, continue to recommend breast shells and believe that many women have been helped by them. Further studies of their use are needed.

The Niplette. A new device, the Niplette, claims to permanently correct flat and inverted nipples within two to three months of

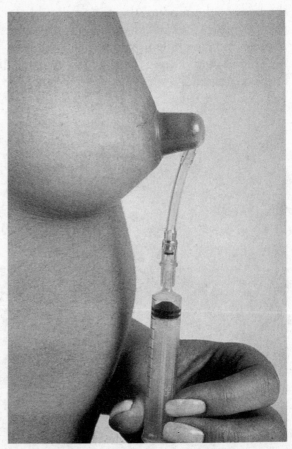

The Niplette, shown with attached syringe, is reported to correct flat and inverted nipples.

daily use (see Resource List, page 450). Invented by a British plastic surgeon, the Niplette consists of a thimble-shaped, transparent nipple mold and a small syringe used to create a comfortable level of sustained suction. When the syringe is removed, the nipple cup remains in place over the nipple for hours at a time, gradually everting it. The device is reported to have been used successfully by thousands of women in Europe, usually for the cosmetic correction of inverted nipples in nonpregnant women. However, it is also recommended for use through the seventh month of pregnancy to correct inverted nipples in preparation for breastfeeding, under your doctor's supervision. The Niplette is not recommended in late pregnancy and while lactating, since leaking milk will break the seal and make the device ineffective. The Niplette has only recently become available in the United States and is being marketed by Avent America, Inc. directly to the public, principally through ads in women's magazines. While the Niplette sounds promising for correcting flat or inverted nipples, few U.S. practitioners have experience using the device, especially during pregnancy, and little data is available about its safety and effectiveness. Discuss the Niplette with your doctor or lactation consultant before trying it.

If inverted nipples are not recognized prenatally or treatment has not corrected the problem by the time the baby is born, see chapter 7, pages 222–225, for additional strategies for breastfeeding with inverted nipples.

Breast Secretions. In the latter months of pregnancy, many women notice that their breasts secrete a small amount of early milk, known as colostrum. You might see a few clear or yellow drops appear at the nipple openings when you compress your nipple between your thumb and forefinger. Or you might notice yellowish stains on your maternity bra. Women vary in the amount of colostrum they produce during pregnancy. Some never observe any breast secretions, while others can express measurable amounts of colostrum (although there is no need to do this).

Rarely, the colostrum contains blood and ranges from a bright red to a brownish, rusty appearance. While bloody nipple discharge always is alarming and raises fears of cancer, the cause usually is benign when the bleeding evident from *both* breasts occurs in late pregnancy or the first two weeks postpartum and doesn't persist. Such cases of temporary blood-tinged colostrum are believed to be related to the tremendous proliferation of blood vessels in the breast during pregnancy and the rapid development of milk ducts and glands. In my experience, the blood gradually clears as the milk comes in abundantly, and usually is gone by one to two weeks, resulting in the descriptive name, "rusty pipe" phenomenon. *Of course, you should notify your doctor if you ever notice an abnormal discoloration of your colostrum or milk or any evidence of blood.* Never dismiss such a symptom as normal without getting your doctor's opinion.

Another cause of bloody nipple discharge is intraductal papilloma, a benign tumor within a milk duct. If such a tumor is suspected, your physician may recommend further diagnostic tests, such as ultrasound, surgical removal, or close follow-up.

Breast Lumps or Masses. One in nine women will be diagnosed with breast cancer in her lifetime. Early diagnosis of breast cancer depends on routine breast self-examinations, screening mammograms, and regular medical checkups. Unfortunately, many cases exist where the diagnosis of breast cancer was tragically delayed due to pregnancy or lactation. During these times, new breast lumps are easily overlooked or attributed to milk glands, clogged ducts, or other lactation-related explanations. Although mammograms are hard to interpret when performed on dense lactating breasts, that doesn't mean diagnosis of a suspicious lump has to be delayed. Ultrasound is an excellent way to distinguish solid lumps from cysts, even during pregnancy and breastfeeding. Biopsy of any suspicious lump should *not* be postponed. Modern breast biopsy no longer requires surgery. Definitive answers are now easily obtained with ultrasound guided core biopsy, a special type of needle biopsy. If you detect a breast lump, notify your doctor immediately and have it checked. If your doctor dismisses it without an ultrasound, biopsy, or close follow-up, *get a second opinion.*

Making Pediatricians Aware of Breast Variations

I must emphasize the importance of communicating with your baby's pediatrician-to-be about the presence of any potential breastfeeding risk factors. Pediatricians seldom examine mothers' breasts and may be unaware of variations in appearance that could affect the success of breastfeeding. Not uncommonly, a pediatrician is left wondering why a breastfed baby isn't gaining weight when the mother seems to be feeding often enough. For example, the unsuspecting doctor might be uninformed about the woman's previous breast biopsies that may have cut milk ducts. Or she or he may be unaware that the woman has tubular breasts and might not be able to produce a full milk supply. I find it ironic that the pediatrician responsible for the baby's growth seldom is informed about breast variations in the mother that could affect the success of breastfeeding. Make sure your baby's doctor is aware of any condition that could affect your baby's ability to obtain milk with breastfeeding.

Prenatal Plan for Special Circumstances

Many breastfeeding problems can be anticipated prenatally, giving you time to seek out information and make special preparations. Common examples are flat or inverted nipples, chronic maternal illness and medications, or anticipated birth defects or multiple births. When anything out of the ordinary is identified prenatally, I urge you to use every avenue available to acquire information about your particular situation before your baby arrives. While I can't address every possible eventuality, I will give you some examples of how to use the prenatal period to prepare for unique circumstances.

Multiple Births. Breastfeeding of twins and greater multiples poses a unique challenge, and at the very minimum, you will want to arrange for sufficient help after delivery and acquire some specialized information pertaining to nursing multiple babies. Often multiple births occur early, so your babies could be premature and small. I routinely recommend that mothers of multiples plan to rent a hospital-grade electric breast pump to maximize their milk supply until the babies are nursing well and gaining weight appropriately (see chapter 11, pages 393–402). It's a good idea to locate a pump rental station in your vicinity before you deliver. I also suggest you join a Mother of Twins Club (see Resource List, page 449) and talk with other women who have nursed multiples successfully. La Leche League provides valuable support for breastfeeding mothers of twins or greater multiples. The care of twins can be facilitated by an array of baby equipment/supplies designed for multiples, ranging from strollers to twin nursing pillows.

Birth Defects. The increasing use of prenatal ultrasound and amniocentesis allows for the early recognition of various defects that in the past were not identified until after birth. Knowing in advance that your baby has a heart defect, cleft palate, Down syndrome, or other medical problem will allow you to plan prenatally for any unique requirements concerning your infant's care and feeding, instead of being totally surprised at delivery. If the particular problem is likely to affect your baby's ability to breastfeed, you can arrange to meet with a lactation consultant and your baby's doctor prior to delivery to discuss anticipated feeding difficulties and learn how to obtain and use a rental electric pump to bring in and maintain your milk supply after delivery (see chapter 10, pages 360–371). You could join a support group for parents of babies with the same problem, interview surgeons or specialists who might be called to consult, and read at length about your baby's problem.

Medications. Whether a mother's medications are compatible with breastfeeding is a common and perplexing question. Lack of information about this issue often results in delayed or interrupted breastfeeding. A common scenario goes like this: Mother is eager to breastfeed and baby is ready to nurse. Someone notices that the mother takes several prescription medications and inquires whether they pose a risk to the baby. Until a reassuring answer is obtained, nursery personnel are reluctant to let the infant go to breast. Mother and baby become distressed, and bottle-feeding is begun until someone in authority gives the green light to breastfeed.

If you take medication on a chronic basis, such as anticonvulsants, antidepressants, asthma medications, blood pressure medications, and steroids, you should plan to use the prenatal period to track down information about the specific drugs you take (see Maternal Medications and Breastfeeding, chapter 7, pages 266–269). Misinformation about drugs in breast milk is very common. If you are told that a medication is not compatible with breastfeeding, get a second opinion before abandoning your plans to nurse. The American Academy of Pediatrics publishes a list of commonly used drugs, along with recommendations about their safety for breastfeeding infants. A pharmacist, especially one at your local drug consultation center, should be able to knowledgeably answer questions about drugs in breast milk. The Drug Information Service at University of California at San Diego can answer such questions for a small charge (see Resource List, page 448). Often, a safer drug can be substituted for one that could cause adverse effects in nursing babies. By all means, discuss the issue with your obstetrical and pediatric care providers before you deliver to avoid any unnecessary delays in putting your baby to breast.

Maternal Illness. A chronic medical condition in the mother can raise numerous questions about breastfeeding (see chapter 11, pages 415–421). Infectious problems, such as hepatitis or TB, raise issues about the risk of transmission of illness to the baby. Women with health conditions associated with minimal fat stores, such as cystic fibrosis, eating disorders, or chronic diarrhea, may not produce sufficient milk. Lactation can reduce the insulin requirements of diabetic mothers. If you have a chronic medical problem, consult with the physician who manages your condition, as well as your obstetrical care provider and your baby's doctor, about your plans for breastfeeding.

Maternal Employment. If you anticipate becoming employed while still nursing your baby, plan to attend a prenatal class on breastfeeding and working. Locate a pump-rental station in your vicinity (see Resource List, page 446) and begin your search for quality child care. Make sure the person you select knows that breastfeeding is a priority for you and is willing to support your efforts. It's never too early to begin communicating with your employer about ways to accommodate breastfeeding when you return to work. Think about where you might pump privately at the workplace and how you can use coffee breaks and your lunch hour to express milk to maintain your supply. Chapter 8 provides a detailed discussion of breastfeeding and employment.

Previous Breastfeeding Difficulties. If your previous breastfeeding experience was fraught with difficulties, you may worry whether similar problems might recur this time. Perhaps your first baby lost excessive weight after birth or failed to gain adequately with breastfeeding. Maybe you suffered uncomfortable breast engorgement, cracked nipples, or a painful bout of mastitis. It's still possible to have a thoroughly enjoyable breastfeeding experience this time. I suggest that you schedule a prenatal visit with a lactation consultant or other breastfeeding specialist who can review your previous breastfeeding history. Chances are good that she will be able to pinpoint where things went wrong and suggest strategies to assure your success this time around. We can't change the past, but we can learn from it.

Choosing a Hospital

Today, the choice of a hospital at which to give birth is not only influenced by geographic location and personal preference but also increasingly dictated by insurance policies, HMOs, and physician-hospital affiliations. Nevertheless, an extremely competitive market makes hospitals keenly sensitive to consumer preferences, especially when it comes to childbearing. Hospitals are scrambling to renovate their maternity wards and make them more "family centered." Traditional labor, delivery, and recovery rooms rapidly are being replaced by single-room maternity care and LDRs (single rooms where women labor, deliver, and recover). Lactation specialists increasingly are found on staff in hospitals with maternity services.

Despite today's short postpartum hospital stays, I can't overemphasize the impact of the hospital experience on the success of breastfeeding. The twenty-four hours or so you will spend in the hospital can either set the stage for long-term success or seriously undermine your breastfeeding efforts. Plan ahead to deliver in a setting where breastfeeding will be encouraged and protected. Tour the hospital prenatally and inquire about their maternity policies. Wherever a choice exists, select a hospital where mothers and babies are kept together after birth, where rooming-in is unrestricted, where breastfeeding on demand is encouraged, where supplements are not given to breastfed babies except for valid medical reasons or a mother's express desire, and where staff are knowledgeable about breastfeeding and prepared to spend individual time with new mothers (see chapter 4, pages 107–112). If pro-breastfeeding policies are not standard, write out your requests and discuss them with both your obstetrical and pediatric care providers. Enlist their support in agreeing to write specific orders that will assure your baby rooms-in as much as possible, nurses on demand, and is not given unnecessary supplements. Fortunately, a growing number of hospitals are modifying their maternity practices to better promote breastfeeding, so it should be possible to find a setting where you can get an optimum start nursing your baby. In fact, making hospital policies more supportive of breastfeeding has become a worldwide mission.

The Baby-Friendly Hospital Initiative

In September 1990, the United Nations convened a large gathering of heads of state to address the welfare of the world's children and to ask nations to commit to twenty-seven objectives to improve children's status by the year 2000. Because declining breastfeeding rates worldwide have seriously jeopardized the health of children, one of the targeted global priorities was the "empowerment of all women to breastfeed their children." As a direct outgrowth of this resolution, The United Nations Children's Fund (UNICEF) and the World Health Organization (WHO) introduced a worldwide initiative in 1991 to "re-create a world environment that supports, protects, and promotes the practice of breastfeeding." This campaign is aimed at removing the obstacles to breastfeeding that a woman may encounter in the hospital and restoring traditional community support systems that protect breastfeeding. The emphasis on creating a hospital environment friendly to mothers and babies was reflected in the project's name, The Baby-Friendly Hospital Initiative (BFHI).

The campaign acknowledges that widespread hospital practices, such as separating mothers and babies and giving water and formula supplements to breastfed infants, unwittingly undermine breastfeeding and contribute to its decline. The baby-friendly code drawn up by UNICEF and WHO assures that a hospital is on the side of breastfeeding by removing barriers to its successful initiation. In 1992, UNICEF and WHO officially launched BFHI as a worldwide campaign for both developing and industrialized countries. The new code is being communicated to virtually every hospital in the world, and those that comply with its practice standards are being awarded "baby-friendly" status. The following Ten Steps to Successful Breastfeeding summarize the recommended practices for every facility that provides maternity services and cares for newborn infants. At the time of this writing, only a dozen or so U.S. hospitals and birthing centers have earned the official baby-friendly designation. Scores of others have obtained a letter of intent to work toward implementing these ten steps.

1. Have a written breastfeeding policy that is routinely communicated to all health care staff. The written policy should address all ten steps, prohibit the promotion of formula, be available to all staff, and be evaluated for its effectiveness.

2. Train all health care staff in skills necessary to implement this policy. All staff should be trained in the advantages of breastfeeding and the basics of practical management. Selected staff should receive specialized training to allow them to serve as resource people.

3. Inform all pregnant women about the benefits and management of breastfeeding. Those who have never breastfed or who have previously encountered problems should receive special attention.

4. Help mothers initiate breastfeeding within one hour of birth. Healthy babies should be allowed to remain with their mothers for at least the first hour. Mothers who have had cesarean deliveries should be given their babies to hold within a half hour after they are able to respond to their babies.

5. Show mothers how to breastfeed, and how to maintain lactation even if they are separated from their infants. Nursing staff should offer all mothers further assistance with breastfeeding and verify that mothers can demonstrate correct breastfeeding technique. Mothers of babies in special care nurseries should be shown how to express their milk frequently to maintain lactation.

6. Give newborn infants no food or drink other than breast milk, unless *medically* indicated. Staff should know the valid medical reasons for offering supplements to breastfed infants. Formula used in hospitals should be purchased by the facility and not accepted free or promoted in any way.

7. Practice rooming-in—allow mothers and infants to remain together twenty-four hours a day. Rooming-in should start within an hour of a normal birth or within an hour of when a cesarean mother can respond to her baby. Separations should occur only for necessary hospital procedures or medical indications.

8. Encourage breastfeeding on demand. Mothers should be advised to breastfeed whenever their babies show signs of hunger. No restrictions should be placed on the frequency or length of feedings.

9. Give no artificial teats or pacifiers (also called dummies or soothers) to breastfeeding infants. Mothers should be taught to avoid pacifiers and bottle-feeds because they can interfere with breastfeeding.

10. Foster the establishment of breastfeeding support groups and refer mothers to them on discharge from the hospital or clinic. Key family members should be taught how to support the breastfeeding mother at home. Hospitals should have a system of follow-up for breastfeeding mothers after discharge, such as early postnatal visits, home visits, or telephone calls.

I thought it would be helpful for you to know about the Baby-Friendly Hospital Initiative (see Resource List, page 452) and to realize that hospitals the world over are making efforts to better support breastfeeding women. Being aware of these ideal hospital policies should help you know what to ask for at your own hospital so that you get the best possible start with breastfeeding.

Chapter 3

How Milk Is Made and Released

Mammals and Lactation

Before you begin breastfeeding, it will help to know something about the spectacular process by which your body produces milk and makes it available to your baby. The amazing phenomenon of lactation gets little attention in American society, where a disproportionate emphasis on the female breast as a sensual organ creates the distorted view that breasts are designed principally to evoke sexual arousal. But breasts have an important functional role in human reproduction.

Humans are classified as one of more than four thousand species of mammals, or animals who produce milk for their young. Before infant formulas became available within the past century, breastfeeding was indispensable for survival of our species. While breastfeeding now has become an optional, rather than essential, human function, we must realize that artificial feeding on a large scale has occurred for only a short period in all of human history. For other mammals, successful lactation remains a critical part of the reproductive cycle. I find it absolutely fascinating to examine the enormous diversity in mammals that allows each species to be nourished in a manner that ideally meets the growth and developmental needs of its young. Thus, human milk and the mother-baby interaction during breastfeeding represent both ideal *nutrition* and ideal *nurturance* for human infants.

Anatomy of the Human Breast

The External Breast Structures

The paired, dome-shaped *breasts* are situated on the front of the chest. Contrary to the media portrayal of near perfect, symmetrical orbs, women's breasts come in a wide variety of sizes and contours, ranging from tiny to huge, from pert to pendulous, and from rounded to bullet-shaped or tubular. In most women, breasts are not an identically matched pair. Upon close inspection, slight asymmetries in size and appearance can be noted. A few women have a marked difference in breast size or other variations in appearance between their two breasts.

The *nipple* and *areola* are located near the center of the breast and are darker in color than the breast tissue. The nipple is the central protrusion, while the areola is the circular dark area on which the nipple sits. When babies breastfeed, they don't just suck on the nipple. Instead, they draw a large amount of the surrounding areola/breast into their mouths in order to properly extract milk. Thus, we correctly say that a nursing baby *breastfeeds* instead of *nipplefeeds*. Nipples vary tremendously in size and shape. Some are so flat that a distinction from the surrounding areola can barely be detected. Others are extremely long. Inverted nipples retract inward toward the chest wall, so that the tip of the nipple might be hidden from view or pulled inward when the nipple is compressed. The nipple diameter can range from very narrow to extremely wide or bulbous. The surrounding areola also comes in a variety of sizes and shapes. Some are so small that the baby easily takes the entire areola into his mouth while nursing. Others are four to five inches in diameter and couldn't possibly fit into an infant's mouth. The areola is usually round, but it can be eliptical. It contains hair follicles, and many women have some hair on their areola.

The Internal Breast Structures

Internally, the breast is composed of four main types of tissue: *milk glands* that produce milk, *milk ducts* that carry milk, *supporting tissues* that give structure and shape to the breast, and *protective fat* that cushions the breast from injury. Variations in breast size largely depend on the amount of fatty tissue present. Almost all women have sufficient glands to produce enough milk for their infants. The milk glands are arranged in fifteen to twenty-five distinct sections, or *lobes*. The different sections are separated by supporting tissue, known as *connective tissue*. Also present in the breast is a network of *blood vessels* to carry blood to and away from the milk glands. The generous blood supply not only nourishes the breast but also provides the nutritional components for manufacturing milk. *Nerves* make the breast sensitive to touch and cause the nipple to become more erectile when it is stimulated. The nerves also carry the baby's suckling stimulus to the brain where it results in the release of hormones that make and eject milk (see Role of Prolactin and Oxytocin in Lactation, pages 75–78).

Breast Development and Prenatal Breast Changes

The milk glands and main milk ducts actually begin to develop in the breast during fetal life. At birth, many babies have swollen breast buds, due to stimulation of the ducts and glands by the mother's pregnancy hormones. In both girl and boy newborns, the temporarily enlarged breasts sometimes secrete drops of milk, known as *witches' milk*, in the first few days after birth. Thereafter the mammary gland remains inactive until puberty, when estrogen and other hormones cause development of the breast fatty tissue and the milk glands and ducts.

When a woman gets pregnant, development of the milk ducts and glands dramatically intensifies. While a pregnant woman is contemplating how she plans to feed her baby, Mother Nature is single-minded in her purpose. Beginning in early pregnancy, the breasts are prepared for lactation whether or not a woman intends to breastfeed. The pregnancy hormones, including estrogen and progesterone, cause the milk ducts and glands to proliferate and enlarge. *Ducts* branch and rebranch into smaller *ductules*, whose ends bud off into grapelike clusters of small rounded sacs, known as *alveoli*, the milk-producing glands. Alveoli are surrounded by tiny, bandlike *muscle cells* that squeeze the glands to expel milk into the ductules. Each cluster of alveoli makes up a *lobule*, and a

cluster of lobules makes up a *lobe*. Smaller ductules that drain milk
from lobules merge to form the larger ducts that drain each lobe.
Sometimes ducts merge before they exit at the nipple, so the
number of nipple openings might be smaller than the number of
breast lobes. The milk ducts dilate to form larger *milk sinuses*
shortly before they open at the tip of the nipple. Milk that pools in
these reservoirs situated just beneath the areola is easily removed
by the baby during nursing.

All this breast development results in significant enlargement
and varying degrees of breast tenderness within the first few
months of pregnancy. The preparation of the breasts for breastfeeding is so effective that full lactation occurs even when an
extremely premature baby is born. Reports exist of women who
have lactated after experiencing a miscarriage in the second
trimester of pregnancy.

In addition to extensive duct and gland development, the nipple
and areola become larger and more pigmented during pregnancy,
perhaps serving as a visual marker for the infant who must grasp

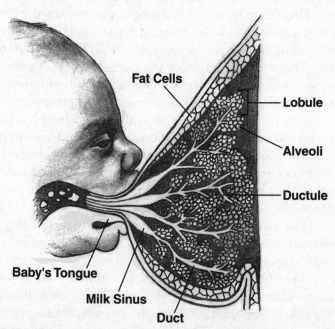

Internal breast structures and view of infant's mouth on breast, with jaws
positioned over the milk sinuses to obtain milk.

both the nipple and a significant portion of surrounding areola in order to feed correctly. Small raised bumps arranged in a ring around the areola become more prominent. These *Montgomery's glands*, as they are known, secrete an oily substance that cleanses and lubricates the nipple and helps keep the areolar tissues healthy, soft, and pliable. The nipple and areola have many nerve endings which, when stimulated, cause the nipple to become erect and trigger the pituitary reflex mechanisms that release oxytocin and prolactin (see Role of Prolactin and Oxytocin in Lactation, pages 75–78). The nipple becomes more sensitive during pregnancy, the blood supply to the breasts increases greatly, and the branching veins on the surface of the breasts become much more prominent. Some pregnant women develop stretch marks on their breasts similar to those that appear on the abdomen or thighs.

Milk Increases in Abundance

On approximately the second to fourth day after giving birth, a woman's breasts will become quite full and firm. Scant colostrum changes to creamy white transitional milk and greatly increases in quantity. This surge in milk production, accompanied by perceptible breast swelling, is often referred to as "milk coming in," an unfortunate phrase that wrongly implies *no* milk was present until this time. The scientific term for the beginning of abundant milk production is *lactogenesis*. The sudden increase in milk production is triggered by the abrupt fall in estrogen and progesterone after delivery of the placenta, coupled with the high blood level of prolactin at the end of pregnancy. Although early and frequent nursing are thought to help increase milk production sooner, the fact is that lactogenesis occurs even in formula-feeding mothers. (Medications to dry up a mother's milk supply are no longer routinely prescribed for nonbreastfeeding women.) Thus, a mother easily could change her mind and switch from bottle-feeding to breastfeeding in the early postpartum period. After milk has come in abundantly, however, what happens in the breasts differs markedly between breastfeeding and nonbreastfeeding women. If a woman nurses her baby or uses a pump to express her milk, production of milk will continue. If milk is not emptied from the breasts, however, ongoing production quickly ceases. Thus, lactogenesis, or milk coming in, is a pivotal point in breastfeeding.

Ongoing Milk Production

As explained above, whether or not a woman intends to breast-feed, Mother Nature sees to it that milk increases in abundance several days after delivery. However, milk rapidly begins to dry up if it is not removed, so that milk production quickly stops in women who formula-feed their babies. Breastfeeding women continue to produce milk as long as they nurse their infants regularly. I know a woman who lactated continuously for twelve years, nursing each previous baby through the subsequent pregnancy. Ongoing milk production in breastfeeding women is known as *galactopoiesis*, and is principally regulated by the hormonal and emptying mechanisms described below. (Both men and nonbreast-feeding women can suffer from spontaneous milk production due to various medical causes, including pituitary tumors and certain medications. This phenomenon is known as *galactorrhea*.)

Role of Prolactin and Oxytocin in Lactation

Many hormones are involved in making and releasing milk. For the purpose of simplifying the explanation, however, I will focus on the role of *prolactin* and *oxytocin*. Both hormones are made by the *pituitary gland* located at the base of the brain. The driving force that controls the release of these hormones is infant suckling. When the infant nurses and stimulates nerve endings in the nipple and areola, a message is carried to the brain that results in the release of prolactin from the anterior pituitary gland and oxytocin from the posterior pituitary.

Prolactin. Prolactin is the hormone believed to be important in stimulating milk to be manufactured from components in the blood. It is particularly important in early lactation. If a woman begins breastfeeding, her prolactin level remains elevated and her milk production continues. If a woman formula-feeds her baby, her prolactin level gradually declines to the nonlactating range and milk production ceases. Thus, prolactin blood levels are higher in breastfeeding women than in formula-feeding mothers. Furthermore, prolactin levels rise markedly during a breastfeeding, often increasing several-fold from their baseline level. Although prolactin gradually declines until the next nursing, blood levels remain much higher in breastfeeding mothers than in nonlactating women. The

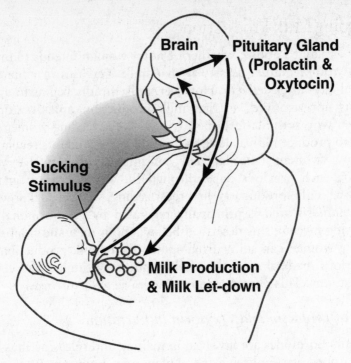

Brain

**Pituitary Gland
(Prolactin &
Oxytocin)**

**Sucking
Stimulus**

**Milk Production
& Milk Let-down**

Hormones involved in milk production and milk release.

high baseline prolactin and frequent daily prolactin spikes stimulate continued milk production in breastfeeding women. Generally, the more a baby nurses, the more prolactin will be released and the more milk will be produced. This is why frequent, unrestricted nursing is so important to successful breastfeeding.

As long as a woman is fully breastfeeding, her estrogen levels remain low and prolactin levels high. This combination usually prevents her periods from returning for many months, a phenomenon known as lactational amenorrhea. In addition to decreasing her chances of conceiving (see Lactational Amenorrhea Method, chapter 6, pages 191–192), lactational amenorrhea postpones menstrual blood loss and thereby helps the breastfeeding woman rebuild iron stores depleted by pregnancy and delivery.

Prolactin blood levels are elevated in pregnant women, but it is believed that the high progesterone levels during pregnancy prevent milk from being produced until after birth. Within a couple of days after delivery, progesterone and estrogen levels quickly fall while prolactin remains high. This is the hormonal combination that triggers the dramatic increase in milk production after delivery. Years ago, I had a patient whose milk inexplicably had not increased by three weeks after delivery. When she suffered a severe postpartum hemorrhage, a large piece of retained placenta was discovered and removed by performing a D & C. Presumably, the retained placental fragment produced enough pregnancy hormones to interfere with lactogenesis. The woman's milk came in abundantly thirty-six hours after the placental fragment was removed and she went on to nurse her baby successfully for over a year.

Oxytocin. Oxytocin, the hormone that causes the uterus to contract during labor, also plays a key role in lactation. When a baby starts suckling at the breast, oxytocin is released and causes tiny octopus-like muscle cells that surround the milk glands to contract. This squeezing action of the tiny muscle cells forces milk and fat globules out of the milk glands and into the ducts. Oxytocin also causes muscle cells along the milk ducts to contract and propel milk through the duct system. The main role of oxytocin in breastfeeding is to expel the milk that is manufactured in the milk glands. Thus, prolactin is involved in milk production, while oxytocin is involved in milk extraction. The effect of oxytocin on milk release is known by two common terms, the *let-down reflex* or the *milk ejection reflex* (*mer*). In humans, little milk can be obtained without the milk ejection reflex operating.

When milk lets-down into the milk ducts, the dilated sinuses beneath the areola rapidly fill with milk. This milk is easily available to the nursing infant if the baby is attached correctly to the nipple and surrounding areola. With the nipple positioned well back in the baby's mouth, the infant's tongue and jaws compress the areola and underlying milk storage areas, thereby pressing the milk from the sinuses into his mouth (see the illustration on page 73).

When a woman begins breastfeeding after delivery, oxytocin not only causes milk to be ejected from the breast but also triggers uterine contractions that help shrink the enlarged uterus back to its normal size. Thus a nursing mother might feel some abdominal cramping while she breastfeeds during the first week or so postpartum. This temporary discomfort, known as *afterpains*, is a strong indicator of oxytocin release, which will help her milk to flow.

After about two weeks, the let-down reflex usually becomes

quite brisk and the volume of milk is rather abundant. The sudden stretching of the milk ducts as they fill with milk creates a sensation in the breasts when let-down occurs. Many women describe this feeling as a "pins-and-needles" sensation, or as "tightening," "stinging," "burning," or "tingling." Some women do not perceive a dramatic let-down response, yet produce plenty of milk. When milk is letting-down, it may drip, or even spray, from the breast, and the baby may gulp rapidly or pull away to catch his breath. Because stress and anxiety can interfere with the let-down, it is helpful to try to relax during nursings and to develop a familiar routine that will condition the let-down reflex. Most nursing mothers soon are able to condition their let-down to be triggered by the sight, sound, or smell of their baby. Simple maneuvers like sitting in a favorite chair, pouring a glass of juice to drink, or gently massaging the breasts can evoke the milk ejection reflex and start milk flowing before the mother actually begins feeding. Pain, embarrassment, fear, anxiety, interruptions, or the presence of a disapproving relative can impede the let-down reflex in some women. Typically, a mother's milk will let-down several times during a single feeding.

Role of Milk Removal in Ongoing Milk Production

Hormones alone don't fully explain how milk production is regulated in breastfeeding women. Some women, for various reasons, breastfeed from one breast only. In such instances, the unsuckled breast soon stops producing milk, even though both breasts have the same exposure to prolactin and oxytocin while the mother nurses on one side. Scientific evidence now exists to confirm that the amount of milk produced in each breast principally is governed by the amount of milk that is removed. Residual milk contains a protein substance known as *FIL* (*feedback inhibitor of lactation*). When FIL builds up in residual milk remaining in the glands, further milk production is suppressed. Residual milk also can cause excessive pressure and distension of the milk ducts and glands. Sustained pressure from residual milk eventually can damage milk-producing glands and further decrease milk supply. Thus, a woman will produce more abundant milk when her baby nurses efficiently and frequently, removing much milk from her breasts. The same woman will produce less when her baby nurses poorly or infrequently, removing little milk. Whenever feeding practices prevent the efficient extraction of milk, production can decrease. It is especially important that the breasts not be permitted to become overly full, uncomfortably tight, and lumpy in the first postpartum week. Every effort should be made to relieve excessive pressure and to help milk flow freely once it starts being produced in abundance.

Unfortunately, many common breastfeeding problems result in failure to drain the breasts well, which leads to diminished milk supply. Examples include infant difficulties latching-on correctly to nurse, severely sore nipples that interfere with feedings, or mother-baby separations that prevent a woman from nursing on a regular routine. When regular, effective milk emptying cannot be provided by the nursing infant, milk should be removed by mechanical means or by hand expression to prevent an unwanted decrease in milk supply. Generally, the most efficient, effective, and comfortable breast pumps available are the hospital-grade, rental-quality models that can empty both breasts well in about ten minutes. Many references will be made throughout this book to the use of such pumps in the management of breastfeeding difficulties.

Drying Up

Lactation will continue in each breast as long as milk continues to be removed. The drying up, or *involution*, process can occur rapidly (as in a bottle-feeding mother after delivery) or very gradually (as in a woman still nursing a toddler occasionally). Millions of bottle-feeding mothers experience their milk coming in a few days after delivery and provide models for the involution process. If these women do not nurse their babies or pump their breasts, their milk dries up within a matter of days. Their initially high blood prolactin level soon declines to the nonlactating range. Suppressor proteins present in residual milk in the glands send a powerful message to decrease the volume of milk produced. The sustained pressure of unremoved milk in the breasts causes the glands to shrivel and stop secreting milk. The same process occurs if a woman in full lactation weans abruptly.

Involution of lactation also can occur gradually. For example, as an older baby weans slowly over many months the breasts may never become uncomfortably full as milk production gradually declines. Involution can occur at different rates in each breast depending on the baby's nursing habits. In fact, it is possible to wean completely on one side while continuing to nurse from the other breast.

As the volume of milk decreases during weaning, the milk composition changes to again become more colostrum-like, with higher levels of protein and minerals and lower levels of fat and the milk sugar lactose. Some women can express drops of milk from their nipples for many months after they stop breastfeeding. Although this can be quite normal, women should report any nipple discharge to their doctor to determine its origin.

Beginning when a woman is about thirty-five years old, the milk glands in the breast progressively decrease in number and are replaced by fatty tissue. While most women in their late thirties and forties certainly can breastfeed successfully, it has been my impression that a few women in this age range have unexplained difficulty producing sufficient milk for their babies. Perhaps in these women the decrease in milk glands has progressed more rapidly. After all, wide variations also occur in the onset of puberty or menopause. Following menopause, the breasts have progressive loss of their functional components and fatty tissue as they go into "retirement." Nevertheless, amazing stories exist of postmenopausal grandmothers who were able to relactate and breastfeed a grandchild when the infant's mother died in childbirth (see Relactation and Induced Lactation, chapter 11, pages 404–407).

Milk Composition

Colostrum. The early milk produced during pregnancy and the first few days after delivery is known as *colostrum*. It is present in scant volume and can range in appearance from watery to thick yellow. Some women leak drops of colostrum prenatally, while others do not notice any milky discharge until they start breastfeeding. Colostrum differs in composition from mature milk. Colostrum is higher in salt and protein, including many immune components, but it is lower in the milk sugar lactose and lower in fat content. Although colostrum has fewer calories per ounce than mature milk, it is the perfect first food for babies. The small volume makes it unlikely that a baby will choke when she is learning to suck, swallow, and breathe in synchrony after birth. Colostrum is easily digested, has a gentle laxative effect, and contains important growth factors that prepare the intestines to digest and absorb milk. Colostrum also is rich in antibodies, white blood cells, and other immune properties that coat the lining of the infant's immature intestine and help protect the baby against swallowed bacteria and viruses. Babies who are fed formula drink milk of the same composition at every feeding, while breastfed babies receive a very dynamic fluid that changes in composition day by day during the first week or two.

Transitional Milk. The sudden increase in milk production that begins a few days after delivery is accompanied by changes in milk composition as well. The milk produced from about four to ten days is no longer true colostrum and not yet mature milk. Since the composition of breastmilk is changing daily during this time, it is commonly known as *transitional milk*. The volume is climbing, while the protein content declines and the fat and lactose contents increase.

Mature Milk. The breast milk produced after about ten to fourteen days is known as *mature milk*. It not only looks quite different from colostrum but also has a much different composition. Mature milk is whiter and is present in much greater volume than the early milk. While gradual changes in composition may occur over several weeks, composition of mature milk becomes rather consistent, except for the fat content that varies throughout the feeding (see Foremilk and Hindmilk, page 82).

Mature milk looks thinner than infant formula, which causes some mothers to mistakenly believe that their milk isn't rich enough. When expressed and left to stand, the fat will separate and rise to the top. Despite its watery appearance, mature human milk contains all the nutrients a baby requires. It is so well utilized by babies that breastfed infants consume less volume than formula-fed infants, yet grow as well or better in the first several months. After about six months, the protein content of milk drops off a little, but babies are normally eating solid foods by this time and are obtaining other sources of protein in their diet.

Foremilk and Hindmilk. Not only does milk composition change over time, but the fat content of milk changes throughout a single feeding. The milk a baby first obtains during a breastfeeding is low in fat content and is somewhat watery. This milk is known as *foremilk*. When the let-down reflex is triggered, the milk glands release large fat globules into milk, raising its fat content considerably. The milk obtained after the milk ejection reflex, or milk let-down, has been triggered is known as *hindmilk*. On average, fat makes up about 4 percent of the content of human milk and provides more than half of its calories and energy. Foremilk may be only 2 percent fat, while the fat content of hindmilk can be 10 percent or higher. The increased fat content of milk consumed toward the end of the feeding is like having dessert. As a baby nurses on the first breast, he obtains a higher fat milk as the feeding progresses, eventually finishing with creamy hindmilk. By the time he switches to the second side, some mixing of foremilk and hindmilk already has occurred in the second breast when the let-down reflex was triggered while nursing on the first side. Nevertheless the baby begins by drinking a more watery milk than he finished with on the first breast, somewhat like taking a sip of water during his meal. As he continues nursing at the second breast, the fat content of his milk climbs steadily, leaving him full, sleepy, and thoroughly satisfied.

Common Myths about the Production of Breast Milk

Mʏᴛʜ: As long as you intend to breastfeed, you can always count on having plenty of milk.

Fᴀᴄᴛ: Certainly most women are capable of breastfeeding successfully and producing adequate quantities of milk if given proper guidance in nursing technique and routines. Yet, many parents do not appreciate the basic principles that regulate milk production in women who desire to nurse. They just assume that their feeding "intentions" will automatically translate into a ready supply of milk for their baby. Although you can count on your milk coming in abundantly after delivery, continued adequate production depends on regular infant suckling that effectively removes milk. In order to keep producing plentiful milk, you need to nurse your baby often (eight to twelve times a day for a newborn). The baby needs to suck effectively during feedings and empty much of the milk in the breasts. Sufficient milk will not continue to be made if a baby feeds on a restricted schedule, if supplemental bottles are routinely given, or if an infant's sucking doesn't extract very much milk. Thinking and wishing to have milk won't guarantee an adequate supply. It is only when the breasts receive frequent, effective suckling and when milk is removed regularly that full milk production continues. You can see why it is so important to get help quickly if nursing isn't going well. The better your baby is able to *take* your milk, the better your breasts are able to *make* more milk.

MYTH: Breast size predicts one's ability to breastfeed. Flat-chested women don't produce as much milk as large-busted women do.

FACT: An old wives' tale claims that women with small breasts don't make as much milk as women with larger bosoms. It's understandable how such a notion could become popular since most people naturally assume that breast size would predict breast function. However, breast size tends to be related to the amount of fatty tissue in the breast, rather than the quantity of milk-producing glands. In recent years, most breastfeeding books adamantly refute the belief that flat-chested women will have trouble making milk. They argue that breast size has nothing to do with lactation ability.

Actually, it's probably true that *prepregnant* breast size has little to do with subsequent milk production. In my experience, most women with small breasts experience remarkable breast enlargement during pregnancy or when their milk comes in. By the time their breasts become engorged after delivery, these women no longer would be considered to have small breasts. Thus, I believe that dramatic prenatal and postpartum breast changes reflect optimistically on a woman's milk-producing potential.

A few women have small or poorly developed breasts that do not enlarge much with pregnancy or after delivery. In my experience, such women may be at increased risk for making insufficient milk, but this has not been proved conclusively. Such women may not have enough functioning milk glands in their breasts to produce an abundant milk supply. Often, they have small breasts that are more tubular and less rounded. Perhaps cases such as these have contributed to the origin of the myth about breast size. Unfortunately, we know little about how variations in breast appearance relate to lactation potential.

Myth: To produce high-quality milk, your diet must be strictly regulated because your milk reflects what you eat.

Fact: Many women are reluctant to breastfeed because they mistakenly believe that they must eat a "perfect" diet in order to make nutritious milk for their baby. They fear that skipping a meal, drinking soda, eating junk food, or disliking vegetables might make it preferable for them to formula-feed. This simply isn't true. Women all over the world manage to produce milk of excellent nutritional quality while eating diets that vary widely. The different nutritional components in milk are taken or manufactured from substances in the mother's bloodstream. Whether the protein in your diet comes from peanut butter or the most expensive steak, your milk will have the right quality and quantity of protein.

Busy mothers might not eat the right amount of every nutrient every day. If a mother's diet is temporarily deficient in one constituent, such as fat, her own body stores of fat will supply the necessary amount to keep making nutritious breast milk. The quantity of most nutrients in milk is regulated at the desired level no matter how much the mother takes in. For example, the salt in milk doesn't increase if a mother eats salty potato chips. Of course, the more healthful diet you eat, the better you will feel now and the healthier you will be years later. Proper nutrition for breastfeeding is little different from proper nutrition for pregnancy. Chances are good that you already are eating what you need.

Women who chronically eat a poor diet, such as women in countries where food supplies are inadequate, eventually will produce less milk. Also, if a woman has a vitamin deficiency, her milk may be low in proper vitamin content. This is quite rare, however, in the United States, where most nursing mothers have enough to eat and are advised to continue taking their prenatal vitamins while they lactate. Women who suffer from eating disorders or who have minimal fat stores due to chronic illnesses like cystic fibrosis will need to be monitored closely when they breastfeed.

MYTH: Breastfeeding makes your breasts saggy and less attractive.

FACT: Whether the breasts become more saggy after breastfeeding is disputed. Most experts argue that breastfeeding has a minor impact on subsequent breast appearance compared to the dramatic breast changes that result from pregnancy alone. Probably the greatest influence on how much a woman's breasts will sag over time is something beyond our control—the effects of heredity. Some women develop sagging breasts in their twenties after having just one baby. Other women may have delivered and nursed multiple children, yet their breasts show little sagging at fifty years. These differences are largely due to genetic influences, such as breast shape and the type of breast-supporting tissues we inherit. Wide-based breasts may be less prone to sagging than breasts that are narrow at the base.

It has been suggested that because breasts look larger and firmer during lactation, they naturally seem smaller and more saggy after weaning. In reality, the breasts might have changed very little from their original appearance, now long forgotten! Generally, flat-chested women prefer their breast size during lactation, while some large-busted women prefer the appearance of their breasts when they are no longer lactating. I suspect that women who are comfortable with their body image before becoming pregnant are more likely to remain satisfied with their physical appearance after becoming a mother and nursing their baby. Regardless of how your breasts look later, you can take pride in the knowledge that your body carried and provided the ideal nourishment for your precious child, for whom your breasts were an unmatched source of security and comfort.

Meanwhile, it probably helps to provide adequate support to your breasts during pregnancy and lactation by wearing a properly fitted maternity or nursing bra. Because breasts are heavier during pregnancy and lactation, they are more susceptible to gravity forces pulling them down and stretching the supporting ligaments. Custom-made bras can be ordered for women in hard-to-fit sizes (see Resource List, page 451).

Chapter 4

Getting Started –
The Hospital Experience

After months of preparation and anticipation, your baby has finally arrived. Exhausted and exhilarated, you are ready to begin your breastfeeding experience: your pregnancy has culminated in this special moment. After nourishing your baby in the uterus, your body is prepared to continue to provide all your baby's nutritional needs outside the womb.

Most babies are vigorous and healthy at birth and require little immediate care beyond drying them off and clearing the mouth and nasal passages. Unless you or your baby has a medical problem, the two of you ought to be able to be united right after delivery. A large number of U.S. hospitals now offer LDRs (labor-delivery-recovery rooms) that allow women to stay in the same room for labor, birthing, and immediate recovery. Instead of being whisked off to a nursery, your baby can remain with you and undergo any required assessments after birth right in the presence of his family. This practice gets breastfeeding started on the right foot.

Your First Feeding

You will want to start breastfeeding as soon as possible after delivery. Generally, earlier opportunities to nurse are linked to greater breastfeeding success. In most situations, the first nursing can take place within thirty to sixty minutes of giving birth, when a baby's sucking instinct is most intense. Try not to hold rigid expectations for this first breastfeeding experience. Instead, view it as a relaxing, intimate, get-to-know-you time. Your baby may only lick your nipple and act content to be snuggled at your breast. He may attach to your breast, suck briefly, then stop and look around. Or, he may latch-on and suck rhythmically as if he's done this many times before. Any one of these responses is perfectly normal. What's important is that the two of you remain together after delivery during a precious time of mutual exploration.

Correct Breastfeeding Technique

When beginning any new activity, whether swinging a golf club, typing at a keyboard, playing a musical instrument, or nursing a baby, it pays to learn and use proper technique from the very start. It's easier to establish and reinforce the right habits from the outset than to try to correct errors in technique once bad habits are ingrained.

Many new mothers are surprised to learn that breastfeeding isn't pure instinct for them or their babies. Even though babies have innate reflexes, like rooting and sucking, that serve them well in seeking and obtaining food, the fact is that correct breastfeeding is a learned art. In most societies, the art of breastfeeding is passed from mother to daughter and sister to sister. At present in the United States, when so many contemporary grandmothers lack personal breastfeeding experience, new mothers are left to learn how to nurse their baby from a postpartum or nursery nurse. Such one-on-one instruction is essential if you are to leave the hospital confident and capable of nursing your baby on your own at home. Don't be shy about asking for extra help! You're the best judge of whether you have learned all you need to know before you are discharged.

The Basics of Positioning

Many women who begin breastfeeding are so preoccupied with having their baby grasp their breast that they skip right over the fundamentals of getting themselves and their babies into proper position for nursing. Your body position might not seem relevant until you consider that you will spend many hours breastfeeding each day for many months. Positioning yourself properly will reduce the likelihood of any physical discomfort while nursing and make it easier for your baby to breastfeed. Correct positioning of your baby will improve her attachment to your breast and increase her intake of milk. It's definitely worth spending a little time getting it right!

Getting Comfortable

The first breastfeeding may occur while you're reclining or sitting in your hospital bed or sitting in a chair in your room. The reclining position will be discussed a little later. If you sit up in bed, elevate the head of your bed as much as possible. You will probably need to tuck some pillows behind you to keep your back straight. If you sit up in a chair, select one with ample back and arm support and an appropriate height. It shouldn't be so low that your knees point up nor so high that your feet can't reach the ground. If necessary, tuck one or more pillows behind your back to help you sit upright. A rocker sounds enticing but it's preferable not to have movement while you and your baby are learning.

A pillow placed on your lap will help elevate your baby to the level of your breast. If no pillow is available, crossing your leg on the side you are nursing will bring your baby closer to your breast. A lap pillow is essential for women who deliver by C-section to keep the baby's weight from pressing against their incision. A footstool beneath your feet will also decrease the distance between your lap and your breast and make your back more comfortable. These simple measures can reduce neck, shoulder, and back strain. Some women purchase and use a special nursing pillow to make breastfeeding more comfortable and may even bring their pillow on outings.

Sitting upright is important, both for your comfort and to help your baby attach to your breast correctly. Leaning forward or backward changes the position of your breasts in relation to the baby and makes it more difficult for your baby to grasp the breast correctly. When you breastfeed, you always want to bring the baby to your breast, not your breast to the baby. When your breast has to be pulled to reach your baby, it is more easily dislodged from the infant's mouth during feeding. If your breasts are very large, you may want to roll up a diaper or receiving blanket and put it under your breast to elevate it.

Positioning Your Baby

No matter which breastfeeding position you use, a few basic principles apply. Your baby should be well supported throughout the feeding to help her relax and to provide her with a sense of security. You can use pillows, cushions, or your arm to maintain good support for her head, neck, shoulders, back, and bottom. Your baby's head, neck, back, and hips should remain in alignment. Her body should not be flexed or curved when positioning her to feed. When first learning to nurse, you'll want to keep her hands out of the way so they don't wind up in her mouth or next to your nipple. You can do this by swaddling your baby in a blanket. Or, you may be able to hold her arms against her body as you position her to nurse.

Supporting Your Breast

During pregnancy, most women experience remarkable breast enlargement as a result of the development of the milk glands and ducts. When abundant milk production begins, the breasts get even heavier. A newborn infant can't be expected to keep the breast correctly positioned in her mouth during nursing unless you support your heavy breast from beneath. Use the hand opposite from your arm that is supporting the baby to cup your breast so you can present the nipple to your baby. Place four fingers underneath your breast and your thumb on top—the C-hold—to gently support your breast. The placement of your fingers on your breast is very important. They should be well behind the areola, far back from the nipple, so that they don't get in the way of the baby's mouth. Some women successfully use a "scissor" hold, or V-hold, to support the breast between their index and middle fingers. However, it is difficult with this hold to splay the fingers far enough apart to keep them behind the areola. The C-hold not only provides better breast support, but it makes it easier for the baby to grasp sufficient breast without impediment. Eventually, most babies learn to breastfeed without requiring the breast to be supported throughout the feeding. In the beginning, however, breast support will be a big help to your baby.

Breastfeeding using football hold.

Football Hold. The football hold, also known as the clutch hold, is used to position the baby to nurse on the same side as the supporting arm. The position is a popular choice for mothers who have had a cesarean birth, as it keeps the baby's weight off the mother's incision. Begin by sitting your baby up at your side, facing you with her head near your breast. Tuck her body under your arm against your side, like a football, with her feet pointing toward your back. If you are seated in a chair, the baby's body can be flexed at the hips, with her bottom at the back of the chair and her legs pointed up. Her shoulders, neck, and head are supported by your hand and fingers, while her upper back rests against your forearm. Typically a pillow is placed beneath the arm supporting the baby to elevate her to the level of the breast and to provide comfortable support for the mother's elbow. The football hold is another popular position for small babies or those having trouble latching on. It also works well for women with large breasts or flat nipples. The position allows a mother to see her nipple and the baby's mouth and to control the baby's head. It is important not to apply too much pressure to the baby's head, however, as this can cause the infant to arch her head against your hand.

Reclining Position. It is not necessary to get into a sitting position in order to nurse your baby. Women who have a cesarean birth often prefer to nurse while lying down to avoid pressure against their incision. Other women may not feel well enough to sit upright for long. At home, you may want to nurse your baby while lying in bed at night or while napping during the day. To nurse while lying down, roll onto one side and have a helper place several pillows against your back. You'll probably want a pillow under your head, and some women like to have a pillow placed between their knees. Try to keep your back and hips in a straight line. Place your lower arm around your baby and draw her close to you so that your bodies are touching. Your baby should be on her side

Breastfeeding in reclining position.

facing your breast, with her mouth lined up with the nipple. Use your opposite hand to support your breast.

It is actually possible to nurse from either breast in the reclining position without turning over. Place the baby on the bed next to you to nurse from the lower breast. Or, elevate the baby on a pillow to bring him to the level of the upper breast. You will want to have several other pillows handy to help you get into optimal position. Placing a pillow against the baby's back will keep him from rolling over if you want to remove your lower arm and put it under your head.

Helping Your Baby Attach Correctly

A baby is born with several reflex actions that help him learn to breastfeed. For example, an infant will automatically turn his head toward a stimulus that brushes against his cheek, a reaction known as the rooting reflex. He will open his mouth wide and put his tongue down and forward when the lips are touched. When a nipple touches the roof of the baby's mouth, it triggers rhythmical cycles of sucking in which the tongue compresses the nipple and areola. Despite all these built-in reflex actions, you should not expect your baby to latch on correctly to your nipple without some extra help on your part. Many mothers admit that they aren't sure how to breastfeed and that they were hoping the baby would know! They hold the baby in the vicinity of the breast and expect the infant to take over from there. You can be a great help to your baby by performing a few simple maneuvers.

Once you are positioned comfortably with your breast supported, and your baby is well supported and positioned with her mouth aligned with your breast, you are finally ready to help your baby latch on. Your baby's hands should be out of the way and her body pulled close to you so the breast is within easy reach. You don't want the breast pulling away from her as she tries to nurse.

Lightly touch your nipple against the midpoint of your baby's lower lip to stimulate her to open her mouth WIDE. Many women make the mistake of trying to push their nipple into their baby's mouth, just like we do with bottle-feeding. Instead of trying to insert your nipple, concentrate on bringing your baby to your breast. Lightly tickle her lip, and patiently wait until she opens very wide (see illustration, page 96). Then quickly pull her toward you so she grasps your breast. A common error at this step is to attempt to latch a baby on when her mouth is not open wide enough. Usually this problem occurs because a mother is so anxious to get her baby attached that she doesn't take the time to keep tickling her baby's lower lip until she opens really wide, like a yawn. A baby who grasps the nipple without opening wide will end up grasping only the tip. Correct latch-on involves taking the entire nipple plus about one to one and a half inches of surrounding areola and breast. To understand why this is so important, review what you learned in chapter 3 about the milk glands and ducts. Remember how the ducts dilate into larger sinuses or reservoirs of milk just beneath the areola? In order for your baby to properly compress these sinuses and obtain milk, she must grasp sufficient areola and breast to allow her jaws to be positioned over the location of the dilated milk ducts. Since the size of the areola can vary tremen-

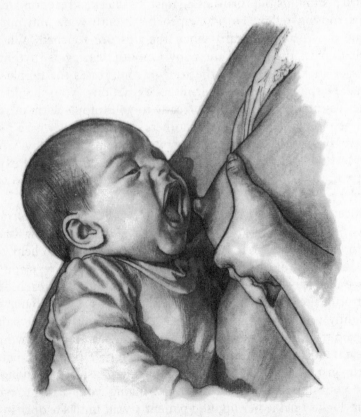

Lightly tickle the baby's lips until she opens WIDE like a yawn.

The infant should grasp the entire nipple
plus about an inch of surrounding areola.

dously from woman to woman, a baby may need to take it all into
her mouth (if the areola is small) or may leave a margin visible
beyond her lips (if the areola is large). What's important is that the
baby takes the entire nipple and a large mouthful of breast (see
illustration, above). This will assure that the nipple is far back in
the baby's mouth so that it won't experience any friction or pressure and, thus, won't get sore.

Latch-on can be made easier for some babies if the mother uses
a C-hold and then gently compresses her fingers and thumb to
make the areola more narrow. The fingers and thumb should be
aligned with the baby's mouth by positioning them parallel to the
infant's jaws before squeezing them together. The result is a more

narrow and more protuberant areola area that may be easier for the infant to grasp properly.

When your baby is attached correctly, her jaws should be open wide, her lips flanged out, her nose resting against the upper breast, and her chin pressed against the underside of the breast (see illustration, below). You should feel her jaws compressing the breast at a point well past the nipple. Her sucking should not be uncomfortable. The tip of her tongue might be visible between her lower lip and the breast as it lies over the lower gum. Even with her nose touching the breast, your baby can breathe comfortably because her nostrils are flared. If you attempt to press your breast away from your baby's nose, this can change the angle of the nipple in your baby's mouth, creating friction and soreness. If her breathing seems obstructed by your breast, try pulling her lower body closer to you.

Signs of Proper Technique. You can assume your baby is latched on correctly if you observe the following:

- Her mouth is open wide and her lips are flanged out.
- She has taken a good amount of the areola into her mouth.

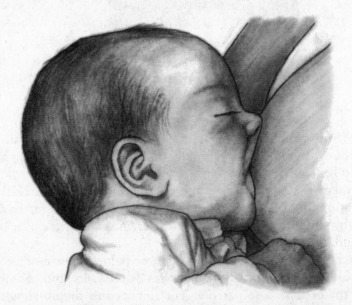

Correct positioning of the infant's mouth on the breast, with jaws open wide, lips flanged out, and nose and chin touching the breast.

- She sucks deeply and rhythmically, with several sucking bursts separated by pauses.
- You hear your baby swallow regularly (a soft "kaa, kaa, kaa" sound when the baby exhales).
- Your nipple is comfortable after the first few sucks.
- Her cheeks don't sink inward, and you don't hear any clicking sounds as she nurses.

Signs of Incorrect Technique. You should suspect that your baby is *not* attached to the breast properly if any of the following are present:

- She is grasping just your nipple and no surrounding areola.
- The baby's chin and nose are away from the breast.
- Her lips are curled in.
- She keeps falling off.
- She doesn't suck deeply and regularly (a rapid, light, sucking action—flutter sucking—is wrong).
- You seldom hear swallowing.
- Her cheeks are tugging inward or you hear clicking noises.

You also should assume that the latch-on is incorrect if you experience significant pain while nursing. Brief, slight nipple discomfort often is present during the first few sucks for the first couple of days, but thereafter breastfeeding should be comfortable. Significant pain usually means the baby is not grasping the surrounding areola properly. If she isn't latched on correctly, don't continue the feeding. Instead, remove her, correct your positioning, and latch her on all over again.

Removing Your Baby from the Breast. When a baby has fed well and is satisfied, he usually will stop sucking and come off the breast on his own. Do not attempt to remove your nursing baby from the breast by pulling him off. Breaking suction in this way is likely to cause trauma to your nipple and result in soreness. Instead, slide your finger into your baby's mouth and press down on the breast to break suction in order to remove your nipple.

When Breastfeeding Becomes Second Nature

All these details you're trying to learn make breastfeeding sound like a lot of fuss and bother. You might wonder if breastfeeding is going to be terribly restrictive, since it seems so very complicated. But remember, when you are busy learning the basics, everything seems painstaking and awkward. Before long, however, you'll be nursing without thinking about the fundamentals at all. A toddler learning to walk has to concentrate on every step. In a matter of weeks, the child becomes more surefooted, and before long, walking is second nature. Breastfeeding is like that. You and your baby have so much to learn in the first days that you wonder if you will ever go through the motions automatically. Before your baby is a month old, I predict you'll be breastfeeding while performing all kinds of activities: reading, talking on the phone, eating your lunch, comforting an older child, watching a soccer game, sitting at your computer terminal, or putting the dog out.

Tips for C-Section Moms

Although a cesarean birth poses unique challenges, successful breastfeeding certainly is possible for mothers who have a C-section. Disappointment and anger over an unplanned cesarean delivery may leave you with less emotional energy to devote to breastfeeding unless you are able to safely vent any negative feelings you may have about the loss of your hoped-for birth experience. If your C-section is planned, inquire in advance about hospital policies that promote successful breastfeeding (see The Baby-Friendly Hospital Initiative, pages 67–69) and present any special requests that you would like honored, like the avoidance of artificial nipples and ready access to your baby. Ask to have a support person stay in your room at all times to help you with your infant. Arrange to share this responsibility among several people, such as your partner, your mother, and your sister.

If you are able to have an epidural anesthetic, you can be awake for your baby's birth and can breastfeed shortly after delivery. Even if you require a general anesthetic, you can start breastfeeding with assistance as soon as you feel ready. You will want to choose one of the nursing positions that keeps the baby's weight off your incision, such as the side-lying position or the football hold. Resist suggestions to have your baby fed in the nursery, and be assertive about asking for the extra help you need at each feeding.

Although the medications you take will pass into your milk, generally the antibiotics and pain relievers prescribed after cesarean delivery are safe for breastfeeding newborns. If the effects of a drug on your infant are in question, ask whether a safer medication might be substituted.

Frequency of Breastfeeding

New mothers want to know how often they should breastfeed. When your baby is just learning to nurse, it's best not to think about how far apart to space "feedings." The very term implies meals being consumed at predictable intervals. But an early breastfeeding session is less a meal than it is a learning experience that needs to be repeated at frequent intervals.

You and your baby each have a lot to learn, and the way you learn is by practice. You are learning how to position your baby and how to present your breast. Your baby is learning how to correctly grasp your nipple and areola, how to extract milk, how to suck and swallow and breathe without choking, and how to soothe and pacify herself at your breast. Until your milk comes in abundantly on about the third day, your baby may obtain only a couple of teaspoons of milk when she nurses. Instead of waiting an arbitrary number of hours between feedings, plan to offer your breast as often as your baby shows interest (see Infant Signs of Readiness to Feed below) in order to give your baby as much breastfeeding practice as possible. Expect to nurse your baby at least eight, and as many as twelve, times each twenty-four hours during the first month. If your baby doesn't wake or demand to nurse after about three and a half hours have elapsed since the beginning of the last feeding, you should try to arouse her. Ideally, your baby will be with you in your hospital room, but if she must stay in the nursery, request that she be brought to you whenever she stirs.

Infant Signs of Readiness to Feed

Many new parents expect their baby to cry when she is hungry. Few realize that crying is actually a late sign of readiness to feed. If you wait until your baby is crying loudly before you prepare to nurse her, both she and you may experience unnecessary frustration if you are unable to satisfy her need fast enough. Worse yet, some babies become exhausted from crying too long and end up nursing poorly by the time they are brought to the breast. Instead of waiting for your baby to cry, look for earlier, more subtle clues that she is ready to nurse. Babies signal readiness to feed during arousal from sleep, by increased alertness, flexing their extremities, bringing a hand to their mouth, turning their head, or moving their

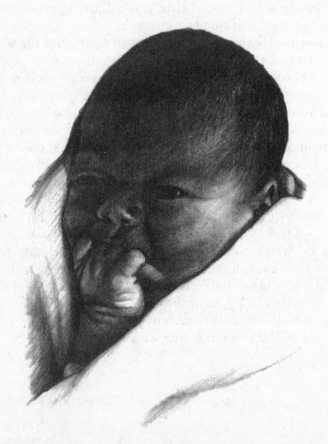

Sucking on fingers or hands can signal readiness to feed.

mouth or tongue. One or more of these signs can usually be observed long before the baby cries out loud.

Early Infant Elimination Patterns

The first bowel movement your baby passes, known as meconium, will look tarry black and is present in the baby's intestines during fetal life. Because colostrum is a natural laxative, frequent nursing will help expel the meconium. During the hospital stay, your baby's stools may change to a greenish-black. As the volume of milk your baby drinks increases, his bowel movements will turn yellow-green. By the fourth or fifth day, they should look yellow-gold, with little seedy curds, and the number of movements should increase to four or more each day (see Infant Elimination Patterns, chapter 5, pages 139–141).

Your baby may urinate only a couple of times a day on the first two days when the volume of colostrum he drinks is low. Once your milk increases in abundance (around the third day), he obtains a greater volume with each feeding, and the number of wet diapers increases to six to eight each day. Begin during your hospital stay to notice your baby's elimination habits. Keeping a record of your baby's feeding times, wet diapers, and bowel movements can be very helpful in monitoring his progress with breastfeeding.

Burping Your Baby

All babies swallow some air during feeding. Although many will burp easily without any special positioning, most parents make a ritual of helping their baby burp after taking the first breast and at the end of the feeding. A few babies need to be burped more often to remain comfortable. Trapped air in the stomach can cause a baby discomfort, making him restless partway into the feeding. Releasing the air may allow a baby to proceed with feeding more comfortably. A bubble of air in the stomach also can make a baby feel full too soon and cause him to stop feeding before he has taken enough milk. Burping the baby after the first breast not only makes room in the stomach for more milk, but the positioning and handling involved in burping can help arouse a sleepy infant to take the second side.

If your baby is sucking well, don't interrupt him to burp. Rather, take advantage of natural pauses for burping and use the time to socialize with your baby as you gently pat and stroke him.

Several good techniques are suitable for burping your baby. My favorite position for burping a newborn is to sit the baby upright on your lap, with your hand cupped under his chin to support his chest and head. Lean him forward slightly while you rub and pat his back. If he doesn't burp after a few minutes, you don't need to persist in your efforts. Another popular position is to support your baby upright over your shoulder (protected with a cloth diaper) and pat his back. Or you can lay your baby across your lap, with his head slightly higher than the rest of his body, and gently rub and pat his back.

Clothing

When you first start to breastfeed, adequate exposure of the breasts will make it easier for your baby to latch on correctly. You'll have plenty of time later to learn to nurse discreetly. It helps in the beginning to wear a gown that opens in the front. Those lovely nursing gowns with the slits for exposing your breasts will serve you well once breastfeeding is going smoothly. In the beginning, however, clothing often gets in the way of your baby's efforts to latch on. It's best to forgo modesty in favor of technique. Pull the curtain around your bed or ask the nurse to put a *Do Not Disturb* sign on your door if you are concerned that someone might enter your room unannounced while your breasts are exposed. You are not expected to nurse in the presence of anyone who makes you uncomfortable. During the learning stage, feel free to ask anyone to step out of the room if you feel awkward in their presence. Eventually, most women become comfortable nursing almost anywhere without feeling self-conscious, but you probably won't want an audience when you and your baby are still figuring things out.

Drink a Beverage While You Nurse

Another good habit you will want to start before you leave the hospital is making sure you have something available to drink each time you breastfeed your baby. Milk production requires extra fluids, and nursing mothers get thirsty often. Let your friends and relatives help out by getting you a glass of water or juice. Placing a straw in the glass will make it easy for you to take a drink when the glass is offered, since at first both your hands will be occupied during nursings. Many breastfeeding mothers find that the habitual practice of drinking a beverage as they prepare to nurse also helps to trigger their let-down reflex.

Night Feedings

Don't make the mistake of bypassing night nursings so you can get extra sleep in the hospital. Night nursings are important to your baby and to you. No one gets much sleep in a hospital whether or not they feed their baby at night. The best way to assure that you get the maximum possible sleep in the long run at home is to leave the hospital knowing how to feed your baby. A breastfed baby who is kept in the nursery and bottle-fed by the nurses at night may not nurse as well when the mother desires to resume breastfeeding in the morning. Today, hospital stays are so short that mothers can't afford to miss even one opportunity to practice their breastfeeding technique before they go home. Don't view night nursings as an inconvenient interruption. Doing the feedings yourself at night ultimately benefits you and your baby.

Learn All You Can in the Hospital

During your brief hospital stay, there's so much to learn about baby care that it's hard to take it all in. Still exhausted from labor and delivery, you may be tempted, indeed encouraged, to delegate as much care as possible to the nurses. But remember, although the nurses may give expert care for the moment, they're not coming home with you! Your top priority in the hospital is to transfer as much of the nurses' expertise as possible to yourself and your partner before you take your baby home. Let the nurses know that you want to do much or all of your baby's care so you will be prepared to "go it alone" after discharge. Don't be afraid to ask even the most basic questions. Plenty of mothers have asked the same thing before you!

Closed-Circuit TV. Many hospitals have educational programming for new parents on closed-circuit TV. Such programming ranges from in-house productions aired at specific times to continuous commercial programming aimed at new parents. I am amazed how often the TV is on when I enter a patient's room. We certainly are a visually oriented society, and TV viewing is an integral part of daily life. Instead of watching your favorite soaps, talk shows, sitcoms, or drama features, vow to use the TV for educational purposes until you are comfortable in your new parent role. Baby care and breastfeeding videos won't substitute for one-on-one guidance from an experienced nurse, but the information you gain from watching these programs will make your interactions with the nurses even more worthwhile.

Classes. Many hospitals offer group instruction, such as bathing demonstrations or infant-feeding classes before discharge. Make every effort to take advantage of such instruction before you go home. Some hospitals offer classes a few days after discharge, when parents often are even more receptive now that they are "flying solo."

One-on-one Instruction. Reading materials and videos are valuable resources, but when it comes to latching your baby on, it really helps to have an experienced professional at your side. While you are in the hospital, ask for personal, expert assistance as often as you need it. Before you are discharged, ask a knowledgeable nurse to observe your breastfeeding technique to make certain you can correctly position, latch, and nurse your baby on your own at home.

Breastfeeding Specialists. Many hospitals that offer maternity services have a breastfeeding specialist or lactation consultant on their staff. Sometimes this individual is able to meet and assist every breastfeeding mother on the ward. In other hospitals, she might be called upon to help only those women having difficulties. Ask whether your hospital has a lactation consultant and don't leave without getting her phone number! If you are having any difficulties, ask to be seen by the specialist. Often, these experts are able to continue to help women on an outpatient basis after they are discharged.

Hospital Policies That Promote Breastfeeding Success

It's no great mystery which hospital policies promote breast-feeding and which ones jeopardize its success. Fortunately, most U.S. hospitals have made great strides in becoming more "baby-friendly" (see chapter 2, pages 67–69). The higher the breast-feeding rates where you live, the more likely the hospital where you deliver will have supportive maternity policies that foster breast-feeding success. On the other hand, hospitals with high bottle-feeding rates may be geared to a bottle-feeding norm. The following policies are known to help get breastfeeding off to the best possible start. Even if these desired practices aren't standard policy at your hospital, ask whether an exception can be made in your case. Hospital staff often make special concessions for informed, assertive patients who ask for what they want. Request that your own and your baby's doctor write hospital orders that help assure favorable breastfeeding practices.

Continuous Rooming-in. Many studies have shown that one of the best ways to promote successful breastfeeding is to keep mothers and babies together in the same room. Close proximity of her infant helps a mother learn to read her baby's cues and respond promptly to her baby's needs. Breastfeeding on demand occurs more readily when a mother and baby are together. A baby cared for in the nursery probably won't be considered to be "de-manding" until she is crying out loud. An astute mother with her baby in her room can pick the infant up to nurse as soon as she starts to stir. Studies show that babies are less stressed and don't cry as much when they are cared for in their mother's room. Mothers whose babies are kept in the nursery often admit that they worry more about their infants. Rooming-in can be a great confidence-builder. The new mom who succeeds in providing most of her baby's care herself in the hospital leaves knowing she will be able to meet her baby's needs at home. Ask to keep your baby in your room at all times unless you need the staff to watch your baby while you shower, for example. If your baby is not allowed in your room at night, request that she be brought to you for all nursings at night and ask your baby's doctor to write an order to that effect.

Usually, hospitals with liberal rooming-in practices also have the most liberal visitation policies. The popular trend toward family-centered maternity care is highly commendable, and certainly a vast improvement over the arbitrary rules in place when I was having babies. It can be a wonderful thing to bring a child into your family surrounded by all your loved ones, but I must warn you about turning your room into a block party. Having all your extended family and friends can be fun for a time, but you may be left feeling like an entertainment coordinator. Limit visitors to those you really want to have present, and then keep visits short. Remember, the purpose of your hospital stay is to learn to care for and feed your baby, not make small talk with visitors.

Demand Feedings. Be prepared to nurse your baby at the first sign that she is interested in feeding. Put her to the breast as often as necessary to satisfy her. You may nurse as frequently as every hour or so, but don't let more than about three and a half hours elapse without attempting to get your baby to breastfeed. Frequent feedings are important to help your baby become proficient at latching on and sucking properly and to help bring in a milk supply that matches your baby's requirement. The best advice is "watch the baby, not the clock."

Unrestricted Duration of Feedings. In the past, it was common hospital policy to restrict the duration of feedings when a woman first started breastfeeding. Typically, a mother might be advised to nurse only three to five minutes on a side, perhaps increasing the length of feedings by a minute each day. This misguided policy was based on the mistaken belief that sore nipples could be prevented by keeping feedings short at first and building up the sucking time slowly. This common policy was flawed for several reasons. We now know that the most important cause of sore nipples is improper infant latch-on, rather than prolonged duration of feedings. Severe restrictions on the length of feedings can cause mothers to become preoccupied with watching the clock. By restricting feedings to five minutes or less, many frustrated babies were removed from the breast before the let-down reflex was triggered!

Numerous breastfeeding experts today insist that no restrictions should be placed on the length of feedings. They argue that an infant who is latched on correctly will not cause any nipple trauma regardless of how long she suckles. Certainly, a newborn should be allowed to nurse at least ten to fifteen minutes if she desires, once a nurse has verified that the baby is latched on correctly. However, I have encountered some women who nursed for prolonged periods in the first two days and developed severe nipple trauma and pain, despite having their infants positioned correctly. I think this results because some babies create excessive negative pressure when they nurse before the milk comes in abundantly. For this reason, I prefer to aim for moderation in feeding times, say perhaps twenty minutes maximum per side at each feeding during the first three days. If your nipples are becoming painful, I suggest you make sure the infant is latching correctly and then shorten feedings to about ten minutes per side. Frequent shorter feedings are preferable when nipple tenderness is developing (see chapter 7, page 237).

Avoidance of Pacifiers. Many hospitals routinely issue a pacifier to every newborn. Health professionals who care for babies have been taught that infants have a strong sucking urge that is not necessarily satisfied by feeding alone. Physicians and nurses rely on pacifiers to soothe an upset baby so they can perform necessary assessments like listening to the heart. It never occurred to most medical professionals that a pacifier might be an impediment to getting started breastfeeding. But a recent study has shown an increased risk of early weaning among young infants who frequently use a pacifier. I can think of several explanations why early use of a pacifier could interfere with the successful initiation of breastfeeding. First, a pacifier is an artificial nipple that is longer and more rigid than the breast nipple and areola the baby needs to learn to use. For some babies, frequent exposure to an artificial nipple might interfere with learning to breastfeed. Another argument is that newborns need to suckle the breast frequently to obtain sufficient milk and to give the breasts sufficient stimulation. The whole concept of supply and demand is that the breasts produce milk in response to how much the baby nurses. Sucking on a pacifier does nothing to stimulate the mother's milk, and it is a nonnutritive activity for the baby. In the early weeks of life, most, if not all, of a baby's sucking effort should produce food for the infant and trigger milk production in the mother. Furthermore, the less experienced a mother is, the less skilled she will be in distinguishing how well her baby nursed and whether he still might be hungry. Many hungry babies will calm down and appear satisfied when given a pacifier when they really need to be breastfeeding and obtaining milk. For these reasons, I discourage new mothers from using a pacifier in the first weeks of breastfeeding. During this time, the baby should be encouraged to nurse in an unrestricted manner without interference by artificial nipples. All sucking should provide nutrition and be channeled toward stimulating the mother's milk production.

Once the baby is latching on without difficulty, is gaining weight steadily, has surpassed his birth weight, and breastfeeding has become well established, then the mother can introduce a pacifier if she chooses. By waiting four to six weeks, a mother will be much more experienced in distinguishing infant signs of hunger from comfort sucking needs. She will be less likely to overuse the pacifier once she has learned to interpret her baby's cues accurately. Ask the hospital nurses not to give your baby a pacifier, or to use one sparingly. For those of you who need a comeback response to the infamous, "He's just using you for a pacifier!," try this one: "I'd rather have my baby use my breast as a pacifier than to substitute a pacifier for my breast."

Availability of Necessary Breastfeeding Equipment and Resources. A hospital that provides maternity services ought to be able to meet the needs of its breastfeeding clients. In addition to providing accurate information and direct assistance with breastfeeding, hospitals should make necessary breastfeeding equipment available to nursing mothers. Many mothers will need a hospital-grade rental electric pump to solve a breastfeeding problem, to express milk for a premature baby, or to pump after returning to work. If your hospital doesn't have a pump-rental program of its own, ask where you can obtain a rental pump should you need one (see Resource List, page 446). Many hospitals stock breast shells for inverted or sore nipples (see pages 222–225), USP Modified Lanolin (medical grade) for sore nipples, small breast pumps, dual collection kits for rental-grade electric pumps, the Supplemental Nursing System (see pages 114 and 347–349), and other breastfeeding supplies. Before you leave the hospital, request the phone numbers for several sources of support and information about breastfeeding. Good resources to request include your hospital's breastfeeding specialist, local private lactation consultants, a local breastfeeding referral center, La Leche League, Nursing Mothers' Counsel, and local WIC Programs.

No Supplements for Breastfed Babies Unless Medically Necessary. Years ago, it was common hospital practice to offer a bottle of water or formula to a newborn following each breast-feeding until the mother's milk came in. This destructive policy had a very negative impact on breastfeeding success. In many cases, breastfeeding was sabotaged before a woman even left the hospital because babies received numerous bottle-feedings while they were still learning to nurse. Not only was the longer, more rigid bottle nipple easier to grasp than the soft breast, but the contents of the bottle flowed much more rapidly than the trickle of colostrum. No wonder many new babies began to prefer bottle-feeding over breastfeeding! Even when supplemented babies appeared to still nurse well, many failed to breastfeed as often as recommended since their tummies stayed full longer due to the extra fluids they were given. Since her baby didn't nurse frequently, a mother's milk supply might never become well established, thus perpetuating her use of the supplemental feeds. All too often, breastfeeding just fizzled before it ever got going.

Today, breastfeeding advocates around the world recognize that routine supplementation of newborns can place successful breast-feeding in jeopardy for all the reasons just mentioned (see The Baby-Friendly Hospital Initiative, pages 67–69). Ideally, your baby will be solely breastfed during your hospital stay, without receiving any additional fluids. On the other hand, I must emphasize that sometimes a valid medical reason, such as prematurity, severe jaundice, or low blood sugar, makes it necessary to temporarily give extra milk to certain newborns. In such cases, the benefits of giving the required supplement outweigh the potential risks of under-mining breastfeeding. The obvious prudent thing is to tend to the baby's welfare first and work on perfecting breastfeeding once the health of the baby is assured (see When Supplementation of a Breastfed Newborn Is Medically Necessary, pages 112–116).

Withhold Gift Packs Containing Formula. Some infant-formula companies supply hospital nurseries with free formula and gift packs for new mothers. The practice is a cost savings for the hospital and a marketing opportunity for the formula manufac-turers who recognize that new mothers are likely to purchase for-mula brands that are most familiar to them. Both breastfeeding and formula-feeding mothers routinely receive formula-company gift packs, although the contents of the packs are different based on the mother's feeding method.

Most breastfeeding proponents believe that formula-company marketing practices have a negative effect on breastfeeding success. They are legitimately concerned that giving expectant or new breastfeeding mothers anything with a formula logo on it can imply a subtle endorsement of formula-feeding and undermine breastfeeding. Many breastfeeding advocates insist that hospitals should stop accepting formula-company giveaways, and instead should bid on and purchase their own infant formula, just as they buy other supplies. A few baby-friendly U.S. hospitals who embrace the Ten Steps to Successful Breastfeeding (see chapter 2, pages 68–69) already have stopped accepting free formula. Many hospitals have stopped giving formula-company gift packs to nursing mothers. If you do receive any formula to take home, make sure you understand when, if ever, to use it. As a new breastfeeding mother, you need to appreciate that giving your baby formula without a valid reason could reduce your chances of succeeding at breastfeeding. There's probably no harm having formula in your house as long as you don't use it inappropriately.

When Supplementation of a Breastfed Newborn Is Medically Necessary

Sometimes, parents who are highly motivated to breastfeed will become alarmed when their baby's doctor prescribes formula supplement. They wrongly fear that their chances of breastfeeding will be ruined if their baby gets any formula. I have witnessed distressing power struggles between well-meaning parents and physicians over the matter. This always make me sad because parents and health professionals should be joint advocates for their child, never adversaries. Please understand that judgments about supplementing a baby are difficult to make. Giving some formula sometimes becomes necessary when a baby is premature, has low blood sugar, loses excessive weight after birth, or has severe jaundice. Ask your baby's doctor to explain the reasons why she recommends supplement for your baby and how long she expects it to be needed. Make it clear that breastfeeding is important to you, and request expert help for working out any breastfeeding problems that either contribute to the need for supplement or result from its use. With such assistance, chances are excellent that, even if your baby does require supplemental milk temporarily, you eventually will be able to breastfeed exclusively.

Nipple Confusion. Much has been written about the popular belief that early bottle-feeding of breastfed infants will result in "nipple confusion." Stories abound of babies who were exposed to bottle-feeding before breastfeeding was well established and who then displayed a preference for bottle-feeding over breastfeeding. A typical scenario goes something like this: An infant nurses well right after delivery, then stays in the nursery at night where she is fed by bottle one or more times. The next morning the baby fusses and frets at the breast, acts like she doesn't know what to do, and will not latch on to nurse. However, when offered a bottle, the baby takes it eagerly.

Having heard these stories, some parents become convinced that even a single bottle feeding during the early weeks of life will seriously jeopardize their breastfeeding attempts. Such parents may be hesitant to provide supplemental milk to their babies even when a valid medical reason exists because they fear that nipple confusion inevitably will result. However, the notion that a single bottle is likely to cause subsequent difficulty with breastfeeding never has been proved. Many breastfed infants receive one or more supplemental feedings by bottle during the first week of life, and yet go on to breastfeed exclusively. Other infants, including some whose mothers work outside the home, accept a bottle readily when the mother is absent and resume breastfeeding without apparent difficulty when the mother returns.

My own conclusion is that nipple confusion does occur in some, but certainly not all, babies. I think newborns are more susceptible than older babies to the negative effects of bottle-feeding because they are just learning to breastfeed and the volume of colostrum they obtain is relatively low. If a new baby who doesn't yet breastfeed well is allowed to take a bottle, he may perceive the longer and more rigid artificial nipple that yields a higher volume of fast-flowing milk to be easier and more rewarding than attempts at the breast. I also believe, however, that it is possible to predict which babies are more susceptible to nipple confusion. Anything that interferes with correct attachment to the breast or the free flow of milk from the breast is likely to make a baby prefer bottle-feeding to breastfeeding. Thus, the baby who is having difficulty attaching due to his mother's flat nipples and who obtains little milk due to her low supply will be more vulnerable to nipple confusion if allowed to bottle-feed than another infant who has nursed well numerous times and whose mother has protuberant nipples, with a generous, free-flowing milk supply. The important thing to remember is that even when bottle-feeds have caused a baby to nurse less well, all is not lost. By adhering to the basics of proper breastfeeding technique, using a pump to assure your own supply of milk remains abundant (see pages 124–125), and obtaining help from a breastfeeding specialist, you still can expect your baby to learn to nurse correctly and to breastfeed exclusively.

Options for Providing Necessary Supplemental Milk to Breastfed Babies. By far, the most common method for giving a breastfed baby supplemental milk is to use a bottle and nipple. Most parents and many health professionals are unaware that other options exist for feeding milk to a baby. If supplemental milk is necessary and you want to avoid bottle-feeding, ask your baby's nurse if one of these alternative methods is available in your hospital.

Supplemental Nursing System (SNS). If your baby can latch on and breastfeed but requires supplemental milk for a legitimate medical reason, it is possible to feed the supplement while your baby nurses at the breast by using the SNS device. This method causes no disruption of nursing and actually enhances breast-feeding by giving the baby an immediate reward for her efforts. Convenient starter SNS kits are available for short-term use. Ask whether the lactation specialist at your hospital or one of the newborn nurses has experience using the SNS and could assist you. The SNS works best when a baby has learned to latch on correctly to the breast, but still requires additional milk. Babies with significant latch-on problems may not be able to correctly grasp the SNS tubing while taking the breast. (For more information on the SNS, see pages 347–349.)

Cup, spoon, dropper, syringe. In other parts of the world, newborns who require supplemental milk frequently are fed by cup or other method that avoids the use of bottles. Some experts claim that alternative feeding methods are preferable to bottle-feeding, especially when a baby who does not yet know how to breastfeed effectively requires supplemental milk. Cup feeding is not difficult and several options exist, ranging from one-ounce plastic medicine cups available in every hospital to specially made cup-feeding devices designed for supplementing breastfed newborns. Inquire whether one of these methods might be used to give your baby the prescribed supplement and ask that the technique be taught to you.

To cup feed, the baby is held upright and the brim of the cup rests gently on the lower lip. The cup is tipped slightly so the milk just touches the baby's lips. The milk is not poured! Rather, the infant is allowed to lap and then sip the milk at his own pace.

Because babies need to suck, both for comfort and for proper development of the oral structures and speech, I don't advocate cup feeding for the long term. Rather, I see it as a temporary method of giving necessary supplement that is unlikely to interfere with learning to breastfeed. Once a mother's milk increases in abundance, supplement may no longer be necessary if a baby has learned to nurse effectively.

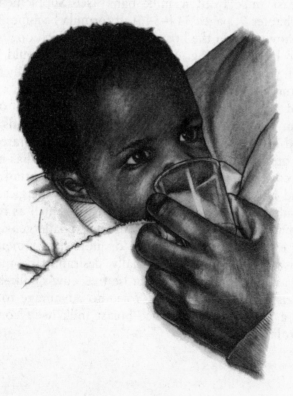

Newborn being fed by cup.

A baby also can be fed with a plastic spoon used in a similar manner to a cup. Some health care providers use an eyedropper to feed milk the same way oral medications are given to a baby. Others have experience feeding newborns with a regular syringe (without the needle, of course) or a periodontal syringe that has a curved plastic tip. If your baby needs supplement, and you prefer a bottle not be used, one of these options might be suitable when an SNS is not available. *Don't try using any of these alternative methods yourself without receiving firsthand supervision from a health professional experienced in their use.*

Deciding What Type of Supplemental Milk to Use. A mother's own expressed breast milk makes the ideal supplement. You may be able to obtain sufficient colostrum or milk using a hospital-grade electric breast pump. If a larger volume of milk is needed than can be expressed, formula will be necessary (unless you are fortunate enough to have access to screened, processed donor breast milk from a milk bank (see Supplemental Milk Options, chapter 9, pages 344–346). If formula becomes necessary for your baby while in the hospital, deciding which one to use can leave your head spinning. Ideally the decision would be made jointly with your baby's doctor and based on your family history of allergies and other medical factors. Hopefully, only a minimal amount of supplement will be necessary until your own milk increases in volume. In addition to the multiple brands of cow's milk–based infant formula available in the United States, several soy-based options also exist. However, soy formula has no advantage over cow's milk–based formula for supplementing breastfed infants and has no proven value in preventing allergies. When a strong family history exists for allergic disease, such as food allergies, asthma, or eczema, I prefer to use a hypoallergenic formula, despite its extra expense. When one or more family members has allergic disease, it becomes especially desirable for mothers to breastfeed as long as possible. A lactose-free, cow's milk–based formula also is available. However, I see no advantage to avoiding lactose in a breastfed baby, since breast milk itself contains the milk sugar, lactose.

Common Problems When You Begin Breastfeeding

The following problems are not uncommon during the get-acquainted phase of breastfeeding. Fortunately, such problems are usually worked out successfully before you leave the hospital or by the time your milk comes in abundantly. Don't be discouraged if things aren't picture-perfect; it's all part of the learning process. With patience and practice, both you and your baby will become more proficient in your roles. If you continue to have difficulty after you go home, you should seek expert help without delay. The sooner you detect a breastfeeding problem and get help, the easier it is to remedy.

Baby Won't Awaken to Nurse. Some newborns sleep longer than desired in the early days of life, perhaps as a result of a long labor, medications used during childbirth, birth trauma, or other events. You might be anxious to begin breastfeeding, only to realize it takes two cooperative partners to make the process work. If more than about three and a half hours have passed without a feeding attempt, ask your baby's nurse to help you awaken your infant. Don't wait for your baby to cry to try to feed her. Instead, keep her with you in your room and try to arouse her from light sleep—look for eyelid movement, facial twitches, movements of her arms or legs, or mouthing motions. Unswaddle her from her blankets, change her diaper, remove some clothing, wipe her bottom with a wet washcloth, stroke her head, or massage her feet. Babies naturally open their eyes when placed upright. You can put her in a sitting position on your lap, with your hand supporting her chin, or hold her over your shoulder. Try dimming the lights if bright lights make her close her eyes. (For more information about how to arouse a sleepy baby, see, How Do I Arouse My Sleepy Baby? chapter 5, pages 153–155.)

Infant Has Difficulty Latching on to the Breast. Even when the infant is awake, alert, and demanding, he may not latch on to your breast right away. Often the baby cries, acts distressed, and doesn't seem to know what to do. This can be enormously frustrating, especially when a mother has the misperception that breastfeeding should be as easy as falling off a log. It also can feel like outright rejection, and often a distraught mother will announce, "My baby doesn't *want* my breast." Nothing could be further from the truth. Of course your baby wants to breastfeed, but he doesn't yet know how to grasp your nipple/areola and obtain milk. If your baby is having trouble latching on, try the following measures:

• Stop your efforts that have made you and the baby upset. Take a deep breath and calm down. Soothe your baby with your voice and by swaddling him. Try settling him down by letting him suck on your clean little finger inserted with the palm side (fleshy part) upward against the roof of his mouth. Tell yourself that latch-on difficulties are common and that many women have felt as you do right now. Keep your baby with you so you can try again as soon as he shows interest.

• Help your baby enjoy being close to your breast. Keep him cradled at your breast even when you are not attempting to breastfeed. Remove your top and provide as much skin-to-skin contact as possible. These "breast-friendly" measures will help offset any frustration that either of you might experience from unsuccessful breastfeeding attempts.

• Review the basics of breastfeeding technique: positioning yourself, positioning your baby, and supporting your breast. Correct anything in your technique that could be improved (see pages 88–99).

• Squeeze a few drops of colostrum onto your nipple to entice your baby or drip a little sugar water onto your nipple from a bottle.

• Enlist a skilled nurse or hospital lactation consultant to help your baby attach correctly to your breast. Then you can apply the effective techniques she demonstrates when you are on your own.

• Use a breast pump to express some milk. Offer this milk, or a small quantity of formula, preferably by cup or spoon, to calm your baby sufficiently to work with him at the breast again.

• If your nipple is flat, use a pump for a few minutes to draw your nipple out and start some milk flowing before trying to attach your baby.

• If your baby is using a pacifier, this could be reinforcing the expectation of a long, rigid nipple (see pages 109–110). Discontinue the pacifier until breastfeeding is going well.

• As a last resort, start pumping your breasts approximately every three hours with a rental-grade electric pump to keep up your milk supply. Offer your expressed milk by bottle or other method to keep your baby well nourished. Continue to try to attach your baby at every available opportunity. As long as your baby remains well fed and your supply is maintained, your baby can eventually learn to breastfeed. Don't give up! You will need to arrange close follow-up with your baby's physician and a lactation specialist after discharge. (See My Baby Won't Latch On, chapter 5, pages 152–153, for additional strategies for latch-on problems.)

Baby Won't Suck. Some babies will initially attach to the nipple/areola, but then take only a few sucks before coming off the breast and crying. Usually these babies are frustrated at not receiving an immediate reward. Perhaps they have had one or more bottle-feedings and expect a rapid flow of milk as soon as a nipple enters their mouth. If an SNS device is available (see pages 114 and 347–349), it can be used to provide supplemental milk while the baby nurses, and thus keep the baby interested in breastfeeding. Usually, once the baby starts sucking rhythmically while using the SNS, the mother's own breast milk begins to flow. The device might be needed for only a feeding or two until the baby starts nursing effectively.

Another reason babies may not suck is that they may "shut down" when put to the breast. If previous attempts at feeding have been negative experiences, perhaps due to rough handling of the baby or aggressive efforts to push the nipple into his mouth, the baby may react to such distress by shutting down and refusing to feed. Other possible signals that your baby may be experiencing sensory overload and needs you to back off include hiccups, yawning, and the "stop sign," raising his hand with palm facing outward. Don't let any feeding session turn into a power struggle. Hold your baby tenderly, speak reassuringly, and let him rest securely against your breast. It might become necessary to pump and feed your expressed milk until feedings, in general, become a pleasant experience before resuming attempts at the breast. Since poor feeding can be a sign of infant illness, I must also caution that it's always essential for the hospital staff to evaluate a baby who isn't feeding well.

Baby Takes One Side Only. Often, the baby latches on more readily to one breast than the other. Perhaps one nipple is easier to grasp, or the milk on that side flows more freely. It is important to keep working with the baby to take the less-preferred side as quickly as possible, to assure that both breasts receive adequate stimulation and emptying. You can start feedings on the "difficult" side and see if the baby cooperates more when he is hungry. If he starts to fuss too much, switch to the preferred breast and let him settle and nurse. Then, building on this success, resume your attempts on the other side. If your baby isn't taking both breasts well by the time your milk comes in abundantly you should start using a hospital-grade rental electric breast pump to regularly remove milk from the breast that isn't being suckled. (I actually recommend pumping both breasts simultaneously since it takes no longer than pumping one side and will help keep the overall milk production generous.) Breast preferences very quickly can cause a lopsided milk supply, which only aggravates the problem. The baby's preference for using one breast results in greater milk production on that side, which in turn makes the baby prefer the better-producing breast even more. Many mothers attest to the effectiveness of a simple maneuver to entice the baby to take the less-preferred breast. Start nursing on the favored side (a cross-cradle hold works well) and then slide the baby over to the second breast without changing his position. As one woman explained, "My baby just thinks I have two left breasts."

Nipple Pain. During the first couple of days of breastfeeding, women often will complain of slight nipple discomfort for the first minute after latch-on. Severe nipple pain that lasts throughout the feeding, or nipple discomfort that doesn't improve once your milk comes in, suggests that the baby is either attached incorrectly or is sucking improperly. You shouldn't need a high pain threshold in order to breastfeed. Severe pain means something is wrong, so don't ignore this important clue. Get help right away with your nursing technique. The most common problem is that the baby is not opening wide enough and is latching on to the tip of the nipple instead of taking a large mouthful of breast. Other strategies to improve sore nipples include patting the nipples dry after feeds and applying USP Modified Lanolin (medical grade); nursing for shorter periods at more frequent intervals; and starting feedings on the least-sore side, then moving the baby to the more painful side once let-down has been triggered (see My Nipples Hurt, pages 160–161).

Baby Isn't Satisfied After Nursing. Some new mothers become frustrated because their baby nurses for prolonged periods but doesn't seem satisfied. Often these are larger babies, over eight or nine pounds, who act persistently hungry until the mother's milk increases around the third day. Sometimes the baby will settle when swaddled snugly, held by his mother or father, or allowed to sleep on a parent's chest. Despite what I said earlier about not using a pacifier, such a baby might need one for a day or so. As long as the baby nurses well and often, short-term use of a pacifier is not likely to interfere with subsequent breastfeeding. If supplemental milk is temporarily required until your milk increases in volume, it can be offered by SNS, cup, or bottle. (Ask about using a hypoallergenic formula if you have a family history of allergies, asthma, or other allergic disease.) If the baby is already a proficient nurser, he probably will continue to breastfeed just fine. Be sure to nurse as often as possible and try to discontinue any supplements as soon as your milk starts to increase. If the baby still isn't being satisfied by the fourth day, notify your baby's doctor and seek additional help with breastfeeding. It's possible the infant isn't nursing correctly and may not be obtaining the milk he needs.

Uncomfortable Breast Engorgement. Few mothers these days are still in the hospital when their milk starts coming in abundantly. More typically, postpartum breast engorgement occurs once a mother has gone home. Exceptions to this include some mothers with C-section deliveries and those with longer stays due to medical complications. Milk coming in abundantly typically causes noticeable breast swelling, tenderness, and firmness. Latch-on may become more difficult due to flattening of the nipple and firmness of the areola. The result can be improper attachment and nipple pain. For some women, engorgement can be a source of discomfort and frustration, especially when excessive pressure interferes with milk flow. When engorgement is unrelieved, the residual milk and pressure can cause the mother's milk supply to decline rapidly.

Early and frequent nursing (at least every two to three hours) is the best way to prevent excessive breast engorgement. Applying warm compresses before nursing often helps start milk flowing, while cool compresses between feedings help relieve pressure and discomfort. Express some milk before nursing, preferably using a hospital-grade electric breast pump, to soften your breasts and draw out your nipples. Pay careful attention to proper nursing technique to assure your baby latches on correctly and obtains the maximum amount of milk. Since engorgement usually occurs after hospital discharge, the topic is covered in more detail in chapter 5, pages, 159–160. (Also see Postpartum Breast Engorgement, chapter 7, pages 225–233.)

Early Discharge and Early Follow-up

Too many new mothers are discharged to go home before they feel confident about breastfeeding or other aspects of their own or their baby's care. Unfortunately, the recent trend toward shorter and shorter maternity stays largely has been driven by financial considerations rather than the health and well-being of the baby and family. In an attempt to curb the problem of "drive-through deliveries," national legislation has been passed requiring insurance companies to extend coverage for normal deliveries to forty-eight hours. But even a two-day hospital stay doesn't guarantee that babies will be nursing proficiently by the time they go home. Early follow-up remains a crucial step in assuring breastfeeding success by identifying mother-baby pairs who need extra help shortly after going home. In late 1995, the American Academy of Pediatrics published a policy statement containing minimum criteria to be met before a newborn should be discharged. The statement strongly emphasized that all infants discharged before forty-eight hours of age should be examined by an experienced health care provider within the next forty-eight hours. In addition to the standard medical assessments performed at the follow-up visit, the encounter should include an observation of breastfeeding to assure the infant latches on and suckles properly.

While all these recommendations make the system sound fail-safe, the fact remains that most mothers go home before breastfeeding is really going smoothly. Early follow-up within two days is *absolutely essential* to assure that your baby is nursing effectively, especially once your milk comes in abundantly. Many pediatricians now see newborn babies in their offices a couple of days after hospital discharge, while other mother-baby pairs receive a follow-up home visit by a nurse. Still others return to a hospital-based follow-up program. While a telephone call from a nurse to check on your breastfeeding progress makes a nice *addition* to one of these visits, it is not an adequate substitute for being seen in person.

If you don't feel ready to go home when your doctor thinks you are, explain your concerns and request more time. If your baby isn't nursing well, ask if you can stay even an additional twelve hours to give you several more breastfeeding sessions where assistance is available. If that isn't possible, see if you can arrange for an appointment the following day with either a lactation specialist on staff at the hospital or a private lactation consultant in the community. Whenever you seek breastfeeding help from someone other than your baby's doctor, it goes without saying that the doctor must be kept informed of all such encounters and feeding recommendations. Your baby's doctor should be the one to coordinate all aspects of your baby's health care.

Babies At-Risk for Inadequate Breastfeeding

Doctors, nurses, and parents alike usually assume that because breastfeeding is "natural," it will proceed naturally. They expect that any problems experienced in the hospital will magically clear up once the family gets home and the mother's milk comes in abundantly. For most women, things do go better with each subsequent feeding and each passing day. But for a few mother-baby pairs, early small problems become serious chronic matters that threaten the success of breastfeeding and the baby's well-being.

After years of evaluating breastfeeding problems, I believe I can predict with some accuracy which mother-baby pairs are at increased risk for inadequate breastfeeding. These couples deserve closer follow-up and monitoring to help them be successful. Anything that could affect the mother's milk production or her baby's ability to latch on to her breast and suckle well can have a negative impact on breastfeeding. Some typical examples are listed below, and many of these are discussed in more detail in chapter 9.

Lactation Risk Factors in the Mother

Previous breastfed baby who didn't gain weight well
Flat or inverted nipples
Variation from normal in breast appearance (such as marked
    asymmetry)
Previous breast surgery that may have cut some milk ducts
Previous breast abscess
Extremely sore nipples
Minimal prenatal breast enlargement
Failure of milk to come in abundantly after delivery
Severe postpartum breast engorgement
Medical problems, such as hemorrhage, high blood pressure, or
    infection

Breastfeeding Risk Factors in the Infant

Small (less than six pounds) or premature (less than thirty-eight
    weeks) infants
Babies having difficulty latching on to one or both breasts
Babies who don't suck well for any reason
Babies with any abnormality of the tongue, jaw, or palate
Twins or greater multiples
Babies with medical problems, such as jaundice, heart or
    breathing difficulties, infections
Babies with neurologic or muscle tone problems

Indications for Using a Rental Electric Pump

The preceding are just a few examples of mother-baby pairs who should receive extra help with breastfeeding after discharge. Some mothers will require only simple modifications in their breastfeeding routines. Others will benefit from using a hospital-grade rental electric pump to empty their breasts immediately after they nurse their babies. By regularly extracting any residual milk at the end of feedings, you can establish and maintain a generous supply even though your own infant might not nurse effectively. A baby who doesn't nurse very well is likely to obtain more milk during his feeding attempts if his mother manages to keep an abundant supply. By "drinking from a fire hydrant," an ineffective nurser still may be able to obtain sufficient milk.

Without the pumping regimen just described, a mother's milk production may decline quickly when her infant nurses poorly. You will hear more about pumping after feedings to extract residual milk in other chapters of this book.

If you or your baby have any of the risk factors mentioned, your baby's doctor should monitor your infant closely after discharge until it is clear that breastfeeding is going well. Since few physicians have the time to evaluate and manage breastfeeding problems, you should ask to be referred to a lactation consultant who can give special assistance with breastfeeding technique, help you decide when and how to taper pumping, and communicate with your baby's physician about feeding pumped milk to your baby.

In-Home Weighing of Infants

In-home weighing of infants is another option to help new parents when close monitoring of breastfeeding is desired. New technology now makes it possible for concerned parents to follow their baby's weight at home, thus taking much of the guesswork out of breastfeeding. Parents can rent an accurate, portable, user-friendly, electronic scale to weigh their baby periodically between medical visits until they are confident that their infant is thriving with breastfeeding. Certainly a scale cannot substitute for your baby's health care provider. Rather, the information it provides is meant to make you and your health care professional a stronger team. Report the weights you obtain to your baby's doctor, who can interpret the results with you. (To locate a rental-grade electronic infant scale, see Resource List, page 450.)

Special, highly accurate rental electronic scales also are available that allow you to measure your baby's milk intake during a breastfeeding by weighing him (identically clothed) before and after nursing. This procedure is known as infant-feeding test weights (see Infant-Feeding Test Weights, chapter 9, pages 333–335, and Measuring Your Baby's Milk Intake, chapter 10, page 389). The information obtained from in-home test weighing of babies can be very helpful in monitoring infants at risk for inadequate breastfeeding. If you have a breastfeeding problem and decide to perform infant feeding test weights at home, I strongly recommend that you also work with a lactation consultant who can help you modify your baby's feeding plan based on the information gathered from the test-weighing procedures. Of course, your breastfeeding specialist will need to communicate closely with your baby's doctor.

Chapter 5

Off to a Great Beginning—
The First Weeks
of Breastfeeding

If my own experience is typical of others, you no doubt felt frightened and insecure upon first arriving home after delivery. I brought my fifth baby home at twenty-eight hours, which was considered "early discharge" at the time, but is routine by today's standards. Despite being a fully trained pediatrician and an experienced mother, I recall becoming worried and upset several hours later. My baby was beginning to look jaundiced and I realized he hadn't urinated since earlier that morning. Why had I insisted on leaving the hospital so early? I was tired and overwhelmed with four other excited children between two and seven years of age. I could have used a word of encouragement and a second opinion from an experienced nurse right about that time. Suddenly, I wished I had stayed in the hospital longer or could check myself back in.

Fortunately, my baby awoke a short time later, nursed well, and wet his diaper. I decided he didn't look very jaundiced after all, and I could tell my milk was starting to increase. While my own anxiety quickly subsided, I tried to put myself in the place of less experienced parents who might face a more prolonged period of insecurity after leaving the hospital. This chapter is devoted to giving you the information you need to remain confident about breastfeeding once you're on your own at home and to set the stage for the long-term success you desire and deserve.

Home Alone with Your Breastfed Infant

Your first days and weeks at home with your new baby are a precious, yet precarious, time. You'll probably alternate between feeling confident and overwhelmed, overjoyed and anxious, exhilarated and exhausted. Initially, learning to care for and getting to know your baby is a full-time job. Breastfeeding will consume the most hours in your day, and will be the most intimate and, if all goes well, the most satisfying aspect of new motherhood. Getting breastfeeding off on the right foot is one of the most important things you can do to smooth your adjustment to new parenthood.

Make Nursing Convenient and Comfortable

At first, most of your nursings will probably occur in a few specially chosen locations around the house, such as your bed, the living room sofa, or a rocker in the baby's nursery. While you and your infant are learning the art of breastfeeding, a convenient and comfortable location is important. For first-time mothers, privacy may be a priority, while those with small children often prefer a central location. Eventually, you'll find you can nurse with ease almost anywhere. In the beginning, however, the setting for your nursing stations, or nursing nooks, can make a big difference. Review what you learned about comfortable positioning (see chapter 4 pages 88–95), and plan to have several pillows and cushions, as well as a footstool, on hand.

To simplify your duties during the first few weeks, keep a supply of clean diapers, infant wipes, and extra infant clothing on a table nearby, so you can feed and change your baby without having to leave your nursing corner. You also will want to stock your area with some enjoyable reading materials for leisurely nursings. (Yes, you eventually will be able to breastfeed without feeling like you need a third hand.) If you have older children, fill a basket or box with a few favorite toys and storybooks to occupy them in your presence while you nurse. Finally, keep a tall glass of water or a filled sports bottle handy to allow you to sip fluids while you breastfeed.

Despite all the effort that went into the preparation of your baby's nursery, she'll probably be more content in a bassinet at your bedside during the early weeks at home. Night feedings will be less disruptive if you can just reach over and bring your baby into bed to nurse. I found a large overstuffed reading pillow with armrests to be a godsend. I kept the cushion propped against my headboard and just sat up in bed and leaned back against it while I nursed in the middle of the night, half-asleep. With a stack of diapers on the nightstand, I could change my baby, often without getting out of bed, and return him or her to the bassinet with minimal fanfare.

Enlisting Support

Breastfeeding is easier when you have a strong support system. Ideally, your partner will be prepared to fulfill many aspects of this important role. Maybe your mother or your mother-in-law or a sister might also be able to help out for a period of time. This helper role is so critical that it is known by a specific name in many cultures and some animal societies. The term *doula* describes the one who "mothers the mother." This individual serves as the primary source of nurturance and support for the new mother, thus enabling her to fulfill her role as principal caretaker of the infant. Today, it is possible to hire a professional doula to nurture postpartum women and ease their transition to new motherhood (see Resource List, page 449).

I have served as a doula myself and expect to do so again many times when my grandchildren are born. On eight occasions, I have had the privilege of being present for several days when my sisters or sisters-in-law brought home new babies. As a result of these experiences, I have concluded that easing the adjustment of vulnerable new parents is a daunting task. Your helper's mission is to jump in and do whatever seems necessary at the moment, to defuse inevitable tensions, to offer advice without undermining the new parents' efforts, to keep a low profile, to serve as a sounding board, and to provide a continuous infusion of emotional support.

If possible, arrange for a friend or relative (preferably one who has breastfed her own babies) to come and stay with you for a week or so. At the least, try to have such a person available during the daytime or consider hiring a professional doula. Ask your partner or other helper to ease your burden by bringing the baby to you for nursings, offering you a beverage, burping and changing the baby after feedings, insisting that you nap, preparing meals, occupying an older child, doing laundry, keeping visitors at bay, and bolstering your spirits.

Don't invite relatives, no matter how well intentioned, with whom you are not completely comfortable, who tend to be hyper-critical, or who aren't likely to be genuinely helpful. Now is not the time to feel like you need to entertain someone or put on a good display. Instead, choose a helper with whom you can let it all hang out, perhaps your sister or mother. Surround yourself with like-minded relatives or friends who can be counted on to encourage you and assist you in every way possible. Even if you have no one who can help you in your home, you can obtain support over the telephone by calling the hospital nursery, your doctor's office, an experienced friend, your local WIC program, or a peer support group.

Restricting Visitors

During your get-acquainted period with your baby, keep visitors to a minimum except for those who truly will help. I have witnessed firsthand how a steady stream of visitors inevitably interferes with unrestricted breastfeeding. Nursings easily get inter-rupted or postponed because of the presence of guests. Discourage drop-in visits. Use your telephone answering machine or ask your partner or doula to screen calls. Have them protect you with comments like "She's with the baby now," or "She's finally napping and I don't want to disturb her," or "The doctor insists that we delay visitors for at least a week or so." I recommend an intimate family honeymoon when bringing your new baby home and launching your breastfeeding. Once your baby is nursing well and gaining weight steadily, you'll have more time and energy to receive visitors and truly enjoy their company.

Getting Enough Sleep

In the first postpartum weeks, sleep deprivation and sheer fatigue plague all new parents. The burden of night feedings, the enormity of baby care, and physical depletion after delivery take their inevitable toll. Remember, exhaustion can make your entire situation seem bleaker, while a little rest can change your whole perspective and improve your outlook. Many parents make the mistake of coming home from the hospital and diving into projects like finishing the nursery, lining the baby's dresser drawers with contact paper, writing birth announcements, completing work assignments, and so on. Your top priority when you aren't feeding your baby or doing other essential care is simply to rest and sleep. Since your nighttime sleep will be interrupted, you need to get in the habit of napping when your baby naps. Wearing your bathrobe during the day may serve as a physical reminder to slow down and rest. Once breastfeeding is going smoothly and a daily routine begins to emerge, you can find time to get other things done. In the first few weeks, however, rest and sleep should take precedent over any other activity you think you "ought to do."

What to Expect During the Early Weeks of Breastfeeding

Normal Breastfeeding Routines

Each baby is a unique individual, with his or her own nursing habits. Breastfed babies can thrive within a wide range of normal feeding patterns. Even in the same family, mothers observe that different siblings have different nursing styles. Some babies breastfeed at closer intervals than others or take longer to complete a feeding. Some like to nurse leisurely, while others get right down to business. Mothers often find a nickname for their baby's particular nursing style, ranging from the "nibbler" to the "barracuda."

While no two babies are alike, the following typical feeding routines should let you know what to expect, help you recognize the ranges of normal, and give you guidance about when to seek help.

Breastfed newborns nurse frequently, at least eight times each twenty-four hours. In fact, ten or twelve feedings a day are not uncommon during the early weeks. *On average,* your baby will awaken to breastfeed every two to three hours. Feedings are timed from the *beginning* of one nursing to the *beginning* of the next. After your baby finishes a feeding, she'll probably be ready to nurse again within the next two hours. In fact, don't be surprised if she sometimes wants to nurse only an hour or so after her last feeding. Babies often cluster several nursings close together, especially in the evenings, and then sleep for a longer stretch at other times, such as the middle of the night.

Frequent
breastfeeding helps
your milk supply
become adjusted to
meet your baby's
requirements.

Many new breastfeeding mothers are not prepared for the normal frequency of feedings. They assume they must not have enough milk because their baby wants to feed so often. New breastfeeding mothers often complain, "It seems like all I do is breastfeed." My response is, "Good for you. Frequent breastfeeding is the most important thing you can do right now!" Getting breastfeeding off to a successful start is indeed a high priority; everything else can wait.

To better understand your baby's needs, try writing down everything you eat or drink for one day, including full meals, snacks, and even sips of water. I'll bet you make at least eight to ten entries. Well, some nursings are more like sips or snacks, while others are full meals. Human milk is digested more rapidly than formula, so the breastfed baby is hungry sooner. Unfortunately, many contemporary parents, grandparents, and even physicians, are more familiar with the typical three- to four-hour feeding schedule of formula-fed infants. Despite the appealing convenience of an infrequent feeding schedule, it's simply unrealistic to expect a breastfed baby to thrive without frequent, round-the-clock nursings.

The best advice is don't focus much attention on the clock. Instead, follow your baby's cues about how often she needs to nurse. If she just fed an hour ago and is acting hungry again, respond to her signals and offer your breast. Feeding frequently during these first weeks is the principal way your milk supply becomes adjusted to meet your baby's requirements. This is known as the breastfeeding law of supply and demand.

Generally, babies can be counted on to let us know when they are hungry. Some babies, however, need to be awakened to nurse because they just don't demand as often as they should. During the daytime, if three and a half to four hours have elapsed since your baby last nursed, you should gently arouse her to feed. Pick her up, change her diaper, and remove some of her clothing to try to awaken her to breastfeed (see How Do I Arouse My Sleepy Baby? pages 153–155). At night, don't let her sleep longer than five hours without breastfeeding until she's at least a month old. To assure she breastfeeds often enough each day, don't allow more than a single four- to five-hour interval without nursing during each twenty-four-hour period.

WHEN TO SEEK HELP: *If your baby often sleeps through feeding times, seldom demands to be fed, or frequently needs to be awakened to nurse, contact her physician. If your baby nurses more than twelve times each day and acts perpetually hungry, arrange to have her weighed promptly to see if she is obtaining enough milk. Ask to be referred to a lactation consultant who can evaluate your breastfeeding technique and make suggestions for improving your baby's intake of breast milk.*

Breastfed newborns should latch on correctly to both breasts and suck rhythmically for at least ten minutes per breast at each feeding. By the time you arrive home, you should be comfortable latching your baby on to each breast. It's not uncommon for a baby to prefer one side or to have an easier time latching on to one breast. However, you need to keep trying to get the baby to take both breasts well. Unsuccessful attempts to nurse don't count as a feeding.

Once your baby is latched correctly, allow her to suck for as long as she wants. She may pause periodically and need some gentle prodding, but, in general, she should suck rhythmically throughout most of the feeding. Allow her ample time at the first breast to help assure that she gets the rich, high-fat hindmilk. She'll probably start sucking less vigorously, fall asleep, or come off the first breast after ten to fifteen minutes. This is a good time to burp her, change her diaper, and help arouse her to take the second side. A baby usually obtains more milk by nursing at both breasts than by taking one side only. Thus, it's generally preferable to nurse from both breasts at each feeding whenever possible. Allow her to stay at the second side as long as she wants, although a baby may nurse only five minutes at this breast, which will probably be less

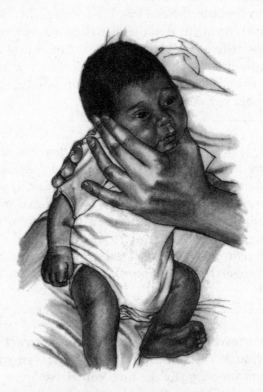

Burping the baby after the first breast helps
arouse the infant to take the second side.

well drained than the first. An infant nurses more vigorously at the first breast and usually takes more milk from that side. Thus, you should alternate the side on which you start feedings, so both breasts receive about the same stimulation and emptying. A lopsided milk supply can develop in a matter of days if you consistently start feedings on the same breast.

WHEN TO SEEK HELP: *If your baby is unable to latch on to one or both breasts or latches briefly but does not suck effectively, try the strategies on pages 117–119. If these techniques don't remedy the problem promptly and allow your baby to start feeding well, seek assistance right away (see Getting Help for Early Breastfeeding Problems, pages 169–171, and How to Obtain Help for Breastfeeding Problems, pages 277–280). It's not only distressing and frustrating to have a newborn who doesn't feed well, but it can place your baby's welfare at risk. Furthermore, if your breasts don't get drained sufficiently, they can become uncomfortably engorged, and your milk supply may be jeopardized. Don't allow your baby to miss feedings and don't allow your breasts to go without regular stimulation and removal of milk. If the latch-on problem can't be remedied quickly, your baby will need to be fed by another method until she learns to breastfeed effectively. In addition, your breasts will need to be pumped at regular intervals in order to keep your supply from declining. The expressed milk can be fed to your baby.*

Both very short or extremely long nursing sessions can signal a feeding problem. If a baby suckles too briefly (less than ten minutes per feeding), she probably won't receive enough milk. On the other hand, if nursings last more than about fifty minutes, or if your baby often seems hungry again shortly after feeding, it could mean that she is not being satisfied. Infants who need to nurse almost continually may not be obtaining adequate volumes of milk. The problem can be due to either ineffective breastfeeding technique or low milk production. Often it is a combination of both. Contact your baby's doctor and have your infant weighed promptly.

Breastfed babies should swallow regularly while nursing. A baby first starts nursing with short, fast bursts of sucking. As milk flow begins, the sucks get longer and slower. Swallowing is triggered when the mouth fills with milk. Before your milk comes in abundantly, your baby may not swallow often during nursing, as the volume of colostrum is rather low. Once your milk starts increasing in volume (usually on the second to fourth day), you should start to hear your baby swallow after every one or two sucks. Swallowing is indicated by a soft "kaa, kaa, kaa" sound when a baby exhales. When your milk ejection reflex is triggered, your baby may swallow after every suck in order to handle the rapid flow of milk. You should hear suck, swallow, pause, suck, swallow, pause. Audible swallowing after every couple of sucks should continue for about ten minutes. As milk flow slows down, the frequency of swallowing will decrease. When your baby goes to the second breast, rapid swallowing should begin again. Other signs that your baby is getting milk include seeing milk in her mouth or dripping from the opposite breast while she nurses.

WHEN TO SEEK HELP: *You should be concerned if you don't hear frequent swallowing when your baby nurses, especially when you have other reasons to suspect your baby isn't feeding well. Infrequent swallowing may be due to a low milk supply or ineffective sucking that prevents your baby from obtaining adequate milk. Signs that your baby is sucking incorrectly include opening and closing her mouth in rapid tremorlike movements, making a clicking sound or dimpling her cheeks while nursing, or frequently coming off the breast. Contact your baby's doctor if you think your infant is not swallowing much milk. The problem needs to be remedied quickly.*

Breastfed newborns should appear satisfied after nursings. Generally, a well-fed baby is a contented baby. In the first two days, when the volume of colostrum is relatively low, your baby may act hungry very soon after the last nursing. By the third day, however, when your milk starts to come in abundantly, your baby should appear more content after nursings. Breastfed newborns usually fall asleep at the second breast and act satisfied between feedings.

Sometimes new parents don't recognize their baby's hunger cues because they mistakenly assume that an infant who just finished nursing must automatically have obtained sufficient milk. The surprising truth is that an infant can go through the motions of breastfeeding, nurse from both sides, and still not consume much milk. Several explanations are possible. Perhaps the baby has been latched on incorrectly or has a faulty suck. Maybe the milk ejection reflex wasn't triggered, or the mother's milk production is insufficient. Obviously, the first thing to do when a baby appears hungry after nursing is to return him to the fullest breast for another chance at feeding.

Of course, not all fussiness in a breastfed baby is due to hunger. Babies need human contact as much as they need food. An infant may cry because he wants to be held and doesn't want to be separated from his mother. Even a well-fed baby may want to be carried and held to make him feel safe and secure.

WHEN TO SEEK HELP: *Breastfed infants who appear hungry after most feedings (e.g., crying, sucking on their hands, rooting, requiring a pacifier to be consoled) may not be getting enough milk. Signs of apparent hunger in an infant should not be ignored, even if the baby is feeding on a proper routine. Contact your baby's doctor and have your infant weighed. If your baby really isn't getting enough to eat, the sooner the problem is recognized, the more readily it can be remedied.*

Demand feeding should mean frequent feeding. Decades ago, when bottle-feeding was the predominant method of feeding infants in the United States, scheduled feedings became popular. Babies were fed by the clock, usually at four-hour intervals. A baby who showed signs of hunger sooner than four hours often was made to wait until the appointed feeding time. Because such rigid scheduling of feedings didn't account for babies' unique needs, some experts began to advocate more flexibility in feeding infants. The term *demand feeding* was used to describe feeding a baby whenever he showed signs of hunger instead of feeding by a rigid schedule.

In recent decades, feeding babies on demand has become the norm. Certainly, feeding a baby when she shows signs of hunger seems appropriate and empathetic. However, some well-meaning parents misapply the concept by allowing a sleepy, nondemanding baby to feed too infrequently. Feeding on demand was meant to give a parent permission to nurse again if their baby seems hungry sooner than expected. A newborn shouldn't be allowed to sleep five or six hours without feeding just because he "hasn't demanded." Nor should "demand feeding" be used to justify a newborn going all night without breastfeeding, even if he is willing to sleep through. In summary, demand feeding reminds us to feed hungry babies *more often* than we might expect them to need to be fed. It shouldn't be misinterpreted to let sleepy babies go too long without nursing.

Postpone pacifier use for breastfed newborns. The use of pacifiers is a widespread childrearing practice, both in the United States and in other countries. Although many experts have cautioned that early pacifier use can undermine the successful establishment of breastfeeding, little scientific evidence has existed to support this claim. Now several recent studies have confirmed that early pacifier use is linked to early weaning. In one study, infants using pacifiers at one month of age were three times more likely to have discontinued breastfeeding by six months of age. The risk of early weaning was greater for "frequent" users (during the whole day and night to help them fall asleep) as compared to "partial" users.

Based on my experience, I agree that early pacifier use before breastfeeding is well established can sabotage long-term breastfeeding. A baby who is "corked" or "plugged" with a pacifier may not learn to nurse as effectively as the baby who does all, or most, of his sucking at the breast. While some hungry babies will spit out their pacifier and vociferously demand a feeding, other underfed infants are more passive. They fool us by acting content to suck nonnutritively on a pacifier when they really need to be obtaining milk. The younger the infant, the harder it is for parents to interpret their baby's cues. It's just not possible in the early weeks to reliably distinguish when a baby only needs "comfort sucking" and when the infant needs "nutritive sucking." Once a pattern of consistent weight gain has been achieved, it is much less risky to introduce a pacifier. After four to six weeks of successful breastfeeding, a mother will have acquired much experience in interpreting her baby's cues. She will be more adept at recognizing signs of hunger and evaluating the quality of a feeding and will be less likely to confuse hunger with the urge to suck.

Infant Elimination Patterns

During the early weeks of breastfeeding, the contents of your baby's diaper will be of surprising interest to you. The fact is that your baby's early elimination patterns can provide a powerful clue to the success of breastfeeding. In the first few weeks, it can be very helpful to keep a daily record of his wet diapers and bowel movements.

Breastfed babies should urinate six or more times a day. In the first two days, your baby may wet only a couple of times in twenty-four hours. As your milk comes in more abundantly, the number of wet diapers steadily increases. By the fourth or fifth day of life, your infant should urinate after most feedings, producing at least six to eight wet cloth diapers each twenty-four hours. The urine should be colorless (dilute), not yellow (concentrated).

Because disposable diapers are so absorbent, it can be difficult to tell whether or not your baby has wet. Even if you anticipate using disposable diapers in the long run, you might want to have your baby wear cloth diapers for the first week or two. Or, you can place a piece of tissue paper in your baby's disposable diaper to help tell whether she has urinated. To get an idea of how a wet diaper feels, you can pour one to two ounces of water onto a dry diaper.

A red or pink "brick dust" appearance on the diaper suggests your baby is not getting enough milk. "Brick dust" on the diaper results when uric acid crystals form in concentrated urine. It is not an uncommon occurrence among breastfed infants during the first day or two, when the quantity of colostrum the baby drinks is low. Once your milk starts increasing in abundance, however, a breastfed baby should be able to consume sufficient volume of milk to produce clear urine.

WHEN TO SEEK HELP: *The presence of uric acid crystals in a baby's urine after the fourth or fifth day raises the suspicion of inadequate milk intake. Unfortunately, both parents and health professionals often misinterpret this valuable clue and mistake it for other phenomena. For example, little girls sometimes have a slight amount of vaginal bleeding a few days after birth as a result of the mother's high hormone levels during pregnancy. When handling a telephone inquiry, a health professional might attribute a parent's report of a reddish color in a little girl's diaper to slight vaginal bleeding. If a boy baby has been circumcised, urate crystals on the diaper might be confused with blood from the circumcision site. If your breastfed baby has a "brick dust" appearance in the diaper after your milk has come in, contact her physician and ask to have her weighed to determine whether she is getting enough to eat. You also should notify your baby's doctor if your infant has fewer than six wet diapers each day after the fourth or fifth day, or if her urine is dark yellow or scant in quantity.*

A breastfed baby's bowel movements should start to turn yellow in color by the fourth or fifth day of life. These yellow "milk stools" appear shortly after your milk comes in abundantly and your baby is consuming generous quantities of milk. The movements are loose, about the consistency of yogurt, with little seedy curds. Some people describe their appearance as a mixture of cottage cheese and mustard; others liken them to butterscotch pudding. Milk stools generally are a large cleanup job, not just a dot or streak.

WHEN TO SEEK HELP: *If your baby is still having dark meconium or green-brown "transition" stools by five days of age and has not yet had a yellow bowel movement, this is a probable sign that she is not getting enough milk. Contact your baby's doctor and arrange to have your baby weighed.*

Breastfed babies usually pass four or more sizable bowel movements each day for at least the first month of life. Many breastfed newborns will pass a yellow milk stool with every nursing during the early weeks of life. This frequent stooling pattern is not diarrhea. It is entirely normal and suggestive of adequate milk intake.

Beginning around one month or so, the number of bowel movements usually starts to decrease. By a couple of months of age, it is not uncommon for an exclusively breastfed infant to go days— even a week or more—without having a bowel movement. This pattern is not considered constipation because when a stool is finally passed, it often is loose and large (indeed, a mudslide!). Unfortunately, some parent education materials I have read inappropriately blur the two distinctly different stooling patterns of younger and older breastfed infants. Parents often are taught that breastfed infants can stool as often as every feeding or as infrequently as once a week. While both extremes can be normal, they are normal at different ages. The breastfed *newborn* has the frequent stooling pattern, while the *older* fully breastfed baby may go days without a bowel movement.

<u>WHEN TO SEEK HELP:</u> *If your newborn is having fewer than four stools each day, or if the bowel movements are scant in amount (just a stain on the diaper), it could mean she is not getting enough milk. Contact your baby's doctor and arrange to have her weighed. I am impressed that parents typically are excellent observers of the contents of their baby's diaper. But health professionals don't always do our part in communicating to parents what's normal and what's not. The simple observation of a baby's stooling pattern is a valuable, yet often overlooked, clue to a baby's nutritional well-being.*

Expected Changes in the Nursing Mother's Breasts

Your breasts will change significantly during the first week after giving birth as they begin their job of making and releasing milk. As stated previously, a wide range of normal exists for when milk comes in abundantly, the amount of milk women produce, the magnitude of breast enlargement or firmness that occurs, and the ease of milk flow. Make it a point to pay attention to your breasts and the clues they can offer about the success of breastfeeding. The following guidelines will let you know what to expect and when to seek help.

A mother's milk usually starts being produced in abundance two to four days after delivery. Colostrum, the early milk produced by the breasts, is present in relatively small amounts, beginning months before delivery and continuing for the first few days after giving birth. The process of abundant milk production (known as lactogenesis) begins approximately two to four days after delivery. In the past, lactogenesis occurred while a mother was still in the hospital. At the time of a mother's discharge, her milk already had increased and the nurses assisting her could be reasonably certain whether breastfeeding was off to a satisfactory start. Today, however, most women are already home when lactogenesis occurs. They may encounter unexpected discomfort or difficulty latching their baby on correctly when their breasts are engorged.

The breasts become larger, firmer, heavier, and warmer when milk increases in abundance approximately two to four days after delivery.

A woman's breasts become larger, firmer, heavier, warmer, and even uncomfortable when her milk starts increasing in volume. While these changes are more dramatic in some women than in others, the large majority of mothers can readily tell whether their milk has come in abundantly. The scant clear or yellow colostrum changes in appearance to whitish milk and greatly increases in quantity. The sudden increase in milk production may be evident by spontaneous leaking from the breasts or by seeing milk in the baby's mouth.

Most often, increased milk production begins two and a half to three days after delivery. Milk tends to come in earlier among women who have given birth previously and those who delivered vaginally, compared to first-time mothers or women who had C-sections. Occasionally, however, milk starts coming in abundantly as late as five to seven days. Often the delay is due either to medical problems in the mother or to severe emotional upset. For example, I have seen lactogenesis be delayed or diminished in some women with high blood pressure, excessive blood loss at delivery, serious infections, severe pain, or extreme emotional stress.

For many women, postpartum breast engorgement is uncomfortable, and in a few it is downright miserable (see chapter 7, pages 225–231). For most women, it is an unmistakable occurrence, but for a small minority, it is barely perceptible. While some women who scarcely notice whether their milk has come in go on to breastfeed successfully, I consider lack of significant postpartum breast engorgement to be a red flag worthy of investigation.

WHEN TO SEEK HELP: *In a tiny percentage of women—sometimes those who are very ill postpartum—milk fails to come in normally and full lactation is not possible. Such a woman may experience little, if any, breast engorgement, and her milk production may not climb sufficiently to nourish her baby. That's why I never ignore a mother's statement, "I'm not sure if my milk ever came in." If your baby seems hungry after most feedings and you do not think your milk has come in by four days postpartum, you should contact your baby's doctor and have your infant weighed to make sure she has not lost excessive weight from birth.*

If you experience severe breast engorgement, with hard, painful, swollen breasts, you should also be concerned. Severe engorgement makes it difficult to get milk flowing well, and the resulting pressure can lead to decreased milk production (believe it or not!). Excessive engorgement can also cause extreme discomfort, problems getting the infant latched on, sore nipples, and poor milk intake by the baby. Contact your own and/or your baby's doctor if your breasts are severely engorged. Ask to be referred to a lactation consultant who can help you obtain and use an electric breast pump to express milk and soften your breasts (see My Breasts Are Swollen and Painful, pages 159–160, and Postpartum Breast Engorgement, chapter 7, pages 225–231).

A mother's breasts usually feel full before each feeding (suggesting milk is present) and become softer after the baby has nursed (suggesting that milk has been emptied). Earlier, I recommended that you alternate the breast on which you start feedings. Some counselors advise women to move a safety pin from one bra strap to the other to remind them on which side to begin. Successful nursing mothers usually admit that they need no such reminder because the fuller breast is so obvious to them. Try to learn to pay attention to such changes in your breasts as long as you breastfeed.

After your longest night interval between feedings, your breasts should feel particularly full. Often, a woman will leak milk onto her bed sheets or become so full that she awakens before her baby demands. These are additional indicators of plentiful milk production.

WHEN TO SEEK HELP: *Generalized breast fullness that doesn't decrease with feeding could suggest that your baby is not extracting the milk effectively. On the other hand, soft breasts that don't feel fuller before nursings could imply that little milk is available at a feeding. Patchy, or localized, breast fullness also can suggest a problem. Obviously, these observations are rather subjective and are less precise in predicting a problem than many of the other breastfeeding criteria described in this chapter.*

A mother's nipples might be mildly tender for the first several days of nursing. Nipple tenderness usually is present only at the beginning of feedings and subsides as the feeding progresses. Discomfort should not interfere with feedings and usually improves once milk starts to come in abundantly. By the end of the first week, breastfeeding is usually comfortable.

WHEN TO SEEK HELP: *Severe nipple pain that makes you dread nursing your baby, pain that lasts throughout a feeding, or pain persisting beyond one week all are considered abnormal. Most likely, your baby is not breastfeeding correctly. If your infant isn't latched on properly or sucking correctly, not only will your nipples hurt, but your baby may not obtain sufficient milk. Thus, if you have severe sore nipples, you should obtain help with your nursing technique and have your baby weighed (see My Nipples Hurt, pages 160–161, and Sore Nipples, chapter 7, pages 233–248). Severe cases might require using a hospital-grade rental electric breast pump until your nipples are healed.*

After two or three weeks, nursing mothers usually notice the sensations associated with the milk ejection, or milk letdown, reflex. One of the hormones released from your pituitary gland during nursing is known as oxytocin. Oxytocin is important to the success of breastfeeding because it causes tiny muscle cells around the milk-producing glands to squeeze milk out of the glands and into the milk ducts. This propelling of milk from the milk ducts is called the milk ejection reflex or the let-down reflex (see Oxytocin, Chapter 3, pages 77–78). Oxytocin release helps milk produced in the glands become available to the baby. Once a woman's milk supply is well established, the milk ejection reflex causes noticeable breast sensations, such as tingling, tightening, stinging, burning, or a pins-and-needles feeling. It can take a couple of weeks to perceive these breast sensations. When your milk ejection reflex is triggered, your baby may start to gulp milk, and milk may drip or spray from the other breast. Just hearing your baby cry or holding your infant can cause your milk to "let-down," even before your baby latches on.

WHEN TO SEEK HELP: *Although many women breastfeed just fine without noticing signs of the milk ejection reflex, failure to perceive the typical let-down sensations by three weeks postpartum could mean that your milk supply is low. Generally, the more abundant the milk supply, the more dramatic the signs of let-down, but this is not a hard-and-fast rule. If you are in doubt about your milk supply, have your baby weighed.*

Normal Weight Patterns in Breastfed Newborns

The most reliable indicator of the success of breastfeeding is your baby's weight. A baby who is thriving is sure to be getting enough milk. On the other hand, a baby who has lost excessive weight or who is gaining too slowly most likely is consuming too little milk. Not only is the baby's welfare of immediate concern, but the mother's milk supply can decline rapidly if her baby isn't removing the milk from her breasts effectively.

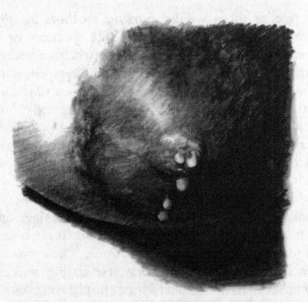

Milk drips and sprays from the breast when the milk
ejection reflex is triggered.

Contact your health care providers if you do not see the following things. They may instruct you to supplement with formula or pumped milk (not water) if your baby is not wetting his/her diaper or having stools as noted below, or is still hungry after frequent nursing. One half to one ounce of supplement is probably adequate after breastfeeding on the second to third day of life. Once your milk has come in, your breastfed baby should gain an ounce a day for the first few months of life.

	First 8 hours	8–24 hours	Day 2	Day 3	Day 4	Day 5	Day 6 onward
Milk supply	You may be able to express a few drops of milk.	→	→	Milk should come in between the 2nd and 4th day.		Milk should be in. Breasts may be firm and/or leak milk.	Breasts should feel softer after nursing.
Baby's activity	Baby is usually wide awake in the first hour of life. Put baby to breast within a half to one hour of birth.	Wake up your baby. Babies may not wake up on their own to feed.	Baby should be more cooperative and less sleepy.	Look for early feeding cues such as rooting, lip smacking, and hands to face.	→		Baby should appear satisfied after feedings.
Feeding routine	Baby may go into a deep sleep 2–4 hours after birth.	Feed your baby every 1½ to 3 hrs, as often as wanted, a minimum of 8–12 times each day.	Use chart on following page to write down time and length of each feeding.	→	→	May go one longer interval (up to 5 hours) between feeds in a 24-hour period.	→
Breast-feeding	Baby will wake up and be alert and responsive for several more hours after initial deep sleep.	As long as Mom is comfortable, nurse at both breasts as long as baby is actively sucking.	Try to nurse both sides each feeding aiming for 10 minutes each side. Expect some nipple tenderness.	Consider hand expressing or pumping a few drops of milk to soften the nipple if the breast is too firm for your baby to latch on.	Nurse a minimum of 10–15 minutes each side every 2–3 hours for the first few months of life.		Mom's nipple tenderness is improving or is gone.
Baby's urine output		Baby must have a minimum of 1 wet diaper in first 24 hours.	Baby must have at least one wet diaper every 8–12 hours.	You should see an increase in wet diapers to 4–6 times in 24 hours.	Baby's urine should be light yellow.	Baby should have 6–8 wet diapers each day of colorless or light yellow urine.	
Baby's stools	Baby should have a black-green stool (meconium stool).		Baby may have a second very dark (meconium) stool.	Baby's stools should be changing color from black-green to yellow.		Baby should have 3–4 yellow, soft stools a day.	The number of stools may decrease gradually after 4–6 weeks of life.

Prepared by Lisbeth Gabrielski, RN, BSN, IBCLC, Lactation Support Service, The Children's Hospital, Denver, CO. Copyright © 1994. All rights reserved. Revised 4/95. Used with permission.

Record number of minutes of active sucking on each side, and the number of wet and dirty diapers your baby has each day.

Time of Day	BREASTFEEDING CHART Date:			BREASTFEEDING CHART Date:			BREASTFEEDING CHART Date:			BREASTFEEDING CHART Date:		
	Minutes/Side (Left/Right)	Number of Urines/Stools	Comments	Minutes/Side (Left/Right)	Number of Urines/Stools	Comments	Minutes/Side (Left/Right)	Number of Urines/Stools	Comments	Minutes/Side (Left/Right)	Number of Urines/Stools	Comments
MNight	/	/		/	/		/	/		/	/	
1:00	/	/		/	/		/	/		/	/	
2:00	/	/		/	/		/	/		/	/	
3:00	/	/		/	/		/	/		/	/	
4:00	/	/		/	/		/	/		/	/	
5:00	/	/		/	/		/	/		/	/	
6:00	/	/		/	/		/	/		/	/	
7:00	/	/		/	/		/	/		/	/	
8:00	/	/		/	/		/	/		/	/	
9:00	/	/		/	/		/	/		/	/	
10:00	/	/		/	/		/	/		/	/	
11:00	/	/		/	/		/	/		/	/	
Noon	/	/		/	/		/	/		/	/	
1:00	/	/		/	/		/	/		/	/	
2:00	/	/		/	/		/	/		/	/	
3:00	/	/		/	/		/	/		/	/	
4:00	/	/		/	/		/	/		/	/	
5:00	/	/		/	/		/	/		/	/	
6:00	/	/		/	/		/	/		/	/	
7:00	/	/		/	/		/	/		/	/	
8:00	/	/		/	/		/	/		/	/	
9:00	/	/		/	/		/	/		/	/	
10:00	/	/		/	/		/	/		/	/	
11:00	/	/		/	/		/	/		/	/	

• **Infant weight loss after birth.** All babies lose some weight in the first days after birth. On average, breastfed babies lose a little more than bottle-fed infants. This is probably because the volume of colostrum, or early milk, is relatively low before mother's milk comes in abundantly. Many health professionals consider it acceptable for babies to lose up to 10 percent of the original birth weight within the first three days after birth (see Weight Loss and Weight Conversion Chart, below). I consider 10% to be the very outer limit of acceptable loss, as most babies will not lose this much weight before they start to gain. Larger babies can lose a greater number of ounces than smaller babies, yet still be considered to fall within the range of normal.

WEIGHT LOSS AND WEIGHT CONVERSION CHART

Birth Weight		10% Weight Loss	
lbs., oz.	Kilograms	lbs., oz.	Kilograms
4 lbs., 8 oz.	2.04	4 lbs., 1 oz.	1.84
4 lbs., 10 oz.	2.10	4 lbs., 3 oz.	1.89
4 lbs., 12 oz.	2.15	4 lbs., 4 oz.	1.94
4 lbs., 14 oz.	2.21	4 lbs., 6 oz.	1.99
5 lbs.	2.27	4 lbs., 8 oz.	2.04
5 lbs., 2 oz.	2.32	4 lbs., 10 oz.	2.09
5 lbs., 4 oz.	2.38	4 lbs., 12 oz.	2.14
5 lbs., 6 oz.	2.44	4 lbs., 13 oz.	2.19
5 lbs., 8 oz.	2.49	4 lbs., 15 oz.	2.25
5 lbs., 10 oz.	2.55	5 lbs., 1 oz.	2.30
5 lbs., 12 oz.	2.61	5 lbs., 3 oz.	2.35
5 lbs., 14 oz.	2.66	5 lbs., 5 oz.	2.40
6 lbs.	2.72	5 lbs., 6 oz.	2.45
6 lbs., 2 oz.	2.78	5 lbs., 8 oz.	2.50
6 lbs., 4 oz.	2.84	5 lbs., 10 oz.	2.55
6 lbs., 6 oz.	2.89	5 lbs., 12 oz.	2.60
6 lbs., 8 oz.	2.95	5 lbs., 14 oz.	2.65
6 lbs., 10 oz.	3.01	5 lbs., 15 oz.	2.70
6 lbs., 12 oz.	3.06	6 lbs., 1 oz.	2.76
6 lbs., 14 oz.	3.12	6 lbs., 3 oz.	2.81
7 lbs.	3.18	6 lbs., 5 oz.	2.86
7 lbs., 2 oz.	3.23	6 lbs., 7 oz.	2.91
7 lbs., 4 oz.	3.29	6 lbs., 8 oz.	2.96
7 lbs., 6 oz.	3.35	6 lbs., 10 oz.	3.01
7 lbs., 8 oz.	3.40	6 lbs., 12 oz.	3.06

Birth Weight		10% Weight Loss	
lbs., oz.	Kilograms	lbs., oz.	Kilograms
7 lbs., 10 oz.	3.46	6 lbs., 14 oz.	3.11
7 lbs., 12 oz.	3.52	7 lbs.	3.16
7 lbs., 14 oz.	3.57	7 lbs., 1 oz.	3.21
8 lbs.	3.63	7 lbs., 3 oz.	3.27
8 lbs., 2 oz.	3.69	7 lbs., 5 oz.	3.32
8 lbs., 4 oz.	3.74	7 lbs., 7 oz.	3.37
8 lbs., 6 oz.	3.80	7 lbs., 9 oz.	3.42
8 lbs., 8 oz.	3.86	7 lbs., 10 oz.	3.47
8 lbs., 10 oz.	3.91	7 lbs., 12 oz.	3.52
8 lbs., 12 oz.	3.97	7 lbs., 14 oz.	3.57
8 lbs., 14 oz.	4.03	8 lbs.	3.62
9 lbs.	4.08	8 lbs., 2 oz.	3.67
9 lbs., 2 oz.	4.14	8 lbs., 3 oz.	3.73
9 lbs., 4 oz.	4.20	8 lbs., 5 oz.	3.78
9 lbs., 6 oz.	4.25	8 lbs., 7 oz.	3.83
9 lbs., 8 oz.	4.31	8 lbs., 9 oz.	3.88
9 lbs., 10 oz.	4.37	8 lbs., 11 oz.	3.93
9 lbs., 12 oz.	4.42	8 lbs., 12 oz.	3.98
9 lbs., 14 oz.	4.48	8 lbs., 14 oz.	4.03
10 lbs.	4.54	9 lbs.	4.08
10 lbs., 2 oz.	4.59	9 lbs., 2 oz.	4.13
10 lbs., 4 oz.	4.65	9 lbs., 4 oz.	4.18
10 lbs., 6 oz.	4.71	9 lbs., 5 oz.	4.24
10 lbs., 8 oz.	4.76	9 lbs., 7 oz.	4.29

WHEN TO SEEK HELP: *If your infant loses more than 8 to 10 percent of his original birth weight or continues to lose weight beyond four days, it is very probable that he is not obtaining sufficient milk by breastfeeding. If a baby doesn't take sufficient milk, a mother's breasts won't continue to make sufficient milk. Your baby's doctor should evaluate your infant, assure that he starts to receive adequate nutrition, and help you obtain assistance with breastfeeding technique and proper breast emptying.*

• *Rate of weight gain.* An infant should stop losing weight once the mother's milk comes in. At this point, a baby should be consuming adequate quantities of milk to begin steady weight gain.

Young breastfed infants gain weight at a surprisingly rapid rate, especially during the first six weeks of life. Most will regain their lost weight and surpass their birth weight by ten to fourteen days. Although every baby's growth pattern is unique, an average weight gain of an ounce each day (beginning by four or five days) is typical during the first three months of life. Between birth and three months, most babies will gain two-thirds of a pound to one pound (ten to sixteen ounces) every two weeks. Thereafter, the rate of weight gain tapers somewhat.

WHEN TO SEEK HELP: *If a breastfed baby is under birth weight by two weeks of age or has not started to gain at least five to seven ounces a week once the mother's milk comes in, the infant should be evaluated and breastfeeding assistance provided. Inadequate weight gain is a strong indicator of low milk intake by a baby and requires prompt investigation. Taking a wait-and-see approach can lead to diminished milk supply and an underfed, unhappy baby.*

• **In-home weighing of your baby.** Several commercial electronic infant scales are available for in-home weighing of your infant (see In-Home Weighing of Infants, chapter 4, pages 125–126). In the past, new parents commonly used in-home baby scales, even though some were notoriously inaccurate. Many contemporary health professionals discourage the use of in-home scales because they assume they are still inaccurate. Some of the modern instruments, however, are accurate to ten grams (just one-third of an ounce) and even to two grams. While a few parents find an in-home scale to be intimidating, most who have used the new, state-of-the-art, digital instruments report that they can breastfeed with greater confidence knowing their baby is gaining weight. As mentioned earlier, your baby's weight is closely linked to the adequacy of breastfeeding. The early recognition of inadequate infant weight gain not only protects your baby's well-being but also improves your chances of succeeding at breastfeeding by identifying potential problems early. Of course, a scale can never substitute for visits with your baby's doctor, but it can provide valuable information about the success of breastfeeding and alert you to the need for medical attention or additional assistance with breastfeeding.

Lightweight, user-friendly, affordable, accurate baby scales can be rented for home use (see Resource List, page 450).

Common Concerns During the Early Weeks of Breastfeeding

My Baby Won't Latch On

During your hospital stay, the nurses probably assisted you in latching your baby on to your breast. Without such expert guidance, you may be having difficulty getting your baby to attach correctly now that you are home. Even infants who once nursed well may have difficulty latching on if the mother's breasts become swollen and firm when her milk comes in abundantly. In addition to the extreme frustration a latch-on problem causes, both your baby's well-being and your milk supply can be placed in jeopardy if your infant is unable to nurse correctly.

Try the strategies outlined in chapter 4 (pages 117–119). If you are not having success getting your baby to nurse well within a few hours, you need to call your baby's doctor and make a plan for assuring your infant receives adequate milk. I strongly advise you to seek assistance promptly from a lactation consultant or to call the nursery at the hospital where you delivered. Ask a neonatal nurse if you can return right away for assistance in getting your baby to breastfeed. The hospital probably has an efficient electric breast pump that you can use while you are there. If your breasts are engorged, expressing some milk will soften your nipple and areola and make it easier for your baby to grasp your breast. Any milk you express can be fed to your baby. Even if you have to pump and feed your expressed milk for a day or so, with patience and practice, your baby can learn to latch on and nurse correctly.

Some babies have overcome latch-on problems with the use of a silicone nipple shield placed over the mother's nipple. The shield is stiffer and more protuberant than the mother's own nipple, and most babies accept it readily. Your nipple is drawn into the shield as your baby breastfeeds. After nursing with the nipple shield for a while, you should try to remove it and attach your baby to your breast. A nipple shield should be used only with the direct supervision of a lactation consultant or other breastfeeding specialist who can assure that your infant obtains adequate milk nursing with the shield and closely monitor your baby's weight gain. I also recommend pumping your residual milk after you breastfeed using a nipple shield, since nursing with the shield is not as effective as direct breastfeeding. Your baby's doctor needs to know that your infant is having difficulty breastfeeding.

How Do I Arouse My Sleepy Baby?

While some newborns awaken on schedule and act hungry, others fail to demand feedings as expected and must be coaxed to nurse. The parents of such infants often mistakenly conclude that they have "such a good baby." At a time when new parents are exhausted and overwhelmed, an apparently contented, nondemanding infant can seem like a blessing. Uninformed health professionals often reinforce this misperception by telling new parents how fortunate they are to have a newborn who sleeps through the night.

But a nondemanding infant is not a blessing. Such a baby can create a false sense of success at first because the infant seems so satisfied. Before long, however, ineffective and infrequent nursing can result in an underweight infant and an inadequate milk supply. If your newborn is not demanding at least every three and a half hours, you need to try to awaken the infant to nurse. Try the following measures to arouse your baby from light sleep (look for rapid eye movements, arm and leg movements, facial twitches, or mouthing motions) and entice her to nurse:

• **Dim the lights.** Babies are more likely to open their eyes in subdued room lighting and will close their eyes in the presence of bright lights.

• **Unswaddle the baby.** Babies get drowsy when they are overly warm and swaddled. You may need to undress your baby down to her diaper to make her less cozy and stimulate her interest in feeding.

• **Position your infant upright,** either sitting on your lap with your hand under her chin or placing her over your shoulder as if you were going to burp her. When positioned upright, most babies will reflexively open their eyes.

• **Perform "passive" sit-ups with your baby.** While supporting your baby on your lap in the sitting position with one hand behind her head, gently lean her backward until she is fully supine (lying on her back). Slowly rock her back and forth at the hips, going from sitting to reclining, about four to six times. This usually will cause her eyes to open.

• **Talk to or sing to your baby.** Use a high-pitched voice and exaggerate your intonation and accentuate each syllable. "You're a h-u-u-u-n-g-r-y b-a-a-a-a-b-y."

• **Massage your infant.** Gently rub her arms and legs, stroke her head, wipe her face with a warm wet cloth, or massage the soles of her feet. Gently run your finger along her upper lip. Start in the midline and move toward the outer edge, one side at a time.

• **Change her diaper or perform cord care.** The stimulation involved in changing your baby's diaper and washing her bottom may suffice to arouse her. If that doesn't work, applying alcohol to the base of the umbilical cord is a pretty surefire way to awaken a sleepy baby. The cold alcohol against the baby's abdomen almost always gets a response.

• **Offer a little expressed milk to your baby by spoon, cup, or dropper.** Hand express or pump as much colostrum or early milk as you can. You can dribble a little milk onto your nipple to entice your baby to nurse. Some drowsy babies who appear disinterested in feeding actually have borderline low blood sugar. Giving them a little nourishment can perk the baby up and bring her to an alert state in which she can nurse effectively.

• **Stimulate sucking activity using your clean little finger.** After washing your hands, place the nail side of your little finger against the baby's tongue and stimulate her palate with the fleshy part of your finger. After your baby starts sucking, remove your finger and offer your breast.

Many nondemanding, sleepy babies do better with a few simple breastfeeding modifications. If the infant does not sustain suckling very long, it is preferable to restrict her nursing to only five minutes per breast. Babies generally take more milk nursing for a shorter duration at both breasts than nursing a little longer on one side only. An exception to this recommendation is the sleepy infant who cannot be enticed to take the second breast after being removed from the first side. In this case, letting the baby nurse longer on the first breast is preferable to interrupting nursing on the first side and then having the baby refuse the second side altogether.

If your baby sucks vigorously for only a few minutes and then stops, try arousing her and switching her to the other breast. You can keep her on the first breast as long as she swallows after every couple of sucks. When her swallowing slows down or she starts to doze off, remove her from the breast, try to bring her to a more wakeful state, and switch her to the other side. This "switch nursing" method will provide her with more milk than allowing her to drift off at the first breast.

Is My Baby Getting Enough Milk?

Even though you can't see exactly how much milk your baby takes while nursing, observant parents usually can tell whether breastfeeding is off to a good start. If your baby can latch on to both breasts well, nurses often with frequent audible swallowing, seems contented after feedings, wets six or more diapers, and has at least four yellow bowel movements each day, she is probably thriving. The following questionnaire developed at the Lactation Program in Denver has proved useful in distinguishing whether breastfeeding is off to a successful start or whether additional help is necessary. If you have any concerns, call your baby's doctor and arrange to have your infant weighed. Remember, if a problem is caught early, it is easier to solve.

EARLY BREASTFEEDING SCREENING FORM

Please complete this screening form when your baby is four to six days old. If you circle any answers in the right-hand column, call your baby's doctor to arrange for further evaluation. The earlier problems are identified, the easier they are to correct. Ask your doctor to refer you to a lactation consultant who can observe your nursing technique and provide one-on-one assistance.

1. Do you feel breastfeeding is going well for you so far?   Yes No
2. Has your milk come in yet? (That is, did your breasts get firm and full between the second and fourth postpartum days?)   Yes No
3. Is your baby able to latch on to your breast without difficulty?   Yes No
4. Is your baby able to sustain rhythmic sucking for at least ten minutes total per feeding?   Yes No
5. Does your baby usually demand to feed? (Answer "No" if you have a sleepy baby who needs to be awakened for most feedings.)   Yes No

6. Does your baby usually nurse at both breasts at each feeding?	Yes	No
7. Does your baby nurse approximately every two to three hours, with no more than one longer interval of up to five hours at night? (at least eight nursings each twenty-four hours?)	Yes	No
8. Do your breasts feel full before feedings?	Yes	No
9. Do your breasts feel softer after feedings?	Yes	No
10. Are your nipples extremely sore? (for example, causing you to dread feedings?)	No	Yes
11. Is your baby having yellow, seedy bowel movements that look like cottage cheese and mustard?	Yes	No
12. Is your baby having at least four good-size bowel movements each day? (that is, more than a "stain" on the diaper?)	Yes	No
13. Is your baby wetting his/her diaper at least six times each day?	Yes	No
14. Does your baby appear hungry after most feedings? (that is, crying, sucking hands, rooting, often needing a pacifier?)	No	Yes
15. Do you hear rhythmic suckling and swallowing while your baby nurses?	Yes	No

Copyright © Lactation Program, Denver, CO. Used with permission.

When Is Poor Feeding a Sign of Infant Illness?

One of the most important clues to infant well-being is the frequency and quality of feedings. Parents, especially mothers, quickly become attuned to their baby's usual feeding pattern and readily notice any changes in feeding frequency, duration, or vigor. Young infants have few ways to communicate illness. Poor feeding is one of the strongest indicators of a medical problem, and it *must not be ignored*. Sleeping through feeding times, showing less interest in feedings, suckling for a shorter period of time, or nursing with less stamina all could indicate some type of medical problem, such as an infection or a heart condition. You should promptly report any change in your baby's feeding pattern to your infant's doctor.

What Does Infant Jaundice Have to Do with Breastfeeding?

Many newborn babies develop a yellowish color to the whites of their eyes and their skin, a condition known as jaundice. Parents often wonder about the significance of newborn jaundice. In adults, jaundice rarely occurs and represents an important sign of illness, such as hepatitis. Jaundice in adults must never be ignored; its cause always must be investigated. Unlike adults, some degree of jaundice is evident in nearly half of all newborns, usually by the third day of life. Most cases of newborn jaundice are mild and require no treatment. The yellow color results from a substance known as bilirubin, a breakdown product of hemoglobin, which is present in red blood cells. Normally, the liver metabolizes bilirubin and excretes it in a modified form into the intestines where it gets passed from the body in bowel movements.

Many factors contribute to higher bilirubin levels in newborns during the first week of life. First, babies are born with more red blood cells than adults and these cells have a shorter life span than that of adult blood cells. In addition, many babies experience bruising during the birth process, and the red blood cells trapped in a bruise quickly add to the bilirubin load. Thus, newborns must handle proportionately more bilirubin than normal adults. Ironically, the immature newborn liver is less effective in metabolizing bilirubin. Furthermore, even when the liver does its job and excretes bilirubin into the gut, bilirubin can be reabsorbed from the infant's intestines into the bloodstream, especially if the baby stools infrequently. Since breastfed babies often obtain less milk compared to formula-fed babies during the first few days of life, breastfed babies may stool less often and develop higher levels of bilirubin. In fact, many studies have confirmed that breastfed babies, on average, have higher bilirubin levels than bottle-fed babies.

Now you can appreciate why so many healthy newborns develop some visible jaundice. Numerous medical disorders can further exaggerate the bilirubin level, such as blood type mismatches between mother and baby that cause the baby's red blood cells to break down faster than normal; liver disease that impairs the metabolism of bilirubin; infection; heart disease; or a low level of thyroid hormone. Thus, whenever jaundice is present, it is important not only to monitor the level of bilirubin but to identify the cause of its elevation as well. Normal, or physiologic, jaundice must be distinguished from serious underlying causes of jaundice that require treatment.

Another reason we worry about jaundice is that high levels (usually over 25 milligrams percent) are toxic to the newborn brain and can cause brain damage and/or hearing loss. Permanent damage can be prevented by monitoring bilirubin levels carefully with blood tests, searching for and treating any identified causes, and using phototherapy (in the form of bilirubin lights or phototherapy blankets) to bring the level down. (Rarely, the bilirubin level rises so high that an exchange transfusion becomes necessary to lower the level rapidly.) Proper treatment of jaundice involves more than just "making the yellow go away." It should include finding and treating any underlying medical conditions contributing to the problem. *Inadequate breastfeeding is a common cause of newborn jaundice that needs to be recognized and treated.*

If you observe any yellowish color to your baby's skin or the whites of her eyes, notify your baby's doctor, who will decide whether to order a bilirubin level. Ask to have your infant weighed. Many doctors don't appreciate that inadequate breastfeeding can contribute to jaundice in a breastfed infant. When breastfeeding is going poorly for any reason, the result can be insufficient caloric intake by the infant, excessive weight loss from birth, inadequate weight gain, infrequent stooling, and an elevated bilirubin level. If your baby has jaundice, your doctor can help you determine whether the level is high enough to pose any danger and whether inadequate breastfeeding might be contributing to the problem.

Review the expected normal patterns for breastfed infants described earlier. Is your baby latching on correctly and feeding on an appropriate schedule? Is she wetting and stooling normally? Has your milk come in? Is she emptying your breasts well? Has she lost excessive weight or started to gain consistently?

Bilirubin levels usually peak around three to five days of age, just when your milk is coming in abundantly and your breasts are maximally engorged. At the point when your breasts need to be drained well, your sleepy, jaundiced baby may not be the most effective candidate for the job. I usually recommend a hospital-grade rental electric breast pump for mothers whose jaundiced infants are not nursing vigorously. By pumping after nursing, you can stimulate a generous supply, improve milk flow, and obtain expressed milk to be used to supplement your baby if necessary.

Unfortunately, many doctors mistakenly believe that it is necessary to discontinue breastfeeding temporarily when a baby's bilirubin level gets high (see Breast-milk Jaundice, chapter 7, pages 248–250). In fact, this is almost never necessary. Most often, exaggerated jaundice in a breastfed baby is due to inadequate breastfeeding. What's needed are measures to improve the baby's intake of milk, not a temporary switch to formula (which often turns out to be permanent).

Why Do I Get Cramps When I Breastfeed?

The hormone oxytocin that plays a role in breastfeeding is the same hormone that causes your uterus to contract during labor. In the first days after delivery, oxytocin released during breastfeeding causes the still-enlarged uterus to contract. The resulting cramps, known as afterpains, help the uterus shrink to its prepregnant size. The discomfort usually is worse for women who have given birth previously than for first-time mothers. While afterpains can be quite uncomfortable, they are short-lived, usually lasting only seven to ten days. These uterine cramps not only help you recover from childbirth, but they are a good sign that your milk ejection reflex is working well.

My Breasts Are Swollen and Painful

One of the most frequent early difficulties encountered by breastfeeding women occurs when their milk comes in abundantly and their breasts get larger, firmer, and tender. These breast changes that coincide with the beginning of copious milk production are known as postpartum breast engorgement. Engorgement results from hormone fluctuations after delivery that cause a sudden increase in milk volume. Tissue swelling, lymph drainage, and increased blood flow to the breasts also contribute to the dramatic breast changes.

It is generally believed that frequent, unrestricted nursing during the first days postpartum will relieve milk congestion and prevent severe engorgement. In my experience, however, the severity of engorgement cannot always be explained by a woman's early feeding practices. Some women begin nursing right away and feed often, yet still experience excessive engorgement, while others don't start breastfeeding for a day or so without getting severely engorged. Most experts agree that engorgement is more remarkable in first-time mothers than those having subsequent babies. In addition, I have observed that engorgement is often greater in women whose breast size increased dramatically during pregnancy.

Fortunately, postpartum breast engorgement is a temporary condition, usually lasting only a few days until your body adjusts to the process of making and releasing milk. By the end of the first week after delivery, milk flow is usually well established and breast engorgement has subsided. In the meantime, it is very important that your baby be helped to latch on correctly and to nurse often (at least every two to three hours) while your breasts are engorged. You may need to express some milk to soften your nipple and areola and make it easier for your baby to latch on. Frequent milk emptying will make you more comfortable, keep your baby well fed, and assure continued generous milk production.

For specific strategies to help your baby nurse well when your breasts are swollen, to relieve uncomfortable engorgement, and to improve milk flow, see chapter 7 (Postpartum Breast Engorgement, pages 225–231).

My Nipples Hurt

Sore nipples are one of the most frequent complaints of breast-feeding women. Early, mild nipple tenderness, beginning on the second day, is so common as to be considered normal. Usually the first minute after your baby latches on is the most uncomfortable. Try your Lamaze breathing techniques to help you relax prior to nursings, so you won't tense up in anticipation of pain.

First and foremost, pay attention to proper nursing position and the infant's attachment to the breast (see chapter 4, pages 88–99). Early sore nipples are usually due to improper infant latch-on. Another helpful strategy is to begin feedings on the least sore side, since your baby suckles more vigorously at the beginning of a feeding until the milk ejection reflex has been triggered. Once your milk begins to flow and nursing is more comfortable, you can move your infant to the more painful side. However, try to assure that both breasts get equal stimulation and emptying. Frequent, shorter feedings are preferable to long nursings at wider intervals. Most mothers find that a soothing emollient applied to their nipples promotes healing. I recommend USP Modified Lanolin (medical grade), such as Lansinoh for Breastfeeding Mothers or PureLan. These products can be obtained from breast pump manufacturers, La Leche League, lactation consultants, maternity shops, and other locations (see Resource List, page 449). Pat your nipples dry and apply a thin coating of lanolin after each nursing. You do not have to remove medical grade lanolin before feeding your infant.

Because the volume of colostrum is low, some babies create a strong vacuum when sucking during the first few days and cause nipple soreness. Once abundant milk production begins, the baby generates less negative pressure during nursing, and nipple pain usually starts to subside. By the end of the first week, you should have little, if any, discomfort with feedings.

Severe or persistent nipple pain is not normal. If your nipples are so painful that you dread feedings, if discomfort persists throughout a nursing, if you have open cracks or fissues, or if your pain does not improve after your milk comes in, you need to seek assistance. Notify your own and your baby's doctor and request to be referred to a lactation consultant. For additional information about the causes and treatment of sore nipples, see chapter 7, pages 233–248.

Can I Feed My Baby on Schedule Instead of by Demand?

The vast majority of breastfeeding proponents strongly attest to the importance of round-the-clock demand feedings for young breastfed infants. However, some parent educators emphasize the value of creating structure and order in a young baby's life by the early establishment of predictable patterns of feeding and sleeping. Other parenting experts consider this philosophy of ordering a baby's life to be somewhat controversial. In my opinion, parents should make every effort to meet their infant's needs promptly in order to help their baby feel loved, safe, and secure and to build trust in the world. Meeting your baby's individual needs as quickly and effectively as possible forms the basis for a strong love bond with your infant. A baby's emotional development can be harmed when her needs go unmet because her parents adhere to an arbitrary feeding schedule. Those who advocate the desirability of regular routines in infant care make attractive claims of successfully feeding babies on predictable schedules and getting them to sleep through the night at an early age.

Obviously, a wide range of parenting styles can be effective in raising healthy, happy children. However, some babies develop regularity in their feeding and sleeping patterns more easily than others. I strongly believe that the unique needs of an infant take priority over parents' desires for predictability and order. While some breastfed babies can thrive well with a regular schedule, it is my impression that the great majority do best on a demand schedule. Breastfeeding is most successful when infants remain in close contact with their mothers and are allowed to nurse in an unrestricted fashion. In some instances, rigid scheduling of feedings has resulted in an infant's failure to thrive.

How Can I Express Some of My Breast Milk?

Many new lactating mothers will need to express some milk in the early weeks of nursing, for example, to relieve uncomfortable engorgement if the baby doesn't empty her breasts adequately. I believe all breastfeeding women should be taught hand expression. In this way, even if they have no pump or can't use their pump effectively, they can still express some milk. After all, you always have your hand with you!

Hand Expression. Hand expression takes practice, so be patient with yourself. Always wash your hands before handling your breasts or collecting expressed milk. For best results expressing milk, first gently massage your breasts, going from the outer areas toward the nipple. A good time to practice learning how to express is when your milk is letting-down. Warm compresses or a warm shower are useful in starting milk flow. Place your thumb above your nipple and your first two fingers below, positioning them about one to one and a half inches behind the base of your nipple. Your fingers should be situated over the milk sinuses, or dilated milk ducts, beneath your areola (see the illustration on page 73 of chapter 3). Next, press your thumb and fingers back toward your chest wall. Then gently roll your thumb and fingers together (as if you were simultaneously making thumb and fingerprints). The rolling motion will extract the milk pooled in the dilated ducts beneath your areola. Lean forward slightly and collect your dripping milk in a clean cup or other widemouthed container. Try to avoid letting your milk roll over your fingers as you collect it. Repeat the push and roll motions until milk stops flowing. At first you might obtain only a few drops with each compression, but soon you should be getting sprays from several duct openings. Rotate your thumb and finger positions around your nipple to empty milk from all the lactiferous sinuses. Storage guidelines for expressed breast milk are covered in chapter 8 (page 306).

Manual Breast Pumps, Battery-Operated Pumps, and Small Electric Breast Pumps. Many breastfeeding women purchase a

Hand expression of breast milk, using a commercial funnel attachment
for a standard baby bottle.

breast pump to remove some milk when their breasts get engorged,
to occasionally express milk when they must miss a feeding, or to
collect extra milk to leave for their baby if they must be absent. A
dizzying variety of breast pumps are available for purchase,
including simple hand pumps, battery-operated types, and small
electric options. Each has its own unique features and price
range. Women have varying success using different types of breast
pumps, making it difficult to generalize about which is the most
effective, comfortable, or convenient in each category. Thus, I suggest you review several pump options with a lactation consultant
who can help guide your decision. Before purchasing one of the
smaller breast pumps, however, consider whether a hospital-grade
rental electric pump would better suit your needs.

Hospital-Grade Rental Electric Breast Pumps. It is generally
agreed that the most effective, efficient, and comfortable breast
pumps available are the hospital-grade rental electric pumps
equipped with a double collection system that empties both breasts
at once. In addition to being fast and comfortable, these pumps are
remarkably effective in maintaining and even increasing your milk
supply. Many of them offer fully automatic cycling and feature a
control mechanism to allow you to regulate both the speed at
which the pump cycles and the amount of vacuum it generates. A

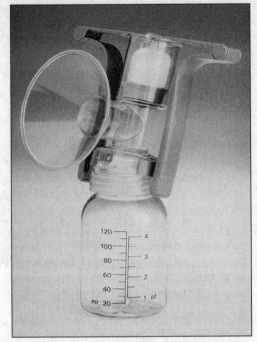

Ameda One-Hand Breast Pump.

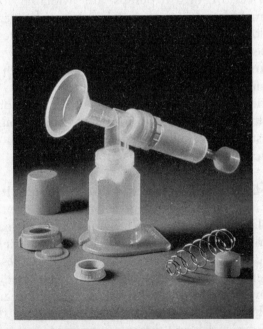

Medela SpringExpress Manual Breastpump.

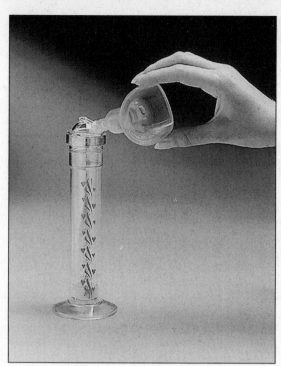

White River Concepts
Manual Pump
with Soft-Cup Funnel.

hospital-grade electric breast pump can be extremely helpful in many situations, including the following: to relieve severe engorgement; to maintain your milk supply when you work outside the home or when your baby cannot nurse due to prematurity or illness; to increase a low milk supply; or to pump after ineffective nursings (for example, if your baby has a sucking problem). You must purchase your own set of collection containers, in addition to paying the pump-rental fee. The rate is more cost effective when you rent the pump for longer periods than at a daily rate. Most women agree that the effectiveness, convenience, and comfort of these pumps make them well worth the expense. In many instances, such as premature birth, the cost of the pump rental is covered by insurance when your health care provider documents that breast milk is medically necessary for your baby's health. To locate an electric breast pump–rental station near you, call the manufacturers listed in the Resource List, page 446. Hospitals, lactation consultants, La Leche League, Nursing Mothers Counsel, WIC clinics, and physicians' offices also can refer you to a pump-rental outlet.

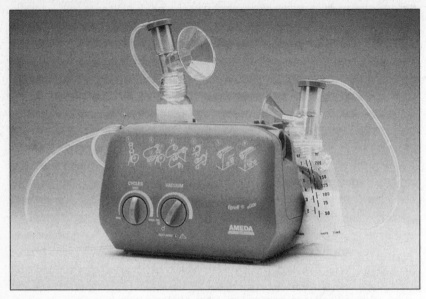

Egnell Elite hospital-grade rental electric breast pump.

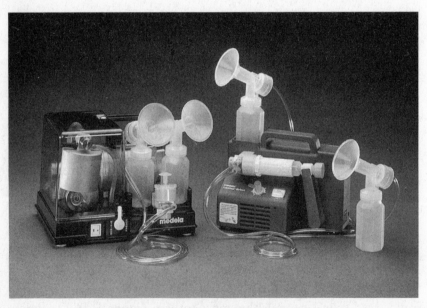

Medela Classic and Lactina Select hospital-grade
rental electric breast pumps.

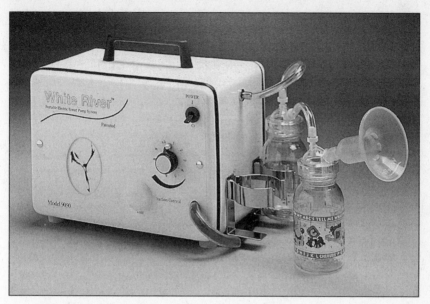

White River Concepts hospital-grade rental electric breast pump.

What If My Baby Needs Supplemental Milk?

Despite all the admonitions you will hear about not giving a breastfed baby any supplemental milk, the fact is that some newborns do not obtain sufficient milk by breastfeeding. If your baby has lost excessive weight after birth or has not started to gain an adequate amount of weight, your baby's doctor might prescribe extra milk feedings. Your baby's welfare must be your top priority. Meeting your baby's nutritional needs will indirectly help your breastfeeding, as a well-nourished baby will nurse better than an underweight infant.

My first preference is to pump the mother's breasts after nursings and try to obtain high-fat residual hindmilk for the baby's supplement. If the volume of breastmilk is inadequate, then some quantity of infant formula (or screened, processed donor breast milk where it is available) might be necessary to correct your baby's underweight condition (see chapter 9, pages 341–346).

If bottle-feedings are not desired, other options exist for feeding supplemental milk to babies, including the SNS device (see chapter 4, page 114, chapter 9, pages 347–349, and chapter 10, page 388), cup, spoon, or dropper. I certainly don't recommend giving supplemental milk without a valid medical indication. On the other hand, I cannot condone withholding essential nutrition from a baby who is being underfed. Obviously, whenever supplemental milk is prescribed, ongoing efforts should be made to keep the baby breastfeeding as effectively as possible, to increase the mother's milk supply, and to ultimately return to full breastfeeding.

The Importance of Early Infant Follow-Up After Discharge

Mothers who give birth today are being discharged much earlier than in past decades. Going home in twenty-four hours or less after a vaginal birth has become commonplace. Opponents have criticized the popular trend toward shorter and shorter hospital confinements, now being referred to as "drive-through deliveries." Controversy abounds about the safety of early discharge for mothers and infants, and recent national legislation now requires insurance companies to extend coverage for normal deliveries to forty-eight hours.

Much of the media attention given to this issue has focused on breastfeeding complications that resulted from too-early discharge and too-late follow-up. Several tragic cases of life-threatening infant dehydration that resulted from unrecognized inadequate breastfeeding were spotlighted in the news. These cases are unlikely to occur when close follow-up after discharge is provided. Telephone counseling can provide *additional* postdischarge support, but it is *not an adequate substitute* for a visit in person, where the infant is weighed and examined.

In the recent past, most newborns remained in the hospital several days and weren't seen after discharge until two weeks of age. Now that babies are being discharged earlier, the American Academy of Pediatrics recommends that infants who go home before forty-eight hours of age should be seen within the following forty-eight hours. This type of close follow-up should eliminate unfortunate cases of excessive weight loss in breastfed babies.

However long your baby stays in the hospital, I urge you to have your infant seen within a few days of discharge for a weight check and physical examination. Delaying follow-up until 10 days or 2 weeks while you guess about how your breastfeeding is going is just too risky. Breastfeeding problems need to be identified and remedied as early as possible. Many options exist for the early follow-up assessment, including a home health visit, an appointment at the clinic or office where your baby will receive her regular care, a hospital follow-up program, or a consultation with a lactation specialist.

Getting Help for Early Breastfeeding Problems

Many new parents mistakenly believe that sheer willpower and determination can overcome any difficulties they encounter in the early weeks of breastfeeding. Instead of seeking professional help as soon as problems become evident, these highly motivated individuals may be convinced that dogged perseverance eventually pays off. Certainly, their never-give-up attitude is admirable considering that many new parents quickly become discouraged and discontinue breastfeeding. But contrary to popular belief, early breastfeeding problems don't automatically correct themselves as a result of perseverance and wishing very hard for it. On the other hand, even the best advice can't guarantee breastfeeding success unless the parents are willing to continue their efforts. What's needed is a suitable balance of expert help and strong motivation.

If breastfeeding doesn't seem to be going well, don't delay taking action. Your problem may not self-correct despite endurance and trying harder. Instead, your difficulties are likely to become compounded by low milk or an underweight problem in your baby. Infant latch-on troubles or sucking problems, severe nipple pain, unrelieved breast engorgement, excessive infant fussiness, inadequate infant weight gain, or apparent infant hunger all require immediate attention. The earlier you obtain help for a breastfeeding difficulty, the more likely it can be overcome. The old adage "An ounce of prevention is worth a pound of cure" most certainly holds true for breastfeeding. Getting help promptly (see chapter 7, pages 277–280.) gives you the best chance of successfully breastfeeding for as long as you desire. You can request help from one or more of the following sources:

• **Your baby's physician.** He or she may have experience managing early breastfeeding problems. If not, ask for a referral to a private or hospital-based lactation consultant or other breastfeeding counselor for specialized advice about your situation. Most importantly, your baby's physician needs to weigh your infant and make sure that no underlying medical problem is present that might be contributing to your baby's breastfeeding difficulties. If you seek advice from other health workers or from breastfeeding support groups, it is essential that your baby's physician remain the primary coordinator of your infant's overall care. Good communication among the various individuals who counsel you is paramount to your baby's welfare.

• **The hospital where you delivered.** Many hospitals that serve mother-baby pairs have a lactation consultant or lactation nurse specialist on staff. The hospital also may have an electric breast pump that you can use on site to relieve severe breast engorgement. You can call the nursery any time night or day to discuss your problem with a staff nurse. Ask if you can talk with or be seen by the lactation consultant. Many hospitals offer follow-up services for new mothers and babies.

• **Lactation consultants at hospitals, clinics, or in private practice.** A lactation consultant (L.C.) is a relatively new member of the health care team who focuses on providing breastfeeding education to parents and on helping nursing mothers overcome breastfeeding problems. Many L.C.'s are registered nurses who have pursued additional training to work with breastfeeding mother-baby pairs. A lactation consultant can provide personal assistance with breastfeeding technique, teach you how to use a breast pump and other breastfeeding supplies, recommend ways to increase your milk supply, demonstrate alternative methods for feeding supplemental milk when necessary, and offer essential support and education. Credentialing as an International Board Certified Lactation Consultant (I.B.C.L.C.) identifies individuals who have attained voluntary certification by the International Board of Lactation Consultant Examiners. To receive the I.B.C.L.C. credential, applicants must complete academic prerequisites and required practice hours assisting breastfeeding mothers, in addition to passing a comprehensive examination. The I.B.C.L.C. designation is the most widely accepted standard for lactation consultants, although some highly skilled breastfeeding specialists have not pursued this designation.

Your obstetrician, family physician, or pediatrician may work with one or more lactation consultants to whom you can be referred. You also can locate an L.C. in your community by contacting the International Lactation Consultant Association or Medela, Inc. (see Resource List, page 445). Nurses, midwives, dietitians, educators, and other individuals from a wide variety of disciplines work as lactation consultants. I recommend that you ask about the professional background and training of the person with whom you work. I cannot overemphasize the importance of good communication between your lactation consultant and your own and your baby's physicians.

• **La Leche League (LLL) International and Nursing Mothers Counsel.** These volunteer organizations are excellent sources of information and mother-to-mother support for breastfeeding women (see Chapter 2, pages 41–45, and Resource List, pages 446 and 448). If these reputable groups are present in your community, they should be listed in the white pages of your phone book. Both groups provide telephone counseling, and La Leche League holds regular meetings. LLL also offers recorded information on selected breastfeeding topics and provides telephone assistance to health professionals and others, including mothers, through its Center for Breastfeeding Information (see Resource List, page 447). While knowledgeable counselors are present in both organizations, you should realize that these peer support groups are not a substitute for professional medical guidance.

• **The WIC Program (Special Supplemental Nutrition Program for Women, Infants, and Children).** Local WIC clinics provide helpful counseling for their breastfeeding clients, and many offer peer support. In addition, some WIC programs provide electric and manual breast pumps for mothers who need them. WIC clinics also can refer clients with complex breastfeeding problems to other community resources. (See chapter 2, page 45 and Resource List, page 447).

• **Lactation centers.** Some breastfeeding mothers are fortunate enough to live in communities where a lactation center is available. These lactation programs often are sponsored by hospitals and may offer complimentary breastfeeding services for mothers who deliver there. In addition, they may provide outpatient consultation (for a fee) for mothers in their community who have breastfeeding difficulties. Most lactation centers also offer telephone advice, operate a pump-rental program, and sell breastfeeding supplies.

Common Myths and Realities About Early Breastfeeding

MYTH: *He can't be hungry again. He just finished feeding a while ago.*

FACT: Breastfed babies, especially newborns just learning to nurse, may appear to have fed well, without actually having taken much milk. It can be hard to tell whether a nursing infant consumed an adequate amount of milk, since the breasts don't have calibrations on them. If your baby acts hungry a short while after feeding, it's best to assume that he genuinely is hungry. Going by the clock ("He shouldn't be due to eat again") isn't as reliable an indicator of the need to nurse again as your baby's obvious hunger signs. Instead of concluding "He shouldn't be hungry again already," consider this possibility: "He must not have taken all he needed last time. He acts like he wants to try again."

MYTH: *I must not have sufficient (or rich enough) milk. He wants to eat every couple of hours.*

FACT: Breastfed babies feed at closer intervals than bottle-fed babies because breast milk is digested faster. This design probably was nature's way to assure that babies would get their mothers' attention every couple of hours around the clock. Breastfed newborns typically nurse every two to three hours from the beginning of one feeding to the beginning of the next. This frequent feeding pattern can make new breastfeeding mothers doubt the adequacy of their milk. Review the criteria for adequate breastfeeding (see pages 131–146) before attributing your baby's frequent feeding to a deficiency in the quality or quantity of your milk. Abnormalities in milk composition are exceedingly rare. Almost all mothers make milk that is sufficiently rich in nutrients.

MYTH: *You should expect some pain with breastfeeding. It's not easy, you know. You'll just have to tough it out.*

FACT: During the early days of breastfeeding, some nipple discomfort at the beginning of feedings is not uncommon. Variable degrees of breast tenderness also can occur during the period of engorgement when the breasts become full and firm. Once your milk has come in and is flowing well, nipple pain and breast tenderness usually diminish. By the end of the first week, breastfeeding generally should be comfortable. Nipple pain that persists beyond a week, that lasts throughout a feeding, or that causes you to dread nursing your baby is distinctly abnormal. (See chapter 7, pages 233–248.) Such pain probably means that your baby is latched on incorrectly to your breast or is sucking in an inappropriate fashion. You need to seek help right away. Ask your baby's doctor to evaluate your breastfeeding technique, or to refer you to a lactation consultant or other breastfeeding specialist who can assist you with breastfeeding. Remember, improper infant positioning at the breast not only creates nipple pain, but it also prevents the baby from obtaining sufficient milk. Thus, sore nipples often go hand in hand with a low milk supply and a fussy, hungry baby. Just as chronic or severe nipple pain shouldn't be considered a normal part of breastfeeding, persistent or extreme breast tenderness also is abnormal and can signal a treatable problem like a breast infection (see chapter 7, pages 254–260).

MYTH: *Don't worry if nursing isn't going well at first. It usually takes four to six weeks for breastfeeding to get well established.*

FACT: The popular statement that breastfeeding takes many weeks to become well established probably originated as a tactic to encourage women having early problems not to become disillusioned and give up. The truth is that early problems don't always work themselves out, just given a few more weeks. While it might take four weeks for feeding routines to become more predictable and nursings to be more efficient, the hallmarks of successful breastfeeding usually are evident within a week postpartum. When warning signs are present, delays in seeking help often lead to diminished milk supply and worsening of the infant's status. The false belief that many weeks must pass before breastfeeding should be going smoothly does women and their babies a disservice. It fosters a risky wait-and-see approach that contributes to inappropriate delays in seeking help for breastfeeding problems.

Myth: *I'm so glad I chose the natural way to feed my baby. Breastfeeding's sure to be convenient, and I won't have to spend a penny.*

Fact: While I'm all for enthusiastically promoting the benefits of breastfeeding, this Pollyanna approach to nursing can set a woman up for disappointment. Certainly, in the long run, breastfeeding usually proves to be highly convenient, enormously enjoyable, and cost effective. In the early weeks, however, mothers with unrealistic expectations may find it more difficult than they had counted on. Feedings seem less convenient when no one else can do them. Nursing seems less "natural" when it involves uncomfortable engorgement and sore nipples. Instead of being totally cost-free, breastfeeding may require that you spend money for nursing bras, breast pads, a rental breast pump, other breastfeeding aids, and professional consultation. Don't get me wrong. I definitely believe any extra investment of time, effort, or money is well worth it. I just think women should be given a realistic view of the commitment breastfeeding requires—especially in the early weeks.

Myth: *You're so lucky your new baby already sleeps through the night! Think of all the extra rest you're getting.*

Fact: Contrary to popular belief, a breastfed newborn who sleeps through the night (longer than a single five-hour stretch) is not a blessing. With rare exception, such an infant is unlikely to gain sufficient weight or to stimulate an adequate milk supply in the mother. Nighttime feedings are a natural, normal part of early breastfeeding. Round-the-clock feedings are necessary to bring in and preserve an abundant milk supply. Newborns need to receive nighttime nutrition, and the breasts need to be emptied regularly, including at night. If your new baby sleeps longer than five hours at night, you should try to arouse him and entice him to nurse.

Myth: *Don't worry about using formula supplements now and then to keep nursing from tying you down. An occasional bottle will give you a break, and it won't interfere with breastfeeding.*

FACT: Supplemental bottles *can* interfere with the success of breastfeeding by upsetting the delicate law of supply and demand. Simply stated, the law goes like this: "The more milk the baby takes, the more milk the mother makes." If a baby drinks a bottle of formula instead of taking breast milk, the mother's breasts will not get the normal amount of stimulation and emptying. Her supply probably will decline in proportion to the supplement she gives, making her dependent on the continued use of formula. What starts out as a "convenience" bottle can result in a great *inconvenience*—the undermining of successful breastfeeding. If you want to offer an occasional bottle after three to four weeks, use expressed breast milk whenever possible.

MYTH: *Don't give formula or use a bottle at any cost. Nipple confusion can occur with even a single bottle-feeding, and giving any supplement will ruin your chances to succeed at breastfeeding.*

FACT: This is the type of dogmatic advice that has placed some babies in jeopardy. Certainly, offering unnecessary formula or giving bottles as a matter of convenience should be discouraged. These practices are known to threaten the success of breastfeeding. But it is a gross oversimplification to insist that no breastfed baby should be given formula or a bottle. The inescapable truth is that *some breastfed babies are unable to obtain sufficient milk by nursing to meet their fluid or nutrient requirements.* Although uncommon, some breastfed babies have lost an excessive amount of weight and become dangerously dehydrated or malnourished. Our first priority always must be the baby's well-being. A healthy, well-nourished baby is more likely to breastfeed effectively than an undernourished baby in a debilitated state. Formula and bottles are not anathema when they are used to restore a baby to good health. If supplements truly are required, you can be sure that you also need to obtain consultation to improve breastfeeding. A rental-grade electric pump will likely be needed to increase your milk supply. Numerous other breastfeeding aids are available to help solve breastfeeding problems.

MYTH: *Don't worry about your baby's slow weight gain. Everyone knows bottle-fed infants grow much faster than breastfed babies do.*

FACT: When breastfeeding is off to a good start, young infants obtain plenty of milk and gain weight rapidly—about an ounce each day during the early months of life. Young breastfed infants typically grow *above the average* on national growth curves. Only after the first three months do breastfed babies taper in their rate of growth compared to bottle-fed infants. If a young breastfed infant is not gaining weight well, it is very likely that the baby is not obtaining sufficient milk by nursing. Not only is the baby at risk for being undernourished and chronically hungry, but the mother's milk supply can be jeopardized. Early intervention to improve breastfeeding will help the baby gain weight more rapidly and increase the mother's milk supply.

Chapter 6

Daily Life
While Breastfeeding

General Guidelines for Breastfeeding Women

The period of lactation is a relatively brief and very special time in a woman's life that is fondly remembered with a measure of pride. During this unique phase in the childbearing cycle, a breast-feeding mother will need to take some extra care to assure that she produces and provides to her infant abundant, high-quality milk. Unfortunately, many misinformed women decline to breastfeed because they worry that they don't "know all the rules" or they fear they will have to make drastic changes in their lifestyle to accommodate nursing. Actually, most women find that few modifications in their daily life are required to breastfeed successfully. The few who do need to make significant lifestyle changes almost always discover that the rewards of nursing their baby far outweigh any temporary inconvenience in their usual routines. Once you survive the early weeks of new parenthood and get breast-feeding well established, you'll begin to appreciate just how convenient it can be to fit a nursing baby into your life. And the healthy practices you adopt while breastfeeding can become the foundation for a lifetime of increased health consciousness.

A Healthful Diet for Lactating Mothers

Because human milk represents the ideal food for young infants, it's only natural to focus first on the type of diet a mother needs to consume in order to produce nutritious milk for her baby. Concerns about the adequacy of their diet cause many women to doubt the quality of their milk. But a mother's diet doesn't have to be perfect in order for her to make adequate milk and to nourish her baby well. Human milk produced by women all over the world is amazingly uniform in its composition. When mothers are poorly nourished, the *quantity* of milk they produce may be reduced, but the *quality* of milk tends to be fairly consistent. The process of lactation assures that human milk will have the right amount of nutrients—even at the mother's expense, if she doesn't eat a balanced diet on a given day.

Keep It Simple and Build on Your Success. Since lactation follows pregnancy, chances are good that you already are familiar with the basics of sound nutrition. If you gained at least twenty-five pounds during your pregnancy and delivered a baby weighing more than about six and a half pounds, you probably already have an adequate diet. Just keep up the good work! Women who require additional nutrition counseling include those who gained less than twenty pounds during pregnancy or who gave birth to a baby weighing less than six pounds at term. Other women who should receive special dietary advice include those who are underweight with little body fat; who are on restricted or specialized diets; who have chronic health problems (such as diabetes) or medical conditions causing malabsorption (such as cystic fibrosis or inflammatory bowel disease); who suffer from eating disorders; or who delivered twins.

Specific Nutrition Recommendations for Breastfeeding Women.

• **Eat three balanced meals a day and nutritious snacks.** Consume a variety of foods in as natural a form as possible to obtain the calories, protein, vitamins, minerals, and fiber you need for optimal health. Eat plenty of fruits, vegetables, and whole-grain breads and cereals. Limit your intake of sugar, salt, fat, and highly processed foods. The Food Guide Pyramid shown on page 180 has replaced the former Four Food Groups as a suggested outline for daily eating. Because most American diets are too high in fat and saturated fat, the Food Guide Pyramid emphasizes food choices that help reduce fat intake. The layout of the guide visually reinforces the relative number of servings from each of the five major food groups. The largest number of daily food choices (six to eleven servings) should come from the bread and grain group. Whole-grain breads and cereals contain more vitamins and minerals and provide more fiber to prevent constipation. At least five servings of fruits and vegetables (two to four servings of fruits; three to five servings of vegetables) are recommended each day— most Americans fall short of this recommendation. Fruits and veggies are a nutritious, low-fat source of calories, vitamins, minerals, and fiber. Make an effort to eat vitamin A–rich produce often, such as carrots, spinach, sweet potatoes, and cantaloupe. Three servings of milk or other dairy products are suggested for breastfeeding women (four servings for teen mothers). Recent evidence has confirmed the importance of adequate calcium intake in the prevention of osteoporosis (brittle bones) in later life. Dairy products are the best source of dietary calcium. Milk and milk products also provide protein, vitamins, and minerals. If you don't like milk or have a milk allergy or milk intolerance, I advise you to get nutrition counseling and, if deemed necessary, to take appropriate supplements to replace essential nutrients in milk. Lactating mothers also should eat three servings of meat, poultry, fish eggs, nuts, or dry beans each day. Meat or meat alternates provide protein, vitamins, iron, and zinc. The small tip of the Pyramid serves as a reminder that fats, sweets, and soft drinks should be consumed only sparingly.

• **While your body is producing breast milk, it requires more calories than usual.** Most lactating women will need to consume about 500 additional calories above their normal prepregnancy food intake. An individual mother's calorie requirements can vary widely depending upon her basic metabolism and level of activity. Nutrition experts recommend that breastfeeding women consume 2,700 calories per day. However, recent studies of healthy lactating women in the industrialized world showed their actual intake of food to be approximately 2,200 calories per day while breastfeeding, or about 15 percent less than the recommended value. Most nursing mothers will need to consume at least 2,200 calories per day to provide necessary nutrients and to maintain milk pro-

Food Guide Pyramid

A Guide to Daily Food Choices

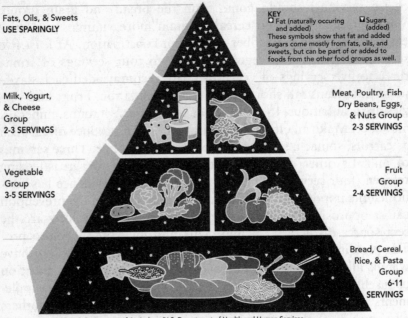

Fats, Oils, & Sweets
USE SPARINGLY

KEY
☐ Fat (naturally occuring and added)   ☑ Sugars (added)
These symbols show that fat and added sugars come mostly from fats, oils, and sweets, but can be part of or added to foods from the other food groups as well.

Milk, Yogurt, & Cheese Group
2-3 SERVINGS

Meat, Poultry, Fish Dry Beans, Eggs, & Nuts Group
2-3 SERVINGS

Vegetable Group
3-5 SERVINGS

Fruit Group
2-4 SERVINGS

Bread, Cereal, Rice, & Pasta Group
6-11 SERVINGS

SOURCE: U.S. Department of Agriculture/U.S. Department of Health and Human Services

Use the Food Guide Pyramid to help you eat better every day . . . the Dietary Guidelines way. Start with plenty of Breads, Cereals, Rice, and Pasta; Vegetables; and Fruits. Add two to three servings from the Milk group and two to three servings from the Meat group.

Each of these food groups provides some, but not all, of the nutrients you need. No one food group is more important than another – for good health you need them all. Go easy on fats, oils, and sweets, the foods in the small tip of the Pyramid.

duction. At this level of calorie intake, a lactating mother can still expect to lose weight gradually during the course of breastfeeding. This is because the body contributes an additional 500 calories each day from body fat stores to help subsidize lactation. Thus, it is nature's plan to store up extra fat during pregnancy so it will be available to contribute to lactation after delivery. Body fat stores are decreased during breastfeeding, particularly in the thighs and hips.

• **Drink plenty of liquids each day, since milk production uses additional water.** Pour yourself a glass of water or nutritional beverage each time you sit down to nurse. Pay attention to your body's thirst cues. For example, some women report that their mouth goes dry as they start to nurse. Feeling thirsty is an important signal that you need to drink extra fluid. Constipation is another common indicator of the need for additional water. Staying well hydrated helps keep your bowels regular. Drinking scant fluids or becoming dehydrated can diminish your milk supply. However, contrary to popular belief, consuming excessive quantities of liquids offers no advantage over drinking to satisfy thirst.

• **In general, you do not have to restrict the kinds of foods you eat while you are nursing.** One of the most popular myths related to breastfeeding is the widespread belief that nursing mothers must refrain from eating spicy foods, chocolate, beans, onions, and a host of other foods that could upset their infant's digestion and cause their baby to be fussy. The perpetuation of this misbelief only serves to make women view breastfeeding as excessively restrictive. The fact is that women all over the world breastfeed their babies while eating local diets that represent a wide diversity of foods, including curried and spicy foods and other fare that nursing mothers in America are cautioned to avoid. Ordinarily, you do not need to eliminate any specific foods from your diet if you are breastfeeding. Certain dietary restrictions are recommended, however, if you, the baby's father, or another of your children suffers from food allergies, asthma, eczema, or other type of allergic disease. A baby whose close relatives have allergic symptoms is at greater risk for developing allergic disease himself. Prolonged, exclusive breastfeeding is important for infants at high risk for allergic disease. The protective benefits of breastfeeding are further enhanced when the mother excludes common allergenic foods— milk and other dairy products, egg, fish, peanut, soy—from her diet during pregnancy and lactation. The allergic risk to her baby is also reduced if the mother rotates her foods, avoiding eating any single food on a daily basis (see Infant Reactions to Maternally Ingested Foods, chapter 7, pages 269–272.) I must emphasize that women who eliminate major food groups, such as dairy products, from their diet will need nutrition counseling by a registered dietitian or their physician.

• **Continue to take your prenatal vitamins.** Breastfeeding women risk depleting their reserves of vitamins and minerals. The vitamin content of milk depends on the mother's vitamin intake or stores. Ideally, foods, not supplements, are the preferred source of all nutrients. But for extra assurance, breastfeeding women usually are advised to continue taking any multivitamin-mineral supplements that were prescribed for them during pregnancy. Strict vegetarian mothers, in particular, should take a supplement of vitamin B_{12}.

Getting Your Figure Back. Immediately following delivery, women lose about twelve pounds, which represents the weight of the baby, placenta, amniotic fluid, and blood. In the following weeks, excess water is lost, amounting to approximately another five pounds. After the first month, breastfeeding women can expect to lose about one to two pounds each month while they nurse. The reason for the steady weight loss is that the process of lactation uses the extra body fat that was stored during pregnancy. Each day you breastfeed, your body subsidizes lactation with about five hundred calories from fat stores. After the first three months, breastfeeding women generally lose weight more rapidly than bottle-feeding mothers and return to their prepregnancy weight sooner.

• **Avoid rapid weight loss during breastfeeding.** Many new mothers are preoccupied with their body image and find the idea of rapid weight loss highly desirable. But trying to return too quickly to your prepregnancy weight by drastically reducing your calorie intake is likely to result in diminished milk production. Women who were at normal weight prior to their pregnancy are advised not to lose more than two pounds per month after the first month of breastfeeding. Overweight women can lose up to four pounds a month. More rapid weight loss, or consuming fewer than 1,800 calories per day, places a woman at risk for reduced milk production. Remember, lactation is the body's only *elective* process. Inadequate caloric intake is perceived by the body as a form of stress. Your body might try to conserve energy in reaction to this stress condition by reducing the energy needs of lactation. Inadequate milk supply can result. It is far preferable to lose weight gradually after pregnancy (after all, it took you nine months to gain it!). Increasing your physical activity through moderate exercise and adhering to a healthy diet will result in steady—and more permanent—weight reduction, without compromising your breastfeeding goal. Instead of resorting to drastic dieting measures, just focus on reducing the total fat and saturated fat in your diet and on reducing your intake of high-calorie snack foods. For most women, breastfeeding provides an ideal time to accomplish *gradual* weight loss because of nature's plan to use body fat for milk production.

• **Seek professional help if you think you could have an eating disorder.** Our society's preoccupation with thinness has contributed to an epidemic of eating disorders, principally among young women. Anorexia nervosa is one of the most extreme eating disorders. Life-threatening emaciation can result from the relentless pursuit of thinness by active food-restricting practices and severe weight-control measures. Bulimia is another common eating disorder that is characterized by episodes of binge eating (rapid consumption of a large amount of food in a short period of time). Binge episodes are frequently followed by self-induced vomiting and use of diuretics and laxatives to rid the body of food. Obviously, such eating behaviors can severely interfere with successful breastfeeding. Reduced body fat stores and highly erratic eating patterns can prevent a mother from producing an adequate milk supply. It is beyond the scope of this book to offer specific help for women with eating disorders, but I feel compelled to mention the problem because it is so prevalent and so devastating. Countless women remain chronic victims of eating disorders and the often incapacitating psychological difficulties that accompany them. If I am speaking to you, I urge you to obtain a referral for professional help from your physician. As a new parent, you owe it to yourself and your baby to reclaim your health.

• **Let the nutritional implications of breastfeeding renew your emphasis on lifelong healthy eating.** Many women, myself included, are particularly receptive to nutrition information during pregnancy and the course of breastfeeding. I found I was more motivated to eat in a healthful manner while I was nursing a baby. Somehow, my conviction to give my baby ideal nutrition served to heighten my awareness of my own and my family's eating habits. The increased attention I gave to learning more about good nutrition had a positive ripple effect on my whole family's long-term health.

Exercise During Lactation

Being physically active is an important aspect of a healthy lifestyle and helps create a positive outlook on life. Women who exercise regularly may wonder whether breastfeeding imposes any restrictions on their level of activity. Research has shown that moderate aerobic exercise has no adverse effect on lactation, and it significantly improves the cardiovascular fitness of mothers. Some breastfeeding women report that their babies are fussier and even refuse to nurse after they exercise. One study has shown that babies prefer preexercise milk over the milk their mothers express following strenuous physical activity. Presumably, babies temporarily were turned off by the increased levels of sour-tasting lactic acid present in milk after mothers worked out. Plan to nurse your baby just before you exercise, since lactic acid remains elevated in milk for approximately ninety minutes afterward. Another reason it is preferable to nurse before exercising is that vigorous jostling of the breasts when they are full can cause leakage of milk into the tissues. This, in turn, can produce a local inflammation that predisposes a woman to a full-blown breast infection (mastitis). In my experience, lactating women are more prone to mastitis following vigorous upper body activities such as jumping rope, rowing, raking, vacuuming, scrubbing, and aerobic exercise. The risk can be reduced by exercising after the breasts have been emptied well by nursing or pumping. You should wear an athletic bra that provides good support. If you experience one or more bouts of mastitis (see chapter 7, pages 254–260) that occur within a day or so after vigorous upper body exercise, you should switch to a lower-impact activity and see if the problem resolves.

Hygiene for Breastfeeding Women

Every new mother has days when she wonders where she'll find the time to shower, let alone dress. Feeding and caring for a newborn can be all-consuming at first. When a mother is nursing, feedings initially take longer, are closely spaced, and can't be delegated to anyone else. It's easy for a mother to doubt that she will ever have time to put on makeup, fix her hair, take a bubble bath, or do her nails again. Many a new mother is still wearing her bathrobe by midafternoon, having found no time to spend on her personal care and appearance. In addition to the time crunch, some new mothers are so preoccupied with their baby's welfare that they are reluctant to shower while leaving their baby unattended and out of earshot in another room.

Remember, we parent and nurture others from our own emotional overflow. Taking time to attend to your daily hygiene needs is fundamental to self-care. And self-care is not *selfish*; it is self-preservation. Structure your time to allow for a daily shower or bath at the minimum. I recall one woman who got up early for a leisurely bath and personal time before her husband awoke to go to work. Another—a frazzled mother of twins—postponed her shower each day until her teenage daughter came home from school and could watch the babies. Many depleted mothers find a shower to be thoroughly rejuvenating, no matter how exhausted they are. Enlist the help you need to spend some precious time each day refreshing yourself.

A daily shower or bath provides sufficient cleansing for your breasts and nipples. You also should wear a clean nursing bra every day, as long as you are leaking milk. Most nursing mothers need to wash their bra daily because it inevitably becomes soiled with milk. If you wear breast pads, change them frequently, as moist pads can harbor germs.

It's surprising how many people don't adhere faithfully to the basic principles of hygiene taught in kindergarten: Wash your hands *before* meal preparation or eating and *after* using the bathroom. If you have grown lax in this area, now is a good time to begin reinforcing sound hygiene habits. For a breastfeeding mother, this also means washing your hands *before* you nurse your baby or pump your breasts and *after* all diaper changes. With a new baby in your home, you're probably worried about the risk of illness in your infant, and frequent handwashing is one of the best ways to reduce infections in your family. Don't be shy about telling relatives and guests that the doctor says they should wash their hands before holding the new baby and after changing her diapers.

Getting Sufficient Rest

New parenthood and sleep deprivation go hand in hand, since the night feedings that are essential for newborns inevitably disrupt the parents' sleep. Although new parents are wisely admonished to "sleep when the baby sleeps" during the day, most succumb to the temptation to do laundry, address baby announcements, prepare and clean up meals, or perform other chores whenever their baby dozes off. Too often, parents underestimate the magnitude of their exhaustion and the vital importance of rest. Even if things are going relatively smoothly, round-the-clock care of a new baby day after day, week after week, takes a physical toll. When breast-feeding isn't going well, you can bet that parental exhaustion is even greater. Troubled feedings can take an inordinate amount of time, yet fail to satisfy the baby's hunger, leading to chronic infant fussiness and poor family sleep patterns (see chapter 9, page 342). Profound parental fatigue can cloud one's judgment, cause depression and discouragement, and squelch the joys of new parenthood. To keep from getting so depleted, temporarily curtail any activity that isn't absolutely essential, go to bed earlier, take your daytime naps like a prescription, sleep with your baby if it makes nighttime feedings easier, or arrange for a relief caretaker for a few hours.

Personal Habits

Expectant mothers typically are conscientious about modifying any lifestyle habits that could pose a risk to their developing baby. Most are eager to comply with advice to abstain from alcohol or illicit drugs, stop smoking, avoid caffeine, decrease their consumption of junk foods, and eliminate unnecessary medications. Basically, the same health principles recommended for pregnant women continue to apply during lactation. I have encountered many women who are so committed to their babies' welfare that they are able to overcome destructive personal habits on behalf of their infant even when they previously have been unsuccessful in doing so for their own good. Many women acknowledge that the positive lifestyle changes they make while carrying and nursing a baby represent a significant bonus to their own well-being.

Alcohol. The risks to the fetus of alcohol consumption during pregnancy have been well publicized. Fetal alcohol syndrome can result in stunted growth, mental retardation, and abnormal appearance. Fortunately, most women are motivated to abstain from alcohol during pregnancy.

Following delivery, many women wonder whether they can safely drink any alcoholic beverages while breastfeeding. Advice concerning alcohol consumption during breastfeeding has been very confusing. For years, nursing mothers were reassured that a glass of beer or wine would help them relax and facilitate their milk ejection reflex. Beer was believed to raise prolactin levels and improve a mother's milk production. Recently, however, a study showed that babies obtained less milk when nursing after their mothers drank some alcohol. Alcohol is passed readily into human milk, and consumption of large quantities can sedate the nursing infant and cause other adverse effects. Both binge drinking by nursing mothers and daily drinking of even small amounts of alcohol now is believed to be harmful to breastfed infants. One study has shown lower motor developmental scores at a year of age in breastfed babies whose mothers consumed one or two alcoholic drinks daily.

Current recommendations are that nursing mothers can drink an occasional beer or glass of wine. To completely forbid alcohol during breastfeeding would probably discourage some women from nursing. On the other hand, permitting some alcohol intake during lactation should never be misinterpreted to condone heavy consumption among women with a drinking problem. I advise breastfeeding mothers to limit their consumption of alcoholic beverages to two drinks per week. You should not breastfeed for at least 2 hours per drink consumed to mimimize the presence of alcohol in your milk. I no longer suggest a glass of beer or wine to relax an anxious mother or to enhance her milk production or improve her let-down reflex.

If you are struggling with an alcohol problem, I urge you to face it. Don't put off any longer getting the help you need and deserve!

Recreational Drugs. Recent studies have shown that up to 10 percent of babies are exposed to an illicit substance while still in the uterus. This distressing statistic is a sad testimony to the rampant drug abuse that plagues our society. I must take a rigid stand on illicit drug use by breastfeeding women. Marijuana, speed, crack, cocaine, heroin, and the other mood-altering drugs of abuse do appear in breast milk and pose a very serious threat to the nursing baby. Several instances have been documented in which breastfed infants were harmed when they ingested an illicit drug through their mother's milk. Infant fatalities have occurred, and a few mothers have been charged with felony child abuse—and even murder—because they used illicit substances that endangered their breastfed babies. The American Academy of Pediatrics strongly insists that no drug of abuse, including amphetamines, cocaine, heroin, marijuana, and PCP, should be taken by nursing mothers. I can't say it emphatically enough: **substance abuse is incompatible**

with breastfeeding! In addition to posing a serious hazard to nursing infants, drugs of abuser are detrimental to the physical and emotional health of mothers (whether they breast- or bottle-feed). A drug-abusing mother is emotionally unavailable to her baby and is incapable of meeting her infant's emotional and physical care needs.

Having stated this, let me make it clear that I do support *former* substance-abusing women in their desire to nurse their babies while staying clean. Such women may be able to breastfeed provided they: remain drug-free; are enrolled in a drug treatment program; receive close follow-up, with regular postpartum urine drug screening; and test negative for HIV. Discuss your situation with both your own and your baby's doctors.

Tobacco. Most adult smokers began using cigarettes while still in their teens and never expected to get hooked. The majority of smokers want to quit, and nearly half try to do so each year. But nicotine is highly addictive, and it can take several attempts until you succeed in quitting for good. Smoking has been shown to increase the risk of prematurity and low birth weight. If you have been a smoker, it's likely that your pregnancy provided the impetus for you to stop or cut down significantly. I certainly hope that was true for you, and if so, I commend you for your efforts. While women who smoke can still breastfeed their babies, it is far preferable for you to quit. Few habits pose as great a risk to your own health as smoking. You can add years to your longevity and vastly improve your quality of life by kicking the habit. Furthermore, evidence is mounting that secondhand smoke causes irritation of the lungs, eyes, nose, and throat and poses a major health risk to children. Among the most seriously affected are young infants whose parents smoke. These passive smoking babies are more likely to suffer a host of harmful effects, including infections of the lower airway, such as bronchiolitis and pneumonia; chronic respiratory symptoms; asthma and wheezing illness; acute ear infections and chronic middle ear fluid; and childhood behavior problems. Passive smoking also is a risk factor for sudden infant death syndrome (SIDS), the unexplained death of an apparently healthy infant.

The risk is greater for increasing number of cigarettes smoked, as well as the total number of smokers in the household. Breast-feeding offers some protection against SIDS for infants of non-smokers, but not smokers. For your baby's sake, make every effort to abstain or at least reduce your smoking habits. If you do smoke, NEVER smoke around your child, and resolve to make your home (and car) smoke-free because smoke can linger in the air and affect your baby even if she isn't present when you light up. Remove all ashtrays from your home as a reminder not to smoke inside.

In addition to the risks of passive smoking, breastfed infants also get exposed to the breakdown products of nicotine and pesticides used on tobacco plants that pass into human milk. Furthermore, some studies have demonstrated that women who smoke produce less milk than nonsmokers. Nevertheless, breastfeeding may still be preferable to formula-feeding for babies of moderate or light smokers. For one thing, the risks of passive smoke are the same for breast- or bottle-fed babies. The protective effects of breastfeeding against wheezing, ear infections, pneumonia, and upper respiratory illness can help mitigate the adverse effects of secondhand smoke.

Caffeine. Most women limit their caffeine consumption during pregnancy or give it up completely because of the remote possibility of caffeine harming the fetus or causing the baby to be underweight. Now that you've gotten caffeine out of your system, it just makes good sense to consume it in moderation while you nurse your baby. You can probably drink two caffeinated beverages each day while you breastfeed without bothering your baby. A cup of coffee has more caffeine than tea, caffeinated soft drinks, or hot chocolate. Some infants may be very sensitive to even small amounts of caffeine, so if your baby seems more irritable after you drink a caffeinated beverage, you will want to cut back.

Medications. Both prescription and over-the-counter medications can pass into breast milk to some degree and be ingested by the nursing infant. Fortunately, the amount of drug that appears in milk usually is too small to adversely affect the baby. Only rarely is a prescribed medicine incompatible with breastfeeding. Nevertheless, it is important to make your physician aware that you are breastfeeding whenever you need to take a medication. The prescribing physician can usually select a drug to treat your condition that will not pose any risk to your nursing baby. You also need to notify your baby's doctor about any medications you plan to take in case you need to observe your baby for possible side effects. The Drug Information Service at University of California at San Diego is a good resource for up-to-date information about the passage of drugs into breast milk. Center personnel handle toll-call phone inquiries from health professionals nationwide, as well as from parents themselves (see Resource List, page 449). You may have a similar drug consultation resource in your own region that can offer the latest information about drug excretion in breast milk. Another helpful resource that provides such advice to health professionals is the University of Rochester Lactation Study Center (see Resource List, page 448). For additional information about maternal medications and breastfeeding, see chapter 7 (pages 265–269).

Contraception and Lactation

Spacing children at least two or three years apart has several advantages. Your first infant can enjoy the luxury of your undivided attention throughout his babyhood before having to share your time and energies with a sibling. Sibling adjustments usually are easier when the older child has acquired sufficient language skills to communicate his natural ambivalence about a baby brother or sister. Two or three years between births gives couples ample time to renegotiate their relationship before the family dynamics shift once again. And spacing pregnancies allows a mother time to replenish her nutrient stores. Most new parents agree that family planning gives them the peace of mind to thoroughly enjoy their new role before contemplating another pregnancy.

Breastfeeding and contraception are very interwoven. For one thing, breastfeeding has an effect on a woman's fertility. The return of menstrual periods is delayed in breastfeeding women compared with women who formula-feed their babies. In addition, various contraceptive methods can have an effect on breastfeeding by diminishing a mother's milk supply. Finally, becoming pregnant during lactation has an effect on breastfeeding because the prenatal hormones markedly diminish milk production. The following information should help you, together with your partner and your physician, select a contraceptive method that is most suited to your needs.

Lactational Amenorrhea Method. It has long been recognized that breastfeeding has an inhibitory effect on ovulation and fertility after childbirth. Fully breastfeeding women sometimes go a year or longer without having a menstrual period. Until recently, however, the contraceptive effect of breastfeeding had not been formally studied. Recent research has documented that a woman who continues to fully breastfeed her infant and who has no vaginal bleeding after fifty-six days postpartum (i.e., her menstrual periods have not returned) has less than a 2 percent risk of pregnancy during the first six months postpartum. The delay in both ovulation and return of menstrual periods after childbirth that is attributed to breastfeeding has been called "lactational amenorrhea." Using lactational amenorrhea as an introductory method of contraception after childbirth is known as the Lactational Amenorrhea Method (LAM). LAM is now recognized as a highly effective temporary family planning method for breastfeeding women in the early months after delivery. By providing natural protection against pregnancy for up to six months postpartum, LAM gives a nursing mother time to choose a more permanent method of contraception with which she is comfortable. It is critical that a woman meet *all three criteria* for LAM before using it as protection against pregnancy. The three conditions are: (1) less than six months postpartum; (2) amenorrheic (no periods yet); and (3) fully breastfeeding. It must be emphasized that when any one of these three conditions change, the woman needs to begin using another family planning method to continue her protection against pregnancy. You also should use another family planning method if you are unwilling to accept even a small risk of pregnancy. (See chapter 1, page 20.)

Nonhormonal Methods of Family Planning. In addition to LAM, other nonhormonal methods of preventing pregnancy include condoms, diaphragms, cervical caps, vaginal sponges, spermicides, intrauterine devices (IUDs), and natural family planning (rhythm method or periodic abstinence). Permanent options include tubal ligation or vasectomy. These nonhormonal family planning methods have no effect on breastfeeding and pose no risk to the nursing infant. You will want to discuss the respective pros and cons of these options in greater detail with your health care provider and your partner.

Combination Oral Contraceptive Pills. Combination birth control pills contain both estrogen and progestin and are the most effective method of birth control. The main concern about using combination oral contraceptives during breastfeeding is the fact that estrogens may reduce a mother's milk supply. Although hormones may pass into breast milk, no immediate or long-term negative effects on infants have been proved. Ideally, combination birth control pills should be delayed at least six months to minimize their potential impact on breastfeeding. I also believe that mothers who take these pills should be warned about the possibility that their milk supply could decrease. Despite the possible risk of diminished milk production, some nursing mothers choose this method of family planning because of its effectiveness. If you decide to take combined oral contraceptives, try to avoid other behaviors that could decrease your milk supply. For example, I have encountered women who started taking a combined oral contraceptive just as they went back to work, started giving their baby supplemental formula, and allowed their baby to sleep through the night. When their milk supply diminished significantly, it was difficult to sort out which of the various "insults" was most responsible.

Progestin-Only Hormonal Methods. Included in this category of contraceptives are the minipill, implants (such as Norplant), and injectables (such as Depo-Provera). These progestin-only hormonal methods are thought to avoid the adverse effects of estrogen on milk supply. When possible, it is best to delay their use at least six to eight weeks postpartum until breastfeeding is well established. Although some hormone passes into breast milk, no adverse effects on breastfed babies have been shown. While implants provide up to five years of protection, the injectables last only about three months.

Return of Menstrual Periods. Most bottle-feeding mothers will be menstruating by the third month postpartum, while fully breastfeeding women are often amenorrheic (not having periods) for many months after delivery. The duration of amenorrhea generally is related to the amount and frequency of infant suckling at the breast. Amenorrhea is shorter for women who breastfeed in a token fashion or on a rigid schedule. Menstrual periods are delayed longer in women who breastfeed their babies on demand, around the clock and who delay the introduction of solid foods for about six months. Typically, menstrual periods resume within a month or so of interrupting full breastfeeding (i.e., when a baby starts sleeping through the night or the mother starts replacing breastfeedings with formula supplements). The return of menstrual periods may be associated with diminished milk supply and a declining prolactin level (the hormone related to milk production). Since decreased milk supply can cause a baby to lose interest in nursing, a woman may find she is unable to breastfeed as long as she had wanted (see chapter 7, pages 262–265, chapter 8, pages 315–316, and chapter 9, page 351).

A few women experience early return of their menstrual periods despite nursing frequently, through the night, and without supplements. Many of these women continue to produce abundant milk while having periods each month. Other menstruating women perceive that their milk supply diminishes just before and during their periods. They feel they have more milk at other times in their cycle. I recall one woman who experienced sore nipples each month around the time of her period. I speculate that her cyclic nipple pain might have been due to a temporary decline in milk, causing her baby to nurse more vigorously. The return of menstrual periods does *not* mean a woman needs to wean her baby. However, she should assume she is fertile and could conceive, even if she is less than six months postpartum. The early return of menses (less than six months) should prompt a woman to evaluate her breastfeeding routines and consider whether her milk supply might be low. Even if that is the case, continued partial breastfeeding is still possible.

Nursing in Public

Recently, national attention has been focused on the rights of women to nurse their babies in public places. In less industrialized countries, where breastfeeding is a community norm, nursing babies accompany their mothers everywhere and breastfeed at will. These societies have traditional slings and other garments that allow infants to be carried, or more accurately, *worn* on their mother's bodies. In many other countries, breastfeeding is considered so natural that people scarcely take notice of it.

In the United States, even though the majority of women begin breastfeeding their newborns, many mothers discontinue nursing within a few weeks or months, with relatively few women managing to breastfeed the whole first year or more, as recommended. The period when most American women do nurse—the early weeks after delivery—is a time when new mothers are least mobile and most sheltered. The result is far fewer breastfeeding role models in the United States than in many other societies. While breastfeeding is talked about and encouraged, it enjoys minimal visibility in our society. A foreigner visiting our country would never guess that most new mothers choose to nurse their babies, because breastfeeding is seldom witnessed outside the home. Parents don't think twice about bottle-feeding their babies in virtually any setting, but few American women are willing to nurse in front of others, and even fewer partners of breastfeeding women are comfortable with public nursing. To avoid nursing in public, many breastfeeding women plan short excursions to shop or run errands based on their baby's predicted feeding pattern. They nurse their baby in the privacy of their home, dart out on their mission, and try to get back before the next feeding. If a mother does get caught with a frantically hungry baby, she is likely to try to "hold the baby off" with a pacifier, retreat to a rest room or her car, or perhaps even give a bottle of expressed milk or formula. Those who do venture to nurse in a highly trafficked area like a mall risk feeling self-conscious or being the recipient of passersby's judgmental glances. The topic has come into the spotlight on a number of recent occasions when mothers who were breastfeeding their hungry infants were asked to leave public places because exposing their breasts to nurse might be offensive to other patrons. In each case that has been challenged in a court of law, the right to breastfeed in public has been upheld. Several states even have passed legislation that excludes breastfeeding from public nudity laws and defends a woman's right to nurse in public. Nevertheless, some people still view breastfeeding as something to be done in private or in a public rest room. Even if you have the *right* to nurse your baby at the mall, you might not feel comfortable doing so unless you are convinced that it is possible to breastfeed discreetly. This type of confidence comes only with experience, maturity, and practical information.

Breastfeeding Clothing. When I was nursing my first baby at the age of twenty, I almost never ventured to breastfeed when away from home. I had never seen anyone else nurse in public, and besides, I didn't know the basics about a breastfeeding wardrobe. I usually wore a shift or dress that had to be unzipped and pulled down to nurse. No wonder I found the prospect unthinkable in public! I wish someone had suggested that I wear two-piece outfits so I could simply lift my blouse to breastfeed or unbutton it from the bottom up. If a woman doesn't feel she can nurse spontaneously when the need arises, she tends to feel restricted in her activities. She may feel obligated to retreat from company and retire to a back bedroom to breastfeed. When a woman is confident that she can nurse discreetly, she can choose to remain with the group, throw a receiving blanket over her shoulder, and breastfeed her baby without missing anything.

While you don't need special clothes to breastfeed, you might be interested in knowing that many maternity shops and specialty catalogs sell clothing that has been altered specifically for breastfeeding women. Professional and even formal wear is available with Velcro flaps and other discreet modifications that make it possible to expose the breasts for nursing. A variety of nursing shawls also are available to shield your breastfeeding baby from public view while allowing you to readily observe your infant. A wide selection of breastfeeding apparel is available from the member companies of the Association for Breastfeeding Fashions (see Resource List, page 450). Even if you don't own any special breastfeeding garments, you easily can put together outfits that let you breastfeed discreetly and with confidence in any setting. Wearing a vest over your blouse is a convenient way to keep your midrift covered when you lift your shirt to nurse. A simple receiving blanket can be as effective as a fancy shawl. Many of the various infant slings that are so popular today allow an infant to nurse while being carried without a casual observer even being aware. Before venturing out in public, practice latching your baby on to nurse in front of a mirror until you have your technique perfected. You'll be amazed how little anyone can really see once you learn the art of discreet nursing.

Being Separated from Your Nursing Infant

Ideally, breastfed babies should accompany their mothers wherever they go and nurse at will. Such unrestricted breastfeeding assures that the baby's needs are promptly met and that the delicate balance between milk supply and infant demand is preserved. If you must be separated from your baby for a short period, you will want to nurse her just before your departure, leaving her with a full tummy. Ideally, you would be able to time your absence to your baby's usual feeding pattern and return before she is ready to nurse again.

If you will be gone past a feeding time, it is preferable for your baby to be fed your expressed milk rather than infant formula. Many nursing mothers learn to express their milk by hand or with a pump shortly after their milk comes in (see chapter 5, pages 162–165). By removing residual milk after several nursings, a mother can accumulate a couple of ounces of expressed breast milk which can be fed to her infant in her absence. It's a good idea to have a stockpile of frozen breast milk on hand in case you cannot be present to nurse your baby for some reason (see chapter 8, pages 305–307 for milk-storage guidelines). If you do miss a feeding, it is important to empty your breasts when you are away from your baby so your milk supply won't decrease. If your breasts remain full past a feeding time, it sends a message to your body to produce less milk. Thus, skipping nursings without emptying your breasts can decrease your milk supply.

Numerous breast-pumping options are available, ranging from inexpensive hand pumps to battery-operated, small electric, and even hospital-grade rental electric pumps that empty both breasts simultaneously (see chapter 5, pages 162–168). If you will miss a nursing only occasionally, you can plan ahead to leave a bottle of expressed milk in your absence. Don't expect to pump a full bottle after first nursing your baby, as your supply is closely matched to your baby's needs. Many women pump only an ounce or less of residual milk after nursing their baby. Hand expression or a manual pump can be adequate for collecting milk after several nursings until you obtain sufficient volume for a full feeding. You will get more milk when pumping after an early-morning nursing than you will later in the day. The second breast used at a feeding usually has more residual milk. You can pour the milk you collect from multiple pumpings on a single day into the same bottle. Keep the storage bottle capped and refrigerated, and use the contents within forty-eight to seventy-two hours. Ideally, women who will miss multiple feedings should use a hospital-grade rental electric pump with a double collection system to pump their breasts at their baby's usual feeding time. Hospital-grade rental electric pumps are not only more convenient but also provide maximum efficiency in preserving your milk supply.

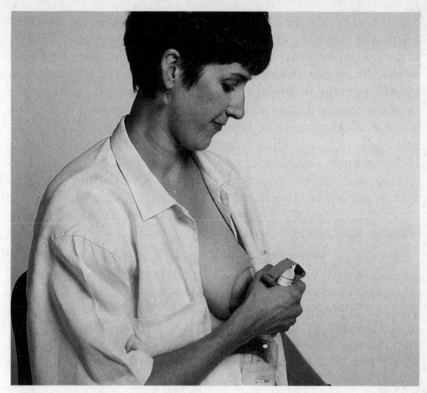

You can plan ahead to leave a bottle of expressed milk in your absence by collecting the milk that remains after several breastfeedings.

General Guidelines for Breastfed Infants

Growth of Breastfed Infants

Human milk is nature's ideal diet for infants. When breast-feeding goes well, a baby will consume adequate quantities of human milk to meet all her nutrient requirements for about six months of life. Breastfed babies grow rapidly in the early weeks and months of life, putting on weight at least as fast as bottle-fed babies. Once a mother's milk comes in abundantly, her breastfed baby should start gaining about one ounce each day, or one and a half to two pounds each month, for approximately the first three months. Most babies double their birth weight at about four and a half months of age. Their early rapid weight gain pattern gradually tapers off (or else we'd all eventually be as big as elephants!).

Babies don't triple their birth weight until about one year, and they quadruple it around age two. After the first three to four months, breastfed infants may gain weight less rapidly than bottle-fed babies during the remainder of the first year. The differences in growth patterns of breastfed and bottle-fed infants can give the false impression that an older breastfed baby's growth is faltering when it might actually be normal. I need to emphasize, however, that "faltering" growth in a breastfed infant during the first three to four months should *not* be considered normal. Early difficulties gaining weight probably reflect unresolved breastfeeding problems that should not be ignored.

Vitamin and Mineral Supplements

In the past, physicians routinely prescribed vitamin and mineral supplements for breastfed infants. Not only was this practice costly and usually unnecessary, but it also undermined women's confidence by implying that their milk was deficient. I recall being confused about why my first baby, Peter, required supplemental vitamins and iron if my milk was supposed to be "perfect nutrition." "How did babies in ancient times thrive without such supplements?" I wondered. Ironically, formula-fed babies don't require extra vitamins and minerals because formulas are fortified with them. Expectant and new parents can get the wrong message that breast milk is less nutritious than artificial baby milk if supplements are given to breastfed infants and not to formula-fed babies. Let me review the current recommendations for supplementation of healthy breastfed infants.

Multivitamins. The milk produced by a well-nourished woman has ample amounts of vitamins. However, poorly nourished women with vitamin deficiencies will produce milk that is deficient in vitamins. A few cases of vitamin-deficient milk and poor infant growth have been linked to a strict vegetarian diet in lactating mothers who weren't taking vitamin supplements.

Human milk is relatively low in vitamin D, but this vitamin is synthesized in the skin in ample amounts if a person is exposed to sunlight. Dark-skinned individuals require more sunlight exposure than light-skinned persons. Vitamin D deficiency can cause rickets (softening of the bones producing bowing of the legs and other bone deformities). A few cases of rickets have occurred in exclusively breastfed babies. The babies in whom rickets occurred were at particular risk because they were dark-skinned and received very little sun exposure. To prevent any chance of rickets, some physicians prescribe multivitamin drops for all breastfed infants instead of singling out those who get little sunshine exposure. Multivitamin preparations are used for this purpose because they actually are cheaper and more accessible than plain vitamin D.

Vitamin and/or mineral supplements may be required for premature infants and those with special health problems. Ordinarily, no vitamin or mineral supplements are necessary for healthy, breastfed infants of well-nourished mothers. Nevertheless, some doctors routinely prescribe liquid multivitamin preparations for breastfed infants "just in case." This practice probably does no harm beyond the added expense and hassle of trying to get your baby to take the vitamins. However, a few mothers report that their infants react adversely to vitamin preparations, either refusing them or acting fussy afterward. If that is the case with your baby, ask your doctor whether a valid indication exists for prescribing the supplements.

Iron. Iron is an important mineral necessary for making red blood cells that carry oxygen to all parts of the body. When infants don't get enough iron in their diet, iron deficiency and anemia can occur and result in impaired development. Years ago, scientists noted that breast milk contained very little iron, compared to the amount present in iron-fortified formulas. The implication was that human milk was deficient in iron and that breastfed babies needed to be supplemented with this mineral. Yet, iron-deficiency anemia is seldom observed in breastfed infants. Several years elapsed before it was proved that the small amount of iron in human milk is exceptionally well absorbed by breastfed infants. Eventually, experts conceded that the relatively small amount of iron present in breast milk was sufficient for young infants. Mother Nature was vindicated again. After about six months of exclusive breastfeeding, infants deplete their iron stores and require additional sources of iron to prevent iron deficiency and anemia. Once semisolid foods are started, however, iron-fortified infant cereal is usually an adequate source of the extra iron needed by breastfed infants. No prescribed iron drops are ordinarily necessary for healthy, breastfed infants. Premature babies, infants born with low red blood cell counts, and babies with other special health needs might require supplemental iron on an individual basis.

Whenever you have iron supplements in your home, keep them out of the reach of children! Many parents don't realize that an overdose of iron supplements can be deadly poisonous. Iron ingestion accounts for a number of childhood deaths each year. Infant drops, children's vitamin/iron tablets, and adult vitamin/iron preparations all are highly toxic when an overdose is taken.

Fluoride. One of the greatest public health discoveries of all time was the recognition that naturally occurring fluoride in drinking water supplies drastically reduces the incidence of dental caries, or cavities. Today, fluoride is added to many community water supplies. In low-fluoride areas, fluoride supplements are recommended for children, and until recently, some practitioners were starting supplements in the early months of life. Since human milk contains little fluoride, even where drinking water supplies are optimally fluoridated, supplements commonly were prescribed for exclusively breastfed infants under six months of age. In addition to the fluoride consumed from community water supplies or fluoride supplements, young children swallow fluoride-containing toothpaste during brushing.

Recently, increased numbers of American youngsters have been found to have dental fluorosis as a result of consuming excess fluoride. Fluorosis is a cosmetic problem in which the tooth enamel is discolored as a result of excess fluoride intake, especially in the preschool years. The appearance of fluorosis can range from barely perceptible chalky white specks to larger areas of pitting or brownish-gray staining. To prevent dental fluorosis, the Council on Dental Therapeutics and the American Academy of Pediatrics recently revised their recommendations for fluoride supplements for infants and children. Babies, even those exclusively breastfed, should NOT be given fluoride supplements in the first six months of life. Thereafter, infants whose families reside in nonfluoridated areas should receive fluoride supplements, although the recommended dosage has been reduced over the first six years of life. The drops can be prescribed by a physician or dentist.

If your community water supply is adequately fluoridated, your baby should NOT receive any supplemental fluoride, even after six months of age.

Water. I wish I knew the origin of the popular myth that breastfed babies require extra water. This widespread belief has no doubt done more harm than good. I suppose the practice originated decades ago when newborns were hospitalized for many days after birth. During this era, mothers and babies routinely were separated, feedings were rigidly scheduled and timed, and round-the-clock demand nursing almost never occurred. In this unsupportive environment, few babies obtained sufficient fluids from breast-feeding alone. Thus, it became common practice to offer newborns supplemental water after each nursing before the mother's milk came in abundantly.

The fact is that human milk is about 87 percent water. A baby who drinks enough milk to meet her other nutritional needs automatically will receive sufficient water. On the other hand, if a baby doesn't drink enough milk, giving extra water might prevent infant dehydration, but it won't make up for the shortfall in calories, fat, protein, vitamins, and minerals. Instead of water, what an underfed baby needs is more *milk*—human milk or infant formula if the breast milk supply is low. Ordinarily, healthy, thriving breastfed babies shouldn't need any extra water. When you find yourself thirsty on a hot day, be sure to nurse your baby more often to provide her extra fluids.

Appetite Spurts or Growth Spurts

An appetite spurt is the name given to describe a period of increased frequency of demand feedings by an apparently hungry baby. Other names for appetite spurts are "growth spurts" or "frequency days." These episodes occur with some predictability at approximately three weeks, six weeks, and three months, although they can happen at any time during breastfeeding. Unless a mother is forewarned about the occurrence of appetite spurts, she is likely to interpret her baby's hunger cues to mean she no longer has enough milk to satisfy him. She will be tempted to start supplemental formula or introduce solid foods in order to satisfy her baby's appetite. But when weaning foods are started too soon, the usual result is a gradual decline in breast milk supply. Don't let this happen to you.

You need to know that appetite spurts are a common, normal part of breastfeeding—they represent the law of supply and demand in action. If your baby suddenly is hungry more often, you just nurse more often to readjust your milk supply to your baby's demand for food. Instead of being caught off guard by these inevitable frequency days, expect them to happen periodically and be prepared to cut back temporarily on your other activities and to increase your nursing to stimulate more milk production.

You may have to feed every two hours or so for a couple of days until your milk supply increases and your baby resumes his former schedule. We tend to talk about growth spurts as if the baby suddenly changed his rate of growth or his nutritional needs. In some cases, I suspect that a mother's change in activities may have decreased her milk supply from its previous level, leaving her baby hungry. No matter what has triggered an appetite spurt, your response is the same: stay home as much as you can with your baby for a few days, nurse as often as necessary, drink extra fluids, get extra rest, and don't let your confidence get shaken!

Supplemental Bottles

In an ideal world, every nursing mother-baby pair would constantly remain in one another's presence, and no breastfed baby would ever need to take a bottle. I had the privilege of enjoying this ideal with my fifth baby, Mark, and I can attest to its many advantages and rewards. Unrestricted and exclusive breastfeeding gives a baby the guarantee of his mother's continual presence and the instant availability of optimal nourishment and nurturing. It gives a woman the best chance of having a continuous abundant supply of milk and of being able to nurse her baby a year or more. Whether by necessity or personal choice, however, the reality is that most breastfed babies in the United States do take bottles from time to time. In many cases, regular bottle-feedings of expressed milk or formula become necessary when nursing mothers daily are separated from their babies due to employment or schooling. Supplemental bottle-feedings are sometimes required for babies whose mothers produce insufficient milk.

Some parents choose to give a bottle occasionally because the father, grandmother, or other relative wants to share in feeding times. Other parents elect to familiarize their baby with bottle-feeding to allow the mother the option of leaving her infant with another caretaker. If you do plan to give your breastfed baby some bottle-feedings, the following guidelines should help minimize the risk of bottles interfering with successful breastfeeding:

• **Delay the introduction of bottles for at least three to four weeks.** It is highly tempting at times to offer a bottle in the early weeks of breastfeeding to let a tired new mother get some badly needed rest. But early use of bottles before breastfeeding has become well established can undermine breastfeeding success. When a baby is first learning to nurse, he may find it easier to obtain milk from a bottle and, thus, develop a preference for bottle-feeding (see Nipple Confusion, chapter 4, pages 113–114). Due to the close balance of breast milk supply and the infant's demand, it is important to nurse as often as your baby acts hungry. Displacing nursings with bottle-feedings can jeopardize the establishment of an abundant milk supply.

If you are considering giving a bottle in the early weeks of breastfeeding because your baby seems persistently hungry, promptly seek medical advice (see chapter 5, pages 169–171). When a baby is not obtaining sufficient milk the situation needs to be evaluated and remedied quickly. Feeding supplemental milk may be essential until the breastfeeding difficulties can be overcome (see chapter 9, pages 341–344). Never be afraid to give a bottle if your baby's welfare depends on it.

• **Put expressed breast milk in the bottle whenever possible.** Feeding expressed breast milk is far preferable to giving supplemental bottles of formula. Infant formula provides inferior nutrition compared with human milk. Not only do formulas lack the immune benefits in human milk, but adding formula to a breastfed baby's diet actually decreases the protective effects that exclusive breastfeeding provides against infant illness. Babies readily can develop allergies to both cow's milk–based and soy formulas, especially when a parent or sibling has a history of food allergies. By feeding milk that has been expressed from your breasts, your baby will be receiving what your body has produced for her. When a breastfed baby drinks a bottle of formula that the mother's breasts didn't produce, the delicate balance of "breast milk supply and demand" can be upset.

• **Pump your breasts whenever you substitute a bottle-feeding for a nursing.** Skipping a few nursings might seem convenient at first glance, but it can soon lead to diminished milk supply. If your breasts are not emptied at a regular feeding time, chemical inhibitors in the accumulated milk and unrelieved pressure in the breast provide a powerful message to your body to decrease milk production. Ideally, if your baby misses a nursing, you should use an effective breast pump or hand expression to empty your breasts in order to keep up your milk production. So you see, giving bottles really isn't very convenient after all.

• **When possible, offer a small amount of milk, instead of replacing an entire feeding.** If you just want to keep your baby familiar with bottle-feeding in preparation for going back to work or in case of an unanticipated separation, you can do so without disrupting breastfeeding. Many women mistakenly assume that the bottle must replace an entire feeding. Instead, you can offer as little as a half ounce of expressed breast milk to reassure yourself that your baby will accept a bottle and can use it effectively. Most women have less milk later in the day. If your baby still seems hungry after an evening nursing, that might be a good time to let Daddy offer a little of your expressed milk in a bottle. You can easily capture some extra milk after the early morning nursings, when your supply is more plentiful. You can either use a pump during or after feeding your baby (the second breast usually has not been as well-drained) or simply place a clean cup under one breast while you nurse on the other. When your milk lets-down, the breast that isn't being nursed may spontaneously drip a half ounce or more. You should refrigerate all collected milk and use it within about forty-eight to seventy-two hours.

If your baby refuses to accept a bottle, see Introduce Your Baby to Bottle-Feeding (chapter 8, pages 292–299) for specific strategies to deal with this frustrating situation.

Starting Solid Foods

When my first baby was born, it was common practice to start solid foods in the first weeks of life—a time when nature intended for toothless babies to be fed solely breast milk. The false belief that human milk needed to be complemented with other foods before a month of age served to undermine a mother's confidence and to sabotage successful breastfeeding. By giving solids too early, parents like myself unknowingly started replacing nature's perfect food—breast milk—with inferior nutrition. We wasted unnecessary time and money buying baby food and dutifully shoveling it into our infant's mouth, only to watch it be reflexively expelled by the thrusting action of the baby's tongue, an innate reflex designed to keep foreign substances out of the mouth. Undaunted, we meticulously scraped the messy contents from the baby's chin and diligently refed it. Part of my own persistence in this endeavor was

based on the mistaken assumption that eating solids was an important developmental milestone and a sign of infant intelligence.
Upon hearing that a neighbor's month-old baby was eating peas, I
determined that Peter, my firstborn, would master this feat at three
weeks. But it's not a competition! If this misguided commitment of
time and effort had been properly channeled into breastfeeding on
demand, I am convinced that far more women would have been
able to breastfeed successfully in earlier eras.

Today, infant feeding experts agree that exclusive breast milk is
the preferred diet for approximately the first six months of life. Premature introduction of solids can expose a baby too early to potentially allergenic foods, displace breast milk in the baby's diet, and
interfere with the immune benefits of human milk. If the quantity
of breast milk is insufficient to support proper infant growth and if
the supply cannot be increased, then supplementing with formula is
preferable to starting solids prematurely.

Infant Signs of Readiness for Solid Foods. A baby will display certain cues to let her parents know when she is ready for
solid foods. Most babies start showing signs of readiness between
five and six months of age. Some will be ready for solids as early as
four months, while a few won't need, or be interested in, solid food
until seven months or so. Solids are meant to complement, or be
added to, the breast milk diet, not to replace breast milk. A baby
around five or six months who consistently acts hungry after
nursing from both breasts and who is showing great interest in the
food you eat is probably ready to begin solids. At this stage, she
will watch you bring food from your plate to your mouth and may
even try to grab it. She will demonstrate the ability to bring objects
to her mouth and lose the tongue-thrust reflex that causes her to
push food out of her mouth when it is introduced too early.

How to Offer Solid Foods. Solid foods provide a baby with
additional calories, protein, minerals, and other nutrients, as well
as new tastes and textures. Starting solids begins the gradual transition to an eventual adult diet of table food. Iron-fortified, single-
grain infant cereal, such as rice cereal, makes an excellent first food
because it is easily digested and is relatively hypoallergenic.
Breastfed babies need additional sources of iron in their diet after
about six months, and iron-fortified infant cereals will meet this
requirement. Infant cereal can be mixed with your own expressed

milk or infant formula. Many parents think of rice cereal as a breakfast food, and so they offer it in the morning. I often hear parents say they give the solids *before* nursing because the baby won't take them afterward. But remember, solids are meant to *add to*—not replace—breast milk. Most women have plentiful milk in the mornings and produce less later in the day. It makes sense to begin giving solid foods in the late afternoon or evening when the baby is more likely to still be hungry after nursing. Begin mixing the cereal very thin so it is easy for your baby to handle. Then gradually thicken the texture as your baby gets used to solids.

Most experts recommend starting a single new food at a time and giving it for several days to be sure your baby tolerates it. If a baby's parents or siblings have food allergies, however, a rotating diet (in which the same food *isn't* given two days in a row) helps reduce the risk of allergies. Parents usually start strained fruits or vegetables after infant cereals. Infant cereals can be mixed with strained fruit, such as applesauce, bananas, pears, or peaches. Popular choices for first vegetables are carrots, sweet potatoes, squash, and peas. Strained meats are the most nutrient-dense foods and are high in protein, vitamins, and minerals. Chicken and turkey make good first meat choices. You also can prepare for your baby some simple and natural foods you eat yourself, like a mashed overripe banana. When you use baby foods, select a predominance of nutritious single-item foods, such as plain fruits, vegetables, and meats, instead of combination dinners and desserts.

Night Nursings

Because breast milk is so rapidly digested, breastfed infants awaken to nurse often, including at night. Although this means that your sleep will be disrupted, night nursings in the early weeks and months are essential to provide your baby with adequate nutrition and to maintain a generous milk supply. At least there is no formula to mix and no equipment to get ready! Initially, your baby will probably sleep in a bassinet at your bedside, where you can simply scoop him up and bring him in bed with you to nurse. You can feed either lying down or propped up with pillows. No harm will be done if you doze off while nursing. Many parents choose to sleep with their babies, and even their older children—a practice known as the "family bed." Such a choice is highly personal, with some parents finding the idea unacceptable, while others insist it is the ideal way to parent a newborn at night. Bedsharing has been shown to increase the number and length of nighttime breastfeedings and has been speculated to reduce the risk of sudden infant death syndrome (SIDS). Although bringing babies in bed with parents commonly is frowned upon in our society, such sleeping arrangements are highly prevalent in developing countries all over the world. Parents who have a family bed usually attest that night nursings are minimally disruptive.

Infant Sleep Precautions. Do not allow your baby to sleep on a water bed, however: babies have suffocated while sleeping on water beds, either by becoming trapped between the mattress and the sideboard or by creating a sinkhole depression with their heads that caused them to rebreathe their carbon dioxide. I also am compelled to mention here the relationship between infant sleep position and SIDS, the unexplained sudden death of babies under a year of age. SIDS is the most common cause of death in infants between one month and one year of age in the Western world. Most cases occur in babies between two and four months of age. Until recent years, most babies in the United States were put to sleep on their tummies. But mounting evidence now confirms a relationship between the prone (tummy down) sleeping position and SIDS. Based on this evidence, in 1992 the American Academy of Pediatrics began to strongly recommend that babies be put to sleep on their backs or on their sides, but NOT in the prone position. You should know that the side position is less effective in preventing SIDS than sleeping on the back. Public awareness campaigns have been conducted to inform parents that they should not put their baby to sleep in the tummy-down, prone position. This simple change in infant care has resulted in substantial reductions in the number of SIDS deaths in America, as well as in many other countries. I should also add that putting a baby to sleep on soft pillows, comforters, or fluffy bedding is a risky practice. A baby's exhaled carbon dioxide can become trapped in soft bedclothes, causing a baby to suffocate when rebreathing her own carbon dioxide. To protect your baby, put her down to sleep on her back on a firm mattress, without any pillows or soft bedding.

Sleeping Through the Night. By six weeks of age or ten pounds of weight, some infants will sleep up to six hours at night, while others still awaken after three to five hours. If your baby awakens and appears genuinely hungry, it makes sense to nurse him instead of trying to get him to sleep through the night. During night nursings, keep things subdued and "strictly business." Use dim lighting, don't play with your baby, and don't even change his diaper unless he has had a bowel movement or has a diaper rash. As long as your baby is awakening at night, you should make it a priority to nap when your baby naps during the day in order to maintain your physical well-being.

One of the most common explanations for faltering weight gain in a once-thriving breastfed baby in the early months of life is that the infant began sleeping eight or more hours at night. Sleeping through the night is a welcome relief to sleep-deprived parents, but it can undermine breastfeeding when it happens too soon. When a young baby (under about four months) sleeps all night, not only does she miss one or more important feedings, but the mother's breasts go a long interval without being emptied. All too often, the result is diminished milk supply and inadequate infant weight gain. Remember that persistently full, engorged breasts send a powerful message to the body to decrease milk production. The first time a breastfed baby sleeps through the night, the mother usually awakens with hard, uncomfortable breasts. A few days later, she may remark that her breasts are no longer uncomfortably full in the morning. The explanation is that her milk supply has decreased because her breasts are being emptied less frequently. If your baby starts sleeping through the night while you are fully breastfeeding, I suggest you use hand expression or a breast pump to empty your breasts just before you retire. Expressing milk before your bedtime will shorten the interval that your breasts go unemptied. This will help maintain your level of milk production and help assure that your baby gets enough to eat during her waking hours. You can freeze the milk you express and save it for later use. If you choose not to express milk before you retire, make sure both your breasts get *well* drained first thing in the morning. Due to the abundant milk available after a long night interval, your baby may leave significant milk after the first morning feeding, especially on the second side. Hand expressing or pumping the extra milk remaining after he nurses will assure continued generous production the rest of the day.

Changing Breastfeeding Patterns

As you settle into nursing beyond the newborn period, you can expect your baby's routines to become more predictable. Gradually, he will have longer intervals between feedings and nurse fewer times each twenty-four hours. He may nurse with remarkable efficiency at some feedings or linger at the breast for comfort and security. Although babies' nursing patterns vary widely, at least seven nursings a day and one feeding at night will be likely for several months. Your best strategy for long-term breastfeeding success is to remain in your baby's presence as much as possible and continue to nurse him on demand.

Infant Bowel Movements. Sometime between one and two months, it is common for breastfed babies to begin passing bowel movements less frequently. For many mothers, this is a welcome change from the early weeks, when breastfed infants may stool after every nursing. Your baby may go several days, even a week or more, without a bowel movement. This is not considered constipa-

Breastfeeding continues to be important for babies
during the second six months of life.

tion because the infrequent stools are not firm or hard to pass. Instead, they usually are loose and passed without difficulty. Sometimes they are quite large—a "mudslide," according to one mother.

Nursing Habits. As breastfed infants get older, they typically nurse more efficiently, as they perfect their technique and your milk ejection reflex becomes well conditioned. By three months, some babies can empty their mother's breast in five to seven minutes. Busy mothers may appreciate the opportunity to shorten nursing sessions, but I must caution you not to make your infant feel "rushed" through feedings. This can lead to a nursing strike (see chapter 7, pages 262–265). Despite your baby's improved efficiency at extracting milk, he still needs ample time at the breast to leisurely nurse for comfort. When he has emptied the first side well, move him to the second breast to continue the feeding. Allow him to remain at the second side as long as desired.

As the months pass, your baby will become more fascinated by his surroundings. He may be easily distracted during nursings by new sights or sounds or the antics of a sibling nearby. He may either pull off your breast to check things out, or worse yet, turn his head without unlatching—taking your nipple with him! To help your baby stay focused during feedings, many mothers make an effort to nurse in subdued surroundings, like a quiet, semidarkened room.

Biting. Your baby may begin cutting teeth around four to six months. It is a widespread misperception that babies cannot continue to nurse once they have teeth, and the presence of infant teeth has caused many women to wean unnecessarily. The truth is that babies can nurse into toddlerhood with a full set of teeth without causing their mothers discomfort. Sometimes the upper teeth will leave a painless indentation on the mother's areola at the end of the nursing.

An infant may try to bite or chew his mother's nipple when he first cuts teeth. Biting doesn't occur during active nursing because the infant's tongue lies over his lower teeth. Instead, biting tends to occur at the end of the feeding after the bulk of the milk has been taken and the infant is restless or playful. The shock and pain of being bitten usually provokes a big reaction in the mother that startles and upsets her infant. Most infants quickly learn the unacceptability of biting if the mother sharply says "no" and removes her breast. When your baby is first getting teeth, it is wise to remove your breast after rhythmic sucking has stopped and move your baby to the second breast before he has a chance to bite. It won't take him long to learn not to bite. If an infant's bite breaks the skin, this should be reported to your doctor who may decide to treat you with antibiotics. Human bites are easily infected and mastitis can occur.

Care of the Teeth. Before a baby's teeth first erupt, parents need to learn how to keep them healthy and how to prevent *baby bottle tooth decay* (BBTD), which is a major cause of dental cavities in infants. As the name suggests, the problem occurs most often in bottle-fed babies, especially those who take a bottle of formula or other sugar-containing liquid to bed with them. When the teeth are bathed in a sugary liquid for prolonged periods, bacteria in the child's mouth change the sugar to acid. The acid attacks the enamel of the child's teeth (especially the upper front teeth), causing decay. Without early treatment, BBTD can progress rapidly and lead to pain, infection, and destruction of baby teeth. Early loss of baby teeth causes the permanent teeth to be crooked.

Parents are often surprised to learn that BBTD can occur in breastfed infants as well as bottle-fed babies. Almost any liquid other than water that is in prolonged contact with the baby's teeth and gums can cause the problem. The risk is greatest for those breastfed infants who co-sleep with their mothers and keep the breast in their mouth throughout the night, bathing their teeth in milk. Some babies' teeth are more prone to decay than others. The first sign of BBTD is white spots on the upper front teeth, which can be difficult to see without proper equipment. The American Academy of Pediatric Dentistry recommends that babies should see a dentist when their first baby tooth erupts, usually between six and nine months. A pediatric dentist can carefully examine your child's teeth for early signs of decay.

In addition to early and regular dental care, you can help prevent the problem by keeping your baby's mouth clean. Gently wipe your baby's gums and any teeth with a damp infant washcloth or a gauze pad after feedings and before bedtime. Once your baby has seven to eight teeth, begin brushing them daily with water and a soft-bristled infant toothbrush. Don't use a fluoride toothpaste until your baby is about three years old.

Preference for One Breast. Sometimes, after months of nursing, a mother will notice that her baby has developed a preference for one breast. The preferred breast usually produces more milk and releases it more rapidly. It's hard to tell which comes first. Does the baby prefer one side because it has the better supply? Or does the preferred breast produce more milk because it is suckled more often? Sometimes, the preference develops because the mother has unintentionally nursed more often on one breast— usually the left side if she is right-handed. The discrepancy between the two breasts is easily perpetuated because the baby naturally prefers to nurse on the better-producing side.

When your baby has a strong preference for one breast, you should make three important evaluations:

• *Is your baby gaining adequate weight?* Often the infant will be gaining fine despite getting most of his milk from one breast. Sometimes, however, low milk production on one side results in inadequate milk intake, causing your baby to stop gaining weight appropriately.

• *How great is the discrepancy in milk production between the two sides?* If the unfavored breast produces much less milk—say only a fourth of the preferred side—you might be anxious to try to increase production in that breast by using it more often or stimulating it with a breast pump. You may be able to get the baby to take the least favored side by offering it when your baby is drowsy or offering it first. If your baby insists, you can start on the favored breast and then slide him across your lap to the less-preferred side without changing his position.

I must caution you, however, about decreasing use of the preferred breast as you try to focus on the unfavored side. You certainly don't want to risk jeopardizing your high milk production on the preferred side. In my experience, when a marked discrepancy in milk production exists, *it is usually easier to boost milk supply even further on the "good" side than to achieve much increase on the very low side.* You actually might be better off following your baby's lead by letting him nurse as often as he wants on the high-producing breast.

• *Is there any abnormality involving the unfavored breast?* For example, cases have been reported where blood in the milk made the baby reject a breast. Also, milk tastes salty when a mother has mastitis. If you have a painful area in your breast, detect a lump, or note an abnormal appearance to your milk, notify your doctor and schedule a breast exam.

Many older babies thrive just fine using one breast more than the other. As long as your baby is gaining well, you generally can let him be the judge of which breast to use when. He may prefer the side with faster flow when he's most hungry and use the other breast for comfort nursings.

Continued Night Waking in Older Babies. Many breastfed babies continue to awaken at night in the second half of the first year and even beyond. Often the baby will nurse just a short while before falling back to sleep. A common cause of night waking in an older baby is that the infant hasn't learned to fall asleep on his own. Parents' reactions vary widely concerning continued night waking in older babies and toddlers. For many parents, nighttime nursings beyond the first six months represent an important aspect of their parenting style. Many mothers are comfortable nursing an older baby or toddler multiple times each night. Often such mothers allow their children to sleep with them and find the night nursings to be minimally disruptive. It's not important to these parents whether their baby is waking because of true hunger or because he needs his mom to help him get back to sleep.

Other parents are highly motivated to get their baby to sleep through the night. They acknowledge that getting adequate rest at night makes them a better parent and better partner the whole next day. They may resent their baby's frequent wakings and eagerly seek strategies for getting their child to sleep through the night. The following explanation may be very helpful to such parents.

Babies awaken at night, even after they no longer require nighttime nutrition, simply because everyone awakens multiple times each night. However, you and I immediately recognize our familiar bedroom surroundings and peacefully roll over and return to sleep. If a baby has always fallen asleep while nursing and being rocked and sung to, he simply may not be able to go back to sleep on his own after a middle-of-the-night awakening. Instead, the baby needs to call forth all his "bedtime props"—breast, mother, rocker—in order to re-create the environment in which he is used to falling asleep.

If your baby is over six months old and is still waking and needing you several times each night, it could be that he doesn't know how to fall asleep on his own. You can help him by starting to put him in his crib just *before* he dozes off. Let his last waking memory be the crib environment, instead of your breast. That way, when he awakens, he will likely be able to get himself back to sleep without needing to come out of the crib. You'll probably have more success beginning this training during daytime naps. At night, we have fewer reserves and, thus, tend to continue using short-term solutions instead of trying new strategies. At first, when your baby cries, you may have to stand nearby and pat his back for a while. Reassure him with your presence, but try not to succumb to the temptation to take him out of his crib. Once your baby learns to go down for daytime naps on his own, he probably will go back to sleep uneventfully in the middle of the night too.

Role of the Father in the Breastfeeding Family

Many men mistakenly believe that breastfeeding is strictly confined to women and babies. They see their role as that of a passive or neutral outside observer who has little influence on the process. A common complaint from fathers of breastfed babies is that they tend to feel excluded from the intimacy of the nursing dyad. But fathers actually have tremendous potential to either facilitate or undermine the success of breastfeeding. Understanding the importance of their role is the first step in equipping fathers to help their breastfeeding partners.

Setting the Family Tone. The first thing a father can do to promote success is to create a positive family atmosphere toward breastfeeding. If he views breastfeeding as making a positive difference in the health and well-being of his baby and as a high priority for his partner and child, this attitude will set the desired tone for achieving success. As a practical matter, breastfed babies need to accompany their mothers whenever possible. A father who views a baby's continual presence as intrusive will subtly undermine breastfeeding. The father who naturally assumes that his baby will accompany the couple to restaurants, movies, dinner parties, and meetings has given breastfeeding his strong endorsement. While a few men actually persuade their partners to breastfeed, more often the mother's motivation to nurse exceeds the father's commitment. But there's a big difference between a man who agrees *to let* his partner breastfeed and one who deliberately creates an atmosphere of success.

Giving Support and Encouragement. Breastfeeding can be emotionally demanding, physically exhausting, and uncomfortable at times. Virtually all new mothers experience doubts about their ability to care for a helpless newborn. Breastfeeding mothers harbor additional fears about the adequacy of their milk supply or the correctness of their breastfeeding technique, or their ability to overcome lactation problems. Fathers can play a key role in bolstering their breastfeeding partner's confidence by showering them with compliments, praising their efforts, and offering words of encouragement. This support role can be particularly difficult when a woman is profoundly tired and discouraged. When a woman is under extreme stress, a man may not know how best to support his mate. He may be uncertain whether she wants to hear, "Don't give up; you can do it!" or "You've done your best. It's okay to switch to bottle-feeding." If you are not sure how to respond to your partner, try explaining that you don't know exactly what to say, but you want to support her in any way you can. Just being a sounding board might be all she needs on a specific day. You can offer valuable perspective, unclouded judgment, or even a sense of humor that defuses tension. Other times, you might be able to mobilize some specific help for a breastfeeding problem by calling the doctor, a lactation consultant, the hospital where your baby was born, or La Leche League (see pages 169–171).

Providing Practical Help. A father can help in so many ways that it's hard to imagine why many men feel left out when their wives breastfeed. A father can go to the baby when he or she awakens and bring the hungry infant to his wife. While the mother is nursing, he can pour her a nutritious beverage, massage her shoulders, compliment her, and lovingly admire his nursing baby. After the first breast, he can burp the baby and help arouse the infant for the second side. When the feeding is complete, the father can change the infant and put him or her down to sleep.

I recently met a wonderful father who made a commitment to take Mondays off in order to spend more time with his baby and let his wife get some extra rest. On Mondays, he performed all the baby care except for nursings, answered the phone and protected his wife, let her get away by herself for a short period if she desired,

Fathers can contribute to breastfeeding success by providing
emotional support and practical help for their partners.

and was present for moral support and companionship. Mondays
turned out to be more than a gift to his wife: they provided this
man with an opportunity to build his confidence in his role as a
father, and helped him foster a unique relationship with his baby.

Building a Relationship with the Baby. Although the reciprocal interaction between a breastfeeding baby and her mother is
one of the strongest bonds in nature, this doesn't diminish the
importance of a baby's early relationship with her father. Instead
of feeling left out of the nursing relationship, fathers can and
should cultivate their own unique bond with their baby. Much has
been written lately about the enormous problem of "father
hunger" among American children. As a result of divorce, single
parenthood, and emotionally remote fathers, countless children
grow up with little or no contact with their fathers. I can't overemphasize how important a father is in the life of his children.
Today, nearly 40 percent of America's children do not live with
their father. Not only has fatherlessness become the single most
important determinant of child poverty, fatherless children are at
increased risk for violence, criminal activity, drug abuse, school
failure, joining a gang, and other social problems. Children deserve

the right to have a healthy, loving relationship with two parents, and fathers deserve to know the truth about their vital role. We have failed to communicate to men just how important they are in their children's lives, starting at birth.

As a father, begin by connecting with your child through touch, one of the most powerfully developed senses at birth. You can hold, carry, rock, caress, massage, and stroke your baby and let her fall asleep against your bare chest. Newborn babies can see best at a distance of eight to twelve inches. When your baby is in a quiet alert state, she is most receptive to engaging visually. She prefers to look at the human face over any other visual stimulus. She already recognizes your voice from hearing it while in the uterus. Babies respond best to a higher-pitched voice, so don't be embarrassed to use baby talk with her. She'll love it. You can sing to her, read to her, or make silly noises. Within a few months, babies already perceive their fathers as principal sources of play and motor movement, different—but no less important than—mothers. If your wife is more adept at comforting, bathing, diapering, and entertaining your baby, don't be tempted to let her be the main infant caretaker. Instead, explain that you want to become competent at caring for and nurturing your baby. Ask her to show you how to perform certain infant-care tasks. Arrange to care for your baby alone, starting with very brief periods, until you feel you don't need to be

Fathers can cultivate a unique and intimate bond with their infants.

"rescued" by the baby's mother. Fathers tell me there's a big difference between being "on my own—just me and the baby" and merely "helping out," with Mom looking over their shoulder to see if they're doing everything right.

Mom, don't come to your partner's rescue as soon as your baby starts to cry. Allow Dad opportunities to soothe or entertain the baby or sing her to sleep. Worry less about whether he is "doing things right," so long as he is "doing the right thing." One wise mother decided not to correct her husband when he put the newborn's disposable diaper on backward the first time. A loving father's sincere attempt to participate in infant care is more important than whether the clothing snaps are in proper alignment.

Sexuality and Breastfeeding

Having a baby transforms a couple into a family and surely represents one of the most significant transitions in adult life. Despite the temporary upheaval and increased stress and responsibility, most couples ultimately discover that parenthood brings a whole new dimension to their relationship that enhances their intimacy and strengthens their bond. At first, however, personal and couple time is crowded out by the pressing needs of the infant newcomer, who easily becomes the focus of the family. The unencumbered spontaneity once enjoyed by childless couples soon is replaced by the comfortable familiarity of their infant's daily schedule and predictable routines. Former exciting leisure activities give way to new compelling interests in baby matters—the quality of a breast-feeding, the magnitude of a burp, or the color of a bowel movement. A new mother, physically depleted at the end of the day, understandably might prefer a quiet evening at home over a night out with her partner. And weeks of nighttime feedings can make a little extra shut-eye seem more appealing than a romantic interlude with one's mate. Before long, the enormous demands of parenthood can lead to neglect of the marital relationship and create tension between the partners.

No generalities can be made about the impact of breastfeeding versus bottle-feeding on a couple's sexuality because individual differences vary so widely. After giving birth, women generally are advised to abstain from sexual intercourse until they no longer have bright red vaginal bleeding and they feel comfortable. Most couples resume sexual relations between four and six weeks postpartum and eventually manage to enjoy sexual intimacy at their same prepregnancy level.

Because extreme fatigue, depression, and preoccupation can diminish libido, it's not surprising that particularly exhausted or overwhelmed new parents often have little energy for sexual activity. Mothers with medical complications of pregnancy or delivery or those who have C-section deliveries justifiably may take longer to recover from childbirth. The frequent complaint of being "too tired" for sex is more common among new mothers than new fathers, since a disproportionate burden of infant care responsibilities are borne by women. Although breastfeeding gets more than its share of the blame for maternal exhaustion, the truth is that caring for a baby is very demanding, regardless of which feeding method is used. Many, in fact, would argue that breastfeeding is easier on a mother than formula-feeding.

Sometimes, fear of discomfort during lovemaking causes women to avoid sexual intercourse, and fear of hurting their partner makes men reluctant to initiate sex. Excessive vaginal dryness (making intercourse more difficult) is a common complaint among breastfeeding women because estrogen levels are low during lactation. Your doctor can recommend a vaginal lubricant if this is a problem for you. Myths and misconceptions about the lactating breasts also can impact lovemaking. Men sometimes assume that when a woman's breasts are used to nourish a baby, they become off-limits sexually. A nursing mother's nipples may be less sensitive to sexual arousal. Other times, uncomfortable breast engorgement or cracked, painful nipples interfere with lovemaking. The intense physical intimacy of the nursing relationship leaves some breastfeeding women with little interest in their partner's sexual advances. With a baby at her breast much of the day, a woman might perceive additional physical contact as just one more demand on her body. Other women find that breastfeeding makes them more comfortable with and confident about their bodies, making them more sexually responsive than ever.

Breastfeeding is an integral part of the full cycle of reproduction. Lactation is not a random occurrence, but a predictable phenomenon that follows childbirth. The hormone oxytocin, which triggers the milk ejection reflex, is the same natural hormone that causes uterine contractions during labor, that shrinks the uterus back to its normal size after delivery, and that produces uterine contractions during sexual intercourse. Since breastfeeding and

sexuality are seldom discussed in our society, most couples discover quite by accident the startling connection between orgasm
and milk ejection. As a woman climaxes during lovemaking, oxytocin is released and milk spontaneously sprays from her breasts as
an amazing reminder of the inextricable link between the sexual
and nurturant roles of the breast.

When a woman is lactating, it is only natural for her partner to
fantasize about suckling her swollen breasts and tasting the milk. I
suspect that most partners do attempt to nurse from their mates
during lovemaking and that doing so enriches the couple's intimacy.
However, some women feel overly protective about their breasts
when they are nursing a baby. A woman may fear that her husband's mouth will contaminate her nipples, that he may steal milk
from the baby's next meal, or that his attempts at nursing will prove
uncomfortable for her. These concerns are generally unfounded.

Despite your inevitable exhaustion and preoccupation with your
new parental responsibilities, I urge you to make time for being
intimate with your partner on a regular basis. At a time when your
couple relationship is undergoing so much change, maintaining an
active sex life will help preserve and strengthen the love bond
between you. While spontaneous romance is a nice ideal, many
contemporary couples find it useful to *schedule* time for sex just as
they schedule other priorities in their life. Make a bedroom date
with your mate. Choose a time when your baby predictably sleeps
soundly. Then plan ahead to be as rested and renewed as possible
so you will be able to focus on your partner and on giving and
receiving pleasure.

≈ *Chapter 7* ≈

Common Problems Encountered by Breastfeeding Women

Breastfeeding is the way women have fed their babies from the beginning of time, so you should expect the process to proceed uneventfully, right? After all, it seems only fair that a woman who makes the positive choice to breastfeed her baby would be able to nurse as long as she desires. The surprising and disappointing truth is that lactation problems do occur, even among women with the best of intentions and the highest motivation to succeed at breastfeeding. Sometimes problems involve the mother's breasts and nipples or relate to her overall health. At other times, breastfeeding problems involve the baby or impact the baby's well-being. Some problems are due to circumstances beyond our control, while others are the direct result of lack of knowledge or lack of confidence, improper technique, or bad advice. Most problems that cause women to discontinue breastfeeding before they had wanted arise within the first few weeks, but a breastfeeding complaint can present at any point in the course of lactation. Whether breastfeeding problems begin in the hospital or surface months later, they can be the source of great stress and threaten long-term breastfeeding.

The Importance of Getting Help Early

The early recognition and treatment of a breastfeeding problem offers the best chance that the difficulty can be resolved successfully. The chief message is: *Get help as quickly as possible so you can resolve your problem before it becomes complicated by insufficient milk* (see chapter 10). Unfortunately, many health professionals practice a wait-and-see approach to breastfeeding complaints, hoping that any difficulties automatically will self-correct between office visits. This nonintervention approach is understandable considering how little training most health professionals receive about the management of breastfeeding problems. Without corrective measures, however, many problems are compounded by low milk or an underweight baby, making a bad situation worse.

Why Breastfeeding Problems Are Readily Complicated by Low Milk Supply

Breastfeeding difficulties can cause physical discomfort, exhaustion and frustration, as well as infant fussiness and poor infant growth. Furthermore, many breastfeeding problems readily become complicated by low milk supply. Often, complaints in breastfeeding women are linked to ineffective or infrequent emptying of milk. If milk is not removed from the breasts regularly, a chemical inhibitor in residual milk accumulates and decreases further milk production. In addition, excessive pressure from unemptied milk can cause damage to the milk-producing glands. Thus, milk left in the breast acts to decrease further milk production (see chapter 3, pages 78–79). Problems that impair milk removal—infrequent or short feedings, inverted nipples, breast infections, sore nipples, breast engorgement—can quickly result in diminished milk production.

Flat and Inverted Nipples

A flat nipple is one that cannot be made to protrude with stimulation. An inverted nipple retracts inward instead of becoming erect when the areola is compressed. Both flat and inverted nipples can make it difficult for an infant to grasp the breast correctly. They also are more prone to trauma from early breastfeeding efforts, which can result in painful cracks and damaged skin. When flat or inverted nipples are discovered prenatally, several treatment options are available to draw the nipples out (see pages 56–61). The most popular of these is the wearing of breast shells, also known as milk cups, over the nipples inside the maternity bra. These dome-shaped devices have an inner ring that is worn over the nipple. When a breast shell is situated over a flat or inverted nipple, it applies steady pressure at the base of the nipple which causes it to protrude through the central opening (see the illustration on page 59).

When prenatal treatment isn't possible or when the problem isn't detected until after delivery, mothers may need extra help with getting started breastfeeding. Whether or not your flat or inverted nipple(s) was treated prenatally, the most important thing you can do when your baby is born is to get skilled help with proper breastfeeding technique and expert guidance in helping your baby attach to your breast correctly.

Flat nipples can range from those that are only slightly less protuberant than normal, to nipples that are almost indistinguishable from the surrounding areola. Inverted nipples range from those with a slight central crease or dimple to deep central inversions that interfere with infant latch-on and prevent milk from flowing normally (see the illustrations on page 57). Depending on the characteristics of your particular nipples, your baby may be able to latch on and draw your nipples out without any special treatment. If your baby is having trouble grasping your flat or inverted nipples, you can try the following strategies:

• Gently compress and roll your nipple between your thumb and index finger for a minute to try to make it more erect before attempting to feed your baby. With patience and persistence, your baby can probably attach to your breast and nurse effectively even if you have flat or inverted nipples.

• Use a breast pump to draw your nipple(s) out immediately before breastfeeding your baby. A hospital-grade electric pump may be available on the postpartum floor for your convenient use. If an electric pump is not available, a hand pump can be used to create steady, gentle suction for about thirty seconds.

• If one nipple is more protuberant than the other, begin your breastfeeding attempts using that nipple. Once your baby learns to nurse from one breast, he may be better able to draw the nipple out

224 ～ DR. MOM'S GUIDE TO BREASTFEEDING

on the other side. You can build on this initial success as you offer the more difficult side.

• Wear breast shells for about thirty minutes before each feeding to help pull your nipples out. Obviously, the devices must be removed prior to breastfeeding. Some women can tolerate longer periods of wear, but overuse of breast shells can make nipples sore by trapping moisture. They can also cause plugged ducts by pressing against swollen breast tissues once milk comes in. (Any leaking milk that collects in the shells should be discarded.)

• If your baby has not learned to latch on well to both breasts and nurse effectively within twenty-four hours of birth, I recommend that you begin regular milk expression. Use the most effective pump you can obtain, preferably a hospital-grade electric breast pump with a dual collection system. Pump your breasts for approximately ten minutes after each feeding attempt. Pumping serves several purposes. It draws your nipples out with each pump cycle, and it provides effective draining of your breasts to assure you continue to produce a plentiful milk supply. Pumping also obtains expressed breast milk to use to supplement your baby until she learns to nurse effectively.

• While your baby is learning to breastfeed correctly, some experts believe it is preferable not to use a bottle to give the required supplemental milk. They argue that a preference for bottle-feeding can easily develop in babies who haven't learned to nurse effectively. These advocates recommend cup feeding or another alternative method of giving the extra milk. Other breastfeeding proponents insist that using bottles doesn't necessarily interfere with learning to nurse, so long as the mother's milk supply is kept plentiful by frequent pumping, and the baby is guided in correct breastfeeding technique. When a baby is having trouble learning to nurse due to flat or inverted nipples, I suggest temporarily avoiding bottle-feeding, if possible, and choosing an alternative method of feeding supplemental milk, at least during the period you are in the hospital.

Most importantly, keep first things first. Your top priorities are assuring your baby receives sufficient milk and preserving a generous breast-milk supply. With regular pumping and persistent attempts at the breast, your baby will probably be able to eventually breastfeed well. Rarely, a woman might have to pump several weeks until her nipples have been drawn out sufficiently for her baby to learn to nurse effectively. But such extra effort is well worth the benefits gained by breastfeeding.

Postpartum Breast Engorgement

The amount of postpartum breast engorgement women experience is highly variable. Some women can scarcely tell that their milk has come in, while others have extraordinary breast swelling, firmness, and discomfort. The amount of engorgement probably is influenced by the frequency of milk removal, the number of milk glands present, the rate at which hormones fall after delivery, and other individual differences.

Breastfeeding Problems Related to Engorgement

Over fifty years ago, a noted British physician, Dr. Harold Waller, published an insightful article in the medical literature describing the contribution of severe breast engorgement to various breastfeeding problems. He estimated that about 20 percent of first-time mothers experienced very dramatic breast engorgement and had difficulty establishing milk flow. It was his belief that this excessive engorgement, if not relieved promptly, soon led to the problems outlined below and was the chief explanation for early failure of breastfeeding. My own observations match Dr. Waller's conclusions, and I wholeheartedly concur with his hypothesis. In my opinion, severe or unrelieved engorgement in the first postpartum week represents *the greatest single physical cause of unsuccessful breastfeeding*. Severe engorgement, if not promptly relieved, can contribute to each of the following difficulties:

• **Breast swelling and firmness can make the nipple and surrounding areola more difficult (certainly not easier!) to grasp.** As a result, an infant may latch on incorrectly, taking only the tip of the nipple, thereby obtaining little milk and causing nipple discomfort. Babies who have learned to attach correctly in the first day or two when the nipple and areola are soft and pliable will be better prepared to nurse effectively should excessive engorgement occur later. In the past, when new mothers routinely remained hospitalized for several days after delivery, abundant milk production began prior to discharge, and nurses were available to help women position their babies correctly if engorgement was present. Today, however, most women find themselves at home when their milk comes in, and are left to muddle through the experience without benefit of guidance from health professionals. An early follow-up visit within two days of hospital discharge can help identify infants having latching troubles due to severe engorgement.

• **Swelling of the skin of the nipple and areola during engorgement makes the nipple more susceptible to trauma during attempts to breastfeed and contributes to soreness.** The resulting damage— often with cracking, bruising, or abrasions on the nipple—leads to nipple soreness, ranging from mild to severe, that can interfere with nursing. Thus, uncomfortable breast engorgement and painful nipples often go hand in hand, creating what one mother referred to as the "double whammy" blow to breastfeeding.

• **Excessive engorgement leads to residual milk and elevated pressure in the milk ducts that causes diminished milk production.** When the pressure of severe engorgement interferes with milk flow, residual milk in the breasts can decrease further milk production. Thus, a woman can go very quickly from too much to too little milk. Bottle-feeding mothers represent a commonplace example of how quickly unrelieved engorgement can cause decreased milk supply. Bottle-feeding mothers attest that extreme breast firmness and fullness subside substantially within about forty-eight hours, as the milk-producing glands cease to function. Thus, the period of engorgement is a critical time in the initiation of breastfeeding, often the make-it-or-break-it period. If milk flow is easily established and the breasts are drained regularly, then full milk production continues. However, if the pressure in tense, tight breasts cannot be relieved and little milk is removed, a woman's body will react as if she is bottle-feeding. Within a few short days, a woman with unrelieved breast engorgement can suffer diminished milk supply. It can take days, or even weeks, of dedicated effort to restore milk production to its full capacity after only a few days of early difficulties. Sometimes the effect can be permanent. Unrelieved breast engorgement is more than a temporary nuisance or an uncomfortable inconvenience. It is a very real threat to the success of breastfeeding because it is so harmful to milk supply.

• **Severe and unrelieved breast engorgement can make it difficult for the baby to obtain sufficient milk with nursing.** Several factors can limit a baby's milk intake during excessive engorgement. Not only is correct latch-on made more difficult when the breasts are swollen and firm, but excessive pressure can impair milk flow.

A mother may struggle at feeding times to get her baby to latch on and suckle well, while the hungry baby cries in frustration at not being able to properly position her mouth on the tense areola. Or, a baby seemingly may nurse often enough, yet remain underfed because she is unable to effectively extract milk during nursing attempts. As the days go by, a baby may lose an excessive amount of weight, becoming less able to nurse effectively, at the same time that milk production rapidly is declining. This is a dangerous combination that all too often follows severe, unrelieved breast engorgement.

Treatment of Engorgement

Feeding Schedule. Whether or not engorgement can be *prevented* by frequent feedings, I definitely agree that it is *improved* by frequent, effective nursing. By the time milk comes in around the third day, a baby should be nursing every two to three hours, at least eight to ten times in twenty-four hours. It's not uncommon for a baby to have one longer sleep interval (hopefully at night!). Ordinarily, I would allow a newborn one five-hour stretch without feeding in a twenty-four-hour period, but if your breasts are engorged, I wouldn't let this single longer interval exceed about 3½ hours. I recommend you *not* allow your baby to use a pacifier in the early weeks of breastfeeding, and this is especially true during engorgement. It does no good for your baby to suck non-nutritively on a pacifier when your full breasts need to be drained. Even if your baby just nursed forty minutes ago, if she exhibits any feeding cues, put her back to your breast. It's entirely possible that her last feeding was not very effective and that she obtained little milk. Now she wants to try again—and she should! Going by the clock ("Gee, she shouldn't be due to feed yet") is likely to prevent your breasts from getting the stimulation and emptying they need and your baby from getting all the milk she requires.

Correct Positioning at the Breast. Going through the motions of frequent feedings does little good if the baby is positioned incorrectly to nurse. In fact, it can make things worse by causing sore nipples that interfere with subsequent feedings. You may have to use a breast pump (see below) or hand expression (see pages 162–163) to take off some milk before latching your baby on. Expressing some milk first will soften the nipple-areola area and make it easier for your baby to grasp. Also, starting some milk dripping from your nipple will help entice your baby to latch on (see chapter 4, pages 88–99, to review the basics of correct positioning and latch-on). Cupping your breast in the C-hold, with your fingers well behind the areola, you may need to gently compress your thumb and forefinger to make the nipple and surrounding areola easier to grasp. Make sure your baby takes a large mouthful of breast. Her lips should be flanged out, not curled in.

Cold and Heat. Simple measures like cold and heat application can help relieve breast discomfort and improve milk flow. Cold therapy increasingly is being recognized for its value in reducing inflammation and pain. Traditional ice packs, cool compresses, or commercial cold packs—even bags of frozen vegetables!—can be applied to the engorged breasts for fifteen to twenty minutes at a time to reduce blood congestion and tissue swelling. This will diminish internal pressure in the breast and help milk move through the ducts to the nipple openings.

Many women attest that their breasts start dripping milk when they stand under a warm shower. This observation has led to the widespread recommendation to apply moist heat to engorged breasts, particularly *before* feedings to increase circulation to the breast and bring the hormone oxytocin to help trigger milk let-down. Wrapping the breasts in warm, wet washcloths or towels for ten to twenty minutes not only feels good but also can start milk dripping. Commercial hot packs are available from a breast pump manufacturer (see Resource List, page 446). These packs can be reused by warming them in the microwave. Be careful not to burn the already stretched, damaged breast tissues, especially in the sensitive nipple area.

Try both heat and cold applications to find which brings you most relief from discomfort and which helps best to improve your milk flow and decrease breast congestion. You can alternate these therapies in a way that is most effective for you.

Cabbage Leaves. For centuries, cabbage has been used in many countries as a folk remedy for a wide variety of ailments. All kinds of medicinal applications have been suggested for cabbage, including eating it raw or lightly cooked, drinking fresh cabbage juice, or applying a raw cabbage leaf poultice. In recent years, a number of lactation experts have suggested that wrapping engorged breasts in cabbage leaves brings rapid, effective relief of discomfort and facilitates milk flow. Many women attest to the benefits of this treatment, but scientific proof is still lacking to confirm whether such therapy truly is effective for breast engorgement. The home remedy is used as follows:

- Thoroughly rinsed and dried, refrigerated or room-temperature, crisp, green cabbage leaves are prepared by stripping out the large vein before applying the leaves over the engorged breast or breasts. The leaves can either be worn inside the bra or as compresses covered by a cool towel. Holes can be cut in the leaves, if necessary, to allow the nipples to be kept dry. The cabbage leaf compresses are left in place for about twenty minutes, or until they have wilted, at which time they can be replaced by fresh leaves. Most women report significant relief within eight hours. Continued application up to eighteen hours has been recommended for mothers who needed to wean abruptly or for severely engorged bottle-feeding mothers who wanted to dry up completely.

- The applications should be discontinued as soon as the desired result is obtained; overtreatment is claimed to reduce milk supply. Practitioners who use cabbage leaves report that women usually require only one or two applications to establish good milk flow.

Breast Pump. Many women are reluctant to pump or express milk during engorgement for fear that they might stimulate too much milk and exacerbate the condition. But engorgement is more a problem of *poor milk flow* than excessive milk production. Removing milk is essential to reducing the pressure in the breasts and the backup of milk that eventually can decrease milk supply. Improving the ease of milk flow from the breasts makes it easier for the baby to obtain milk when nursing. Because the situation so often is compounded by infant difficulties in breastfeeding, a breast pump can be enormously helpful in managing engorgement. A wide array of pumps is available, ranging from inexpensive hand pumps to hospital-grade electric pumps (see pages 162–167). I strongly recommend that you obtain a hospital-grade rental electric pump with a dual collection kit that can empty both breasts simultaneously if your breasts become severely engorged (see Resource List, page 446). Because unrelieved engorgement can be so distressing and its prompt resolution is so critical to continued success, you will want to have the most comfortable, convenient, and effective means of emptying your breasts. If your baby is not nursing well or if your breasts remain uncomfortably full after breastfeeding, pump after feedings to express any remaining milk and reduce breast firmness. Ten to fifteen minutes of pumping with an electric pump is usually sufficient at one session. Longer pumping times can damage nipples and swollen breast tissues. For severe engorgement, some women obtain better results by pumping one breast at a time, instead of both breasts. Use your free hand to gently massage your breast while pumping. Steady pressure applied to areas of firmness often starts milk flowing, at least briefly. When milk flow stops, switch to the opposite breast. Massage and pump on the second side as long as you are getting results. Then switch again when milk flow stops. After fifteen to twenty minutes of total effort, wait an hour or two before trying again.

Relaxation. Do your best to relax and visualize your milk flowing. Being anxious and uptight is only likely to inhibit your milk ejection reflex. Play calming music or practice relaxation techniques such as Lamaze breathing. Ask your partner to give you a neck massage or back rub. Extend your arms above your head and slowly bring them down to your sides. Repeat this "flying

Using a hospital-grade electric breast pump can improve the ease of milk flow and reduce the pressure in uncomfortably engorged breasts.

angel" exercise several times. Many women find it helps their milk to let-down.

Synthetic Oxytocin Nasal Spray. The hormone your body makes to trigger your milk ejection reflex and start your milk flowing is known as oxytocin (see chapter 3, pages 77–78, and chapter 5, pages 145–146). A synthetic form of this hormone was formerly marketed as a nasal spray known as Syntocinon (Sandoz Laboratories). The drug was prescribed for breastfeeding women to help trigger their let-down reflex and promote milk flow when the milk ejection reflex was thought to be inhibited. Synthetic oxytocin was sometimes prescribed for mothers of premature infants and employed mothers who needed help conditioning their milk ejection reflex when using a breast pump. The medication was also recommended to help relieve severe breast engorgement by triggering the milk ejection reflex and stimulating milk flow. Unfortunately, Syntocinon is no longer being marketed. However, a compounding pharmacist can prepare an equivalent drug with a physician's prescription. A compounding pharmacist is a pharmacist who makes custom-tailored medications from scratch. The International Academy of Compounding Pharmacists offers a referral service for patients to help them locate a compounding pharmacist within a fifty-mile radius of their zip code (see Resource List, page 451). If other measures to relieve engorgement haven't helped, ask your doctor whether synthetic oxytocin nasal spray might be worth trying in your case.

Engorgement Beyond the Postpartum Period

While breast engorgement poses the greatest problem during the first postpartum week, it can reoccur whenever milk removal is delayed. Even with well-established breastfeeding, uncomfortable fullness and firmness can result whenever the breasts are not regularly drained. Allowing the breasts to become markedly engorged places the nursing mother at risk for several complications. First, her supply can diminish as a result of residual milk and excess pressure on the milk glands. Second, a woman is more prone to a breast infection whenever her breasts are not emptied well. Here are some common scenarios that can lead to harmful breast engorgement after the first postpartum week.

• A mother decides to skip a few nursings to rest her sore nipples and finds her breasts become hard and sore (see pages 237–248 for correct treatment of sore nipples).

• A mother returns to work at eight weeks after delivery and doesn't pump her breasts during the workday. By noon she is uncomfortably full and starting to leak milk (see chapter 8 for advice on successfully combining breastfeeding and employment).

• A mother leaves her three-week-old newborn with her sister while she runs some errands and finds she is gone longer than she expected. Her sister feeds a bottle of formula to the baby in the mother's absence. When Mom finally gets home, her breasts are thoroughly engorged, but her baby is sound asleep with a full tummy and won't nurse.

• A fully breastfed two-month-old who previously nursed once or twice each night now starts to sleep through until morning. The mother awakens with uncomfortably hard, full breasts.

Most of these examples leading to potentially damaging engorgement could be prevented by practicing unrestricted breast-feeding. This requires keeping nursing mothers and babies together as much as possible. If you must be separated from your infant or cannot nurse regularly, the next best option is to use an effective breast pump to empty your breasts at regular feeding times. As long as you are fully breastfeeding, you should avoid going long periods without emptying your milk. Allowing your breasts to become hard and lumpy due to infrequent emptying not only causes discomfort but also can harm your milk supply and lead to a breast infection.

Failure of Lactogenesis—Milk Never Came In

Some women suffer extreme engorgement and others fall at the opposite end of the spectrum, leaving them to doubt whether their milk came in. Occasionally, lactogenesis, the onset of abundant milk production two to five days postpartum, is delayed among women who have complications of labor and delivery. Rarely, I encounter women whose milk scarcely comes in at all. Often these women have medical problems such as high blood pressure, infection, or anemia. Others have experienced extreme emotional turmoil. In cases of profound physical or mental stress, a mother's body may fail to lactate fully in order to preserve the health of the mother. Since lactation is the only elective process a mother's body performs, it doesn't surprise me terribly that full milk production occasionally is inhibited when a mother is very ill. Sometimes, as a mother's own health problems resolve, her milk supply steadily increases if she perseveres with breastfeeding.

If you doubt that your milk has come in by the fourth day after delivery, I would advise you to have your baby checked to be sure she hasn't lost excessive weight. Your physician, a lactation consultant, or a nurse with experience helping breastfeeding mothers should be able to tell whether your milk production has increased normally or not. If your milk hasn't come in abundantly by four days postpartum, you should start pumping after each nursing to guarantee that your breasts receive adequate stimulation and emptying to help increase your milk. Your baby's sucking alone may not provide sufficient stimulation to increase your milk supply. Using a hospital-grade rental electric pump after nursings may help increase milk production. Rarely, a woman fails to produce sufficient milk through no fault of her own, making it necessary for her infant to receive regular supplements of formula (see chapter 9).

Sore Nipples

Breastfeeding should be an enjoyable and, after the first week, comfortable experience. I am surprised at how many mothers accept sore nipples as an inevitable, unpleasant part of breastfeeding that must be endured by exceptional women. My colleagues and I evaluated over three hundred first-time mothers at four to eight days postpartum and found that 13 percent were experiencing nipple pain so severe that it caused them to dread feedings. That's more than one in ten breastfeeding women for whom pain was a major drawback to breastfeeding. Most of these women assumed that a nursing mother had to be a stoic in order to succeed at breastfeeding. This simply isn't true.

Although most women experience mild nipple discomfort at the beginning of feedings during the first few days of nursing, severe or persistent nipple pain is not a normal part of breastfeeding. Severe discomfort is almost always linked to improper breastfeeding technique and, when present, requires evaluation and treatment.

Consequences of Sore Nipples

Sore nipples are more than just a nuisance. This complaint is a major cause of early discontinuation of breastfeeding. Most women who choose to nurse imagine that breastfeeding will involve relaxed, rewarding interactions with their child. Feeding-associated pain soon shatters the tranquil image of a contented nursing mother and her satisfied baby. Pain can drive a disruptive wedge between a new breastfeeding mother and her nursing infant. I recall the candidly sad plea of one discouraged mother with exquisitely painful nipples who implored her innocent baby: "Please don't wake up and need me."

Nipple pain not only can interfere with the mother-baby relationship but also can lead to insufficient milk and impaired infant growth. You may be wondering how maternal discomfort can be related to an infant's nutritional intake. In fact, the most common cause of severe or persistent sore nipples is improper positioning of the infant's mouth on the mother's breast. If the infant does not grasp the entire nipple and sufficient surrounding areola, pain will result, and the baby will not extract milk very effectively. If she repeatedly fails to empty the breasts well, subsequent milk production will be reduced.

Other reasons why sore nipples can predispose a woman to insufficient milk include restricted feedings and impaired milk letdown. Women who dread feedings are apt to skip, postpone, or limit nursings, which can lead to diminished milk supply. In addition, pain and other noxious stimuli can impair the milk ejection reflex, thus reducing milk flow during painful feedings. You can appreciate that a combination of factors is at work to make diminished milk supply a common complication of chronic nipple pain. Eventually, persistent sore nipples can lead to inadequate infant weight gain. A vicious cycle can ensue, because a frantic, hungry baby may nurse erratically and produce even more nipple trauma.

Early Nipple Tenderness

Early mild nipple discomfort is often present by the second day of nursing and improves once your milk starts to come in abundantly. The discomfort is greatest at the beginning of feedings and seldom lasts throughout a nursing. Marked improvement is usually noticed beginning around the fifth day. No specific treatment is usually required, and you should expect breastfeeding to be comfortable after the first week of getting started.

Sore Nipples Caused by Improper Infant Latch-on or Incorrect Sucking

The most common cause of severe nipple pain or persistent pain beyond the first week is improper positioning of your infant's mouth on your nipple and surrounding areola. The most common error is to allow the baby to grasp only your nipple, instead of taking at least an inch of surrounding areola and breast tissue. The particular shape of your nipple and areola, the size and configuration of your baby's mouth, and your baby's unique sucking habits also can contribute to nipple discomfort. The problem of improper grasp is so common that I urge you to seek expert help in the hospital to assure that your baby is nursing correctly before you go home (see chapter 4, pages 88–99).

Babies' mouths and oral habits vary tremendously. Some infants have a receded chin at birth, making it difficult for them to position their mouth correctly on the lower portion of the nipple and areola. Others have a high-arched palate that affects the position of the nipple-areola in the baby's mouth. Some babies are born with oral habits they have been practicing in the uterus, such as tongue sucking or sucking their lower lip, that interfere with correct latch-on. When you add to all this the wide diversity of women's nipples—long, flat, inverted, creased, bulbous, large, and small— you can see why I consider that bringing a mother's nipple/breast and a baby's mouth together as a functioning unit is a true art form! Indeed, correct infant attachment is the foundation for breastfeeding success. It should be learned with the assistance of skilled helpers in the hospital, not by trial and error at home.

Some infants have a disorganized or abnormal sucking pattern that can produce nipple tenderness and create feeding problems. For example, some infants tend to clench or bite instead of sucking. Others may ball up their tongue instead of using it correctly to compress the milk duct sinuses and extract milk during breastfeeding.

The attachment of a baby's tongue to the lower mouth, known as the frenulum, can be too tight in some infants. The condition, known as tongue-tie, can prevent the tongue from protruding normally. The baby's tongue may not be able to extend beyond the gums or lips, and sometimes the frenulum extends clear to the tip

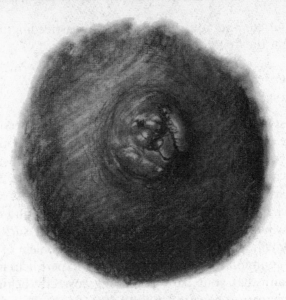

Sore, cracked nipples most often are caused
by incorrect infant attachment to the breast
or improper suckling.

of the tongue, causing an indentation when it is extended. Most tongue-tied babies are not bothered at all by the condition. In a few, however, tongue-tie can cause an infant to have difficulty breastfeeding and a mother to have extremely sore nipples. The limited mobility may prevent the tongue from cushioning the breast against the lower gums during nursing. In addition, limited mobility of the tongue occasionally leads to speech problems when a baby gets older. In cases where tongue-tie is believed to be causing sore nipples, surgically clipping the tight frenulum sometimes results in immediate, or gradual, improvement in breastfeeding and reduction of nipple pain. Clipping a short frenulum usually represents a simple procedure that is performed in a doctor's or dentist's office, although it is sometimes done under general anesthesia. Some controversy surrounds the practice, which was commonplace in past decades, but is seldom performed today. Since few physicians are aware that tongue-tie can cause breastfeeding difficulties, some may be reluctant to recommend clipping it. Among those practitioners who have experience performing the procedure are ENT specialists (otolaryngologists), oral surgeons, pediatric surgeons, and some dentists, pediatricians, and family physicians.

Routine Treatment of Sore Nipples

• **Assure that your infant is properly positioned to nurse and grasps your breast correctly.** Carefully review the detailed guidelines for correct positioning and latch-on (see chapter 4, pages 88–99). Cup your breast in a C-hold, with four fingers below and thumb above. Make sure your fingers are placed well behind the areola. With your baby well supported, aligned with your breast, and turned completely to face you, gently tickle her lips with your nipple. When she opens her mouth *wide*, quickly pull her toward you so that she grasps a large mouthful of breast, with the nipple centered in her mouth. Do not let your baby munch onto your nipple or just grasp the tip without any surrounding areola. That is a sure setup for discomfort and ineffective milk extraction. It's always better to remove your baby and let her reattach to your breast than to continue to let her nurse with an improper grasp. The football hold makes it easier for a baby to attach correctly since this position affords the mother a good view of the baby's mouth on her nipple (see illustration page 238).

• **Begin feeding on the least sore nipple to trigger your milk ejection reflex.** Once milk flow has begun and your baby has taken part of her feeding, she will be less hungry when brought to the second, more painful side. Your baby will nurse less vigorously after the letdown reflex has been triggered, making breastfeeding more comfortable. As soon as possible, resume alternating the breast on which you begin feedings to prevent a lopsided milk supply.

• **Frequent, shorter feedings are preferable to lengthy nursings spaced at wider intervals.** Temporarily, limit feedings to ten minutes per side if your nipples are very sore. Many women with sore nipples postpone feedings because they dread the pain associated with nursing. However, this can result in a ravenously hungry baby who nurses more frantically and produces more trauma. Also, the longer feedings are postponed, the more engorged the breasts become, and the harder it is for the baby to correctly grasp the breast. Finally, less frequent feedings can diminish a mother's milk supply, which already has a tendency to be low in women with sore nipples.

• **Gently pat your nipples dry with a clean cloth after nursing to remove surface wetness.** Excessive moisture on the skin surface can delay healing and cause chapping. If you wear breast pads, change

Correct infant latch-on can be made easier using the football hold, which allows the mother better visibility of the infant's mouth on the breast and better control of the infant's head.

them as soon as they become wet, and remove surface moisture after each feeding. However, don't go to extremes and excessively dry your nipples, as this can worsen the condition of your skin. In the past, many breastfeeding experts gave erroneous advice that led to excessive drying and cracking of nipples. Women were advised to use a hair dryer on a low setting or to expose their nipples to prolonged air drying in low-humidity environments. We now recognize that, just as excessive drying can crack and split chapped lips, it can contribute to breakdown and delayed healing of damaged nipple skin.

• **If you have cracks or other breaks in the skin, keep your nipples covered with a soothing emollient to maintain internal moisture.** Applying a soothing ointment to sore, cracked nipples will protect them from excessive moisture loss and will speed healing. A coating of USP Modified Lanolin (medical grade) is the superior emollient to use on your nipples. This ultrapure grade of lanolin is sold as Lansinoh for Breastfeeding Mothers and PureLan. Apply the lanolin to your nipples after each feeding just as you would keep chapped lips covered with lip balm to maintain the normal moisture present in the skin and promote healing. Emollients like medical-grade lanolin are particularly effective in climates with low humidity to protect nipples from excess drying.

Many breastfeeding experts tout the well-known healing properties of milk itself. They recommend expressing a few drops of milk after each nursing, and gently coating the nipple with it, then allowing the milk to dry on the nipples. Although I have little first-hand experience with this practice, the many proponents of the technique claim it promotes healing of sore nipples. However, the nipples of nursing mothers inevitably are bathed in milk much of each day, affording them the benefit of milk's anti-infective properties. The reason I don't routinely recommend coating damaged nipples with milk after nursing is my belief that cracked nipples are similar to chapped lips. The constant wet-to-dry effect that results from frequent licking of chapped lips only provokes more drying and cracking. Rather than allowing milk to dry on nipples, it would seem prudent to remove surface wetness and then keep nipples protected with lanolin to avoid the wet-to-dry cycles that further damage skin.

Health professionals who specialize in wound healing have found that the use of moisture-retaining occlusive dressings are effective in promoting healing of wounds in other body sites. Recently some physicians and lactation specialists have tried this treatment with sore nipples. They are reporting good results using hydrogel dressings applied to the nipples between feedings to maintain a moist environment for nipple healing.

• **Wear wide-based breast shells over your nipples between nursings.** These devices minimize discomfort from a crack or open wound and accelerate healing by preventing direct contact with nursing pads or your bra. Without these devices protecting your nipples, your bra or nursing pad might stick to a cracked or irritated area of nipple skin, causing the wound to reopen every time you remove the covering.

• **If your nipple pain is so severe that you are unable to tolerate nursing your baby, a hospital-grade rental electric breast pump can be used to express your milk comfortably.** Pumping provides a convenient means of emptying your breasts and maintaining or even increasing your milk supply, while allowing your nipples to heal. Previously, I had been taught to believe that "no pump is as gentle or as effective as your nursing baby." We now appreciate that not every baby necessarily nurses correctly or effectively. Persistent pain during feedings is a sign that healing is not occurring. Trying to be tough and enduring the pain just subjects your nipples to continued trauma. In this case, the best electric pumps probably will be more gentle and more efficient than your baby's improper, uncomfortable sucking. We are fortunate to have highly effective hospital-grade electric pumps to break the devastating pain cycle, preserve milk production, promote healing, and provide the option of returning to breastfeeding after calm has been restored to a family. I recall one woman whose nipple pain was so excruciating that she admitted in private: "I expected breastfeeding to make me feel more connected to my baby. Instead, I look at her and dread the thought of having to feed again. The discomfort of breastfeeding is straining my relationship with my baby." This distraught woman was elated when pumping proved to be pain-free. Her whole attitude improved and she began to enjoy her baby more when she stopped associating her infant with pain. While her nipples healed, she fed her expressed milk to her infant, then cautiously resumed breastfeeding with expert guidance to assure proper technique. For this woman, breaking the pain cycle was the key to her ultimate breastfeeding success.

Blood in breast milk. I also recommend pumping instead of nursing when the breast milk contains blood from a cracked nipple (or other causes). Although many babies ingest blood-tinged milk without parents or health professionals ever knowing about it, drinking bloody breast milk is not entirely benign. For one thing, blood is irritating to the gut and can have a purgative effect. I recall a newborn who was admitted to the hospital for "bloody diarrhea" and was subjected to numerous diagnostic tests to determine the cause before it was found that the blood being passed was the mother's and not the infant's. The mother had been unaware that her painful, cracked nipple was bleeding, nor that her baby was obtaining bloody milk with breastfeeding. Ingested blood also can increase a newborn baby's bilirubin level, worsening infant jaundice (see chapter 5, pages 156–158). Furthermore, blood in breast milk can increase a baby's risk of acquiring certain infectious diseases while breastfeeding (if the mother is infected herself).

In general, hand pumps, battery pumps, and small electric pump models are not as comfortable or effective as the hospital-grade rental electric pumps. To find the nearest pump rental depot, call the manufacturers listed in the Resource List, page 446.

If you decide to use a pump to interrupt breastfeeding and allow your nipples to heal, plan to pump your breasts every time your baby needs to be fed. This will be a *minimum* of eight times in twenty-four hours. You will want to express *at least* as much milk as your baby requires to be satisfied. A more generous milk supply is even better, and the excess milk can be frozen. When a mother's milk supply is abundant, her baby obtains milk more easily and is less likely to damage her nipples. Beginning about two to three weeks postpartum, the amount of milk you should expect to get from both breasts combined is about an ounce for every hour that has elapsed since you last pumped or fed your baby. Thus, if you pumped after a three-hour interval, you should get about three ounces. If you slept for a five-hour stretch at night, you would expect to pump about five ounces when you awoke. You can feed the expressed milk by bottle, cup, or other method approved by your baby's doctor. Keep in mind that a healthy baby shouldn't require more than thirty minutes to complete a feeding.

If you use an electric pump to heal sore nipples, I must emphasize the importance of obtaining expert help with your breast-

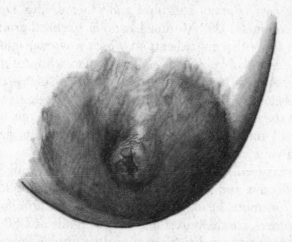

When severe nipple damage prevents continued nursing, breastfeeding can be interrupted to allow the nipples to heal while the milk supply is comfortably maintained using a hospital-grade electric breast pump.

feeding technique when you are ready to return to nursing. I recall one woman who spent nearly a week pumping and healing her severely cracked nipples, only to have the wounds reopen when she resumed nursing her baby using the same inappropriate technique that had damaged her nipples in the first place.

• **Synthetic oxytocin nasal spray can be used to help facilitate the let-down reflex in women with sore nipples.** As mentioned earlier, the pain of sore nipples can cause a woman to tense up at feeding times, resulting in inhibition of the milk ejection reflex. This only compounds the problem of sore nipples because a baby sucks more vigorously before milk lets-down. You can try simple strategies to help trigger your milk ejection reflex, such as breast stroking and massage, drinking a beverage, or using relaxation breathing (see pages 313–314). Synthetic oxytocin nasal spray is an additional aid that might prove helpful to some women with sore nipples by triggering their milk let-down (see page 231 for information on how to obtain synthetic oxytocin nasal spray).

First Do No Harm. One of the most important principles in medicine is "first do no harm." The sad truth is that inappropriate treatments often prove worse than no treatment at all. Over the years, some nipple creams have been marketed that were useless at best or that actually aggravated sore nipples. Many women are sensitive to the additives in various nipple creams. Some that were used in the past contained alcohol and other drying agents. One reason I recommend USP Modified Lanolin (medical grade) is that it is free of any other ingredients to which a woman might react. Although a popular belief exists that women who are allergic to wool will react adversely to lanolin, dermatologists insist that true lanolin allergies are very rare. Most women "allergic to wool" are sensitive to the fibers. If you suspect you may be allergic to lanolin, apply a small amount to your inner arm to see if you react before trying it on your nipples.

Most breastfeeding experts agree that medical-grade lanolin is the most effective and safest substance that can be applied to sore nipples to promote healing. PureLan and Lansinoh for Breastfeeding Mothers are the purest and safest brands of USP Modified Lanolin and do not need to be removed before feedings. I cannot recommend other creams, ointments, or topical applications because they are not as effective and some are not safe for infants.

Some breastfeeding counselors recommend applying ice to sore nipples. They claim that ice treatments temporarily desensitize sore nipples sufficiently to allow some women to tolerate nursing. While I advocate ice in the treatment of engorgement, mastitis, sports injuries, and other conditions, I do not recommend it for sore nipples. First, I don't believe in numbing the pain to make nursing tolerable. Discomfort while nursing is a warning sign that the baby is latched on incorrectly or that mechanical trauma is continuing and is preventing healing. I also think there is some risk of ice causing cold injury to the sensitive skin of the nipples.

Sore Nipples Caused by a Yeast Infection

Persistent nipple pain sometimes results from a yeast infection of the nipples. The problem occurs more commonly than appreciated, as few medical personnel are familiar with yeast infection of the nipples. Most women know about vaginal yeast infections, and new mothers soon learn that a persistent infant diaper rash can be due to a yeast infection. Yeast, also known as candida, thrive in moist environments, such as the mouth, the vagina, the diaper area, and the nipples of a breastfeeding woman. Although yeast commonly are harbored in these areas, they normally live in balance with bacteria and cause no symptoms. Certain conditions make a yeast infection more likely to occur. For example, treatment with antibiotics diminishes the growth of normal bacteria and allows yeast to overgrow and produce symptoms. Yeast aren't likely to invade normal skin, but once the skin barrier has been broken, damaged skin is more susceptible to a yeast infection. An ordinary diaper rash might develop when a wet/soiled diaper is left on too long. Once the rash persists for a few days, you should suspect that a yeast infection is now present.

Because some yeast are present in every infant's mouth, candida can easily be transferred to a mother's nipples. A yeast infection is more likely to develop if a mother has chronic nipple trauma from improper infant latch-on or incorrect suckling or if she has a crack, fissure, or opening in the nipple skin. A crack that has been present for several days may become infected by yeast, which can keep it from healing.

Most breastfeeding specialists recognize the symptoms of a suspected yeast infection of the nipples. Unfortunately, relatively few obstetricians, pediatricians, or family physicians are familiar with the problem, which is seldom mentioned in traditional medical textbooks. An awkward situation often arises when a lactation consultant suggests the diagnosis, and the mother's physician is reluctant to prescribe treatment since he or she is unfamiliar with the condition. Some dermatologists will diagnose and treat yeast nipple infections.

The diagnosis of a yeast infection of the nipples is often based on circumstantial evidence. Proving that yeast are the culprit can be difficult, as culture results may be inconclusive. The following clues will help you suspect that your nipple pain is due to a yeast infection:

- **The timing and nature of the pain.** The pain from yeast nipples typically starts *after* the first couple of weeks, although it can begin anytime. Usually, the mother has weathered early, mild sore nipples and has been nursing comfortably before pain starts anew. Mothers frequently describe their discomfort as burning, shooting, or stabbing pain that radiates from the nipples deep into the breast. Pain is present both during feedings and *after* nursing. Often, discomfort is so severe that the mother decides to wean. Nipple pain can be very chronic, sometimes present for weeks or months, virtually spoiling a woman's breastfeeding experience.
- **Appearance of the nipples.** Yeast infection of the nipples may cause surprisingly little change in nipple appearance. In fact, some practitioners wonder how a mother could complain of severe pain when her nipples may look relatively normal. Occasionally, they will appear pinkish. Rarely, the skin is inflamed with reddened bumps, typical of a baby's yeast diaper rash. I tend to suspect yeast if a crack, fissure, or other irritated area has been present for several days. Any break in the skin can be invaded by yeast.
- **Previous problems with yeast.** Yeast infection of the nipples occurs more commonly among women who have experienced vaginal yeast infections during pregnancy and previous problems with yeast. Some women seem to be more yeast-prone than others.
- **Recent treatment of mother with antibiotics.** Yeast infection of the nipples often starts during or after a mother's treatment with antibiotics. The antibiotics promote an overgrowth of yeast by destroying bacteria. A woman may have received a course of antibiotics to treat a uterine infection, breast infection, or other illness before she began experiencing nipple pain.
- **The presence of yeast diaper rash or oral thrush in the baby.**

The possibility that nipple pain is due to a yeast infection should be considered whenever a baby has thrush (yeast in the mouth) or a yeast diaper rash. Yeast infections in the baby often occur after a course of antibiotics, for example to treat an ear infection. Oral yeast, called thrush, causes white patches on the baby's tongue (often assumed to be milk). It also can look like stringy white matter inside the baby's lips or cheeks (see photograph page 246). A yeast diaper rash looks bright red (common in the thigh creases and between the buttocks), with red bumps at the margins.

• **Other risk factors for yeast.** Diabetic women suffer more yeast infections than others, making them more prone to yeast nipples. Yeast infections are also more common among women taking birth control pills.

Treatment for Yeast Infection of the Nipples

If you suspect that you could have a yeast infection of one or both nipples, you will need to see a practitioner who can diagnose the problem and prescribe medication, such as your obstetrician or family physician. Although a lactation consultant may be more familiar with the problem, she may need to ask your doctor to write a prescription for you. A few pediatricians are willing to treat the problem in lactating women, and occasionally women seek help from a dermatologist. No studies have been conducted to determine the most effective treatment for yeast nipples, but several therapies are commonly prescribed, including a topical antifungal cream or ointment and/or an oral antifungal medication widely used to treat vaginal and other yeast infections (brand name, Diflucan; generic, fluconazole). Sometimes a topical cortisone cream is also recommended to reduce inflammation.

If the baby has a yeast diaper rash or oral thrush, proper treatment of the infant's yeast infections should be considered an essential part of your own therapy. Some practitioners recommend treating the baby even when no infant symptoms are present. Other things that will help combat a yeast infection of the nipples include the following suggestions:

• **Exercise good hygiene.** Wash your hands often, including after changing your baby's diaper or using the toilet and before and after breastfeeding.

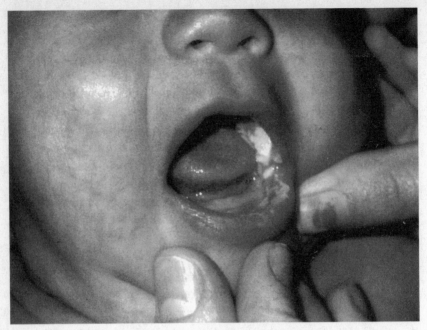

Thrush in a baby's mouth can cause a painful yeast infection
of the mother's nipples.

• **Keep your nipples free from surface moisture.** Remember, yeast thrive best in a moist environment. Change your breast pads as soon as they become wet. Allow your nipples to air dry a few minutes after nursings.

• **Boil pacifiers and bottle nipples at least once daily.** Pacifiers and bottle nipples can harbor yeast and reintroduce it into your baby's mouth while you are trying to treat a yeast infection. If you use a breast pump, boil the breast shield that is placed over your nipple and the bottle at least once a day.

• **Observe your baby for any signs of a yeast diaper rash or oral thrush.** Ask your pediatrician or family physician to treat a possible yeast infection in your infant. Creams and ointments are available for diaper rashes and an oral medication is available for thrush. Babies and mothers often reinfect one another, so simultaneous treatment of the breastfeeding dyad is best.

• **If you have any signs of a vaginal yeast infection, ask your obstetrician or family physician to prescribe treatment for you.** Women with vaginal yeast infections are more prone to nipple yeast problems. One advantage of oral therapy is that it can eradicate yeast from other sites as well as your nipple infection.

• **Consider interrupting breastfeeding temporarily by using a hospital-grade rental electric breast pump.** Sometimes, when nursing is too painful to tolerate, pumping proves to be a comfortable alternative. Temporarily pumping instead of nursing also can speed your recovery from yeast nipples by breaking the mouth-nipple cycle of reinfection.

• **It is popularly believed that yeast infections can be prevented by making dietary changes.** Advocates of this belief recommend reducing one's intake of sugary foods and eating more yogurt with acidophillus.

Fortunately, many women who receive treatment for a yeast infection of their nipples can expect to notice improvement within a few days. However, women vary tremendously in how rapidly and completely they respond to therapy. For some, the pain relief seems nothing short of miraculous, while others continue to have nipple pain, despite persistent attempts to treat the problem. It is possible that some women whose symptoms do not improve with antiyeast therapies actually have another cause for their pain that is wrongly assumed to be yeast. A few women suffer chronic pain attributed to yeast and become so discouraged that they choose to wean rather than endure continuing discomfort. I am convinced that if more enlightened physicians took an interest in this common and frustrating problem, more effective therapies for yeast nipples would be found.

Sore Nipples Caused by Infection with Bacteria

Sore nipples can also become infected with bacteria. When bacteria invade the broken skin barrier, the result can be worse pain, delayed healing, and the risk of progressing to a full-blown breast infection (see pages 254–260). The offending germs that invade a crack or break in the skin usually are those found in the baby's mouth, including staph germs. Germs found in feces also can cause nipple infections, especially when breastfeeding women forget to wash their hands after diaper changes. Yellowish drainage and surrounding redness may be evident in the infected area. A bacterial infection of the nipple is more likely to be present when a mother's nipple pain is severe, when a break in the nipple skin is present, and when the baby is less than one month old. A bacterial infection is also likely when an older nursing baby bites the mother's nipple and breaks the skin. Your doctor can confirm such an infection by taking a culture with a swab or make a presumptive diagnosis by judging from the appearance of the nipple. In addition to correcting any problems with the baby's latching technique, bacterial infections of the nipple should be treated with a course of oral antibiotics to assure prompt healing and to prevent mastitis. If you are prone to yeast infections, your health care provider may prescribe an anti-fungal medication to be taken simultaneously.

Sore Nipples Caused by Sensitive Skin

In addition to the causes of sore nipples just described, differ-ences in skin sensitivity make some women more prone to nipple discomfort during breastfeeding. In the past it was commonly accepted that redheads and fair-skinned women were more likely to have sore nipples. While some experts dispute this popular belief, others, including myself, find some truth in it. In my experi-ence, women who have very sensitive skin on other parts of their bodies often have more trouble with sore nipples. I think seasonal and geographic differences have an influence as well. In Denver, we see more women with nipple complaints in the fall and spring. Our humidity is so low that excessive drying of the nipples contributes to nipple breakdown. You might accurately guess that lanolin is very popular here!

Breast-Milk Jaundice

Jaundice is a yellowish skin coloration that becomes evident in more than half of all newborns. The yellowish color results from a substance in the blood known as bilirubin, which is released when red blood cells break down. Newborn jaundice can be due to many causes, ranging from benign to serious. The yellow color always should be reported to your baby's doctor (see chapter 5, pages 156–159).

It is generally agreed that breastfed newborns have a higher inci-dence of jaundice than formula-fed babies. There are two distinct reasons for increased levels of jaundice in breastfed babies. The most common explanation is known as *breastfeeding* jaundice. In this case, jaundice becomes exaggerated due to poor breastfeeding and low milk intake. Usually the baby is not nursing often enough or is not breastfeeding effectively. The infant may have lost excessive weight after birth or be failing to gain weight. Jaundice is noticed around the third day of life and continues for several days. The treatment of breastfeeding jaundice should be aimed at improving breastfeeding technique and assuring that the baby gets adequate nutrition (see What Does Infant Jaundice Have to Do with Breastfeeding? chapter 5, pages 156–159). The bilirubin level falls rapidly once the baby is well fed.

The other type of jaundice that is linked with breastfeeding is called *breast-milk* jaundice. In this case, the bilirubin level becomes elevated as a result of an unknown factor in some mothers' breast milk that increases the absorption of bilirubin from the newborn intestines. This delays the excretion of bilirubin into the stools and causes the baby to remain jaundiced. The problem usually begins toward the end of the first week and can continue for many weeks.

With breast-milk jaundice, the baby nurses well, obtains plenty of breast milk, appears healthy, and gains weight normally. Although low levels of breast-milk jaundice occur quite commonly in breastfed infants, the bilirubin level rarely gets high enough to require specific treatment. If the bilirubin rises to a worrisome level (usually over 20 milligrams percent), or if the baby's doctor is getting anxious about whether some other medical problem could be causing the jaundice, the doctor may recommend that you discontinue breastfeeding for twenty-four to thirty-six hours to see if the bilirubin level drops. A dramatic fall in the bilirubin level within a day or so of interrupting breastfeeding confirms the diagnoses of breast-milk jaundice. During the time that breastfeeding is interrupted, the baby is fed formula. After breastfeeding is resumed, the bilirubin may rise slightly before it gradually declines to a normal level over a couple of weeks.

If your baby's doctor requests that you temporarily stop breastfeeding due to breast-milk jaundice in your baby, it is critical that you use an effective breast pump to empty your breasts at regular feeding times while your baby is formula-fed. This way, you will maintain an abundant milk supply and can resume breastfeeding easily. You don't need to discard your expressed milk while breastfeeding is interrupted. It can be frozen for later use.

Sometimes when a mother must interrupt breastfeeding due to

breast-milk jaundice in her infant, she may assume there is something wrong with her milk and wonder whether she should return to breastfeeding. Please know that your milk provides perfect nutrition for your baby and that breastfeeding certainly is worthwhile! Many babies each year are needlessly weaned because of the diagnosis of breast-milk jaundice. Interrupting breastfeeding should be only rarely necessary for this condition. However, both mothers and doctors can become anxious when jaundice persists in a newborn baby, and your doctor may feel compelled to make a diagnosis and resolve the problem. Even when breastfeeding is interrupted, you should be able to resume nursing your baby within about thirty-six hours.

Excessive Leaking of Milk

Most women experience leaking of milk when their milk ejection reflex is triggered, perhaps upon hearing their baby cry or shortly after starting to nurse. Milk usually drips from one breast while a mother is nursing on the other side. For the majority of breastfeeding women, leaking milk represents little more than a minor inconvenience. Some even find it amusing to watch their milk spray during feedings or in the tub or shower.

I consider leaking milk to be an encouraging sign of a well-conditioned milk ejection reflex. Seeing milk flow freely makes me optimistic that a woman will succeed at breastfeeding. Despite my own enthusiasm over leaking milk, for some women, leaking is an irritating and embarrassing problem that represents a definite drawback to breastfeeding. Excessive leakers may complain of drenched clothing, soiled bedding, and constant wetness. To these women, breastfeeding is more messy than convenient.

Women not only leak to different degrees but also react to leaking in different ways. For example, you may already have observed that your milk lets-down during lovemaking. Some women find this connection between breastfeeding and sexuality to be fascinating, even erotic, while others find it off-putting.

If leaking milk is a problem for you, let me help you reframe the issue so you might view it in a more positive light. You see, leaking is more than just normal—it's a wonderful marker for breastfeeding success. Leaking usually signals a highly effective milk ejection reflex and an abundant milk supply. When milk flows readily, babies usually nurse easily. Of all the breastfeeding problems I've encountered, I think leaking is the preferred one to have.

I don't mean to trivialize your concerns if you are one of those women who leak excessively and are bothered by it. The following pointers will help you better understand and deal with leaking milk:

• **Leaking is usually worst from two to six weeks.** It takes a week or two for the milk ejection reflex to start working well. Within several more weeks, the capacity of the milk ducts increases, so less milk leaks from the nipple openings when milk is letting-down.

• **The sensations of the milk ejection reflex will alert you that your let-down is being triggered.** You can stop milk from leaking by applying pressure against the nipple openings. To do this discreetly in public, cross your arms in front of your chest and press your thumbs against your nipples. No one needs to know what you are doing.

• **To protect your clothing, wear washable or disposable breast pads inside your nursing bra to absorb any leaking milk.** Change wet pads frequently, however, to keep your nipples free of excess surface moisture. Don't try to reuse disposable pads after they have dried, as they get very stiff and rough. Wash reusable pads and your nursing bra daily. If you don't want to purchase nursing pads, you can stitch together reusable ones from 100 percent cotton cloth. Even an all-cotton handkerchief works fine.

• **You can wear plastic breast shells to prevent leaking milk from soiling your outer clothing.** Breast shells, also known as milk cups, can be worn over your nipples and held in place by your nursing bra (see the photograph on page 59). Among their many purposes, breast shells are used by some women to collect leaking milk. (Don't try to save the milk that drips into breast shells.) Some employed breastfeeding mothers wear breast shells to protect their clothing since leaking at the workplace can prove especially embarrassing.

Clogged Ducts (Caked Breast)

Sometimes one or more of the lobes of the breast don't drain very well, causing a temporary backup of milk, known as a clogged duct or caked breast. Unlike generalized breast engorgement, a clogged duct is a localized blockage of milk. A tender, hard knot can form in the affected duct system, and the surrounding area of the breast usually feels full and tender. Most often, the outer lobes near the armpits are involved, since more milk glands are concentrated in those areas. The problem usually results from incomplete emptying of milk from the breast or by going too long between nursings. A clogged duct also can be caused by breast trauma and chronic inflammation from a low-grade, unrecognized breast infection. Women who have an overabundant milk supply are more prone to getting clogged ducts. A few women are plagued by the problem.

A clogged duct can be quite uncomfortable, and if it doesn't get relieved promptly, it can progress to a full-blown breast infection (see pages 254–260). Don't ignore a clogged duct. It's an important warning sign and calls for your immediate attention to prevent a breast infection from occurring. The following simple measures usually provide relief for a clogged duct within eight hours:

- **Nurse more often.** A clogged duct is the result of incomplete or irregular removal of milk from the breast. The best way to counter it is to nurse more often. This is easier if you can be more available to your baby. Cut back on other activities as much as possible so you can concentrate on relieving the problem.
- **Gently massage the clogged area.** Gentle pressure applied to any tender knots or caked portions of the breast will help milk to flow from the obstructed area. Keep your massage gentle, as overly rough manipulation of the breast increases the risk of mastitis. Massage and pressure work best when applied prior to and while nursing your baby.
- **Start several feedings in a row on the clogged side.** A baby's most vigorous nursing occurs at the first breast suckled. To help drain the clogged side, you can start several consecutive nursings on the affected breast. Be careful, however, not to let the second breast remain overly full or you could develop a blocked duct on that side or a decline in your milk supply.
- **Vary your nursing position to empty all lobes well.** Different nursing positions result in better drainage of different lobes of the breast. In addition to the traditional cradle hold, try the cross-cradle hold, the football hold, and lying down to nurse to find

which position works best to empty your clogged area (see chapter 4, pages 91–95). Try pointing his chin toward the plugged duct.

• **Take a warm shower or apply warm compresses to the caked area.** Heat usually helps trigger the let-down reflex and facilitates milk flow. Many women spontaneously drip milk in the shower or bathtub. Try applying warm compresses to the clogged area, especially just before nursing and in conjunction with breast massage.

• **Use a breast pump to empty the engorged area well.** If your baby doesn't nurse well or you are separated from your baby during part of the day, you may need to use an effective breast pump to relieve a clogged duct. Women who have an overabundant supply may need to periodically express some surplus milk to soften their overfull breasts (see Overabundant Milk Supply, pages 260–262).

• **Try to identify and eliminate any risk factors you may have, especially if you have a recurring problem with clogged ducts.** As mentioned earlier, women with superabundant milk supplies are at increased risk for clogged ducts whenever their breasts don't get well drained. Other risk factors include an erratic feeding or pumping schedule—typical of employed mothers—or wearing a constrictive bra. In addition, breast trauma, such as being bitten or kicked by the baby or massaging the breast too vigorously, can produce inflammation in a duct system and interfere with milk drainage. If you suffer frequent clogged ducts, I suggest you review your breastfeeding practices with a lactation consultant.

A Word of Caution. I have encountered more than one woman in my career who had a cancerous breast lump which was mistaken by her physician for a clogged duct. Although the mass persisted for months, proper diagnosis of the malignancy was inappropriately delayed, while treatments were prescribed for the presumed "clogged duct." Please never label a persistent breast lump as a clogged duct. Clogged ducts come on abruptly, are painful, and resolve within a day or so. Only a few things can happen with a true clogged duct. It will clear quickly, and the tender lump will disappear; it will progress to mastitis, which will become painfully obvious; it won't empty well, so the lobe will partially dry up, in which case the lump will disappear; or, it will temporarily resolve, but return at a later date. **Any lump that persists for days or weeks must be accurately diagnosed. It is not a clogged duct.**

Breast Infection (Mastitis)

Mastitis is the medical name for a breast infection. It is a miserable, "flu-like" illness that is accompanied by an area of pain and redness in the breast. The condition seldom occurs in women who are not lactating, but it is not uncommon among breastfeeding women. As many as 10 percent of nursing mothers will have a breast infection during the course of breastfeeding.

A breast infection is usually caused by bacteria, often the same germs that are normally present on the nipple and in the baby's mouth. Many factors can increase a nursing mother's susceptibility to mastitis. Chief among these is irregular or incomplete removal of milk from the breast. Poor emptying can result from many causes, such as too long an interval between feedings; ineffective removal of milk by the infant or by a breast pump; having a clogged duct that prevents proper milk drainage from a particular lobe; or wearing a tight-fitting bra that impedes milk flow. Infecting bacteria can enter the breast through a cracked nipple or duct opening to cause mastitis. Any type of breast trauma will also predispose a lactating woman to mastitis. The trauma can result from infant teething, incorrect infant latch-on or abnormal infant suckling, generating excessive vacuum pressures with a breast pump, or by an older baby pinching the breast. In my experience, maternal exhaustion also leaves a mother vulnerable to mastitis. The infection often strikes employed mothers, sleep-deprived women, or mothers with house guests or holiday plans. The typical symptoms of mastitis are outlined below.

Achy, "Flu-like" Feeling. Women coming down with or suffering from full-blown mastitis mistakenly may assume they have a bad case of the flu. Because flu-like symptoms are so common with mastitis, physicians are taught that "flu" in the breastfeeding mother is mastitis until proved otherwise. Indeed, women unaware that they have mastitis may call their doctor to request treatment for the flu or to inquire whether their baby might catch the flu from them by nursing. Only after gathering more information does it become evident that the mother is really suffering from mastitis. I also recall a woman who telephoned to ask whether the over-the-counter medication she was taking for her flu symptoms could harm her nursing baby. Further probing revealed that she actually had mastitis. If you become ill with body aches and flu-like symptoms, it is possible that you have mastitis, and you should notify your doctor.

Breast Pain, Redness, and Firmness. Most women with mastitis will be able to pinpoint a painful area in one or both breasts. The affected spot is usually pink or red and firmer than other areas of the breast. The pain can range from severe, even exquisite, to a vague achiness or tenderness to the touch. Usually, an entire wedge-shaped lobe of the breast will be involved, starting at the nipple and extending toward the chest. Any portion of the breast can be affected, but the outer areas next to the armpits are common sites, since the milk glands are concentrated in these locations. The skin over the tender area can range from faintly pink to fiery red and tight. The painful area is usually firmer than the surrounding tissues due to obstructed milk flow from the infected lobe. In some cases, the entire breast becomes hard and swollen. I recall one woman in whom the first symptom of mastitis was unexplained diffuse engorgement of one breast. Fever, redness, and flu-like symptoms eventually followed within eighteen hours, but the initial sign of mastitis was sudden obstruction of milk flow from one breast.

Fever and Chills. Mastitis usually produces some degree of fever, but the achiness and breast pain often precede the temperature elevation. While some physicians won't treat mastitis unless a fever is documented, I recommend antibiotics if flu-like symptoms and a red, tender area of the breast are present. I had mastitis once myself when Mark, my youngest, was eleven months old. I awoke in the middle of the night, certain that something was wrong. My nipple and areola were exquisitely tender and by morning my breast hurt and I felt awful. I sought medical attention, convinced that I had mastitis, but my caring, knowledgeable doctor was hesitant to treat since my temperature was barely elevated. By late afternoon, I was much sicker and had a definite fever, so antibiotics were started. I subsequently have seen other women with the same progression of symptoms, so now I recommend treatment even if a fever is not yet present.

Headache. Few physicians or parents associate a headache with a breast infection, but an unexplained headache often is present in women with mastitis. Of course, a headache can have many causes, ranging from sleep deprivation to high blood pressure. If you have a headache along with any other symptom of mastitis, you might have a breast infection. Even if you have no other symptoms of mastitis, any severe or persistent headache should be reported to your doctor.

Nipple or Areolar Pain. A breast infection can start when bacteria enter the milk ducts at the nipple opening. At first, the infection might be contained in one of the lactiferous sinuses under the nipple, before progressing into the breast. An area of the areola that is tender to the touch or painful during nursing can be a symptom of an early breast infection. The infection can quickly spread from the duct system to affect a whole lobe of the breast.

Can I Continue to Breastfeed with Mastitis?

In the past, physicians believed that women with mastitis needed to wean, both to speed their recovery and to prevent their babies from becoming ill. This belief arose in the pre-antibiotic era, when the postpartum hospital stay was lengthy and when severe mastitis often occurred in epidemic form in a large hospital ward. Today, mastitis is milder and occurs sporadically, not in epidemics, and it is readily treatable with antibiotics. Not only is continued breastfeeding allowed, it is preferable. Women who wean abruptly when they have mastitis are at greater risk of developing a breast abscess (a walled-off pocket of pus that must be drained). Most cases of mastitis are caused by germs from the baby's own nose and throat. Medical authorities generally agree that a mother who gets mastitis while nursing her healthy infant can safely continue to breastfeed through the illness. Of course, whenever a mother or other family member is sick, the baby should be observed carefully for any signs of illness, such as poor feeding, irritability, listlessness, difficulty breathing, or fever. It is possible, although not likely, for a baby to develop a serious infection with the same germs that have caused mastitis in the mother.

In a few instances, I believe that a baby should NOT be fed milk from an infected breast. For example, if a mother is pumping her milk for her premature or sick newborn and develops mastitis, this is a different situation from the woman who comes down with a breast infection while nursing her healthy infant. I recommend that mothers who are pumping milk for high-risk infants discard all milk expressed from the infected breast until their symptoms clear up. Meanwhile, the baby can still be fed the milk pumped from the unaffected breast. Such decisions should always be made in consultation with your baby's doctor. I also recommend "pumping and dumping" when the milk from the infected breast contains visible blood or pus.

Treatment of Mastitis

Call your obstetrician or family physician promptly if you have any symptoms of mastitis. The sooner you start treatment, the sooner you will feel better and the less likely complications, such as a breast abscess, will occur. A breast abscess is an exceptionally painful walled-off pocket of pus that cannot be treated effectively by antibiotics unless the pus is drained. Ultrasound may help diagnose a breast abscess. Usually, a breast abscess results from inadequately treated mastitis.

• **Take the antibiotic your doctor prescribes for the full course of therapy, even if you feel much better after a few days.** Mastitis should be treated for ten to fourteen days to be sure the infection is thoroughly eradicated and that an abscess doesn't occur. A number of antibiotics can be used to treat mastitis successfully. Recurrences do occur when the wrong antibiotic has been used, when the infection is treated for less than ten days, or when medication doses are taken irregularly. Although most antibiotics used to treat mastitis are compatible with breastfeeding, you always should let your baby's doctor know what medication you are taking since some of it will pass into your breast milk.

• **Rest in bed as much as possible for a day or two.** Take my word for it, mastitis is a miserable illness. Being run-down probably made you more susceptible to infection in the first place. Now is the time to pamper yourself so you can get well before attempting to resume all your responsibilities. Enlist all the help you can from your partner, extended family, friends, neighbors, or members of your church. For at least two days, arrange to be relieved of all your duties, except breastfeeding your baby, of course, and pumping if necessary. Try to find other caretakers to supervise older children, perform household chores, and care for the baby when you are not nursing. Don't try to be a martyr.

Instead, learn to ask for what you need and to be a gracious receiver of care from others. With full-blown mastitis, it can take thirty-six to forty-eight hours before you notice significant improvement in terms of breast pain, fever, and body aches. Call your doctor if you aren't feeling much better within two days.

• **Drink plenty of fluids, especially if you have a fever.** Fever markedly increases your fluid requirement and places you at risk for becoming dehydrated. Dehydration not only makes you feel worse, but it can reduce your milk supply. Normally, nursing mothers should drink an eight-ounce glass of water or nutritious beverage with every feeding. During an illness, you will need to drink additional fluids. If your appetite is diminished, at least try to consume liberal quantities of juice, soups, and gelatin. If your mouth feels dry or your urine is infrequent or dark, you are probably somewhat dehydrated.

• **You will probably require pain medication the first two days of your illness.** Ask your doctor for a prescription if necessary. Ibuprofen is a good choice for over-the-counter pain medication, because only minimal amounts of this pain reliever are excreted into milk. Furthermore, the anti-inflammatory effects of ibuprofen help reduce the breast inflammation that accompanies mastitis. Rarely, prescription pain medication is necessary for a day or two. Fortunately, after twenty-four to forty-eight hours of antibiotic therapy, the breast discomfort usually improves dramatically.

• **Nurse more often, especially on the affected side, to keep your breasts well drained.** Failure to remove milk from the breasts at regular intervals can make a woman more susceptible to a breast infection. Similarly, leaving the breasts full and engorged during a bout of mastitis makes it more difficult to cure the infection and increases the risk that a breast abscess will form. Although a woman with a breast infection should try to keep her breasts well drained, this can be difficult to do for several reasons. First, the pain of mastitis can make a woman postpone feedings or limit nursing on the infected side. Second, breast inflammation can interfere with normal milk flow, leading to swelling, firmness, and engorgement in one or more areas. So the very thing that's needed—effective milk removal—is more difficult than usual to accomplish. Try to nurse as often as possible. It will probably be more comfortable to start feedings on the good side until the letdown reflex is triggered. Once milk is flowing, move your baby to the infected breast until it is drained well.

• **If nursing your baby on the infected breast is extremely painful, or if you are having trouble getting milk to flow, it might be necessary for you to use a hospital-grade electric breast pump for a couple of days.** Some mothers with mastitis find pumping to be more comfortable than nursing their baby. You can use the pump to regularly remove milk from the infected breast while continuing to nurse on the good side. Pumping will help improve emptying and maintain your milk supply in the infected breast until you are able to tolerate full breastfeeding again. To locate an electric breast pump–rental station near you, see the Resource List, page 446.

• **Consider requesting a prescription for synthetic oxytocin nasal spray if your milk isn't letting-down.** When a woman has mastitis, her milk ejection reflex may not work as well. Not only does pain inhibit milk let-down, but the breast inflammation caused by mastitis also impedes milk flow. Some women report improved milk flow when they use synthetic oxytocin nasal spray before pumping or nursing (see page 231 for information on how to obtain the medication). The potential benefits of the medication must be weighed against the expense. If the infected breast is very engorged and you cannot get milk to flow with the measures described on the preceding pages, then synthetic oxytocin is worth a try.

• **To prevent getting a recurrence of mastitis, search for and eliminate any risk factors that might be present.** All too often, doctors treat mastitis solely by prescribing an antibiotic. Many women suffer recurrent bouts of the illness without ever figuring why they are at increased risk. In my opinion, searching for risk factors that predispose a woman to mastitis is an essential part of the treatment plan. In addition to the more common risk factors listed below, I have found that mastitis often follows some type of vigorous upper-body activity, such as jumping rope, scrubbing a floor, vacuuming, raking, mowing the lawn, rowing a boat, lifting and moving things, or doing jumping jacks. I suspect that vigorous upper-body exercise in women with heavy, milk-laden breasts causes leakage of milk into the breast tissues. Such leakage produces inflammation, which can progress to infection. While I'm not suggesting that a breastfeeding woman *never* exercise or attend an aerobics class, I do think she should only participate in such activities after first nursing and while wearing a good support bra. I have encountered some women who were plagued with recurrent bouts of mastitis that occurred in relation to vigorous upper-body exercise. Most of these women decided to discontinue the mastitis-provoking activities until they weaned their babies.

Factors That Predispose Women to Mastitis

- Infrequent or ineffective removal of milk from the breast
- Cracked or chronically sore nipples
- Fatigue, exhaustion
- Overabundant milk supply
- Trauma caused by infant, especially teething/biting
- Vigorous upper-body exercise
- A constrictive bra (especially underwire types)

Overabundant Milk Supply

I have made so many references in this book to low milk supply that you might wonder whether anyone really produces excessive quantities of milk. While many more women seek help for too little milk than for too much milk, an overabundant supply is a frustrating problem for some women. Obviously Mother Nature prefers to closely match a woman's supply to her infant's need. The process of lactation is not efficient when a woman's body makes surplus milk that isn't needed by her infant. I don't know why some women produce extra, unwanted milk, while others fail to produce enough. Although low-milk problems often result from improper breastfeeding management, overabundant milk production is usually unrelated to a mother's breastfeeding practices.

I am convinced that women vary widely in their capacity to produce milk. In earlier times, some mothers with overabundant supplies sought employment as wet nurses. I suspect that an overabundant supply results from a triple combination: exceptional production capacity, a brisk and well-conditioned milk ejection reflex, and a superefficient nursing baby. While generally preferable to low milk, the problem can still be a source of frustration and discomfort for both mother and baby. Women with an overabundant milk supply often voice the following complaints:

- Breasts that easily become uncomfortably engorged
- Dramatic (sometimes painful) sensations of the milk ejection reflex
- Chronic leaking milk

- Repeated clogged ducts
- One or more breast infections
- Rapid weight loss due to the high metabolic demands of producing so much milk

As if the problems that an overabundant supply cause a mother aren't troubling enough, having superabundant milk can also be frustrating for babies. Many women are more upset by the distress their overproduction seems to cause their infant, including the following:

- Choking and sputtering when milk lets down
- Excessive gas and abdominal discomfort from overeating
- Rapid weight gain
- Inability to enjoy "comfort nursing" since the baby obtains unwanted milk even when trying to nurse to sleep
- Frustration with breastfeeding that leads to early weaning or a nursing strike (abrupt refusal to nurse; see pages 262–265)

Fortunately, the problem of overabundant milk usually improves with time. The baby may "grow into" his milk supply as he gets a little older. Furthermore, the supply tends to gradually diminish since the mother's breasts don't get well drained. Ordinary life stresses like returning to work, becoming ill, skipping meals, or suffering a breast infection all can cause milk production to decrease.

Meanwhile, you can try some of the following strategies to help your baby enjoy nursings better, to prevent the risk of clogged ducts and mastitis, and to gradually reduce your milk production:

- Position your baby so that his head and throat are higher than your nipple. By nursing "uphill," he will be better able to control your overly fast flow of milk. Use the football hold and lean back to elevate your baby's head. Or, try the cradle hold, with your baby elevated higher than usual, while you lean back in a recliner.
- If your let-down is causing your baby to choke and/or cry, temporarily interrupt the feeding until your milk stops spraying. Then allow your baby to resume feeding after the milk flow has slowed.
- The two key ways to reduce milk production are to remove less milk at each nursing and to remove milk at less-frequent inter-

vals. To prolong the interval at which milk is removed, you can try nursing on only one breast at each feeding, alternating the breast you use. Using one breast at each nursing might also make feedings go more smoothly for your baby. After the initial rapid flow tapers, your baby may be able to comfortably handle the milk volume from a single breast. However, the unsuckled breast may be left uncomfortably full and place you at risk for mastitis. If you decide to use one breast, you probably will need to express sufficient milk from the opposite breast to relieve some of the pressure and keep you comfortable. Eventually, the milk supply should decrease.

Another way to modify feedings is to allow your baby to nurse from both breasts at each feeding, but to avoid emptying either side well. The first breast will be left softer than the second, but neither will be thoroughly drained. You'll want to nurse at the first breast for at least five to seven minutes after your milk lets-down to assure that your baby gets ample hindmilk. Once he switches to the second breast, some mixing of foremilk and hindmilk already will have occurred. What isn't desired is to have your baby take only the watery foremilk from each breast.

• Some women with overabundant milk choose to obtain a hospital-grade electric breast pump so they can soften their breasts whenever the need arises. They simply freeze their excess milk for later use—perhaps after they return to work.

• Where feasible, supermilk producers can collect and donate their surplus milk to a Donor Milk Bank (see Resource List, page 451). This is an option available in Denver since we have a large distributing Mothers' Milk Bank. Being able to provide extra milk for infants in need serves to reframe a woman's "problem" and turn it into a positive.

Note: As unlikely as it seems right now, you actually can go from too much to too little milk in only a few days. I have seen this happen a number of times when women started skipping nursings and leaving their breasts engorged. Remember, extra milk is preferable to insufficient milk!

Nursing Strike

Occasionally, a breastfed infant starts refusing to nurse without apparent explanation. *Nursing strike* is an apt term used to describe this sudden breastfeeding refusal. It occurs most commonly between four and seven months of age. In a typical case of nursing strike, a mother will report that when she offers her breast, her baby cries, arches his back, pulls away, and essentially rejects the breast. He may latch on for a few seconds, but does not suckle for any appreciable time. The baby usually accepts a bottle well and is content to bottle-feed. Faced with this frustrating behavior in her infant, it is not uncommon for a woman to give up nursing and explain that her baby "weaned himself." Other women are distressed at the prospect of not being able to continue breastfeeding and seek advice from their doctor or a breastfeeding counselor. With prompt intervention, nursing strikes can often be remedied, thus preserving the opportunity for a woman to continue to breastfeed.

At first consideration, a nursing strike appears to occur suddenly and without obvious reason. Upon more careful examination, however, I find that one or more contributing factors are usually present. Some infants begin their distressing behavior during the course of an upper-respiratory infection. A stuffy nose can create distress when a baby tries to breath while nursing. Or an ear infection can be more painful when a baby reclines to nurse. The refusal behavior sometimes coincides with teething and may be the result of discomfort while sucking. I'm also aware of a few instances of nursing strike that started after a teething infant bit his unsuspecting mother and caused her to shriek in surprise and pain—which, in turn, startled and upset the baby. A busy mother may find she has been hurrying feedings to get to other activities instead of permitting her infant leisurely nursings. Another baby may go on strike because he has been frustrated by an overabundant milk supply or an overactive milk ejection reflex. The common theme in these examples is some type of unpleasantness associated with breastfeeding.

While any number of reasons—recognized or overlooked—may contribute to a nursing strike, I have come to conclude that *many* cases also involve a gradually *dwindling milk supply*. After the early months of frequent, round-the-clock nursing, many mothers begin giving supplemental bottles and spending increased periods of time separated from their babies. A mother's milk supply may decline after her baby starts sleeping through the night, causing her breasts to go eight, ten, or twelve hours without emptying. At first a mother may not even be aware that her supply is less abundant or that her baby is becoming frustrated with the increased effort to obtain milk. Without consciously planning it, she actually may have started weaning, and her baby may decide to escalate the process abruptly through a nursing strike. Thus, I believe the common denominator of nursing strikes all too often is low milk supply. When diminished milk flow is coupled with a baby who has been exposed to the ease of bottle-feeding, abrupt refusal to nurse can result. Low milk volume and bottle use aren't always to blame, however. Other cases have been described in which the mother had an abundant milk supply and the baby was being fully breastfed.

If your baby is manifesting a nursing strike, seek consultation with a lactation consultant or other breastfeeding specialist. You also should let your baby's doctor know that your infant is experiencing this feeding problem. The physician will want to make sure that no illness is present to explain your baby's behavior and that the infant continues to receive sufficient nourishment during the period of breast refusal. Effective treatment of a nursing strike involves three key strategies:

1. First, try to get your baby to return to breastfeeding by attempting to nurse him in his sleep. Fortunately, most infants will cooperate, although some may cry upon awakening and finding themselves at the breast. Eventually, your baby may awaken and continue to nurse without protest. Some mothers have found that they could keep their child nursing by walking with the infant. Bottle-feeding should be avoided if at all possible. If your baby requires supplemental milk, several options are available for providing it without using bottles (see chapters 4 and 5, pages 114–116 and 167–168). If regular bottle-feeding is inevitable, try to have another caretaker give the bottle. If breastfeeding frustrates your baby because it does not satisfy his hunger, you may be able to woo him back to the breast beginning with "comfort nursing" after he has been given supplemental formula to curb his appetite.

2. Eliminate any unpleasantness associated with nursings and remedy any exacerbating factors. If your baby has a cold, nurse your infant after clearing the nasal passages with a bulb syringe. If you think an ear infection could be present, have your child checked and treated. Attempt to nurse in subdued, quiet surroundings to minimize distractions, and let your baby take all the time he wants. If discomfort from teething seems to be contributing to diffi-culty nursing, soothe your baby's gums with a cold teething ring.

3. **Evaluate your milk supply and, if low, attempt to increase your milk production.** Even if your supply was normal prior to the nursing strike, your milk can rapidly decrease if your baby refuses to nurse. Once the original problem is compounded by low milk, it will be even harder to get your baby back to breastfeeding. So, unless your infant immediately can be enticed to resume breast-feeding at the normal frequency and for a suitable duration, you will need to obtain an effective breast pump to maintain (and increase) your milk supply. While hand expression and manual pumps prove highly effective for some women, in general, I recom-mend an efficient hospital-grade electric pump to regularly empty your breasts and keep your milk production up until your baby is nursing well once again.

Pumping can create a potential dilemma since you can't predict when your baby might be willing to cooperate and nurse. It's pos-sible you will finish emptying your breasts with the pump just when your baby acts like he might be willing to breastfeed. On the other hand, if you leave your breasts unemptied while waiting expectantly for your baby to suckle, your milk supply may dwindle. I would advise putting your baby to breast every couple of hours (preferably with the infant asleep or drowsy at first). Then, you should pump both breasts immediately after your nurs-ing attempt to assure they are well drained.

With sufficient reassurance, a strong commitment to nursing, and the temporary discontinuation of bottle-feeding, a nursing strike often can be overcome. Increasing your milk if it is low and nursing your baby in his sleep are your best strategies.

Maternal Medications and Breastfeeding

Nursing mothers naturally are concerned about the potential dangers of medications they take being transmitted to their babies through their breast milk. In fact, all drugs are excreted to some degree in breast milk, and medications should not be taken indis-criminately by nursing mothers. Many factors have an influence on the amount of drug that will be transferred into milk, including the dosage amount and dosing schedule, how the drug is taken (e.g., oral versus by injection), the physical and chemical properties of the drug, the amount of breast milk the baby drinks, how often the baby is fed, and how long the drug is needed. Fortunately, most medications taken by breastfeeding women are safe for nursing infants, because the amount of drug present in breast milk usually is minimal.

However, lack of information about drug excretion into breast milk frequently has resulted in misconceptions and exaggerations about the risks to the infant. Often, nursing mothers are mistakenly advised to wean their infants when the medication prescribed for them actually would have been compatible with breastfeeding. Or, a mother may decide not to take a medication she needs because she is worried that it could have a harmful effect on her baby.

Some drugs may cause temporary side effects in infants when they are passed into breast milk. One study examined adverse reactions in more than eight hundred infants who were breastfed by women taking medications. Although no major adverse effects requiring medical attention occurred in any of the infants, about 10 percent of women reported minor adverse reactions in their infants. Here are the most common reactions according to drug category: antibiotics caused diarrhea; prescription pain medication caused drowsiness; antihistamines caused irritability; and sedatives, antidepressants, and antiseizure medications caused drowsiness. In all cases, the benefits of breastfeeding were felt to outweigh the temporary, minor effects of a maternal medication on the infant.

A few drugs that are necessary to protect a mother's health are too toxic for breastfed babies. Included among those that are considered incompatible with breastfeeding are cancer chemotherapy medications, drugs that suppress the immune system, and lithium, used to treat bipolar disease (although some women have breastfed while taking lithium, without apparent harm to their infants). Other drugs, such as some antidepressants, may also be of concern.

In the past, many prescription drugs were said to be unsafe for nursing mothers simply because little information was available about how much of the drugs entered the breast milk. As medical knowledge about the topic has increased, many drugs that were previously considered to be contraindicated during breastfeeding are now considered to be compatible with nursing. Because knowledge about drug excretion in breast milk changes so rapidly, it is a good idea to get a second opinion whenever you are advised that breastfeeding is not possible with a certain medication. Ask the physician prescribing the drug, as well as your baby's doctor, before concluding that weaning is necessary. Often pharmacists, especially those at drug information centers, have the most up-to-date information. The Drug Information Service sponsored by the University of California at San Diego will answer inquiries from the public about medication use during breastfeeding (see Resource List, page 448). If the drug being prescribed poses a risk to nursing babies, the pharmacist might be able to suggest a safer alternative. The American Academy of Pediatrics (AAP) publishes and regularly updates an excellent reference for health professionals about the transfer of drugs and chemicals into human milk. Ask your doctor if he or she has a copy of the latest version of this AAP publication. Other helpful guidelines for breastfeeding women requiring medications are outlined below.

• Whenever your doctor prescribes a medicine for you, ask whether it is safe for breastfeeding. Whenever you are taking a drug, notify your baby's doctor and observe your infant carefully for possible side effects. Report these to your baby's doctor at once.

• Take only necessary and effective medications. When choosing over-the-counter drugs, avoid multi-ingredient medications to treat minor symptoms.

• When feasible, it is generally preferable to take a medication right after nursing your baby. For most drugs, the peak concentration in breast milk will usually be reached between feedings if the medication is taken right after nursing.

• When once-daily medications are prescribed, the dose can be taken just prior to your baby's longest sleep interval at night. Most long-acting drugs, however, will maintain a fairly constant level without identifiable peaks.

• If you are nursing and must take a medication that is believed to pose a risk to your infant (such as a radioactive compound), you can temporarily interrupt breastfeeding without permanently weaning. A rental electric breast pump can be used to express your milk at regular intervals and maintain your supply until you have completed the course of therapy and can safely nurse once again. (See Resource List, page 446, to locate a pump-rental station near you.)

• When you have advance knowledge of the need to take a medication (e.g., for elective surgery), you can pump extra milk and freeze it prior to beginning your course of therapy. Your baby can be fed the stored breast milk while nursing is interrupted. Of course, you will have to pump and discard your milk while taking the drug that is unsafe for breastfeeding.

I cannot emphasize strongly enough that recreational drugs must NOT be taken by nursing women, both because of the very real risk such drugs pose to a baby as well as the danger that exists when a mother attempts to care for her infant while she is high. Several infant fatalities have occurred when babies ingested tainted milk from their nursing mothers who used illicit drugs.

Some Drugs That Should Not Be Taken During Breastfeeding*

Cancer chemotherapy drugs
Drugs that suppress the immune system
Lithium
All illicit drugs
Radioactive drugs (usually taken for diagnostic scans)

*List is not inclusive.

Some Common Drugs That Usually Are Compatible with Breastfeeding*

Acetaminophen
Antibiotics (most)
Antihistamines (most)
Antiseizure medications (most)
Blood pressure medications (many)
Blood thinners (most)
Diuretics (most)
Ibuprofen
Insulin
Over-the-counter medications (most)
Pain medications (most)
Prednisone
Thyroid replacement hormone

*List is not inclusive.

Some Drugs Whose Effects in Breastfed Infants Are Unknown but May Be of Concern*

Antianxiety medications, such as Valium
Antidepressants, such as Prozac, Zoloft
Antipsychotic medications, such as Thorazine
A few antibiotics, including chloramphenicol and ciprofloxacin

*List is not inclusive.

Infant Reactions to Maternally Ingested Foods

While true allergy to mother's milk has never been proved, some breastfed infants react adversely to certain foods consumed by their nursing mothers. Mothers of these babies typically report that their infant becomes fussy three to six hours after the mother has eaten an offending food. It usually takes one to four hours for allergic components of foods to appear in mother's milk. A baby may react within minutes after nursing, but usually within two to four hours. The reaction can continue as long as the offending substance remains in the mother's system and continues to enter her milk. This can be three to four days or longer after eating certain foods.

Common Offending Foods in the Mother's Diet. The most common foods that provoke allergic reactions in nursing infants include milk and other dairy products, wheat, eggs, peanuts, soy, fish, corn, and citrus. Often the food (or foods) the baby reacts to is something the mother eats daily or something she ate frequently during her pregnancy, such as orange juice or a peanut butter sandwich.

Typical Infant Symptoms of Allergy. Common allergic symptoms seen in breastfed babies include skin rashes, red cheeks, vomiting, diarrhea, runny nose, cough or congestion, fussiness, and "colic." Breastfed babies who are fussy due to allergies to foods in the mother's diet tend to be adequately nourished, or even overweight, rather than underweight. As a result of their frequent fussiness and apparent discomfort, their mothers may try to nurse more often and can end up overfeeding their babies.

Not all adverse reactions to foods the mother ingests are true allergies. Babies can be sensitive to foods in other ways than an allergic reaction. For example, babies might be extra fussy and irritable if their mothers consume too many caffeinated drinks, or they can become gassy due to broccoli, onions, or cabbage in the mother's diet. These unfavorable reactions are not true allergic reactions.

Keeping a Food/Behavior Diary. If you think your baby is reacting to something in your diet, discuss this with your child's doctor. You also should start keeping a meticulous food/behavior diary. Record on this daily log what and when you eat, when you nurse your infant, and the time and type of problem behavior observed in your baby. A sample food/behavior diary is shown on page 271. While you are keeping a record, simplify your meals. Try to eat only three food items at a meal. Avoid multiple seasonings and multiple ingredient dishes. By scanning your daily diary, you should be able to track the relationship, if any, between your baby's symptoms and specific foods you eat.

Eliminate Offending Foods. Don't get overzealous and go on a drastic elimination diet. Instead, be a sleuth as you review your diary to determine the most likely offending foods. This kind of detective work often pays off. Usually, only a few foods in your diet cause a problem for your baby. Completely eliminate the one or two most likely offensive foods for at least four to five days—preferably a week. That should be long enough to get the food entirely out of your system. At the end of a week, rechallenge with the particular food to see if your baby's symptoms reappear. Far too many women arbitrarily eliminate foods in hopes of reducing colicky behavior in their baby. I've met breastfeeding women who have restricted their intake to only half a dozen foods in a desperate attempt to improve their baby's symptoms. A drastic elimination diet is only likely to reduce your milk supply and make you feel like a martyr. Women who eliminate major food groups, such as dairy products, from their diets should receive nutrition counseling from a registered dietitian or their physician. Such women may require appropriate supplements to replace essential nutrients in the eliminated foods.

Prevention of Allergies in At-risk Infants. Infants at high risk for allergic disease include those who have a parent, sibling, or other close relative with food allergies, asthma, or eczema. Pro-

Date: ___/___/___   ## DAILY FOOD AND SYMPTOM DIARY

Time Interval	Actual Time	Breastfeeding Duration (Minutes per Feed)	Urine	Stool	Other Infant Intake (Food or Fluid)	Mother's Food & Fluid Intake	Infant Symptoms—Behavior (1–5 scale, see below) Describe physical symptoms (e.g., rash, cough, congestion, runny nose, vomiting, diarrhea)
12–1 am							
1–2 am							
2–3 am							
3–4 am							
4–5 am							
5–6 am							
6–7 am							
7–8 am							
8–9 am							
9–10 am							
10–11 am							
11–12 noon							
12–1 pm							
1–2 pm							
2–3 pm							
3–4 pm							
4–5 pm							
5–6 pm							
6–7 pm							
7–8 pm							
8–9 pm							
9–10 pm							
10–11 pm							
11–12 midnight							
24-Hour Total							

Scale: 1 = asleep   4 = consolable crying
        2 = quiet awake   5 = unconsolable crying
        3 = slightly fussy

longed exclusive breastfeeding has been shown to reduce the likelihood of allergic symptoms in these at-risk infants. Breastfeeding is especially protective if the mother also eliminates the most common allergenic foods mentioned earlier from her diet during pregnancy and as long as she is nursing. Mothers of potentially allergic babies should also rotate their foods, avoiding eating any single food on a daily basis. Try to resist cravings and avoid eating large quantities of one food. You might be able to eat a small amount of an offending food every three or four days, but not every day. Once your baby starts solid foods, discuss with her doctor the plan for introducing new foods, especially allergenic ones like milk, egg, wheat, peanut butter, corn, citrus, and shellfish. If you have a strong family history of allergic disease or believe your baby displays allergic-type symptoms, I suggest you seek consultation with a pediatric allergist or an environmental medicine specialist. Allergic disease can be a chronic, frustrating problem— even a life-threatening one if anaphylaxis (severe allergic reaction with shock and airway obstruction) occurs.

Colicky Behavior in Breastfed Infants

Few things are more distressing to parents than the sound of their own baby crying. Mother Nature intended it this way, to guarantee that well-meaning parents would promptly respond to their baby's needs. Fortunately, by trial and error and good intentions, most parents soon learn to read their baby's cues and thus manage to keep crying to a minimum. Since human milk is the ideal infant food and is so readily digestible, breastfeeding parents often assume that their babies automatically will be content most of the time. But babies have a wide range of temperaments and differing needs. Some are naturally easy and predictable, while others are extrasensitive and more difficult in general. Babies cry an average of one and a half to four hours a day in the first six weeks of life, but any crying can feel like too much when it exceeds a parent's threshold for coping.

Colic is a vague term that describes excessive crying in an otherwise healthy baby for no apparent reason during the first three months of life. No specific cause or treatment has been identified, and parents are typically advised to use comfort measures to cope with the excessive crying until their baby outgrows the problem.

Often, a baby is labeled as being "colicky" (crying without an explanation) when the infant, in fact, has a reason for crying that hasn't been recognized. If your breastfed baby cries excessively without an obvious explanation, consider the following possibilities:

Hunger. When a breastfed baby cries a great deal, the first thing to consider is the possibility of hunger. Neither the number of nursings nor the length of feedings can provide absolute assurance that your baby has gotten enough milk. Many breastfeeding mothers automatically assume that their baby can't be hungry because "I just fed him." But having nursed recently doesn't guarantee that your baby isn't still hungry. Sometimes babies nurse without having latched on correctly or without sucking properly. Sometimes the milk doesn't let-down briskly or a woman doesn't produce enough milk to satisfy the baby. Thus, an infant might "go through the motions" of nursing without actually getting a full feeding.

If your baby cries excessively and you can't figure out why, start with a weight check to be sure he is gaining at an appropriate rate. Don't settle for telephone advice about your baby's "colicky" behavior unless your infant has been weighed within the last week. Time and time again, we have evaluated a breastfed infant referred to the Lactation Program for "colic" only to find that the baby was very underweight and had been crying due to hunger. In the early months of life, you should expect your baby's height and weight percentiles to be proportionate. If your baby's weight is dropping percentiles, his crying might be due to hunger (see chapter 10). Crying due to hunger is usually accompanied by vigorous sucking on a finger, fist, or pacifier and promptly responds to feeding.

Reaction to Maternally Ingested Foods. Allergies and other adverse reactions to maternally ingested foods can produce colicky behavior in breastfed infants as previously described. In addition to fussiness, these babies often have skin rashes, vomiting, diarrhea, congestion, or other symptoms. Irritable, allergic infants often are overweight, since they are put to breast frequently in an attempt to console them. They may become fussy minutes after nursing or a couple of hours later. Frequently, a family history of food sensitivities can be elicited. (See pages 270–271 for how to keep a food/behavior diary to help pinpoint the offending foods in the mother's diet.)

Overactive Let-Down Reflex. As previously noted, some women are blessed with an abundant milk supply and a brisk let-down (see Overabundant Milk Supply, pages 260–262). Their breasts work like precision machines when it comes to feeding time. As soon as the milk ejection reflex is triggered, milk pours from their nipple openings so fast that it's all their baby can do to handle the flow without choking. It's a little like drinking from a fire hydrant, and some babies find it too much of a good thing. As they gulp and sputter their way through a feeding, they may get overwhelmed. Some infants pull off the breast and cry in frustration until the milk stops spraying. Others make valiant attempts to get through a feeding, but end up swallowing excessive amounts of air. This can cause uncomfortable gas and lead to unexplained crying during or after feedings.

If an overactive let-down is causing your baby distress, try expressing some milk before feeding, and put your baby to the breast after milk flow tapers to a manageable level. Or, you can interrupt nursing for a minute or two once the let-down is triggered and wait for the milk to stop spraying. Babies of mothers with overgenerous milk supplies often do better nursing from one breast at a feeding instead of both breasts. This way, they get more hind-milk and a gradually decreasing flow rate.

Gastroesophageal Reflux (GER). The circular muscle that separates the stomach and the esophagus (food pipe) is loose in young infants, so that stomach contents can easily enter the esophagus during or after feedings and be spit up. This condition is known as reflux or gastroesophageal reflux (GER). Reflux is more likely to occur when a baby is lying on his back with a full tummy. Thus, it is not uncommon for a baby to spit up while lying supine for a diaper change after a feeding. In mild cases of reflux, the baby may spit up a lot, but acts content and gains weight appropriately. Usually, by eight to ten months of age, when babies have learned to sit up well and spend more time in a semiupright position, the frequency of spitting decreases.

In a few infants, GER represents a serious problem rather than a benign condition. These babies may be chronically fussy due to the irritation of acid stomach contents in their esophagus, producing heartburn symptoms. Babies with serious reflux often become distressed and irritable during feedings. They may pull away from the breast, cry, arch, act uncomfortable, and refuse to keep nursing even though plenty of milk remains. Occasionally, reflux is severe enough to impede proper growth and cause choking, coughing, pneumonia, or hoarseness.

If your baby has symptoms that sound like reflux, notify her physician. Generally, babies with GER do better with frequent, smaller feedings that avoid overdistension of the stomach. Spitting up can be reduced by frequent burping during feedings and by positioning the baby upright after nursings. Sometimes medication is prescribed to help the stomach empty more rapidly or to reduce the amount of stomach acids. Rarely surgery becomes necessary to remedy the problem.

Infant Colic. Colic, described earlier, occurs in an estimated 10 to 15 percent of all infants, and it is one of the most difficult and frustrating things for new parents to handle. Crying attributed to colic typically is intermittent and intense, often coming in sudden attacks and lasting an hour or more at a time. There usually is a pattern to the crying, which escalates in the evenings, when parents are most depleted and least able to cope with stress. No definite cause of colic has been found, although common theories include a sensitive temperament, an immature digestive system, and excessive intestinal gas. Colic usually peaks around four to six weeks of age and subsides by three months. It occurs in both breastfed and formula-fed infants. Colicky babies are otherwise healthy, well fed, alert and active, appear happy between crying spells, and show no long-term effects of colic.

Colic is not a telephone diagnosis. If your infant cries excessively without explanation, it is essential that your pediatrician examine him and confirm that no medical problem exists (see below). Other parents have found the following strategies to be helpful in reducing infant crying:

• A baby's cry is a distress signal, and crying babies need to be held and comforted. Holding doesn't reinforce crying any more than feeding reinforces hunger. Responding quickly to a baby's crying doesn't "spoil" the infant. Rather, promptly attending to a crying baby teaches the infant to trust her caretakers. This trust relationship becomes the foundation for communication.

• Gentle rhythmic motion, such as rocking or swinging, and soothing words or repetitive singing will tend to diminish crying.

Steady rhythmic sound, like running the vacuum or fan in the next room, may also settle a crying baby.

• Swaddling a distraught infant in a blanket or cuddling him snugly and providing close physical contact will help him feel secure and may diminish crying. A front-pack, carrier, or sling will allow you to hold your infant for long periods without restricting your activities.

• Avoid vigorous bouncing, jiggling, or jostling, crowds, loud noises, or other boisterous activities that may further upset your baby. When your baby starts to fuss, take him into a quiet room with subdued lighting and minimal stimulation.

• Place your baby across your lap tummy-down and pat her back or carry her facedown on your forearm with her legs draped over either side of your elbow. Pat her back with your other hand while walking, rocking side to side, or squatting and standing.

• Try a car ride. Secure your baby in his car seat and go for a short drive. The motion and motor usually lull the baby to sleep. Another strategy is to push your baby around the block in his stroller until he falls asleep.

• Arrange to take a break when you are feeling especially tense and anxious. Just getting outside and walking around your neighborhood or running a short errand while someone else stays with the baby can renew your perspective. Your baby's crying will not seem nearly as nerve-racking to a relief caretaker.

• Take consolation in the knowledge that other parents have survived colic too. Try to remember the crying is no one's fault, the condition is self-limiting, and your baby is otherwise healthy. Never shake an infant, as violent shaking can cause severe brain injury and even death!

Unrecognized Illness. Any time a baby seems extra fussy, consider whether he might be ill. Both extremes of behavior—lethargy or increased irritability—are common signs of illness in young infants. Other possible indicators of infant illness include fever, poor skin color (pale, dusky, grayish), not feeding well or sleeping through feedings, coughing or difficulty breathing, or a rash. The younger the baby, the more concerned you should be. Never hesitate to call your baby's doctor and describe any change in behavior that could signify an illness.

How to Obtain Help for Breastfeeding Problems

Also see chapter 5, pages 169–171.

Physicians. Virtually all physicians believe that human milk is the preferred way to feed babies. Most have heard lectures during their medical training citing the benefits of breastfeeding. The majority of doctors encourage women to nurse their babies, however few are equipped to provide effective counseling to women who experience difficulties with breastfeeding. The management of breastfeeding problems requires a health professional who can spend sufficient time to observe a nursing, who has specialized knowledge about breastfeeding (usually well beyond what was taught in their training), and who has access to breast pumps and other equipment resources. Most physicians lack both the time and the expertise to solve complex breastfeeding difficulties. Fortunately, a growing number of physicians recognize the importance of lactation management and are becoming aware of the referral resources in their community. Thus, more doctors are working in conjunction with lactation consultants and local lactation centers to help women succeed at breastfeeding. A few physicians have acquired additional expertise in the management of breastfeeding problems and have made breastfeeding consultation part of their medical practice.

Many mothers assume that their doctor won't be interested or able to help them overcome a breastfeeding problem. They bypass their doctor and look for help elsewhere. I must discourage this practice because it is unfair to both the physician and the mother-baby pair. I know of several cases where a nursing mother was being counseled by one or more "experts" while the baby's physician remained unaware that his or her patient was having a problem. Often, a breastfeeding difficulty is related to an underlying medical problem in the infant or mother, making physician input essential to the breastfeeding management plan. For example, a poor-feeding baby could have a serious infection, a heart defect, or low blood sugar, among other possibilities. Even if you decide to obtain help from a lactation consultant or other breastfeeding specialist, always make sure that your baby's doctor knows you are having a breastfeeding problem and that he or she concurs with the treatment plan.

Lactation Consultants. A lactation consultant is a breast-feeding specialist whose practice focuses on providing education to breastfeeding women and helping them solve breastfeeding problems. Lactation consultants are prepared to spend the necessary time observing breastfeeding and helping you with correct technique. Commonly known as L.C.'s, many lactation consultants have pursued voluntary certification by the International Board of Lactation Consultant Examiners. These practitioners can be identified by the letters I.B.C.L.C. after their name, which stands for International Board Certified Lactation Consultant. Although other avenues are available for obtaining certification as a lactation consultant, the International Lactation Consultant Association has acknowledged the I.B.C.L.C. as the professional credential for lactation consultants. This credential is granted only to those who meet certain eligibility criteria and pass a certifying examination. Before selecting an international board certified lactation consultant, it's a good idea to inquire about the individual's educational background, professional preparation, and training. People who function in this role include nurses, dietitians, social workers, childbirth educators, and teachers. It's essential that your lactation consultant remains in close communication with your own and your baby's physicians.

To find a lactation consultant near you, contact the International Lactation Consultant Association to obtain a referral or call the Medela Resource Line, which locates breastfeeding consultants by zip code (see Resource List, page 445).

Lactation Nurse Specialists. A growing number of obstetric, neonatal, and pediatric nurses are taking on an expanded nursing role by serving as lactation consultants or lactation nurse specialists in their particular setting. Many of these nurses have earned the I.B.C.L.C. or other type of lactation consultant credential. Others work as breastfeeding specialists without pursuing the I.B.C.L.C. tredentials.

Lactation Centers. Increasingly, hospitals that provide maternity care are offering specialized lactation services for their maternity patients and the nursing mothers in their community. The Lactation Program, which I cofounded and for which I serve as a consultant, has been in continuous existence since 1985. If such a center is available in your area, it represents an ideal place to seek expertise in dealing with a breastfeeding problem. Most lactation centers are staffed by nurse lactation consultants with specialized training in the management of breastfeeding difficulties.

You should expect to pay a consultative fee for breastfeeding services provided by lactation consultants, nurse specialists, and breastfeeding centers. Be sure your own and/or your baby's physician knows you have sought help with breastfeeding, and ask the practitioner who provides your breastfeeding consultation to fully inform your physician about the appointment. Obtaining a physician referral for the visit may increase your chances that your insurance will cover the cost of breastfeeding services.

La Leche League. La Leche League is an excellent source of breastfeeding information and invaluable support (see chapter 2, pages 41–44, chapter 5, page 171, and Resource List, page 446). Accredited leaders are trained to answer telephone inquiries in a sensitive manner, based on La Leche League–approved materials. The emphasis in their telephone counseling is on providing mothers with information and encouragement rather than dispensing "advice." Leaders sometimes make in-home visits to provide direct help with breastfeeding technique. Mothers appropriately are cautioned to notify their baby's or their own physician about all medical concerns. La Leche League is unsurpassed in the number and quality of breastfeeding educational materials and their network of support. La Leche League can also refer you to a physician in your community who is knowledgeable about breastfeeding and is a member of their Medical Associates. However, I must emphasize that La Leche League is *not* a source of medical advice and is not an adequate substitute for proper medical supervision when you or your baby is experiencing a breastfeeding difficulty.

Presently, too many well-intentioned women quit breastfeeding early due to preventable and treatable problems. Only when prenatal, in-hospital, and follow-up maternity services effectively promote and protect breastfeeding will every mother who chooses to nurse her baby be able to succeed in her goal. I foresee and eagerly anticipate the day when all health professionals will be adequately trained in lactation management—not just the merits of human milk—and when specialized breastfeeding services are a routine part of the medical care provided to nursing mothers and babies. Meanwhile, common breastfeeding problems still threaten women's success. Determination and persistence in overcoming lactation difficulties are well worth the effort.

Chapter 8

Working Without Weaning

In the preceding chapters, I have emphasized that ideal infant nutrition consists of an exclusive diet of human milk for about six months, followed by the gradual introduction of solid foods. Continued breastfeeding is recommended throughout the baby's first year, and thereafter as long as is mutually desired. I have explained that successful breastfeeding is best fostered when mothers and babies are kept in close proximity and when babies are allowed to nurse at will. Yet, mothers of young children are entering the workforce in unprecedented numbers, and most of these women endure lengthy, daily separations from their little ones. Today, whether by choice or necessity, more than half of mothers of infants under a year are employed. When their all-too-short maternity leave passes all too quickly, many new mothers find themselves forced to choose between what they know is best for their baby and what is mandated by their daily circumstances.

I have been one of those women—caught in the awkward paradox between idealized recommendations and my personal reality. I write this chapter with enormous empathy for parents like myself who have been torn between genuine devotion to their baby and seemingly inextricable commitments in the world of work. In my own case, long-term breastfeeding became one of many painful casualties of my work demands—not just once, but four times over. The purpose of this chapter is to help women who desire to breastfeed, and who contemplate being employed, to explore their options for continuing to nurse their babies while working outside the home. Specific strategies will also be outlined to enable concerned partners, relatives, child care workers, and employers to support employed breastfeeding women more effectively. I strongly believe that national breastfeeding rates cannot be raised until we stop viewing these concerns as mere personal dilemmas faced by a few individuals and instead accept them as broad societal issues.

The Impact of Employment on Breastfeeding Success

Many women attempt to combine employment and breastfeeding, and some enjoy remarkable success. Others meet with frustration and disappointment due to lack of support, lack of pumping facilities, lack of time, lack of energy, and eventually lack of milk. Women who intend to return to work after delivery begin breastfeeding at about the same rates as women who do not expect to work outside the home. However, women who return to work while still breastfeeding encounter unique challenges that can make it more difficult for them to reach their breastfeeding goals. While continued breastfeeding certainly is possible for employed women, it is by no means easy. But even women who face daunting obstacles, such as doctors, nurses, flight attendants, factory workers, waitresses, teachers, field hands, road flaggers, and performers, have managed to find workable solutions. The best advice is simply to give it a try. Don't assume that breastfeeding won't be possible under your particular circumstances.

If you are considering combining breastfeeding and working, you will want to equip yourself with practical information, the support of your employer and coworkers, the cooperation of your child care provider, the encouragement of your partner, an effective pump and a place to use it, a cooler to store your milk, a sense of humor, an iron will, and a flexible baby. It takes a big commitment, but I'm confident you will discover that it certainly is well worth the effort.

With each of my babies, I returned to school or work while still nursing. My first child, Peter, was born while I was a pre-med student in college. I had to return to school a week after giving birth. I deliberately squeezed all my classes together between 8:00 A.M. and 1:00 P.M. Monday through Saturday to avoid any prolonged absences. Unfortunately, in those days, I knew nothing about the importance of expressing milk or how to do it. My plan wasn't ideal, but it was workable. I would nurse Peter just before leaving and immediately upon returning. The baby-sitter gave him a bottle of formula in my absence. Of course, my breasts got uncomfortably full in the six-hour (counting commuting time) interval between feedings. If I had known to express my milk mid-morning, I could have obtained breast milk to feed Peter while I was gone. Expressing also would have helped me keep up my milk supply. Nevertheless, I was able to nurse for more than five months until I entered medical school.

Paige, my second child, was born at the beginning of my second year of medical school. I had placed an ad seeking a baby-sitter near the hospital campus and, miraculously, found a capable woman right across the street. Although I had to return to classes when Paige was only a few days old, I brought her to school with me each day and was able to go to the baby-sitter's house periodically to nurse. By this time, I had learned about expressing milk and occasionally used hand expression to empty my breasts when I couldn't nurse. Bolstered by experience, I breastfed with increased confidence and seldom missed a feeding.

I was a fourth-year medical student when my third baby, Tricie, was born. This time, I was assertative enough to request that my schedule be rearranged to allow for a much-coveted maternity leave. For ten glorious weeks, I was inseparable from my new baby and nursed her exclusively, appreciating for the first time the privilege of unrestricted breastfeeding. Then, all too soon, it was time to return to my hospital duties. Although I tried to empty my breasts regularly using hand expression, I found it difficult to adhere to a suitable pumping schedule because I was on a clinical rotation that afforded few breaks. Once I resumed taking night call at the hospital, my stress level soared. With three children under four years, I wasn't getting any rest at home either. My milk supply gradually declined and the frequency of breastfeeding diminished as I struggled to keep all my commitments to others.

Few things are harder than having a baby while doing a medical internship. I spent my entire fourth pregnancy in a state of profound exhaustion. I had expected to be permitted only two weeks off, but I actually was granted four. The first day I returned to work, I was on call and didn't come home for thirty-six hours. Little Heather abruptly had to learn to drink from a bottle, while I attempted in vain to express my milk every three hours. The hospital had an electric breast pump (primitive by today's standards), as well as some now outdated hand pumps for mothers of premature infants. However, no facilities were available for breastfeeding employees. I had no idea where I would store any milk that I expressed, since the idea of handling a "body fluid" at the workplace was not yet accepted. I didn't know anyone else who had pumped and saved their milk. No one asked or knew about my plan to continue breastfeeding, and I didn't solicit any help, although I sure could have used it! Not knowing what else to do, I retreated to a private restroom every time I needed to empty my breasts. With no pump or special equipment, I simply hand expressed into a paper cup. Invariably, my beeper would go off and interrupt me before I was finished. This only accentuated the intense conflict I felt between meeting the needs of my own baby and the needs of the hospitalized children in my care. I felt guilty and selfish about my desire to breastfeed, convinced that I somehow had relinquished my right to nurse when I had committed to an internship. Since I was usually too swamped to eat lunch and I didn't know what else to do with my expressed milk, I drank the cup contents before exiting the restroom. You might guess correctly that breastfeeding was a bittersweet experience this time.

There's a saying in pediatrics, "You keep having children until you get it right." With my fifth child, Mark, I was determined to get breastfeeding right. This baby arrived on the last day of my residency. For the first time on my professional journey, no formal educational training program awaited me. I decided to make breastfeeding my high priority. This time, I resolved not to accept any commitments that might jeopardize breastfeeding. Determined to be present for every nursing, I stayed home for two months before starting to teach a few classes at the University of Colorado School of Medicine. When Mark was five months old, I accepted a half-time academic appointment. I found a baby-sitter a few blocks from the hospital and nursed before going to work and upon returning. By the time Mark was a year old, I was working full-time and still breastfeeding. I ended up nursing well over two years without ever giving a bottle or a drop of formula!

Looking back on my experiences, I am disappointed about some of the choices I made and the high price I paid to return to work too early. If I knew then what I know today, I no doubt would have been able to breastfeed longer after returning to school/work. More importantly, however, I would have delayed the return to work until my breastfeeding success was assured. On the other hand, I am extremely grateful to have been able to nurse my babies as I did under the circumstances I had. I especially count it a privilege to have been able to breastfeed my last baby the full natural course. Today, a breastfeeding woman who returns to work still faces many challenges. But she is more likely than I was to have accurate information, efficient breast pumps, corporate support, and like-minded peers to help her achieve her breastfeeding goal.

The Advantages of Continuing to Breastfeed During Employment

Considering how harried most mothers feel when they work outside the home, it's understandable that breastfeeding women often ask: "Is it really worth the effort to continue nursing?" Only you can make that decision for yourself and your baby, but in my own case, the answer was always an unwavering *yes*! Some of the advantages women have identified include:

• **Improved infant health.** It is clearly to your baby's advantage to be fed human milk for as long as possible, thereby continuing to receive optimal nutrition. In addition, the immune properties in human milk help your baby resist disease and reduce the chances that she will become ill. This is even more important if your baby is in day care since children in day care suffer more infections.

• **Fewer work absences due to infant illness.** Employed mothers who are able to continue nursing will enjoy an added benefit that accompanies a healthier baby—less absenteeism. Few employed mothers experience the luxury of taking off work when they are ill. Instead, they usually drag themselves to the office even when they are feeling crummy so they can use their sick days when their baby gets ill and can't go to day care. Continuing to breastfeed helps decrease the likelihood that you will have to miss work due to illness in your baby.

• **Improved personal health and well-being.** Continuing to breastfeed after becoming employed allows you to reap the maternal health benefits of nursing. Women who breastfeed generally return to their prepregnant weight sooner, have delayed return of menstrual periods, have lower rates of premenopausal breast cancer and ovarian cancer, and a reduced risk of hip fractures later in life.

• **Feeling more connected to your baby during the workday.** Pumping your milk during the workday can help you feel closer and more connected to your baby during the time the two of you are separated. As your breasts swell with milk during the passing hours, you experience a powerful physical reminder of your bond to your baby. The ambivalence most women feel when they leave their baby with a substitute caretaker can be tempered by leaving a part of yourself with your baby each day—your expressed breast milk.

• **Periodic breaks that restore your perspective.** There's nothing like job pressures and the constant turmoil of any workplace to warp your perspective. For eight hours or more each day, your universe tends to shrink to the walls of your office or the hassles of your organization. What a privilege to be able to take periodic lactation breaks that refocus your attention on your larger world— your precious child and family and your "lifework" as a parent.

• **The opportunity to nurse your baby when you are together.** While few employed mothers realistically can enjoy unrestricted nursing throughout the workday, they have the option of resuming breastfeeding each time they are reunited with their babies. The special intimacy of the nursing relationship makes mother-baby reunions extra meaningful after a separation. Your regular absence during the workday is a very real loss to your baby. How sad that many infants not only must endure their mother's routine absence, but they must abruptly relinquish breastfeeding as well. While drinking expressed breast milk is not equivalent to unrestricted breastfeeding, maintaining your milk supply assures that your baby can continue to breastfeed when you are home and receive your expressed milk in your absence.

Preparation for Returning to Work While Breastfeeding

Successfully combining breastfeeding and working should actually begin long before your first day on the job. There are many things you can do during your maternity leave that will improve your chances of continuing to breastfeed after returning to work. Naturally, the more prepared you are, the more confident you will be.

Focus on the Optimal Initiation of Breastfeeding

I find that many prospective parents who anticipate returning to work after delivery are convinced that breastfeeding will proceed uneventfully during their maternity leave. They assume that everything will go well and that all they need to learn is how to use a breast pump at the workplace. The truth is that early breastfeeding problems plague working women at least as often as other mothers. Few things are more discouraging than getting off to a rocky start nursing and then having to return to work before breastfeeding is well established. It is much more difficult to preserve breastfeeding during mother-infant separations when one or more problems are present than when the initiation of breastfeeding has gone smoothly.

- It may sound simplistic, but my first piece of advice for preparing to continue breastfeeding after returning to work is to acquire as much information as possible before you deliver. This means attending (preferably with your partner, prospective babysitter, or other support person) a prenatal class that covers the breastfeeding basics that every parent needs to know. In addition, you will want to acquire specific information about pumping and storing expressed breast milk. One advantage to learning about various pumping options prior to delivery is that you may be able to obtain a personal pump or the collection kits for a rental electric pump while you are in the hospital.
- Next, I urge you to use your brief hospital stay to optimize your early breastfeeding experiences and to prepare for nursing your baby successfully at home (see chapter 4). Ideally, you will be able to nurse your baby shortly after delivery and to room-in with your infant. You should request individualized bedside assistance from the nursing staff to help you position your baby correctly to

nurse. Plan to feed your infant on demand, including throughout the night, and avoid giving your baby a pacifier for at least the first several weeks.

• Early follow-up after hospital discharge should be your next strategy to assure the best possible start breastfeeding during the early weeks at home. Insist that your baby be seen within forty-eight hours of discharge and, if you are having any problems, request to be referred to a lactation consultant for additional help. Once your baby is clearly thriving and you are confident that breastfeeding is well established, you can turn your attention to some of the details of milk collection and storage (see pages 304–307).

Delay Your Return to Work for as Long as Possible

If you already are employed and plan to return to work after your baby is born, give thoughtful consideration to the length of your maternity leave. I know all too well what it feels like to reluctantly go back before you are physically and emotionally prepared. You can't possibly imagine how you will feel when your precious newborn is placed in your arms. And you can't accurately predict whether you or your baby will have medical complications that make you wish you had a longer recovery period. Avoid making a firm commitment in advance about when you will return to work. It's safest to request more time than you think you will need or ask for a range of time (e.g., sixteen to twenty weeks). In general, the longer you can take, the better. Four months is better than three months. Ten weeks is better than eight weeks. Six weeks is better than four. Don't be afraid to ask for more time than you imagine will be granted. You just might get what you ask for, and you certainly won't be offered more time than you request.

A health professional in a hospital's newborn intensive care unit, who daily worked with parents of high-risk infants, subsequently gave birth to premature twins who were being cared for in the nursery where she was employed. As her maternity leave was approaching its end, she realized she was not yet ready to return to work. Her babies were just learning to nurse, and she felt she needed more time with them at this important transition. When we discussed her predicament, she felt she had no options to extend her leave. I pointed out that her own experience as the mother of premature infants in this particular nursery would, no doubt, make her more effective in her professional role than ever before. I

Delay your return to work for as long as feasible after delivery to get the best possible start with breastfeeding.

suggested that employees often are granted educational leave and a stipend to obtain such valuable training experience! I also reasoned that the maternity leave for premature twins ought to be longer than for a single healthy baby. I didn't tell her what to say or do, but I left her feeling entitled to more time and convinced that her personal experience would make her a more desirable employee in the long run. The next time I saw her, she was beaming. She had asked for and been granted an additional three weeks off!

No one else will put your baby's needs first if you don't. Employers and coworkers view your absence mostly in terms of how it affects them. I recall one woman who *resigned* from her job when she left for maternity leave. Refusing to believe she really wasn't returning, her employer sent her flowers after she delivered her baby, with an accompanying note that read, "Hurry back!"

Don't be seduced by such appeals. Keep your own family your highest priority. And don't be afraid to ask, ask, ask.

Speaking of asking, another woman described her intense ambivalence about returning to her full-time position after the birth of her first baby. Deciding she had nothing to lose and a lot to gain, she boldly approached her boss with a seemingly outrageous request. She asked to work only four days a week (thirty-two hours) and to be paid her full salary. Much to her amazement, her boss barely hesitated before granting her request and acknowledging, "You're worth it to me."

Become Familiar with Milk Expression

In much earlier times, breastfeeding babies and their nursing mothers were inseparable. Women simply brought their babies to their place of work and nursed on demand as they went about their daily responsibilities. Babies were "worn" in slings and carriers on their mothers' bodies, and breastfeeding was so natural and so expected that a nursing baby was not viewed as disruptive to a woman's work. Whether engaged in agricultural duties or laboring at handcrafts, periodic nursing breaks were a routine part of a woman's workday.

Following the industrial revolution, gainful employment largely moved from the homestead to an external work site. Today, employed mothers may be separated from their babies during regular work hours, plus the additional time required to commute to their workplace. Too few employed mothers in the United States have accessible, affordable on-site day care arrangements that make it feasible for them to periodically nurse their babies throughout the workday. Instead, most working nursing mothers are forced to maintain lactation by using a breast pump to express their milk at regular intervals during the workday.

If you anticipate going to work while you are still breastfeeding, chances are you will need to use a breast pump. I advise you to become familiar with pumping options as early as possible (preferably prenatally) and to begin expressing milk while you are home on maternity leave. You will want to be thoroughly familiar with milk expression before you return to work. By practicing in advance, you can condition your milk ejection reflex to be triggered by pumping. Your first days on the job probably will be difficult enough without the extra stress of trying to figure out how to use a breast pump on a time-restricted break.

Some women are blessed with an abundant milk supply and a brisk milk ejection reflex that makes them successful expressing milk with any pump, or even with hand expression. In general, however, I strongly recommend that employed women plan to use a hospital-grade rental electric breast pump whenever possible. A rental electric pump with a double collection system allows you to drain both breasts at once, thus saving you valuable time. Most women find these pumps to be the most comfortable and efficient means of expressing milk. The faster and easier you can express, the more likely you will be able to comply with the required schedule of pumping.

If you cannot obtain a hospital-grade rental electric pump, then look into the smaller electric models, the battery-operated pumps, and the manual pumps. Even if you have no pump, you can still empty your breasts with hand expression. This is the method I used when I had to return to work while nursing. Ideally, you should arrange for a consultation with a breastfeeding specialist who can help you outline a pumping regimen that is tailored to your particular situation.

Begin Collecting and Freezing Excess Milk Before Returning to Work

Theoretically, it is possible to pump at work each day the precise amount of milk that your baby will need to drink during your absence the following day. You can leave each day's chilled expressed milk with your baby's caretaker to be fed to your infant the next day. At the minimum, you would need to plan ahead for your first day at work by pumping in advance sufficient milk to be fed to your infant the first day you are separated. The problem with this routine is that it leaves little room for the unexpected. What if you have a particularly hectic day at work and are unable to pump as much milk as usual? What if the sitter accidentally spills some of your precious expressed milk? Or what if you suddenly are called out of town on business? If you were bottle-feeding, you surely would have on hand more than one day's supply of formula at a time. Then why shouldn't you have a stockpile of expressed milk for your breastfed baby? Knowing you have ample stores of your milk frozen for your baby will give you extra peace of mind. Begin by pumping any residual milk after your early-morning and/or midmorning nursings. Most women have more milk at the first morning feeding after they have slept at night than they do later in the day. Their baby may fill up on the first breast and take little from the second. Using a pump immediately after the morning feeding(s) accomplishes two purposes. By getting well emptied in the morning, a woman's breasts will probably produce more milk the rest of the day. In addition, pumping the milk left behind after some feedings allows a woman to obtain several extra ounces each day.

I should caution you that your extra stores of milk should be used for emergencies only. You should never skip pumpings at work, assuming you can just rely on your frozen reserves. The end result could be a dramatic decline in your milk supply and the rapid depletion of your once-generous stockpile of expressed milk. In general, you should try to pump each day approximately as much (or more) than your baby takes in your absence. An occasional setback is to be expected, but don't be tempted to rely too heavily on previously pumped milk. As best you can, try to keep up with your baby's needs. This will require close communication with your child care provider about how much milk your baby drinks during the workday. In general, if you can pump at least one ounce of milk for each hour that has passed since you emptied your breasts, you will probably have sufficient milk to meet your baby's needs. Thus, if three hours have elapsed, you should expect to get about three ounces when you pump. Don't worry about getting more milk than you need. It's always preferable to have too much than too little. Keeping the supply generous also helps keep your baby eager to go back and forth from breast to bottle.

Introduce Your Baby to Bottle-Feeding

Most likely, your baby will drink your expressed milk from a bottle while you are at work. Young infants (under about seven months of age) require liberal sucking, both for emotional gratification and for proper oral development. Using alternative methods of feeding that avoid bottles are appropriate for short periods when a baby is learning to nurse, but my own bias is that young infants should take most of their feedings by sucking. Ideally, bottles should be avoided until breastfeeding is well established (usually three to four weeks). Once breastfeeding is going well, a mother who intends to work outside the home should begin to familiarize her baby with bottle-feeding.

Some breastfed babies accept a bottle easily, while others are very resistant to a new method of feeding. Many breastfeeding mothers become frustrated and discouraged when their baby refuses to drink from a bottle. The following suggestions have been found to be helpful in encouraging breastfed infants to accept a bottle. The most important thing to remember is to stay calm when offering a bottle to your baby. Your baby will probably resist a bit at first by turning away, grimacing or making a face, or pushing the nipple away with her tongue. Don't force the bottle at any time and promptly discontinue your efforts at the first sign that your baby is becoming unhappy with this lesson.

1. Plan a time when you can devote ten to fifteen uninterrupted minutes to this endeavor. Your baby will feel pressured if you are rushed.

2. Choose a time when your baby is alert and slightly hungry so she will be motivated to learn a new way to receive milk. On the other hand, avoid offering a bottle when your baby is very hungry. An upset, frantically hungry baby will be in no mood to try something new.

3. Offer expressed breast milk that you have pumped earlier in the day. Warm the bottle first, taking care not to overheat the milk (see page 307). Because the artificial nipple smells and tastes different than your nipple, having a familiar fluid to drink may encourage your baby to try the new feeding method.

4. There is no particular bottle-nipple unit that works best for every baby. If your baby uses a pacifier, she might prefer a nipple shaped like her pacifier nipple. Stick with one type of nipple for several days. Trying a wide variety of nipples will probably just confuse your baby more.

5. Breastfed babies often accept a bottle more readily when it is offered by an alternate caregiver. If the nursing mother tries to give the bottle, the baby may protest and turn toward the breast to nurse. On the other hand, some breastfed babies actually accept the bottle better when they are in their own mother's arms and can hear her reassuring voice.

6. Go slowly and gently, first touching the baby's lips with the nipple and watching her reaction. Don't force the nipple past her

lips. Instead, let your baby draw the nipple into her mouth at her own pace.

7. Express a little milk from the artificial nipple onto the baby's lips and/or tongue. Remove the nipple before your baby protests. Keep a smile on your face and keep talking in a reassuring tone the whole time. Babies notice their mothers' and caretakers' facial expressions and take their cues from them.

8. If your baby starts to get upset, try to calm her down by talking in a soothing voice. Wait until she starts to settle before you remove the nipple from her lips. Avoid letting her get very upset and then taking the nipple away. This will inappropriately teach her that if she protests enough you will remove the nipple. It's better to remove the nipple before she becomes upset or to try to calm her with your voice before you remove the nipple.

9. If your baby is tolerating the process and does not appear distressed, introduce the nipple a little further into the baby's mouth and let her explore it orally. Keep smiling and offering words of reassurance in a calming tone.

10. Don't spend more than about ten minutes on this process and stop sooner if you or your baby become frustrated. It's better to end the session on a positive note and try again tomorrow.

Frustrating as it is, you can take comfort in knowing that countless women have struggled with the challenge of enticing their breastfed babies to take a bottle. While the same tricks aren't necessarily effective with every mother-baby pair, don't lose heart. Something always works! I'm confident you will find a solution too.

Child Care Arrangements

Long before you begin work, you will want to settle the details of your child care arrangements and enlist the support of your baby's caretaker in your breastfeeding plans. As a practical matter, families usually consider cost, convenience, and proximity to home or workplace in selecting child care. I cannot overemphasize the obvious importance of quality of care and appropriateness of the setting for the individual child. Young infants do best when they have a close, nurturing, positive relationship with a single caretaker or a few consistent caregivers. We all have read or seen accounts of well-intentioned parents who unwittingly hired neglectful or abusive caretakers. The risk is greatest with preverbal infants who are unable to communicate the situation to their parents. Think hard about who you will ask to care for your precious baby. If you don't use a trusted relative or friend, make sure the caretaker is licensed and always check references. Ask yourself whether you enjoy this person's company. If not, do you really want your child spending all day with her? If you use a child care center or a family day care home, choose one that is accredited by the National Association for the Education of Young Children or the National Association for Family Day Care. Anytime something doesn't seem right to you, trust your intuition and remove your child from the setting.

Once you are certain that your child will be physically safe and that her emotional and intellectual development will be optimized in the setting you have selected, you can turn your attention to your breastfeeding plans. Your child care provider is not only responsible for your baby's welfare, but she also needs to be your unwavering ally in your efforts to continue breastfeeding. Ask whether the caretaker has breastfed her own children or cared for other breastfed infants. How does she feel about handling your expressed milk or coping with a baby who may not take a bottle readily? Is she willing to cooperate with you in your attempts to maintain breastfeeding? For example, is she willing to avoid giving a bottle if you are due back shortly and could nurse upon arrival?

I know what it's like to have a sitter who sabotages your breast-feeding efforts and to have one who goes the extra mile to make breastfeeding work. With my second baby, I hired a wonderful mother of a toddler who lived right across the street from the hospital where I was a medical student and who had breastfed her baby. This special woman allowed me to nurse Paige in her living room as soon as I arrived in the morning, so I could "top her off" before going to class. Then, she welcomed my daily drop-in visits to nurse periodically as my schedule allowed. Before I departed after each feeding, we jointly tried to anticipate the next feeding time. If Paige awoke early, she patiently distracted and soothed her until my arrival. I'm sure it would have been easier for this woman to just give Paige a bottle at her convenience, but she made every effort to accommodate my attempts to breastfeed. I'm very indebted to her to this day.

Unfortunately, some months later, this wonderful woman moved out of state, and I had to leave Paige with a more rigid sitter near my home. No longer able to nurse during the day, I still tried to hand express my milk and keep breastfeeding. However, the baby-sitter was an intimidating older woman who complained about Paige's reluctance to accept a bottle in my absence. She made it clear that she thought formula was "richer" than my expressed milk, and she repeatedly urged me to wean. I wish I could report that I found a more enlightened and compatible sitter and that I continued to breastfeed long-term. The truth is that I felt unsupported, trapped by my circumstances, and even guilty for wanting to nurse my baby. Little wonder that my milk supply steadily dwindled and Paige gradually lost interest in nursing. Reluctantly, I stopped breastfeeding a few months later.

Arrange to leave your baby with the child care provider for several hours on one or more occasions before you actually start work. Ask the child care provider to feed your baby while you are gone. These trial sessions give your baby and the caretaker time to get to know one another. The assurance that the caretaker can feed your infant successfully will reduce your anxiety and give you some peace of mind.

Clarify for the baby-sitter what to do if you are late picking up your baby and whom to call in an emergency. Show her how to quiet and comfort your baby when he is upset. Ask if she is willing to spend some time at the end of the day reviewing your baby's eating, sleeping, elimination, and behavior patterns with you.

Workplace Facilities and Scheduled Breaks

Prior to going to work, you will want to make arrangements for when and where you will express milk. In most cases, it is best to inform your employer of your intentions to maintain lactation while at work. Be prepared to cite the advantages of enhanced maternal-child health and reduced absenteeism. It might help you to know that the American Academy of Pediatrics recommends that employers support breastfeeding women to continue lactating after starting or returning to work by providing appropriate facilities and adequate time for pumping. Remind your employer that raising breastfeeding rates is a national health objective and that your baby's doctor is urging you to continue breastfeeding (probably true). Explain that you will be using your "coffee breaks" as "lactation breaks" and that you will pump while you eat lunch. Jokes about pumping, innuendos, and snickering on the part of coworkers are inappropriate and may constitute sexual harassment. Although many women put up with such behavior, you do not need to tolerate it in today's workplace.

An increasing number of modern work sites have lactation lounges equipped with hospital-grade rental electric pumps. All you need to use the workplace pump is your own collection kit. Most women prefer to bring a personal cooler to transport their expressed milk and keep it cold, rather than putting it in a workplace refrigerator.

Enlist Support for Your Breastfeeding Plan

With exceptional motivation, a flexible baby, and a bountiful milk supply, you might be able to succeed on your own. Most of us ordinary people, however, reach our goals more easily when we have the benefit of a cheering squad. Identify your sources of support and allow these people to nurture you emotionally. For most women, the support of their husband or partner has the greatest impact on their success. Perhaps you know a coworker who has breastfed who can encourage you. Maybe your mother or mother-in-law will champion your efforts and smooth the way for you. In my case, getting involved with La Leche League following the birth of my fifth baby proved to be the ticket to experiencing the full course of breastfeeding. By surrounding myself with knowledgeable, like-minded, highly motivated women, I gained the necessary confidence to make breastfeeding Mark one of my highest priorities. No one in La Leche League told me what choices to make about my situation. But the information I gained at meetings and my firsthand exposure to unrestricted breastfeeding are what empowered me to make different choices with this baby that would assure my success. With the support of other mothers in La Leche League, I delayed my return to work longer than I had with any of my previous babies. Then I began part-time work and made child care arrangements that permitted me to be present for every nursing. When my baby was a year old, I resumed full-time work while continuing to nurse uninterrupted. Being present for every feeding was something I had always longed to do. Support is one of the key factors that enabled me to make the choices that gave me the outcome I had long desired.

The Importance of Regular Milk Emptying for Continued Milk Production

Probably the most common mistake made by employed nursing mothers is to wait until their breasts are uncomfortably full before pumping. Workplace distractions are so prevalent and work-related demands so pressing that a nursing mother is tempted to postpone pumping sessions as long as possible. Only when her breasts are painfully hard does she finally stop to express her milk. This is an all-too-common scenario that inevitably leads to diminished milk supply. I have repeatedly emphasized that failure to drain the breasts regularly causes sustained pressure on the milk-producing glands and the accumulation of a protein inhibitor substance in residual milk. The combination of pressure and residual milk gives a powerful message to the body to decrease milk production. If a woman waits to pump until her breasts are uncomfortably full, her milk supply can steadily decline. Faithfully adhering to your pumping schedule probably is the most important thing you can do to keep a generous supply and assure your long-term success. The frequency of pumping will depend on the age of your baby. Because young infants nurse more often than older babies, the sooner you go back to work, the more frequently you will need to pump. If you return to work with a four-week-old, you should plan on pumping more often than if you return when your baby is four months old.

Conscientious employees tend to put everyone else's needs above their own. This urgent phone call, today's staff meeting, the essential memo easily take precedent over pumping. To make breastfeeding successful, you need to be appropriately selfish. Outline a realistic schedule and resolve to stick to it. If you can't do it for yourself, insist on doing it for your baby. Trust me, the memo can wait for ten to fifteen minutes until you finish pumping. One of the most successful employed breastfeeding mothers I recall managed to faithfully pump her breasts on schedule. She let nothing prevent her from taking her lactation breaks precisely at the prearranged time. The office could be in utter chaos, with everyone clamoring for her attention, but this amazingly focused woman simply walked away at her appointed hour to express her milk. And her milk flowed in abundance. Somehow, everything managed to wait for the few minutes it took her to pump. Every day brings

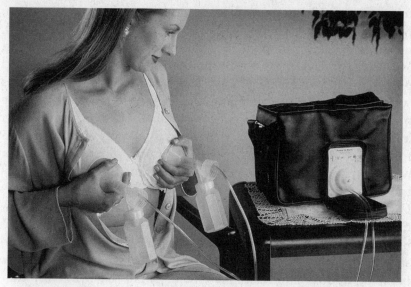

Medela Pump In Style professional performance electric pump.

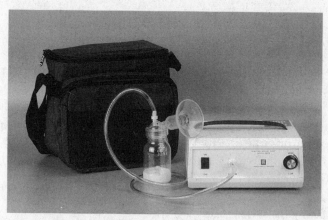

White River Concepts rental electric breast pump
with single or double collection kits.

its own set of crises that threaten to pull you off course if you don't
resolve to adhere to your pumping schedule.

Types of Breast Pumps

Women commonly ask for recommendations about which
breast pump to use. Unfortunately, it is difficult, if not impossible,

to predict which pump will work best for a particular woman. Many types of breast pumps are available, ranging from small, inexpensive hand pumps to hospital-grade rental electric pumps. Women's satisfaction with the different manual or hand pumps, battery-operated pumps, and small electric pumps varies widely. Generally, women find the larger, rental-grade electric pumps to be most effective and comfortable. The double collection kits available for use with the rental pumps allow a woman to comfortably empty her breasts in ten to fifteen minutes. A popular option among working women is a professional performance electric breast pump with dual collection system that can be purchased. Owning such a pump can prove very cost effective if a woman continues pumping for many months or uses it again when the next baby comes along. The best advice is to meet with a lactation consultant or nurse specialist who can help you explore various pumping options and select the type of pump that will meet your needs and budget.

Range of Options for Breastfeeding and Working

You may not appreciate the wide variety of options available for combining working and nursing. Each woman's circumstances are unique. Since no two situations are alike, I would not presume to tell you what to do. But I can give you a range of options and describe the pros and cons of each. Then you can choose a plan that fits your individual circumstances, resources, lifestyle, and motivation.

Nurse Baby at Work Site

Employment is least disruptive of breastfeeding if mothers and babies can remain in contact or if the baby can be brought to the mother for feedings. A few lucky women are able to make arrangements to bring their baby to the workplace, perhaps keeping him with her in a bassinet or having him in an on-site child care setting. Such an arrangement obviously works best if a woman has a flexible schedule that allows her to nurse her baby when he demands or to go to the day care center when her infant requires feedings. Some women pay a child care provider to tend to the baby's needs, perhaps in her own office or an adjacent room. The nanny provides all infant care while the mother performs her work duties. When the infant needs to be fed, the nanny brings the baby to his mother to be nursed.

Obviously, women in executive positions or those who own their own businesses are more likely to work out such an arrangement than women in nonmanagerial positions with little flexibility. The decisive factor, however, seems to be a woman's determination and commitment to explore every avenue for creating such a possibility. Having contact with your baby throughout the workday is especially important for women who must return to work within a few weeks postpartum when a baby is still nursing every two to three hours. My own hairdresser, Tiffany, elected to bring her baby to her shop, beginning shortly after birth. She made this decision with the knowledge that she might lose some clients who weren't willing to incur any inconvenience as a result of having a baby in their midst. The arrangement has been enormously successful. Trent was still being nursed at eighteen months of age! Those of us who frequent the salon have all held, rocked, played with, and kept a watchful eye on Trent. We have followed his developmental milestones with genuine interest. Each time Tiffany greets me with the announcement that she is still nursing, I exclaim, "Good for you!" A few times my appointment took longer than usual because Tiffany needed to attend to Trent. Even though I am generally a hopeless type A, impatient, hurry-up sort of person, I consider the few extra minutes I spend every month or so to be a small contribution toward someone's successful breastfeeding experience. Being at the salon challenges me to put into action the beliefs I have long espoused—that it takes a whole society to support breastfeeding. Over the years, several of my coworkers have brought their babies to work. Of course some compromises had to be made. But any inconvenience was more than offset by the positive effect the babies had on our disposition. I often have witnessed the uncanny ability of a baby's presence to transform a grumpy employee into an animated, grinning entertainer. There's something about an innocent, engaging infant that evokes an instant attitude adjustment which can ripple throughout an office.

Work Part-Time

In my case, I achieved the greatest success combining breast-feeding with employment when I worked part-time. At least one study has found longer duration of breastfeeding among women with part-time employment compared to full-time employees. Part-time work is less disruptive of breastfeeding because it allows a nursing mother more time with her baby. A mother might work fewer hours every day or fewer days each week. With a shorter duration of daily separation, a woman's milk supply is less likely to dwindle and her baby will miss fewer nursings. The woman may need to pump only once during her workday, or perhaps not at all if her baby is older than about four months. For part-time employees who work a full day, but who put in fewer days each week, exclusive breastfeeding can occur on the days the mother doesn't have to work. Thus, a woman might have four or five days each week to breastfeed normally or to build her milk back up after having worked a couple of days.

If a part-time position is not feasible in the long term, I urge you to attempt to negotiate the possibility of temporarily working part-time after your maternity leave. Even a few weeks of part-time employment will ease your transition back to work and your baby's transition into her day care setting. You can begin to incorporate milk expression into your workday before resuming a full-time position.

Pump and Save

The preferred strategy used by employed nursing mothers who are separated from their babies is to pump their breasts at the approximate times their baby typically would feed. The expressed milk is kept refrigerated or stored in a cooler and brought to the baby-sitter to be fed to the infant in the mother's absence. If the mother is able to effectively empty her breasts at frequent intervals, she has the best chances of keeping up a generous milk supply. So long as her milk production is abundant, her baby is likely to remain interested in nursing when Mom and baby are together. Although women manage to pump and save using a wide variety of pumps or hand expression, a hospital-grade rental electric pump or a professional performance electric pump with a double collection system makes a particularly popular option among working mothers. Women pumping both breasts simultaneously can express their milk in ten to fifteen minutes, plus cleanup time. The ease with which pumping can be accomplished makes it more likely that a woman can comply with her pumping schedule.

Pump and Dump

A few working women have no facilities to safely store their expressed milk. They may be field workers or military personnel on maneuvers, for example. Flight attendants might have difficulty storing milk during lengthy travel. Although such situations occur only rarely, the point to be made is that milk expression is still desirable even if the milk cannot be saved and used. Regular expression of milk is essential for continued milk production. Although feeding the expressed milk to the infant is much preferred, it may not always be possible. Even if milk has to be hand expressed over the sink or pumped and discarded, emptying the breasts is critical to preserving a generous milk supply. Leaving the breasts uncomfortably engorged not only predisposes a woman to mastitis (see pages 254–260) but also can diminish her milk supply.

Don't Pump

Some women are unwilling or unable to pump at all during the workday. If that is your situation, partial breastfeeding mornings and evenings is still possible. Some women prefer to start substituting formula feedings for the breastfeedings they will miss while at work, beginning a couple of weeks before their actual employment begins and after breastfeeding is well established. They first substitute formula for a single breastfeeding, then a few days to a week later, they eliminate a second nursing and replace it with a feeding of formula.

Other women prefer to nurse unrestricted throughout their maternity leave, giving their baby the longest period of exclusive breastfeeding possible. If you do this, when you first return to work, your breasts will probably become overly full if they aren't drained during your absence from your baby. Within a few days, however, your milk production will decline and your breasts will soften. Since you won't be pumping, your baby will need to drink formula while you are working. However, you might be able to satisfy your baby with breastfeeding alone while the two of you are together at home. You can nurse during the night as well. Some women report that their breasts adjust to making more milk during the times they are with their babies and less milk when they are away. Other women find that their milk supply diminishes significantly if milk isn't removed from their breasts regularly during the workday. Although breastfeeding when Mom is available can still contribute important nutrition and immune properties to the baby, you need to be prepared to offer sufficient additional formula to satisfy your baby's appetite and growth needs. Nevertheless, "comfort nursing" can remain a highly valuable source of security and emotional gratification.

Collection and Storage of Expressed Breast Milk

Site. Try to arrange for an appropriate workplace setting to meet your pumping needs, preferably one that is nearby so you won't waste precious minutes getting there. You will want a quiet, private location where you can relax and pump your breasts without fear that you will be interrupted by a coworker. Some women use their private office, while others go to a formal lactation lounge or other designated area. Intrusions can be minimized by having a lock on the door or by posting a ROOM IN USE—DO NOT ENTER sign.

Unfortunately, many women are forced to retreat to their car, find an unoccupied office or conference room, or use a storage area. Ideally, the site you select should have an electrical outlet to allow you to use an electric pump. If no wall outlet is available, you can still use an electric pump if it comes with a power pack. When fully charged overnight, these pumps will run by battery for about an hour. Your pumping site should also have a sink and running water so you can wash your hands and clean your equipment. The availability of reading materials helps pass the time while pumping. The presence of a telephone allows you to call and check on your baby. Such contact usually helps trigger the milk ejection reflex. The walls of some corporate lactation lounges are decorated with posters of nursing mother-baby pairs and pro-breastfeeding slogans. Despite the mounting workplace support for today's breastfeeding employees, stories still abound of resolute women who valiantly pump their milk in a restroom lounge or bathroom stall because no alternative pumping site is available. The inappropriateness of expecting a mother to prepare her baby's meal in a bathroom cannot be overstated!

Preparation and Hygiene. Always wash your hands thoroughly before and after pumping your breasts or manually expressing milk. A daily shower or bath is adequate to maintain breast cleanliness. All pump parts that come into contact with your milk should be washed in hot soapy water after each use and rinsed well. Once each day, you should sanitize these parts by washing them in a dishwasher or boiling them for twenty minutes. Follow the specific cleaning instructions for your pump. Ask your child care provider to wash her hands before and after feeding your breast milk.

Collection of Milk. Milk expressed at a pumping session should be poured into a clean container, such as a glass or durable plastic feeding bottle or a disposable bottle bag. Communicate with your child care provider so you will know approximately how much milk to pour into a single feeding container. It's best to have a little more than you think your baby will take. If your milk supply is low, you may need to pool milk from more than one pumping session to make a full feeding for your baby. On the other hand, if your milk supply is generous, you may be able to pump more than your baby can drink at a single feeding. It is always preferable to produce more milk than your baby takes; you can freeze the surplus for later use. If you freeze any milk, be sure to leave enough room at the top of the container to allow for expansion during freezing.

When possible, store milk in the same container from which it will be fed. Cap bottles tightly—do not store them with nipples attached. Bottle bags can be sealed with a clean rubber band or twist tie. Because they easily rupture and leak, place one bag inside another to prevent tears or holes. Another option to protect fragile bottle bags and prevent their rupture is to place multiple bags into a larger zip-lock storage bag. Breast pump companies sell a higher-quality, more expensive milk storage bag that better protects the properties of expressed breast milk when stored (see Resource List, page 450). Label each container (using masking tape or adhesive labels) with your baby's name and the date the milk was expressed.

You may "layer" milk collected on the same day by adding milk from more than one pumping session to the same bottle. If freshly expressed milk is to be added to previously frozen breast milk, chill it first in the refrigerator before adding it to the frozen portion.

Storage of Expressed Breast Milk. Your expressed milk can be safely refrigerated for forty-eight to seventy-two hours. If you anticipate longer storage (because you pump more than your baby takes), your milk should be frozen. Leave about an inch at the top of the container to allow for expansion during freezing. Place your expressed milk in the back of the freezer elevated off the bottom, where the temperature is most stable, not in the door where the temperature fluctuates. Storage guidelines for expressed breast milk are as follows:

Site	Duration
On refrigerator shelf	Up to 48–72 hours
Freezer compartment inside a refrigerator	Up to 2–3 weeks
Separate freezer unit of a refrigerator	Up to 3 months
Separate deep freezer (Kept at –20° C or 0° F)	Up to 6 months

Thawing of Frozen Expressed Breast Milk. Several safe methods are suitable for thawing frozen breast milk. Some are faster than others. Milk may be thawed slowly in the refrigerator. Be aware that volumes of three or more ounces may take several hours to thaw in this manner. Milk can be thawed in a matter of minutes by holding the container under running warm water or placing it in a clean bowl of warm water. It is important that the top of the milk container remains above the water at all times. *Do not* thaw milk at room temperature by letting it sit out for hours. *Do not* refreeze thawed milk. I think it is reasonable to reuse left-over milk at the next feeding, provided it has not been kept at room temperature for more than one hour, is placed in a clean container, and returned to the refrigerator. Any milk remaining after a second feeding should be discarded. Do not add fresh milk to a bottle that already has been used. Instead, let the baby finish the first bottle before offering a fresh bottle.

Warming Chilled Breast Milk. Cold milk is not harmful to an infant, but some babies prefer their milk warmed to body temperature, like breast milk. You can take the chill off refrigerated milk by running it under warm water or by setting the container in a pan of warm water. Do not place the pan over direct heat, as this can overheat the milk. Bottled breast milk can also be warmed in a commercial bottle warmer.

Microwave Heating of Expressed Milk. Authorities generally recommend AGAINST using a microwave oven to either thaw or warm expressed milk. Inadvertent overheating of milk occurs easily in a microwave and infants have accidentally been burned. Furthermore, milk will curdle when overheated, and many of the immune properties of human milk are heat sensitive and can be destroyed by overheating.

Transporting Expressed Milk. An on-site refrigerator is not necessary as long as your expressed milk is placed in an insulated cooler bag or other insulated container. Some mothers who have access to a refrigerator at work actually prefer using an insulated cooler to keep from storing their milk in a community refrigerator. (I have heard at least one account of a coworker who unwittingly used expressed breast milk as a coffee creamer.) Do not leave human milk at room temperature for more than about an hour. While human milk inhibits the growth of bacteria (formula fosters their multiplication), it still is not a good idea to leave milk unrefrigerated for long periods. You should also keep your expressed milk in an insulated cooler when you transport it to your child care provider.

Corporate Support for Breastfeeding Employees

Until recently, corporate America showed little concern for the dilemmas of working parents. Increasingly, company executives have begun to recognize that offering various family support services can reduce the costs of recruiting and training replacement workers for employees who resign their positions at the end of their maternity leave. Prenatal education, on-site day care, flexible work schedules, and lactation programs are some of the innovative family services that are helping family-friendly companies attract and retain valued and competent workers. Many committed nursing mothers once thought continued breastfeeding was incompatible with returning to work. Corporate lactation programs are just one of the latest incentives being used to retain valued employees. More and more companies are providing a private, comfortable work-site location for pumping breast milk and equipping these lounges with rental electric breast pumps. Supervisors are being instructed to allow flexible use of break time so a lactating woman can be absent for fifteen to thirty minutes per pumping session. The most elaborate programs, such as Medela's Corporate Lactation Program, even provide access to a lactation professional who can give expert advice and counseling. One key reason explains the growth of these programs: *companies are discovering that breastfeeding makes good business sense.* With more mothers returning from maternity leave, fewer infant illnesses and less absenteeism, more satisfied and loyal employees, and lower retraining costs, companies are finding that it pays to help employed women reach their breastfeeding goals.

Inquire whether your company offers any lactation support services for breastfeeding women. The more women who ask about breastfeeding, the more companies will consider providing facilities and support. If no formal program exists, request informal support for your breastfeeding plan. Ask your employer to help you find a suitable location to pump and to authorize flexible use of your breaks for expressing milk. Let your employer know you appreciate their support and cooperation. Legislation has been drafted, and may one day be enacted, which will protect a woman's right to breastfeed or pump milk in the workplace, and will encourage employers to support lactation by providing facilities for working women to express milk.

What Will People at Work Think?

Many new mothers experience irrational guilt about taking a maternity leave, and they return to work concerned that their coworkers resent their absence. They may be reluctant to ask for any concessions to allow them to breastfeed. Don't succumb to such inappropriate feelings. Instead, resolve to keep your priorities straight. Your first loyalty must be to your own family. While you are one of many employees at your workplace, you are the ONLY mother to your baby. The smartest employers know that being a good mother is part of being a good teacher, a good nurse, a good secretary, or a good executive. You should not feel the least bit uneasy about spending your breaks expressing milk. Instead, be confident in the knowledge that your willingness to expend extra effort for your baby's welfare is highly praiseworthy and commendable. An enlightened employer will recognize the labor of love involved with pumping milk as an indication of your intense dedication and commitment, sense of priorities, time-management skills, and broad work ethic.

You may need to be politely firm at times. A coworker or supervisor who has never pumped their breasts may not understand why it can't be put off an hour or so. Humor and a quick wit go a long way in getting your needs met. I know an employed mother who was hurrying off to pump her uncomfortably full breasts when her boss called an urgent meeting. "I'll be there in ten minutes," she explained. "I have to pump first." "No, this meeting is important," he insisted. "You can pump afterward." "How would you like to sit through the meeting with an uncomfortably full bladder?" she countered with a grin. The analogy made its point. She pumped *before* the meeting.

Helpful Hints for Employed Breastfeeding Mothers

• **Wear clothing that is convenient for pumping, such as blouses that open in the front and pull up.** Choose clothes that won't show stains from leaking milk (avoid silk!). Keep an extra neutral-colored blouse and a sweater or jacket at work in case milk leaks onto your outer clothing. One veteran mother referred to the telltale signs of leaking as "headlights." Knowing you have a spare blouse or jacket available can give you peace of mind about avoiding embarrassing "accidents." For those who leak easily, you can provide further assurance that clothing won't be soiled by wearing breast pads or breast shells inside the nursing bra. The gentle areolar pressure provided by breast shields also might stimulate some milk release, thereby reducing excessive engorgement. On the other hand, some women find that the pressure from breast shells contributes to clogged ducts.

• **Make a point to drink extra fluids while at work.** You are more likely to adhere to normal breastfeeding routines at home, like drinking a beverage each time you nurse. In the workplace, it's easy to get distracted and inadvertently limit your fluid intake. Constipation can signal that you need extra liquids, and it goes without saying that you should respond to the sensation of thirst. To assure you always have something nutritious on hand to drink, consider bringing a sports bottle or thermos to work and keep bottled water and juice on hand.

• **Set your alarm a half hour earlier each morning to savor a leisurely nursing session before your hectic pace begins.** Allow a little extra time in the morning to begin your day by breastfeeding your baby calmly and unhurriedly. A few extra minutes of sleep can be traded for the quiet, relaxing joy of having a contented baby at your breast. Although the rest of your day may be governed by time constraints, you don't have to start off feeling rushed.

• **Communicate with your baby-sitter so your infant is ready to nurse as soon as you arrive home.** This might require slight alteration of your baby's feeding schedule to make sure he hasn't just finished a bottle when you walk through the door with full, dripping breasts. Nursing your baby at the end of a hectic day can be the most peaceful reunion of all.

• **Keep your focus on the nursing relationship, not the volume of milk you are able to produce.** Under normal conditions, nursing mothers breastfeed their babies on demand and are unaware of slight fluctuations in their milk supply. If their baby seems hungry sooner than usual, they simply nurse again to satisfy the infant. When women pump and measure their milk on a daily basis, however, it's easy to become preoccupied with the amount of milk they produce. Focusing too heavily on the quantity of milk can create sufficient anxiety to interfere with the milk ejection reflex and compound the problem. Some employed women will obtain abundant milk with relative ease, while others will get less through no fault of their own. Regardless of how much milk you obtain with pumping, try to focus on being able to nurse your baby when the two of you are reunited each day. Even if some supplemental formula becomes necessary, a satisfying nursing relationship can continue as long as mutually desired.

• **Attempt to breastfeed exclusively on weekends and days off to build up your milk supply and to restore the nursing relationship.** Many women are motivated to devote extra time outside work hours to resume full breastfeeding. This is a big commitment, considering that employed women usually spend their days off buying groceries, running errands, doing laundry, cleaning house, preparing meals, and so on. However, keeping your baby with you on weekends and allowing unrestricted breastfeeding can help boost your milk supply before the start of a new week. More importantly, both you and your baby can enjoy the emotional rewards of a few days of uninterrupted breastfeeding after making it through another workweek.

• **Consider reverse-cycle nursing, that is, nursing more in the evenings and at night when you are available to your baby.** This strategy is said to be used commonly in other societies where breastfeeding is the norm. It works well for some employed mothers, especially those who sleep with their babies and allow unrestricted nursing through the night. Other women consider adequate nighttime rest to be a necessary prerequisite to working during the day. Many insist their sleep is more restful when their baby is in her own crib, and they can't wait to eliminate night feedings. While some working women appreciate learning about reverse-cycle nursing and use it to foster breastfeeding success, others can't imagine deliberately choosing to nurse often at night to help offset the effects of a daily separation from their infant. You can decide what works best for you.

Common Problems Experienced by Employed Breastfeeding Mothers

The following difficulties are common among all nursing mothers, but employed mothers may be more prone to these complaints. Most can be prevented and/or remedied, and none has to mean the end of breastfeeding. Since each of these problems is covered in detail elsewhere, I will limit my discussion here to those issues unique to working mothers.

Fatigue and Discouragement. New motherhood is challenging whether or not you breastfeed and whether or not you work outside the home. Fatigue plagues all new parents from time to time. Certainly, many women enjoy their jobs and derive fulfillment from their work. Some manage to juggle home and office without getting ruffled. Most, however, admit that their multiple roles occasionally push them into role overload. Caring for a young infant is hard enough without adding the demands of outside employment, a daily commute, unrelenting time pressures, regular milk expression, and running a home. There's a fine line between the glamour of "having it all" and the stifling burden of overwhelming responsibility.

Don't make the mistake of assuming there's something wrong with you if you sometimes get tired and discouraged. Examine your situation to see if there is anything you can do to simplify your life for a few months. Ask your friends and relatives for help. Hire someone to do chores you don't have time for right now. Drop some of your commitments. Lower your standards. Turn off the TV and go to bed earlier.

Often, a nursing mother who admits she is tired and discouraged will be told to stop breastfeeding. Breastfeeding gets wrongly blamed for all kinds of woes. But weaning seldom improves a woman's situation. She still has a baby to feed, diaper, bathe, and care for. Only now she has to buy and mix formula and wash more bottles and nipples. The truth is that fatigued nursing mothers usually describe breastfeeding as one of their few pleasant daily interludes. A harried nursing mother periodically *has* to stop to feed her baby or pump her breasts. Every few hours, she has the chance to renew her perspective and focus exclusively on being connected with and providing milk for her baby. Breastfeeding is such an abbreviated time in your life. Are you sure you want to cut it short? Working causes you to miss out on much of your child's babyhood. Are you sure you want to add breastfeeding to the list of family-life sacrifices you are willing to make?

Before you conclude that weaning would improve your situation, examine the price you will pay by giving up breastfeeding. Weaning may free up some time at work that you would have spent pumping, but the price you pay is the lost opportunity to enjoy leisurely nursing your baby evenings and weekends. Weaning before you had planned to may leave you feeling cheated and deprive your baby of some of the benefits of breastfeeding.

Decreased Milk Supply. One of the most common difficulties voiced by working nursing mothers is decreased milk supply (see also chapter 9). The problem usually results from being unable to pump frequently enough during the workday. At home, women nurse their babies on demand as often as necessary and naturally match their milk supply with their baby's milk requirement. At work, it is tempting to postpone or shorten pumping sessions because of job pressures. When the breasts don't get drained as well by pumping as they would by nursing, then a mother's milk supply can diminish. Several other factors can contribute to the problem of low milk supply, including physical exhaustion, not eating or drinking enough, stress, inhibited milk let-down, or a baby who doesn't nurse well when the mother is available for feedings. The most common ways a mother realizes that her milk supply has decreased are: (1) she expresses noticeably less milk at pumping sessions than previously; (2) she is unable to pump as much milk as her baby wants to drink in her absence; (3) she is no longer able to satisfy her baby by breastfeeding when they are together.

Maintaining a generous milk supply is easier than trying to increase your milk once it has dwindled. But if your milk has already diminished, there are several things you can do to try to increase your supply. First, try to pump more often, preferably with a hospital-grade rental electric pump equipped with a double collection system. Pump at least ten minutes, even if your milk stops flowing sooner. Nurse your baby at least every two to three hours when the two of you are together. Try to nurse exclusively on weekends if possible. If your baby sleeps longer than six hours at night, consider pumping your breasts either just before you retire or once in the middle of the night. Eat a balanced diet and healthy snacks, drink fluids liberally, rest as much as possible, and try to get help with household duties. See pages 335–341 for additional tips on increasing a low milk supply.

Inhibited Milk Ejection Reflex. A mother nursing her hungry baby in the privacy and comfort of her home usually has little trouble getting her milk to flow. Her milk ejection reflex is promptly triggered by the visual image of her infant or the sound of her baby's cry. A mother's milk may begin to let-down as soon as she initiates familiar nursing routines, like sipping a glass of juice or settling into a cozy recliner with her baby. Certainly the work environment is less than conducive to conditioning the let-down response. Milk flow can be impaired when a woman is pumping under time constraints or is wondering whether her privacy will be interrupted or whether her coworkers resent her absence. Inhibited let-down of milk can prolong pumping sessions or lead to poor milk emptying and diminished milk supply (see also pages 77–78).

To help trigger your let-down reflex before pumping, look at a photo of your baby, bring a baby item with your infant's scent, play a tape recording of your baby's cry or vocalizations, or telephone your baby-sitter to talk about your baby. Gentle breast massage or nipple stimulation or drinking a beverage as you would at home before nursing can serve the same purpose. Some working mothers obtain an excellent let-down response with the use of synthetic oxytocin nasal spray. (For information about how to obtain this medication, see page 231.)

Clogged Ducts. A clogged duct often results from an irregular pumping schedule that prevents the breasts from getting well drained (see also chapter 7, pages 251–253). The best treatment of a clogged duct is nursing more frequently on the affected breast, nursing in different positions, and applying heat and gentle massage to the clogged area. These therapies are difficult, if not impossible, to perform during the workday. Certainly, an employed woman with a clogged duct should attempt to nurse (if feasible) or pump more often while at work. Pumping the breasts singly sometimes helps. When using a single collection container, you can use your free hand to apply gentle pressure or massage to the clogged area. Don't overdo any breast manipulation, however, as "trauma" can increase the risk of mastitis, or a breast infection.

Mastitis. The most common predisposing factor for mastitis is incomplete or infrequent breast emptying. Thus, you can see why a working mother would be particularly susceptible to a breast infection if she goes too long without pumping. Other risk factors that frequently are present among employed women include clogged ducts and extreme fatigue. A breast pump that generates excessive suction can cause cracked nipples or other damage that makes a woman more prone to a breast infection. Breast trauma leading to mastitis can also occur from overly vigorous massage or improper manual expression technique. For information about the symptoms and treatment of mastitis, see pages 254–260. To minimize your risks of getting mastitis, do your best to express your milk regularly using a comfortable, efficient pump and make every effort to get enough rest. If you develop a fever or body aches, feel like you are getting the flu, or notice a hard, painful area in one of your breasts, notify your doctor. Mastitis is a very unpleasant illness. I urge you to get antibiotics started as early as possible if you show signs of mastitis.

Baby Loses Interest in Nursing. Some babies of working mothers increase their desire to nurse because they link breast-feeding with their mothers' presence. Others gradually lose interest in nursing as they grow more accustomed to bottle-feeding during the workday (see Nursing Strike, chapter 7, pages 262–265). The problem tends to be aggravated whenever the mother has a low milk supply. Although some babies will nurse enthusiastically, even when the flow of milk is less than the baby desires, most infants quickly become frustrated with breastfeeding when milk doesn't flow as readily from the breast as it does from the bottle. To prevent your baby from losing interest in nursing, try to keep your milk supply up with regular pumping. When you are with your baby, nurse as often as the infant desires, preferably before the baby gets too hungry and is easily frustrated.

If your baby has started to show a loss of interest in nursing, take the following steps to try to correct the problem.

• If your milk supply is low, make an effort to pump more often at work. Use the most efficient pump you can obtain, preferably a hospital-grade electric pump with a double collection container.

• Offer your breast frequently to comfort, settle, or pacify your baby. This will help remind your infant that breastfeeding is more than nutrition—it is a unique source of security and emotional satisfaction. If your baby still seems disinterested, try nursing him when he is drowsy or asleep. Nighttime nursings usually go well and can help entice your baby back to the breast. When your infant does cooperate by nursing, don't rush him or make him come off the breast before he is ready. Instead, focus your attention on your infant and allow him to continue as long as desired. To minimize distractions, nurse in a quiet, subdued environment.

• If your baby doesn't suckle vigorously when nursing or nurses only for short periods, it might become necessary to pump after breastfeedings in order to assure that your breasts receive adequate stimulation and effective removal of milk. Otherwise, your supply probably will decrease, which will only aggravate the problem.

Ideally, every woman who desires to breastfeed would be able to structure her day around her baby's needs and be free to nurse her baby when the infant demands. In reality, women, especially working mothers, juggle many competing priorities that threaten the success of breastfeeding. But countless women are discovering that it is possible to work without weaning and that breastfeeding can still be possible, despite the challenges posed by a daily separation from one's infant. Armed with accurate information, equipped with pumping facilities, and bolstered by corporate and family support, many women are willing to make the commitment of time and energy that will enable them to maintain breastfeeding while working outside the home.

Chapter 9

Insufficient Milk Syndrome and Inadequate Weight Gain in the Breastfed Infant

Few breastfeeding topics are clouded by more misinformation and controversy than the subject of insufficient milk. The very mention of this emotionally laden issue evokes extremes of opinion. Insufficient milk is overdiagnosed by some practitioners, while others deny its existence. Meanwhile, countless women cite low milk as their reason for early weaning. The enigma of insufficient milk is the haunting breastfeeding issue that has captivated my interest and been the focus of much of my professional career.

When I first became interested in helping women solve breastfeeding problems more then twenty years ago, I read everything I could find about lactation and breastfeeding. Over and over, I encountered dogmatic statements about the guaranteed sufficiency of a woman's milk production: "The more the baby nurses, the more milk a woman makes." "A baby's need for milk and his mother's ability to produce it in just the right quantity" was touted as one of nature's most perfect examples of the law of supply and demand. Despite wide variability in breast appearance, women were reassured that "every breast is the perfect breast for breastfeeding." "Breastfeeding is a confidence game," I read, with the implied message that breastfeeding failures were due to lack of confidence, or worse yet, lack of motivation.

At the same time I was reading about the infallibility of breast-feeding, I was encountering numerous women with heartrending stories of breastfeeding failure in the face of heroic efforts to nurse their babies. Not only had their infants' health been jeopardized by undernutrition, the women themselves had been dragged through a psychological wringer and were racked by guilt because the sup-posedly flawless biologic process of lactation had inexplicably gone awry for them. The well-intentioned reassurances found in most breastfeeding books held no consolation for these mothers of per-petually hungry infants. In fact, the glib phrases of optimism only served to rub salt in their raw emotional wounds.

While I can understand the value of promoting a message that insists every woman can breastfeed successfully, I have also wit-nessed the psychological devastation this tact has inflicted on women who, through no fault of their own, have been victims of insufficient milk. The time is overdue to acknowledge that lacta-tion, like any other body function, can sometimes fail or be limited by a whole variety of reasons, many of which are beyond a mother's control. We would never presume to tell a devastated infertility patient that "every woman can get pregnant" or insist to a diabetic woman that "every pancreas can make insulin." Yet, breastfeeding mothers struggling with insufficient milk continue to hear "every woman can breastfeed." Continuing to deny that insuffi-cient milk exists only delays our investigation of possible causes, preventive measures, and potential therapies.

My exploration of insufficient milk has led me to the conclusion that the problem is far from rare. In fact, throughout the world, the chief reason women give for discontinuing breastfeeding before they had wanted to is insufficient milk. Low milk can be related to both mother and infant factors that impact either the *making* or the *taking* of breast milk. Despite the unpopularity of the topic among breastfeeding enthusiasts, I have been outspoken about the magnitude and significance of the problem, which has subjected me to criticism at times. However, if my message has spared even one baby the devastating consequences of malnutrition or softened the psychological blow for even one woman who experienced the dis-appointment of insufficient milk and couldn't understand why, then my crusade has been worthwhile.

"Perceived Insufficient Milk"

One reason some breastfeeding proponents don't like to acknowledge the existence of insufficient milk is that so many women who could have succeeded with breastfeeding end up abandoning it early because they *believed* they had too little milk. There's no doubt that fear of the problem can undermine a woman's confidence and convince her that she truly doesn't have enough milk.

I don't dispute that widespread *misperceptions* about insufficient milk contribute enormously to the early discontinuation of breastfeeding. Many women fail to reach their breastfeeding goals due to the problem of "perceived insufficient milk." Exhausted, insecure, first-time mothers are easily convinced they must not have enough milk because their babies want to nurse so often. I vividly recall one such woman, the daughter of a colleague, whose breastfeeding was almost derailed by perceived insufficient milk. Her father called me when his grandson was ten days old and inquired whether the baby should be given some supplemental formula since the mother was tired and discouraged about the frequency of feedings. Fortunately, I decided not to draw any conclusions over the telephone and opted instead for an in-person encounter with the mother and baby. I invited her to meet me at the clinic where, much to everyone's amazement, the "hungry" baby weighed a full pound above his birth weight and certainly wasn't in need of any formula! Once the baby was confirmed to be thriving remarkably, his mother's whole perspective changed. The every two-and-a-half-hour feeding pattern no longer seemed so exhausting when she learned that her baby was doing exceptionally well with breastfeeding. Her anxiety dissipated and her confidence rose as I explained that this was breastfeeding at its best. Rather than trying to change the baby's pattern, what was really needed was to reframe the family's perception of breastfeeding norms and then help the mother restructure her lifestyle to accommodate unrestricted nursing. That simple strategy, plus a generous dose of well-deserved praise and encouragement, was enough to dispel the mother's perception of insufficient milk and allow her to continue breastfeeding with confidence.

Authentic Insufficient Milk and Its Consequences

While concerns about low milk supply often are unfounded, the unmistakable truth is that some breastfed babies really don't obtain sufficient milk. A mother's perception that her baby is hungry may be a valid one. An underfed infant's welfare can be placed in jeopardy unless adequate nutrition is provided promptly. Giving the mother encouragement and reassurance, without improving her baby's intake of milk, can be disastrous.

The phrase "insufficient milk" can mean either inadequate milk production on the mother's part *or* the inability of the baby to take enough milk during feeding. Either way, the baby receives inadequate nutrition with breastfeeding. Infant consequences of inadequate milk intake can range from hunger and slight malnutrition to life-threatening dehydration. In 1994, a wave of media attention was focused on this problem when several mothers whose babies were harmed by inadequate breastfeeding agreed to go public with their stories.

Many breastfeeding proponents were enraged by the media coverage, arguing that such "negative publicity" about breastfeeding would discourage expectant mothers from choosing to nurse. They insisted that the cases exposed were rare, isolated horror stories deliberately embellished by the reporters. They implied that such unpleasant topics shouldn't be openly aired.

I had been deeply concerned about the issue long before the media blitz because I was personally aware of a number of similar tragic cases and had witnessed other instances of failure to thrive in breastfed babies. I chose to participate in some of the media coverage to publicize the problem in order to prevent other babies from being harmed. I frankly was surprised at the magnitude of the negative reaction from some health professionals who feared that exposing the problem of insufficient milk would irreparably harm breastfeeding promotion efforts. You might ask why I was willing to make myself vulnerable to such criticism. I did it out of respect and empathy for those mothers and babies who had been unsuspecting victims of insufficient milk. The mothers of these infants had been completely unaware that their efforts to breastfeed could conceivably place their babies in jeopardy.

I am convinced that making parents and professionals aware of the problem of insufficient milk intake by breastfed infants was necessary to prevent more infants from suffering complications. I also believe that the media attention given to inadequate breast-feeding has played an important role in preventing the problem by rapidly bringing about many long-overdue changes in the hospital care and early follow-up of breastfed infants.

"Primary" vs. "Secondary" Insufficient Milk

Based on our experience evaluating many hundreds of breast-feeding mothers with insufficient milk, my colleagues and I at the Lactation Program in Denver have found it helpful to divide the problem of low milk supply into two main classifications. We designate these categories as "primary" and "secondary" insufficient milk. Secondary causes are by far the most common. We use the term to refer to low milk that results from—*or is secondary to*—one or more problems in breastfeeding management. Primary insufficient milk, on the other hand, appears to be unrelated to breastfeeding technique. Rather, it describes a low milk supply problem that was present from the outset and that is beyond a mother's control. Certainly, most women are capable of breast-feeding successfully, and primary insufficient lactation occurs very rarely. Estimates are that only 2 to 5 percent of women are incapable of producing an adequate milk supply despite optimal breast-feeding management.

With secondary insufficient milk, the breasts enlarge normally during pregnancy and become engorged after delivery when milk comes in abundantly. The potential to breastfeed successfully is readily apparent to anyone who views the milk-laden breasts on the third postpartum day. All that is necessary for continued generous milk production is a healthy infant who suckles well and empties the mother's milk at appropriate intervals. If something interferes with regular, effective drainage of milk, secondary insufficient milk can occur.

You can correctly guess that secondary insufficient milk is potentially preventable and correctable, especially when it is recognized early and appropriate intervention is started promptly. More than twenty years of evaluating breastfeeding mother-baby pairs have convinced me that the chief cause of secondary insufficient milk is failure to regularly and effectively remove milk from the breasts once abundant milk production begins. In summary, preventable, or secondary, causes of insufficient milk are much more common than primary causes, and failure to empty the breasts effectively and regularly is the most widespread, preventable cause of low milk.

Primary Causes of Insufficient Milk
(Factors Beyond a Mother's Control)

While most instances of insufficient milk are due to problems in the management of breastfeeding, a few mother-related explanations for insufficient milk involve primary causes that are entirely beyond a mother's control. In these cases, a woman produces insufficient milk from the start and may not be capable of making a full milk supply even under the best of circumstances. However, partial breastfeeding is still possible even when a baby must drink some supplemental formula on a daily basis.

With primary insufficient milk, a mother often reports that her breasts did not enlarge appreciably during pregnancy and/or that she experienced only minimal breast changes after delivery. She usually explains that she never felt her milk came in abundantly and has never been able to satisfy her hungry baby despite appropriate nursing technique and routines. Often the problem is attributed to an apparent abnormality in breast development and function. The following examples identify some recognized causes of primary insufficient milk.

Abnormal or Underdeveloped Breasts. Contrary to popular opinion, it simply is not true that "every breast is perfect for breastfeeding." Women's breasts vary widely in appearance and function. Such abnormalities are often overlooked because few pediatricians evaluate breast appearance even when breastfeeding is going poorly. Although obstetricians examine women's breasts prenatally, their exam usually is restricted to the detection of breast lumps rather than the identification of lactation risk factors. In my work with breastfeeding women, I have encountered many whose insufficient milk problem appeared to be linked to an obvious variation in breast appearance, such as tubular-shaped breasts (see chapter 2, pages 53–54, and chapter 11, pages 411–412), marked breast asymmetry, other type of abnormal breast development, or absence of prenatal breast enlargement.

Previous Breast Surgery. Many women have had diagnostic or cosmetic breast surgery that has impaired their ability to breastfeed (see chapter 11, pages 407–414). Research confirms that surgical incisions near the nipple-areola area carry the greatest risk, probably because of the likelihood that milk ducts have been severed. A simple biopsy, augmentation procedure, or breast reduction can limit breastfeeding potential in some women.

Breast Radiation. Radiation of the breast (for example, to treat breast cancer) damages the milk-producing glands and ducts. Little or no milk is produced after radiation therapy to a breast (see chapter 11, page 414). Damage to the milk glands can also occur when other chest organs are treated with radiation.

Failure of Lactogenesis (Postpartum Breast Engorgement). In a few women, milk fails to come in normally and doesn't increase abundantly after delivery. Sometimes the problem is attributed to serious illness in the mother, such as hemorrhage, high blood pressure, infection, or severe emotional stress. Since lactation is a mother's only elective body function, I don't find it too surprising that under great physical or emotional stress, milk production is sometimes inhibited.

Hormone Problems. A few women have hormone disorders that prevent full lactation. For example, pituitary gland tumors can affect blood levels of the hormone prolactin. Untreated thyroid disease has also been linked with insufficient milk.

Older Age. As more older women bear children these days, several lactation experts have observed that some mothers in their late thirties and forties have unexplained insufficient milk. I strongly suspect that some of these cases are due to the aging process. Beginning after age thirty-five, the milk-producing glands gradually decrease in number and are replaced by fatty tissue. Some of the "older" mothers with insufficient milk previously nursed successfully when they were younger. Although many women over forty produce abundant milk, age may explain some puzzling cases of insufficient milk.

Inadequate Body Fat. Lactation uses about one thousand calories a day, approximately five hundred of which come from body fat stores. Women who have gained less than twenty pounds during pregnancy, those with chronic illnesses resulting in low fat stores (e.g., cystic fibrosis, eating disorders, chronic bowel disease), and some athletes with very low body fat may not produce a full milk supply. Sometimes lifestyle changes or referral to a registered dietitian may enable such women to increase their body fat.

Small Breasts with Little Storage Capacity. We are just learning that the capacity of breasts to store residual milk can impact the daily frequency of feedings required for success. While small breasts don't necessarily produce less milk, the amount they can store may be reduced, requiring more frequent removal of milk. Thus, women with small breasts may need to nurse their babies at more frequent intervals than women with greater milk storage capacity. I have observed that women with small breasts seem more vulnerable to the effects of delayed emptying than women with larger breasts, who have the capacity to store more residual milk.

Secondary Causes of Insufficient Milk (Preventable Factors That Often Can Be Corrected)

Countless maternal and infant breastfeeding difficulties are readily complicated by insufficient milk. Many of these management problems are discussed in detail in chapter 7. Whenever milk is not removed from the breasts, the resulting excess pressure along with a chemical inhibitor in residual milk combine to give a powerful message to reduce production in the milk glands. In the next section, I have provided common examples of maternal situations that can contribute to insufficient milk, followed by descriptions of at-risk infants who are unlikely to nurse vigorously or to effectively remove milk from the breasts. Such infants require special attention and closer follow-up after hospital discharge. Mothers of these at-risk infants could improve their babies' intake at the breast and preserve a generous milk supply by expressing the remaining milk after breastfeedings.

Maternal Factors That Can Contribute to Secondary Insufficient Milk

Failure to relieve postpartum breast engorgement. I have repeatedly emphasized my conviction that the most common preventable cause of insufficient milk results from unrelieved postpartum breast engorgement. When the breasts don't get drained well after milk comes in abundantly, rapid decline in milk production occurs.

Inappropriate feeding routines. The breasts are very sensitive to ineffective emptying, especially during the period of postpartum engorgement. Even after lactation is well established, however, ineffective or incomplete removal of milk soon leads to decreased production. Whether the inappropriate feeding frequency or ineffective breastfeeding results from a baby sleeping all night, the elective use of supplemental bottles, temporary infant illness, heavy infant pacifier use, or maternal employment, the ultimate effect is to diminish milk production.

Sore nipples. Sore nipples can contribute to a low milk supply in several ways. First, sore nipples usually result when a baby is latched on incorrectly to nurse. Improper latch-on makes it difficult for a baby to obtain sufficient milk during nursing. Thus the baby is at risk for being underfed, and continued milk production can be jeopardized by incomplete milk removal. Two other reasons sore nipples are so easily complicated by low milk are that mothers may feed less frequently due to discomfort or have impaired milk letdown as a result of their pain.

Mother-baby separation. Whenever breastfeeding mothers and their nursing babies must be separated, diminished milk production can result if infrequent or incomplete breast emptying occurs. Common reasons for maternal-infant separation include sick or premature newborns, maternal employment, maternal schooling, maternal illness, rehospitalization of infants or mothers, or elective separation for travel or vacation.

Illness. If a breastfeeding mother becomes ill, her milk supply can decline either temporarily or permanently. Illness causing decreased milk production can be mild (colds, flu, diarrhea) or serious (heart failure, severe infections, cystic fibrosis). A breast infection can result in low milk production on the affected side.

Asymmetric milk supply. When the milk supply differs markedly between the two breasts, usually the low side is *under*producing rather than the other *over*producing. A very discrepant milk supply places a woman at increased risk for overall insufficient milk since the normal side may not be able to compensate for the low-producing side. I should emphasize that I have found it easier to increase milk production in an already abundant-producing breast than to bring a low-producing side up to normal. Discrepancies in milk production often begin in the first few post-partum weeks. If recognized early, efforts to increase the low side are more likely to be successful.

Stress. Stories abound about successfully breastfeeding women who suddenly "lose their milk" following an intensely stressful event, such as the death of a family member. In other instances, women have continued to make milk despite catastrophic life events. Clearly, some lactating women appear to be more suscep-tible to the effects of stress than others. Poor dietary habits and sleep deprivation may be additional contributing factors that exac-erbate the effects of stress.

Resumption of menstruation. Menstruation is usually delayed for many months in breastfeeding women. Menstrual periods typi-cally resume after a woman is no longer fully breastfeeding (i.e., the baby is sleeping through the night or taking other foods). Often, the resumption of menstruation is linked to a decreased pro-lactin level and diminished milk supply. However, a few fully breastfeeding women have early return of their periods without apparent effect on milk production.

Pregnancy. In my experience, milk production drops off dra-matically in breastfeeding women who become pregnant. Certainly it would be difficult for a woman to grow a baby in her uterus while fully nourishing another infant outside her body. Perhaps it is nature's plan preferentially to provide nutrients to the developing fetus over the older baby. Although many women choose to nurse through a pregnancy, they should be advised that their milk will probably decline. I have seen cases of infant failure to thrive that resulted when a mother mistakenly thought she could continue to fully nourish her breastfed baby after becoming pregnant (see chapter 11, pages 402–403).

Hormonal contraceptives. Some women find that estrogen-containing birth control pills cause their milk supply to decline. Progestin-only "minipills" are less likely to have an adverse effect on milk supply, but a few women may be susceptible. Their use should be delayed until breastfeeding has been well established.

Medications. With the exception of birth control pills, few medications have a negative effect on milk production. Included among those that could decrease milk supply are bromocriptine (Parlodel), antihistamines, blood pressure medication, and Methergine (sometimes prescribed for postpartum bleeding).

Weight-loss diet. Women can breastfeed successfully consuming a wide range of diets. However, severe calorie restriction places a woman at risk for diminished milk production. Lactating women should not attempt a weight-reduction program without medical supervision. In general, I don't advise breastfeeding women who want to lose weight to decrease their caloric intake below 1,800 calories per day. Remember, lactation is an elective process that can be negatively impacted by the stress of a crash diet.

Infants at Risk for Inadequate Breastfeeding

Small, premature, and/or borderline premature babies. A common belief exists that a small baby needs no special help with breastfeeding—that the breasts will produce just what the baby needs. In fact, small and/or premature babies seldom nurse as well as larger, full-term babies. They may have trouble holding the breast in their mouth and they tire easily during feeding (see chapter 10, page 386).

Jaundiced infants. As discussed in chapter 5 (pages 156–159), jaundice in a breastfed infant is often linked to poor breastfeeding and inadequate intake of milk. In addition, a high bilirubin level can cause a baby to be sleepy and to feed less vigorously, further aggravating the problem. Babies being treated with phototherapy often act sleepy and don't feed well.

Twins or higher multiples. Giving birth to twins doesn't automatically signal the breasts to make twice as much milk. Unless both twins nurse well, a mother may find she doesn't produce enough milk for two babies. Unfortunately, twins are often born early and have low birth weights and thus may not nurse effectively. The situation easily is complicated by maternal exhaustion as a result of caring for more than one baby (see chapter 11, pages 393–401).

Infants with abnormal muscle tone or other neurologic problems. Babies with abnormal motor tone can be either somewhat floppy (low tone) or stiff (high tone). Both extremes can interfere with correct breastfeeding. Infants who might have problems with muscle tone include premature babies and those with Down syndrome, cerebral palsy, or low Apgar scores at birth.

Infants with medical problems, such as heart disease or respiratory illness. Infants who have significant heart murmurs, respiratory problems requiring oxygen, infections, anemia, or other medical conditions often tire easily with feedings and nurse less effectively than healthy babies.

Infants with birth defects that affect feeding, such as cleft lip and/or palate. Any abnormality of the oral structures, especially cleft palate, places a baby at high risk for ineffective breastfeeding. While these infants may appear to be nursing satisfactorily, they may obtain little or no milk (see chapter 11, pages 423–425).

Normal infants with minor variations that can interfere with feeding, such as being tongue-tied or having a receding chin or a high-arched palate. Even minor variations in the oral structures can cause a baby to have difficulty obtaining milk. These infant causes of insufficient lactation can be so subtle that they are easily overlooked.

Normal infants who have latch-on problems, are sleepy, nondemanding, or reluctant nursers. Even an apparently healthy baby can be at risk for inadequate breastfeeding if the baby doesn't nurse regularly and effectively. Babies who are having difficulty latching on to one or both breasts, who need to be awakened for feedings, or who fall asleep after nursing only a few minutes are at risk for not obtaining sufficient milk.

Infants who begin sleeping through the night at an early age. Night nursings are important for stimulating a generous milk supply. It is not uncommon for an infant who previously was gaining well to slow her rate of weight gain or even stop gaining altogether shortly after beginning to sleep seven or more hours at night. (See Sleeping Through the Night, chapter 6, page 208).

Suspecting and Detecting Insufficient Milk

Insufficient milk should not be diagnosed without supportive evidence, including infant weights and growth patterns and measures of breast-milk production and intake (see also pages 131–151).

Infant Growth Measurements

When a breastfed infant fails to attain the expected rate of growth, the most probable explanation is insufficient consumption of breast milk. Usually, the mother's milk supply is too low to meet her baby's nutritional requirements. In a few cases, however, the mother actually produces sufficient breast milk, but the infant is unable to obtain adequate milk during breastfeeding, whether due to incorrect latch-on or improper suckling or physical abnormalities. What many people don't appreciate is that a mother's milk supply usually dwindles rapidly if her baby isn't nursing effectively. Thus, an initially normal milk supply can quickly become low if regular, effective removal of milk doesn't occur.

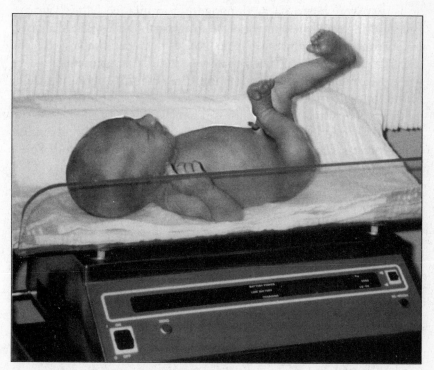

A baby's weight is the best indicator of the adequacy of milk intake.

A few babies suffer from underlying medical problems that either interfere with their ability to consume adequate milk or prevent them from growing properly despite drinking normal quantities of milk. Conditions like malabsorption, heart failure, respiratory difficulties, low thyroid, a urinary tract infection, or other chronic illness can be the cause of growth abnormalities in children. Obviously, whenever a baby isn't growing normally, the infant's physician needs to search for an unrecognized illness. But don't overlook ordinary explanations. Inadequate milk intake is the most common reason why breastfed babies don't gain weight properly.

At each well-baby visit, your infant will be weighed, and her length and head circumference will be measured. These measurements are plotted on a standard infant growth chart to track your baby's individual rate of growth over time. Separate growth curves are used for boys and girls since boys are slightly taller and heavier than girls, even in infancy. At present, both breastfed and formula-fed infants are plotted on the same growth charts.

Fortunately, newly available infant growth charts are more representative of the national population of infants than previous growth grids that were based on predominantly formula-fed babies. We are still awaiting the development of infant growth curves that are based on measurements obtained from solely breastfed babies. Recent research data have confirmed that breastfed babies grow at least as well as formula-fed infants for about the first three months of life. From four to twelve months, however, the growth of breastfed infants tapers in relation to bottle-fed babies.

Normal children and adults vary widely in height and body build. Much of this variation is related to our genetic background. Some babies are naturally longer and heavier than other infants. One child's normal pattern of growth might be along the 95th percentile, while another's normal rate of growth is along the 25th percentile. Thus, each baby has his or her own unique pattern of growth, and deviations from this *pattern* require investigation. The following criteria suggest that your baby is not obtaining sufficient milk:

• **Excess weight loss after birth.** All babies lose some weight in the first few days after birth. Around the time a mother's milk starts being produced in abundance (usually two to four days postpartum), a baby should start consuming larger quantities of milk. At this point, the baby should stop losing weight and begin to gain. Few breastfed babies lose greater than 7 percent of their birth weight before starting to gain. Continued weight loss beyond four days or losing 10 percent or more of the original birth weight is considered abnormal and usually signals that the baby is not obtaining sufficient milk (see Weight Loss and Weight Conversion Chart, pages 149–150). Such babies should be evaluated, and their mothers need to make appropriate modifications in breastfeeding scheduling or technique to assure that the infants begin receiving adequate nutrition. Babies who lose 15 percent or more of their birth weight can develop serious complications, such as severe dehydration, a chemical imbalance in their blood, seizures, and brain damage.

• **Failure to gain approximately one ounce per day in the early weeks of life.** After the brief period of weight loss, well-fed babies will start to gain weight steadily, usually by four to five days of age. Just as babies are born in different sizes, they also grow at different rates. It's not statistically possible for every baby to be "average." Some are larger and grow at the upper percentiles on standard growth grids, while others are smaller than average and grow at the lower percentiles. Generally, breastfed babies gain about one ounce each day during the early weeks and months of life. During this period, babies grow at a more rapid rate than they do later. Between birth and three months, most breastfed babies will gain approximately two-thirds to one pound (ten to sixteen ounces) every two weeks. Boy babies gain slightly more rapidly than girls. When a young breastfed infant is not gaining approximately an ounce each day (five to seven ounces per week), it is likely that the baby is not obtaining sufficient milk.

• **Failure to regain birth weight by ten to fourteen days of age.** If weight loss after birth has not been excessive (<10 percent weight loss from birth weight) and the rate of weight gain is normal (at least five to seven ounces per week), most breastfed babies will surpass their birth weight by ten to fourteen days of age. Larger babies at birth (> nine pounds) may take longer. If your baby is still under birth weight by two weeks, the most likely reason is insufficient intake of breast milk. Prompt medical evaluation is essential to identify and remedy the problem.

• **An infant weight percentile that is much lower than the height percentile.** In general, a child's height and weight tend to be proportionate in infancy, while head circumference follows its own curve independent of height and weight. If a baby is not consuming enough calories for adequate growth, rate of weight gain declines first. If the shortfall in calories continues, height will be impacted next. The last measurement to be affected is head circumference, because Mother Nature tries to protect brain growth even when nutrients are unavailable for optimal body growth. If your baby's height is at the 75th percentile, while his weight is only at the 25th percentile, the infant may be receiving inadequate calories and probably will appear thin and undernourished.

• **A steady decline in weight percentile.** Each baby grows along his or her own unique curve on the infant growth charts. Unexplained changes in a baby's rate of growth could signal a problem such as insufficient intake of milk. For example, if a baby's birth weight was at the 50th percentile, and the baby has grown so slowly that he is only at the 10th percentile by four months of age, this dramatic change in growth percentiles strongly suggests that the baby is not consuming enough calories or that he has an underlying medical problem causing impaired growth. Another baby who had grown along the 10th percentile from birth would not raise the same concern, even though both babies weighed the same amount at the same age.

• **Failure to gain weight between two visits or loss of weight.** Babies grow rapidly in the first year of life. At each pediatric visit, a baby should weigh more than he did at the last visit. Failure to gain any weight, and certainly loss of weight, between two office visits is distinctly abnormal. Inadequate intake of milk is the most likely cause. An ear infection or a bout of diarrhea might cause a baby to stop gaining weight for a few days, but when a week or two has gone by without any weight gain, you should be concerned about your baby's milk intake.

• **Behavioral evidence that a baby is chronically hungry.** When a baby often acts hungry after nursing, fusses and cries excessively, frequently requires a pacifier to be consoled, or nurses with extreme frequency or prolonged duration, it is highly possible that the baby is not obtaining enough milk.

Measuring How Much Milk a Mother Makes or a Baby Takes

Although some mothers and health professionals claim to be able to estimate how much milk a baby takes with nursing, these "guesstimates" often prove to be very inaccurate. Two convenient techniques are available to more precisely estimate the amount of milk a mother makes or a baby takes at a breastfeeding. I cannot explain why these simple, effective techniques are not used more often. They are easy to perform and allow for more accurate measurements of breastfeeding adequacy and for more sensible use of prescribed supplements.

Pumped Milk Volumes. In my experience, most lactating women respond well to hospital-grade rental electric breast pumps and are able to pump milk with relative ease. The volume of milk a mother can express at a usual feeding time with a rental electric breast pump provides a useful estimate of the quantity of milk that would have been available to her nursing infant. Ask your baby's doctor or a lactation specialist to help you interpret the volume of milk you express. When evaluating the adequacy of a pumped volume of milk, it is important to consider the length of the interval since the breasts were last emptied. Milk production can be calculated in milliliters (ml) per hour. A simplified rule of thumb for typical milk intake by breastfed infants between two or three weeks and five months of age is about *one ounce of milk per hour.* An ounce is equivalent to approximately 30 ml of milk. Let's say the mother of a six-week-old infant finished nursing at 10:00 A.M. and then pumped her breasts with a rental-grade electric pump between 12:45 P.M. and 1:00 P.M., obtaining 1¹/₂ ounces (approximately 45 ml) of milk. The interval from the end of her last nursing to the end of her pumping session is three hours. The amount of milk obtained is 1¹/₂ ounces. Thus, her hourly rate of milk production is about ¹/₂ ounce or 15 ml per hour. This is only about half of normal, suggesting her milk supply is low. Of course, this information must be corroborated by other evidence, such as the baby's present weight, rate of weight gain, urine and stooling pattern, and behavior. One should never diagnose insufficient milk based on a single piece of information like a onetime pumping session.

Infant-Feeding Test Weights. Test weighing of infants represents a simple, accurate method of measuring infant milk intake during a breastfeeding. The infant is weighed under the same conditions (identically clothed) before and after nursing. Then, the prefeed weight (in grams or ounces) is subtracted from the postfeed weight. The difference between the two weights equals the volume of milk consumed. One gram is approximately 1 milliliter (ml) of milk, and one ounce is approximately 30 ml or 30 cc. It is extremely important that you don't change the baby's diaper or alter the clothing the baby is wearing between the two weights. If the baby wets or soils his diaper during the feeding, that will not affect the accuracy of the test weight. The urine or stool weighs the same whether in the bladder or bowel or in the diaper. Dividing the amount of milk consumed by the hours that have passed since the breasts were last emptied allows you to calculate the rate of milk production in milliliters or ounces per hour. Remember the simple rule of thumb for milk intake in infants from approximately two or three weeks to five months: *one ounce of milk per hour*. Please keep in mind that this is only a rough estimate and that no firm conclusions should be made about a mother's milk supply based on a single piece of information like a onetime test weight.

A relatively inexpensive, lightweight, and user-friendly commercial scale (The BabyWeigh Scale by Medela) has been designed specifically to perform accurate infant-feeding test weights in the home or office. The scale is marketed principally to lactation consultants who not only use the scales in their practice but also rent them to parents for in-home use (see Resource List, page 450). In my experience, this useful tool greatly facilitates the evaluation and management of breastfed infants with inadequate weight gain.

However, an infant-feeding test weight is just one piece of information. Both pumped milk volumes and test-weighing results

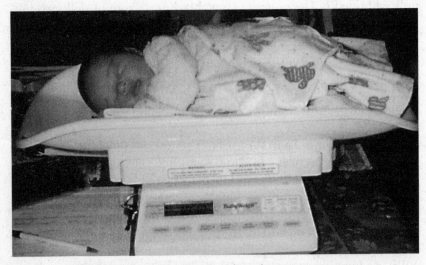

Using an electronic rental scale at home to measure
an infant's intake of breast milk.

must always be interpreted by your baby's physician in conjunction with other data, such as the baby's naked weight and rate of weight gain between consecutive visits.

How to Increase Your Milk Supply

Unfortunately, there is no quick fix for insufficient milk. Primary causes will not be able to be remedied completely. However, when low milk results from problems in breastfeeding management, there are many things you can do to improve your milk production and your baby's milk intake. Generally, the sooner the difficulty is recognized and intervention is started, the better your chances of solving the problem. I urge you to implement some of the following strategies at the earliest opportunity instead of losing valuable time with a wishful wait-and-see approach.

• **Check with your baby's physician or a lactation consultant to see whether you need to make any corrections in your breastfeeding technique or your feeding routines.** Insufficient milk frequently results from insufficient breast stimulation and emptying. For example, a woman may be nursing her newborn at four-hour intervals instead of every two to three hours, or her baby may have slept through the night at an early age. Perhaps her infant nurses only a few minutes at feeding times and doesn't drain her breasts effectively. Or, she may be skipping some nursings and giving supplements that have interfered with her milk supply.

The first step to increasing a low milk supply is to improve the frequency and effectiveness of milk removal. You may need to seek professional guidance from a breastfeeding specialist to assure that you are using optimal nursing technique. Specific recommendations will necessarily vary depending upon your baby's age and condition and whether your milk supply is only slightly low or very low. In general, if you are trying to increase your milk supply, you should try to nurse *more often*—at least every two to three hours from the beginning of one feeding to the beginning of the next. However, I don't advise extending the duration of nursings beyond about thirty to forty minutes. Once a baby has nursed this long, it is unlikely that much more milk will be obtained by prolonging the feeding. Usually at this point, little residual milk remains and the baby's suckling pattern is not very effective in stimulating further milk production. Babies and mothers can become exhausted by marathon feedings without proportionate benefit in a mother's maternal milk production or an infant's intake of milk.

I must interject a cautionary word here about the popular adage you may have heard that goes like this: "The more you nurse the more milk you will make." Certainly there is some truth to this "law of supply and demand," but it is a gross oversimplification to imply that a low milk supply is always or easily corrected by nursing more often. I have seen many tragic cases of severe infant malnutrition that resulted when well-intentioned mothers blindly subscribed to the belief that nursing more often would guarantee that their baby obtained more milk. I have known women who nursed nearly continuously under the assumption that marathon feedings automatically would increase their milk production and their baby's milk intake. I can't overemphasize the importance of using infant-feeding test weights to get an accurate idea of how much milk your baby takes at a feeding if your breastfed infant is underweight.

• **Make sure you are drinking plenty of fluids and eating regular nutritious meals.** Sound nutrition and adequate hydration are important for your overall sense of well-being and may help you make more milk. Certainly extra fluids are needed by lactating women, and a restricted diet can contribute to a low milk supply. On the other hand, you need to know that drinking fluids to excess or eating like a lumberjack won't magically raise your milk production. Most women with insufficient milk have an adequate diet and fluid intake.

• **Cut back on your schedule of activities and determine to do only the bare necessities for the next two weeks.** Most breastfeeding mothers I encounter are under more stress and pressure than they acknowledge. Perhaps our present fast-paced lifestyles make us view all the demands on us as normal. Many new mothers are also juggling the needs of toddlers or preschoolers. Others spend hours every day getting older children to and from various activities. Some are preparing to return to jobs outside the home, while others are facing a move or experiencing marital or financial problems. Maybe you have let yourself get overcommitted with volunteer activities or plans involving your extended family. Step back and examine the stress in your life. See if you can devote the next two weeks to increasing your milk supply. Put everything on hold that can wait a while and ask family and friends to cover for you wherever possible.

• **Try to relax and to adopt a positive, optimistic attitude.** I know that having a low milk supply can put a damper on your outlook. For many women it is an enormous disappointment. Furthermore, a low milk supply often goes hand in hand with a fussy, unhappy baby and inevitable sleep deprivation. I trust that by now you have identified the problem and obtained expert help to put your breastfeeding back on track. If supplemental milk has been prescribed because your baby is underweight, you may experience a huge sense of relief just knowing that your infant is now receiving adequate nutrition. You may actually find you make more milk now that you aren't as worried about your baby's status. Resolve to keep a positive attitude and to get as much rest as possible. Solicit encouragement and support from close friends and family. Try to create a calm, relaxed environment in your home. Play soothing music and visualize an abundant milk supply.

• **Seek treatment for any medical conditions you have that might adversely affect your milk supply.** Remember, for the mother's body, lactation is not an essential process, like breathing. As far as the mother's body is concerned, lactation is elective or optional. The body may cut back on producing milk if it is stressed by some type of illness, such as a breast, uterine, or kidney infection, high blood pressure, or an abscessed tooth. Physical discomfort like sore nipples or incision pain after a C-section can also impair milk supply. I sometimes observe increased milk production when an underlying medical problem in a mother is corrected. So don't ignore your own health or allow any medical conditions or complaints to go untreated.

• **Use a hospital-grade rental electric breast pump to provide your breasts additional stimulation and effective removal of milk.** As discussed earlier in this chapter, your baby can play an important role in causing a low milk supply, for example, by not nursing as frequently as needed or by not sucking correctly. And once a baby is undernourished, he usually nurses even *less* effectively. Early in my career, I remember being taught that a nursing baby was always more effective at draining the breasts than a breast pump. This belief was challenged when I discovered the remarkable effectiveness of hospital-grade electric breast pumps and encountered many babies who nursed very poorly. When dealing with a low milk situation, I commonly recommend that a mother use a rental-grade electric pump to provide additional breast stimulation and effective removal of milk. Most often I advise her to use the pump for ten minutes *after* each nursing. (If milk stops flowing after only a few minutes, she still should continue pumping for the full ten minutes. On the other hand, if milk is still flowing when ten minutes is up, she should continue for about fifteen minutes total). Double collection systems allow women to express milk from both breasts simultaneously, and this saves a lot of time. Since the pump doesn't have to be changed or coaxed back to sleep, it is a relatively simple matter to provide an extra ten minutes or so of mechanical stimulation at the end of a feeding. While the stimulus a baby provides can be highly variable from feeding to feeding, these pumps provide a predictable, uniformly effective stimulus—plus they don't tire, pause, rest, or need to be burped! Ideally, another caretaker can tend to the baby while the mother uses the pump. If she has to postpone pumping until she has finished settling the baby, enough time may have elapsed that she inadvertently could "steal milk" from the next feeding. Thus, it is preferable to pump immediately after the baby finishes nursing. Any residual milk expressed by the pump can be used to supplement the infant. This high-fat hindmilk is calorie-rich!

In most instances, pumping doesn't add to the total time spent on feedings because many women with low milk have been nursing for excessively long periods. Depending on the baby's condition and vigor, I recommend limiting nursings to a reasonable length of time (ranging from five to fifteen minutes per breast), followed by ten minutes or so of pumping.

• **Consider using galactogogues or prescribed medications to stimulate milk production.** Every society has special food supplements known as galactogogues that are popularly believed to enhance milk production. In addition, certain prescription medications used for other purposes have been found to cause a side effect of raising prolactin levels and increasing milk production. While scientific data are lacking to prove that insufficient milk can be effectively treated with specific food supplements or medications, some breastfeeding specialists and physicians will recommend them for women with a low milk supply.

In the past, beer, wine, and other alcoholic beverages were considered to be galactogogues. Many women were advised to drink a beer or have a glass of wine to aid milk production or to relax them sufficiently to improve their milk ejection reflex. This advice is now considered to be outdated and even dangerous. (A memorable quote from my medical school days sums up the dilemma of outdated advice, "Half of what we taught you is wrong, but we don't know which half.") In fact, daily alcohol consumption, even in small amounts, is now forbidden in lactating women because of possible harmful effects on the nursing baby. Some evidence exists to suggest that the lactation-enhancing role of beer or wine actually is found in the malt, not the alcohol. Thus, nonalcoholic beer may offer the same potential benefit that is alleged to be derived from alcoholic beverages. However, I do not recommend it.

Fenugreek. Fenugreek is an annual herb cultivated in India and areas of the Mediterranean. One of the oldest known medicinal herbs, it is a leguminous plant in the same class as soybeans, peanuts, peas, and garbanzos. Fenugreek seeds have long been used as a traditional medicine and as a food spice. Extracts of the seeds are used as a flavoring in artificial maple syrup and curry. Fenugreek seeds are rich in protein and high in fiber and are an important component of a traditional food supplement consumed by nursing mothers in India.

The use of ground fenugreek seeds, available in capsule form at health food stores, has anecdotally been reported to improve milk production in breastfeeding women in the United States. The commonly used dosage ranges from three to fifteen capsules daily, usually taken in three divided doses of one to five capsules. At the higher intakes, women typically notice that their perspiration and urine smell like maple syrup. Milk production is said to increase within a couple of days of beginning fenugreek supplements (see also chapter 10, pages 381–382).

Those who recommend fenugreek for improving lactation insist that it is completely harmless and effective. The fact is that no scientific research is available concerning fenugreek and breastfeeding. Because it is not classified as a medicine in the U.S., fenugreek has not been tested for safety and effectiveness and the amount in different preparations can vary. At least two severe allergic reactions have been reported in the medical literature after just smelling fenugreek or applying it to the skin. Women with known allergies to other leguminous plants are at greater risk for having an allergic reaction to fenugreek. Fenugreek seed has been shown to lower blood sugar levels and blood cholesterol. Presumably, fenugreek appears in the milk of mothers who take it, and the possible effects on breastfed infants have not been studied. Thus, the enthusiasm for fenugreek as a galactogogue should be tempered with a measure of caution. If you want to try fenugreek to increase a low milk supply, you should discuss this decision with your own and your baby's doctor. Make sure no other ingredients are present in the product you purchase, as fenugreek sometimes is sold with added ingredients. Fenugreek is present in Mother's Milk tea, another popular herbal galactogogue that contains several active ingredients that could pose a problem for infants. An excessive intake of any herbal product can have undesirable effects on mothers and their breastfed infants.

Prescription medications. A variety of prescription medications have been used as galactogogues over the years. Each of these drugs is approved by the U.S. Food and Drug Administration (FDA) for the treatment of various medical conditions, but none has specific FDA approval for use to treat insufficient milk. Their effect on lactation was first noticed when the medications were being used to treat other conditions. These drugs presumably work to increase milk production by raising blood prolactin levels.

Probably the first medication to be linked to lactation was the tranquilizer thorazine, which was noted to sometimes cause milk secretion in psychiatric patients taking the drug. Although attempts have been made in the past to use this drug to improve low milk production in lactating women, its heavy sedative effects posed a major drawback. It is no longer used to enhance lactation.

The drug that has been most widely used to try to increase milk production is metoclopramide, marketed under the trade name Reglan. This medication is usually prescribed for heartburn, nausea, and other gastrointestinal complaints. A number of studies have been conducted to test its effectiveness in raising a low milk supply. Several studies demonstrate an increased prolactin level and increased milk production when a mother with low milk takes metoclopramide (usually 10 milligrams three times daily for several weeks). The medication is not a panacea, however. Side effects include sedation, headache, and depression. Many women taking it experience little or no improvement in milk production. Furthermore, both prolactin and milk production may decline dramatically as soon as the medicine is stopped. In prescribing the medication, I have found that women who benefit from metoclopramide can expect their milk supply to approximately double. For some women, this is enough to bring their production into the normal range. For those with profoundly low milk, however, even doubling their supply doesn't allow them to breastfeed without supplements (see also chapter 10, page 382).

Growth hormone is known to be important for milk production in several species. Treating normally lactating dairy cows with bovine growth hormone has been shown to increase their milk production. Recently, studies with human growth hormone (hGH) have been conducted to examine whether it can increase a woman's milk production. In a recent study with mothers of premature infants who were pumping insufficient volumes of milk, daily injections of hGH for seven days resulted in an average 31 percent increase in their milk volume. Further research will be necessary before hGH is recommended for use in women with insufficient milk. A major drawback is that it must be given by injection (see also chapter 10, page 382).

While no miracle cure for low milk exists, it is exciting to contemplate the possibility that in the near future we may be able to routinely prescribe effective therapy to improve a woman's milk production. The fact that this previously neglected area of medicine has finally become the subject of scientific investigation leaves me hopeful that new treatments for insufficient milk will be identified.

When Supplemental Milk Becomes Necessary for a Breastfed Infant

I always feel a little defeated when I am forced to recommend that supplemental milk be given to a breastfed infant. How I wish every case of insufficient milk could be prevented or remedied. How I wish every mother could be helped to achieve her personal breast-feeding goals. But the unmistakable truth is that some women produce an insufficient quantity of milk to meet their babies' essential needs for calories and nutrients. Without the provision of supplemental milk, these babies are at risk for severe and chronic medical complications, including malnutrition, dehydration, chemical imbalance, brain hemorrhage, brain damage, stunted growth, jaundice, infections, and the emotional trauma of chronic hunger. If a mother's milk supply is very low or a baby's welfare is in jeopardy, I consider it unconscionable to withhold from a baby the quantity of milk the infant needs. Yet, I periodically encounter well-intentioned parents who are convinced that human milk represents ideal infant nutrition, *even if fed in insufficient quantity*. They believe it is preferable for a baby to be exclusively fed breast milk, even if the infant is grossly undernourished. When defining ideal infant nutrition, however, we must consider both the *quality* and *quantity* of milk fed to a baby. The ideal infant diet is breast milk fed in adequate quantities. When an adequate volume of breast milk is not available, it becomes essential to supplement an underfed baby with a sufficient quantity of a suitable breast-milk alternative to meet her nutritional needs (see pages 344–346 for milk options).

The adult caretakers in a baby's world are charged with the weighty responsibility of protecting the welfare of an utterly dependent infant. While doing everything possible to increase a mother's low milk supply is highly admirable, such efforts must be coupled with the daily assurance that a miserable, frantic, hungry baby will be allowed to drink her fill. Of course I feel great empathy for a mother's desire to avoid having to give her baby supplemental milk. I know what a disappointment this is to some women. But when a mother's wishes and a baby's needs are not in sync, the needs of a helpless baby always must take precedence over a mother's desires.

Let me make several other arguments for giving an underfed baby the supplement she needs. Anyone who has ever struggled with an insufficient milk problem knows what a strain it can place on the entire family. Everyone becomes preoccupied with the baby's weight and welfare. Weight checks are scheduled at frequent intervals and the parents' fragile sense of competence tenuously fluctuates around every ounce gained or lost. The infant inevitably is fussy and "difficult," leaving the parents feeling anxious and inadequate. Popular labels are misapplied in a futile attempt to make sense of the baby's inexplicable behavior: "colicky," "high needs," "strong-willed," "hot-tempered."

- **The first thing parents notice when their hungry baby is given supplement is that the baby undergoes a striking personality change.** Typically, the baby starts sleeping soundly between feedings, cries little, and is easy to console. Parents quickly begin to feel competent and capable as they are able to please their baby, who they now perceive as "delightful."
- **Next, the baby can be expected to start gaining weight at a remarkable rate.** For example, significantly underweight newborns who are given adequate supplement may gain two to three ounces a day for the first several days. Gaining a pound of catch-up weight

the first week is not uncommon. Documenting appropriate weight gain when a baby consumes adequate quantities of milk provides enormous reassurance about the baby's well-being. It essentially eliminates the need for elaborate diagnostic tests to evaluate the baby's health.

• **A final reason for giving an underweight baby the supplement she needs is that a baby will nurse more vigorously once she becomes better nourished.** I have encountered many underfed babies whose mothers believed they eventually would obtain sufficient milk if they breastfed perpetually. But a baby in a debilitated condition is usually an ineffective nurser who proves incapable of increasing her mother's low milk supply. *Breaking the cycle of underfeeding always is the best advice.* A thriving baby creates an improved outlook and more relaxed parental attitude. Spontaneous increase in milk production often is the net result of a healthier nursing baby and a less-anxious mother.

Parents' Reactions to the Need to Supplement Their Breastfed Babies

Parents vary widely in their reaction to the advice to supplement their breastfed infants. Some are alarmed to discover that their baby is hungry and underweight. Despite their obvious disappointment that breastfeeding isn't going as expected, their overriding desire is to meet their baby's needs. They eagerly feed as much additional milk as required while making every effort to increase their own milk supply.

Other parents react in an entirely different manner by inappropriately placing their own desires over their babies' needs. They may deny that their baby's weight is abnormally low, seeming more concerned about their milk supply than their baby's nutritional status. They may attempt to rationalize the situation by citing other babies they know who weighed the same or less at their baby's age. Or they may reason that they experienced a rough start with breastfeeding and that things are sure to go better from now on. Some deny the problem completely, explaining that their baby cries from colic rather than hunger or insisting that breastfed babies grow more slowly (not true in the early months) or that their previous baby had a similar pattern of growth.

Many mothers actually break down and cry at the prospect of having to supplement their infant. Others cry because they feel so badly about their baby being underfed. Some are distraught because they feel like a failure, as if their bodies have let them down. Many have read breastfeeding materials that promote the myth that every woman can nurse successfully. They are completely caught off guard by the prospect of not having enough milk. Others have read or heard that giving bottles or formula to a breastfed infant always undermines breastfeeding. To them, supplement isn't something to restore their baby's health and their own peace of mind, it is something that ruins all chances of long-term breastfeeding. I can imagine how devastating it would be to desperately want to breastfeed and to be convinced that starting supplement automatically will spell the beginning of the end. But supplement isn't incompatible with continuing to breastfeed. It's not always permanent either, and lots of options exist for giving it.

Supplemental Milk Options

One of the hardest things about having insufficient milk or a baby who doesn't gain enough weight is the loss of control a parent feels. You get no choice about your baby's need for extra milk. But you actually have a great many choices about the kind of supplement you decide to feed and the method of giving it. Exercising some of these choices can restore a measure of control in an uncomfortable situation and help you feel more like a partner in your baby's care. Many options exist for providing supplemental milk when your own supply does not meet all your baby's nutritional needs.

We are fortunate in Denver to have the largest distributing donor milk bank in North America (see Resource List, page 451). *Pasteurized donor human milk* is the ideal supplement for a breastfed infant who is premature, reacts adversely to commercial formulas, has a strong family history of milk allergy, certain digestive or immune problems, or other medical conditions that make human milk essential. Cost is a factor, however, since the milk-processing fee is far more expensive than the price of formula. Insurance usually pays for the milk in cases where the baby cannot tolerate commercial infant formulas. I must emphasize that the only donor milk I can recommend is *screened, pasteurized milk from healthy donors that is provided by a mother's milk bank*. I *cannot* endorse using untreated milk from well-meaning friends and neighbors. Unpasteurized milk could transmit viruses (including HIV, hepatitis, cytomegalovirus) and other disease-causing microorganisms.

In reality, most breastfed babies who require supplemental milk receive iron-fortified infant formula. *Cow's milk–based infant formulas* have the longest track record in artificial infant feeding. They are available in ready-to-feed, concentrated, and powdered preparations. The powdered option is attractive for breastfeeding mothers who may need to feed a relatively small quantity of supplement each day. Cow's milk–based formula might not be my first choice, however, if a close family member (parent or sibling) has an allergy to cow's milk or other allergic disease (asthma, food allergies, eczema). In this case, a hypoallergenic formula should be considered.

Soy-based infant formula represents another popular choice when formula supplement is required, although it has no advantage over cow's milk–based formula for a breastfed baby. Soy formula is often promoted as desirable for infants who are at increased risk for allergic disease; however, it has no proven value in preventing allergies. In fact, many babies who are allergic to cow's milk also are allergic to soy. Soy formula is made with a different sugar than lactose, which is present in both human milk and regular cow's milk–based formula. Some practitioners claim advantages of soy formula for infants recovering from diarrhea or the few infants who have difficulty digesting lactose. Since lactose is present in breast milk, however, I see no advantage to avoiding lactose in the supplement chosen for a breastfed infant.

If one has a family history of milk allergy or other allergic disease, I give strong consideration to supplementing with a *hypoallergenic formula* while the mother works on increasing her milk supply. Using such a formula reduces the risk of having your baby develop allergic symptoms. Because these formulas don't taste very delicious (at least to me!), a baby being supplemented with one of them is unlikely to prefer it over breast milk. They are palatable enough for a hungry baby to drink, however. Hypoallergenic formulas are considerably more expensive than cow's milk–based or soy formulas.

I encounter many parents who hold a highly negative perception of infant formulas because of the commercial industry they represent. Breastfeeding advocates may reinforce this perception when they refer to infant formulas as *artificial baby milk*. A few well-meaning parents actually believe that they can concoct an infant milk more nutritious than those on the market. I must caution you against such dangerous misbeliefs. Infant formulas have been in wide use for more than sixty years, and while less preferable than human milk, the truth is *iron-fortified infant formula represents the most nutritious alternative to mother's milk available today.* Goat's milk, whole, low-fat, or skim cow's milk, evaporated milk formulas, or concoctions promoted at a health food store are *not suitable for infant feeding*!

Options for Feeding Supplemental Milk to Infants

Parents have many options for feeding necessary supplement to their infants. Alternative methods must be demonstrated by a health care provider experienced in their use. It is very important that your baby daily receives the prescribed quantity of milk to meet her growth needs. Each method of supplement carries its own advantages and disadvantages. Whichever method you use, your infant should not spend more than twenty to thirty minutes taking her required extra milk after nursing. If this isn't being accomplished, you need to choose another method of giving the supplemental milk.

Bottle and Nipple Units. Feeding necessary supplement by bottle remains the most common way that extra milk is provided to breastfed babies. Countless bottle and nipple units are available on the market. In fact the choices are so numerous that parents often are confused about how to select among traditional or angled bottles, disposable bottle bags, and nipples with diverse lengths, shapes, openings, flow rates, or an anti-vacuum feature. Each option has arguable merits about its desirability for breastfed infants, and reports vary about how successfully babies switch back and forth from breast to bottle. An angled bottle will allow a baby to be fed in a more upright position and help prevent milk from entering the middle ear. I cannot endorse any particular nipple as being generally preferable for breastfed infants. One baby may feed well with a certain nipple, while another infant using the same nipple may obtain milk too rapidly or have difficulty taking her feeding in a reasonable length of time. Popular choices include traditional straight nipples, orthodontic shaped varieties, tri-cut nipples, and a wide, soft nipple with a patented anti-vacuum air valve. Your baby should be able to take her supplement within about twenty minutes. You don't want her to expend a lot of effort taking the bottle, nor do you want bottle-feeding to be so easy that your baby prefers it over breastfeeding. Many parents make their choice of a bottle and nipple based on such practical matters as which bottle-nipple units are easily available to them, which one their baby readily accepts, or which they have used with previous babies.

The *advantages* of giving necessary supplemental milk by bottle are multiple. In most instances, the bottle proves to be the fastest way to feed a hungry baby. A mother with insufficient milk usually has little time left over between her efforts to improve breast-feeding and to assure her baby is well fed. The greatest and most publicized *disadvantage* of using a bottle with a breastfed infant is the risk that the baby will breastfeed less effectively or lose interest in breastfeeding and develop a preference for bottle-feeding. The magnitude of this risk varies for every baby and every situation. Some babies seem to switch back and forth between breast and bottle with relative ease and to use the correct sucking technique for each feeding method. Some clearly prefer the breast despite being given bottles on a daily basis. Others may quickly show a preference for the bottle and begin nursing only in a token fashion. In my experience, bottle preference is most likely to occur when the mother's milk supply remains very low. In these cases, babies may recognize that their greatest nutritional rewards come from bottle-feeding. If this starts to happen, consider switching to the SNS device for giving your baby her supplement, at least for a few feedings each day.

SNS. The Supplemental Nursing System (SNS) by Medela, Inc., is an ideal way to give necessary supplement to a breastfed infant (see page 114 and illustration on page 348). This device was designed specifically to allow a baby to take supplemental milk simultaneously while breastfeeding. The milk supplement is placed in a plastic bottle which is connected to a thin, silicone tube that is laid next to the mother's nipple. The baby takes both the nipple and the tubing into her mouth when she latches on to nurse. Using the SNS actually enhances a baby's breastfeeding technique by providing the nursing infant with a prompt flow of milk during suckling.

Despite this powerful advantage, the SNS has some drawbacks. For one thing, it is not as widely available as baby bottle and nipple units, although it is carried by electric breast pump rental sites, lactation consultants, many hospitals, and La Leche League (see

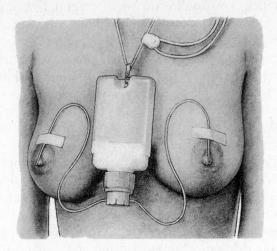

The SNS allows an infant to receive
supplemental milk while breastfeeding.

Resource List, page 450). Although the device is relatively simple,
it still is harder to use and clean than a bottle. A parent should not
be expected to try the SNS without its use being demonstrated and
supervised by a health care provider who has experience using the
device. For a baby who is significantly underweight, I prefer to supplement with a bottle until the infant has achieved critical catch-up
growth. At that point, I invite a mother to switch to the SNS and
phase out the use of bottles if she so chooses. The SNS works best
with young babies, and some infants do better with it than others.
Babies over three or four months of age are more likely to resist its
use or to pull at the tubing while the device is in place. It's certainly
an option worth trying, however.

Some lactation consultants are proponents of a method of supplementing breastfed infants known as *finger feeding*. Finger
feeding involves using the SNS or a similar feeding device by
placing the tubing along the palm (pad) side of the parent's index
finger. The baby suckles the adult finger and tubing simultaneously
to obtain supplemental milk from the attached reservoir bottle.
Those who advocate this method feel that it is less likely to confuse
a baby than bottle-feeding, that a parent's finger is more "natural"
than silicone or rubber, that finger feeding is easier for parents than
using the SNS in its traditional manner, and that the method allows
parents to evaluate their baby's pattern of suckling on their finger.
Some lactation consultants teach parents how to perform "suck

training" with their infant by regulating the flow of milk through the tubing during finger feeding. I have no direct experience with finger feeding and am aware of no scientific data to support this method of feeding over other alternatives.

Cup Feeding. Certainly older infants (beginning around six months) can learn to drink their supplemental milk from a spouted cup. This method avoids the risk of nipple preference sometimes encountered with bottle-feeding. It takes longer at first, but many babies become quite proficient at cup feeding.

In other countries, cup feeding of expressed breast milk is routinely used with newborn infants who are unable to breastfeed. In the United States, newborn infants with cleft palate are often fed by cup. In some nurseries, cup feeding is increasingly being used to offer required supplemental milk to breastfed newborns. Several cuplike devices have been developed for this specific purpose and are marketed by breast pump manufacturers (see Resource List, page 446). Many nurses simply use the plastic one-ounce medicine cups available in every hospital. Parents at home have used shot glasses to cup-feed their babies. The main advantage of using a cup to provide necessary supplement to breastfed infants is the avoidance of artificial nipples that could interfere with a baby's learning to nurse. I have minimal experience with cup-feeding infants beyond the first week of life, and do not recommend the method for the long term. Ample sucking is important for normal oral development in young infants. Your decisions about how to give supplemental milk to your baby should be made in conjunction with your baby's health care provider and not on your own.

Spoon or Dropper. Some health professionals recommend giving necessary supplement to newborns by spoon or dropper. I think this is a reasonable method for the early days of life, when the volume of supplement a baby might need is relatively small and the baby is still learning to nurse. Personally, I do not recommend trying to give a baby necessary supplement by these methods beyond the hospital period, as they tend to be slow and ineffective in getting adequate volumes into the infant. I view them as appropriate only during the first few days after birth.

Duration of Feedings. When a breastfed baby requires regular supplement while his nursing mother is trying to increase her milk supply, the parents may be required to carry out an elaborate and time-consuming infant-feeding plan. At the Lactation Program, we refer to this often-prescribed regimen as "triple-feeding." First, the mother nurses her infant. Following breastfeeding, she uses a rental electric pump to express any residual milk and to provide her breasts maximal stimulation and effective milk removal. In addition, she offers her baby adequate quantities of expressed breast milk or formula by bottle or other method to complete the feeding. If another caretaker is present to help, the baby can be given the supplemental milk at the same time the mother is pumping. This saves valuable time and allows a longer interval between feeding sessions. When no helper is available, however, the mother may choose to feed the extra milk (formula or expressed milk collected earlier) immediately after nursing if her baby is fussing and demanding. Or, if her infant is not protesting, she may prefer to pump her breasts first and then offer the milk she expresses. To avoid stressing your baby and to allow a reasonable break until the next feeding, it is important to set time constraints on triple-feeding.

Generally, your baby should nurse approximately ten minutes at each breast. Dual pumping should be accomplished in about fifteen minutes, and the infant should consume all her supplemental milk in less than thirty minutes. You should have about two hours before starting the process over again. If the entire feeding program is taking more than one hour, you need to talk with your baby's doctor or your lactation consultant to modify the feeding plan. Triple-feeding is an enormous commitment of time and effort. Marathon feeding sessions are distressing to both parents and infants. When feedings take an inordinate length of time, your plan may be self-defeating.

Comfort Nursing

Breastfeeding is much more than a feeding option. It is also a style of mothering and a method of comforting a baby. It's fortunate that we have two terms to describe the process—"breastfeeding" and "nursing." These different words remind us about the dual feeding and nurturing aspects to breastfeeding. When a mother needs to feed her baby supplemental milk because her supply is too low, I emphasize the importance of continuing to nurse as much as possible. If your baby is refusing the breast because she is frantically hungry, you will probably experience more success by offering some supplement first and then nursing "for dessert." Many mothers explain that their babies derive such comfort from nursing that they routinely return to the breast to fall asleep after taking their fill from the bottle. Using breastfeeding as a human pacifier is one of the best ways to keep an infant interested in nursing despite a low milk supply.

Preventive Strategies to Maximize Your Milk Supply from the Outset

It may not be possible to prevent insufficient milk in every instance, but the following recommendations should optimize your chances of bringing in and keeping a plentiful milk supply.

- **Attend a prenatal breastfeeding class.** Most postpartum hospital stays are too short to teach you everything you need to know about breastfeeding. Expectant parents today, more than ever, need to acquire some knowledge about breastfeeding before they arrive at the hospital.
- **Obtain a prenatal breast exam to screen for lactation risk factors.** Before delivery, you will want to identify any breast variations, such as flat or inverted nipples, that could impact breastfeeding. By detecting such risk factors in advance, you can elicit specialized help to prepare for breastfeeding and to tailor a feeding plan for your baby.
- **Select a hospital with supportive breastfeeding routines.** Get the best possible start with breastfeeding by choosing a hospital with supportive breastfeeding policies. Try to nurse within an hour of giving birth. Keep your baby in your room throughout your stay and nurse on demand. Solicit all the help you can to learn correct breastfeeding technique. Ask that your baby not receive any supplemental feedings of formula or water unless a valid medical indication exists.
- **Identify early any risk factors you may have that could interfere with successful breastfeeding.** Seek extra help and advice promptly if breastfeeding doesn't get off to a smooth start, for example, if you aren't sure whether your milk came in abundantly, if your baby has trouble latching on, is smaller than six pounds and/or earlier than thirty-eight weeks, has jaundice, or doesn't

demand to feed regularly. Early intervention can make an enormous difference in achieving successful breastfeeding.

• **Begin using a hospital-grade electric breast pump whenever any doubt exists about whether your breast milk is being removed regularly and effectively.** Preserving a generous milk supply in the face of early difficulties always gives you the best shot at overcoming breastfeeding problems.

• **Arrange follow-up within forty-eight hours of being discharged.** Insist that you and your baby be evaluated by a health professional knowledgeable about breastfeeding within forty-eight hours of hospital discharge. The visit can occur in your home or at a physician's office, clinic, or hospital. Make sure that your baby is weighed at this visit and that her weight loss isn't excessive.

• **Surround yourself with friends and relatives who are experienced and knowledgeable about breastfeeding.** Invite only those individuals who are sure to encourage and support your efforts. Postpone visitors and outings until breastfeeding is going well.

• **Nurse your infant on demand, approximately every two to three hours, or eight to twelve times in twenty-four hours.** Arrange for sufficient help and rest to allow you to devote your energies to round-the-clock breastfeeding. Avoid pacifiers, "relief bottles," or long sleep intervals that prevent your breasts from being drained every couple of hours.

• **Join a mother-to-mother support group, such as La Leche League.** Surround yourself with like-minded women who have breastfed successfully and who can serve as role models for success and as sources of support and information.

• **Avoid breastfeeding "insults" that can decrease your milk supply.** Included among these negative influences are combination birth control pills, separations from your infant, strict weight-reduction diets, and long night intervals without nursing.

• **Keep your baby in your presence as much as possible and nurse whenever your baby demands.** Unrestricted nursing is always your best defense against insufficient milk.

Coping with the Disappointment of Insufficient Milk

For some women, the realization that they have insufficient milk and will be unable to breastfeed exclusively represents a devastating loss. Their sadness lingers long past their infant's babyhood. After many years of hearing and empathizing with women's personal stories, I have come to appreciate that successful breastfeeding, like conception, is not a basic right. Rather, it is a precious gift. Although we all enjoy many blessings, not every woman receives this particular gift. Having to give up your dreamed-about breastfeeding experience is one, often the first, of many parenting disappointments. All parents regularly must reconcile our expectations and our reality and simply do the best we can with the circumstances we have. Despite our real and legitimate grief at the loss of what had been hoped for, we each must resolve to relinquish our claims to what might have been and celebrate the possibility of what still can be.

Chapter 10

Breastfeeding Premature and Other High-Risk Infants

Perhaps this chapter holds so much meaning for me because I first became intimately involved with helping breastfeeding mothers as a young pediatric resident in neonatal intensive care nurseries. I have always felt a special bond with mothers of high-risk infants because my own first child, Peter, developed severe jaundice after birth due to a blood incompatibility between his blood type and mine. I was separated from him for the first four days of his life—an interval that seemed an eternity. Unable to touch or hold him, my concern about his well-being quickly became all-consuming. I so magnified in my mind the seriousness of his medical problem that I was convinced he would either die or be brain-damaged from excessive levels of bilirubin.

I desperately sought to know every detail about Peter's condition and to keep up with every change in his status. Yet, I found it exceedingly difficult to communicate with the attending physicians who made the decisions about his care. As a young navy wife, I had given birth at a military hospital, after seeing a different doctor at each prenatal visit. I had no ongoing relationship with a personal physician and had scarcely met the newborn specialists who were treating my son's severe jaundice. I resolutely waited hour after hour to elicit any scrap of new information—the latest bilirubin level or an update about Peter's feedings. I would station myself in the doorway of our four-bed ward, where I could strategically scan the halls in search of doctors making unannounced rounds. Several times daily, I nearly accosted the pediatricians, pummeling them with questions about my baby. The nearly intolerable stress of those four days eventually culminated in an anguished wait while masked physicians performed a curative, albeit potentially dangerous, exchange transfusion when Peter was three and a half days old. The four-day interval between my giving birth and our being able to hold our newborn baby was an agonizing experience for Larry and me. Time barely crawled, and nothing seemed normal until our baby was finally pronounced well.

When I was eventually permitted to hold Peter and to attempt to breastfeed him, I was blessed with the expert help of a competent and compassionate nurse. With her skilled guidance and Peter's innate instincts, it wasn't long before he correctly grasped my breast and started to gulp contentedly. My engorged, milk-filled breasts craved the relief that his nursing brought. As I held my vulnerable newborn whose life I believed had been hanging in the balance only twelve hours earlier, I felt as if I had been dragged through an emotional wringer and was still sorting out my sensibilities.

Several years later, when I entered a premature infant nursery as an inexperienced young intern, a wave of painful nostalgia reminded me of my brief, frightening introduction to parenthood— that interminable wait to learn whether my baby was going to be okay. Suddenly, I realized that my own experience, intolerable though it seemed at the time, was short and easy compared to the emotional roller coaster that parents of the premature infants around me were forced to ride. Here I encountered babies whose lives truly did hang in the balance, infants who weighed only a fraction of Peter's weight, newborns with birth defects and problems far more complex and life-threatening than a high bilirubin level. Here were infants who might not even survive and who might never be all right. As I worked in neonatal intensive care nurseries, I developed a lifelong awe and respect for those incredible mothers and fathers who endure the indescribable trauma of having a seriously ill newborn. This chapter is devoted to those courageous parents and their precious babies.

Can I Still Breastfeed If My Baby Is Born Too Early or Has Medical Problems?

Whenever a newborn has a medical problem, his immediate care needs can eclipse the importance of breastfeeding. I want to assure you that breastfeeding is not only possible for premature and sick newborns but also is enormously valuable as a component of their overall care. I congratulate you for making the commitment to breastfeed your high-risk baby. Although choosing to breastfeed an infant who is premature, ill, or has a birth defect will require special arrangements, your milk offers your baby immediate and long-term health benefits. Furthermore, breastfeeding will help you feel more involved in your baby's care and more connected to your infant.

Establishing and maintaining a supply of breast milk when separated from your baby will require extra effort on your part. However, many mothers agree that being able to provide their own milk for their hospitalized newborns and to eventually nurse their infants makes all their endeavors worthwhile. Despite how surprised you may be about giving birth prematurely or having a baby with a medical problem, you are not alone. Countless thousands of mothers of high-risk infants have faced the same kinds of questions and concerns you are having right now. This chapter will provide you with the specialized information you will need to succeed at breastfeeding despite being separated from your baby. It provides details about pumping and storing your expressed breast milk, offers practical advice about beginning direct breastfeeding, and helps you make the transition to full breastfeeding after your baby comes home.

Advantages of Breastfeeding Your High-Risk Infant

Breastfeeding offers compelling health advantages for both mothers and babies. You will want to review the numerous benefits of breastfeeding outlined in chapter 1 in order to strengthen your commitment to providing breast milk for your baby. In addition, you should know that human milk provides several unique advantages for premature and high-risk infants.

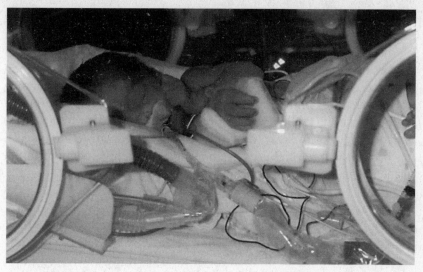

Providing expressed milk for a premature infant offers many health advantages and involves the family in their baby's care.

• **Human milk is the perfect transition food for premature infants who often have trouble tolerating milk feedings after birth.** The nutrient composition of human milk is ideally suited for premature infants. Your own milk is digested more easily than formula, and your baby's stomach will empty faster after being fed human milk. The many growth factors in breast milk help a baby's intestinal tract to mature and absorb nutrients. The proteins in human milk are digested easily, and the fats are particularly well absorbed by premature infants. In fact, when human milk is added to formula, the absorption of fat is improved.

Premature infants have higher requirements for many nutrients than do full-term babies. Interestingly, for the first month postpartum, the milk produced by mothers who deliver prematurely differs in composition from milk made by mothers of term infants. Preterm milk is higher in several important nutrients, including protein and sodium, thus making your own milk even more valuable to your baby.

• **Colostrum and breast milk contain white blood cells, antibodies, and other valuable immune properties to help a baby resist infection.** Babies born prematurely have a weakened immune system that leaves them more susceptible to infectious diseases than term infants. Preterm mother's milk is especially rich in antibodies and other protective factors that help babies resist disease. Numerous studies have shown that feeding human milk to premature infants provides some protection against a variety of common infections. For example, fewer cases of a potentially life-threatening bowel infection, known as necrotizing enterocolitis (NEC), occur in premature infants who are fed human milk compared with those who are solely fed formula. Feeding breast milk to premature infants also has been shown to offer protection against a life-threatening infection of the blood, known as septicemia or sepsis.

• **Breast milk may improve the neurologic development of premature infants.** The long-chain fatty acids present in human milk are known to be important for optimal development of the nervous system and the retina of the eye. In a large multicenter study that followed premature infants for seven and a half to eight years, children who received human milk during their newborn hospitalization had significantly higher IQs than children who received no human milk as newborns. Other studies have shown improved visual performance in premature infants who were fed human milk compared with those fed formula.

• **Feeding expressed breast milk to sick or premature infants involves a family in the care of their special-needs infant.** Many mothers who must be separated from their infants derive great emotional satisfaction from providing their expressed milk for their babies' feedings. At a time when the majority of a baby's care is being provided by nurses, a woman can contribute to her infant's well-being in a uniquely personal way that no health professional could ever match.

I recall feeling so helpless and useless when Peter was being kept in the nursery due to jaundice. I wasn't even allowed to touch or hold him because nursery visitation was so restricted in those days. It was explained to me that if I held my baby, I would "contaminate" him with my germs and prevent him from returning to the nursery for the special care he required. Instead of feeling needed by my baby, I felt like a dangerous intruder. No one attempted to involve me in Peter's care, and although I was planning to breastfeed, no one suggested that I might pump my milk for him. In the nursery, Peter was being bottle-fed formula and water alternately every two hours in an attempt to lower his bilirubin level. As I longingly watched him through the nursery window on the third day after giving birth, I envied the nurse who was feeding him from a bottle while my swollen breasts ached with milk. Although I was grateful for her attentive and affectionate care of my son, I resented the fact that her skill and expertise made her role more valuable than mine. Trying to be friendly, she mouthed a seemingly innocent question through the glass, "What's his name?" "Peter," I blurted out. The name had been chosen as soon as my pregnancy had been confirmed. "Oh," she answered, revealing her disappointment, "I've been calling him Bobby." I can still recall my deep ambivalence about her nicknaming my son. While I appreciated that this nurse had displayed a special interest in my baby, I was also intensely jealous of her opportunity to "mother" him while I had no option but to stand helplessly apart, pressed against a glass barrier.

At a time when you might be feeling like I was, pumping your breasts and providing milk for your baby's feedings is a worthwhile and specific activity that no one else can do for your infant. Feeding your own milk to your baby can preserve a special link between you and your hospitalized newborn.

• **By maintaining your milk supply, you are making it possible to ultimately breastfeed your baby one day.** As long as you are producing milk, you preserve the option to begin breastfeeding once your baby is able to go to breast. When that day comes, your infant will benefit additionally from the close skin-to-skin contact, security, and comfort that breastfeeding affords. By starting to express your milk, you are offering your baby and yourself the chance to benefit from all the advantages of long-term breastfeeding. After all, prematurity is not a lifelong condition. In a matter of weeks or months, your baby will be home with you. By establishing your supply in the first weeks of separation, you may be able to breastfeed as long as you had planned.

Preparation

When a mother delivers prematurely, she may not have had the opportunity to prepare for routine breastfeeding, let alone to learn the details of pumping and storing milk for her baby. Most pregnant women who attend prenatal breastfeeding classes do so in their last two months of pregnancy. If you delivered prematurely, chances are you never got to attend such a class. You may not know anything about how to manage breastfeeding. Women in your situation often feel unprepared for motherhood, unfamiliar with routine baby care, and totally overwhelmed by the highly specialized equipment in a neonatal intensive care nursery.

While most health professionals are supportive of breastfeeding under routine circumstances, a woman's desire to breastfeed can take a backseat when her infant is critically ill or very tiny. Neonatal nurses may be so preoccupied with the moment-to-moment physical care of your baby that they may view breast-feeding as something remote—not really relevant to today's priorities. But it won't be long before your baby's nutrition will be of great concern, and you will need to start now if you want to provide your own milk for his feedings. Make it clear to those caring for your baby that breastfeeding is extremely important to you. Ask to receive specialized help from a lactation consultant or other breastfeeding specialist so you will be sure to receive the information and support you need and deserve. Most hospitals with a neonatal intensive care unit (NICU) have a lactation consultant or nurse specialist to assist breastfeeding mothers. These experts are a wonderful source of information and support.

Maintaining a Breast-milk Supply Without a Nursing Infant

The first step toward breastfeeding a high-risk infant is learning how to successfully establish and maintain a breast-milk supply without a nursing baby. This usually requires the use of an effective hospital-grade electric breast pump to empty your breasts at regular intervals until your baby is able to fully breastfeed. You will find it helpful to review the information in chapter 3 on how milk is made and released. The key objectives of pumping are to obtain milk to be fed to your baby as long as direct nursing isn't possible and to preserve a generous milk supply for eventual breastfeeding. Even if you aren't sure about making a long-term commitment to breastfeeding, I urge you to begin expressing your milk anyway. You can always stop pumping if you change your mind later, and your baby will have benefited from receiving your precious colostrum and early milk. If you delay getting started for more than a few days, you may have difficulty producing adequate milk and spend a lot of effort trying to "catch up." Right after delivery is when your body is ideally suited to start producing abundant milk.

Under normal circumstances, a healthy newborn begins nursing shortly after delivery and breastfeeds eight or more times each day—usually every two to three hours around the clock. Whether or not a woman plans to breastfeed, colostrum begins changing to abundant milk around the second to third day postpartum. If milk is regularly removed from the breasts, more milk continues to be produced. On the other hand, if breast milk is not removed effectively and regularly, continued milk production will cease, just as if a woman were bottle-feeding.

Thus, if you are separated from your baby after delivery, it is crucial that your breasts receive a regular suckling stimulus and regular effective removal of milk that mimics routine infant nursing. This is best accomplished by using a hospital-grade rental electric breast pump to express your milk as often as a nursing baby would have fed.

Obtaining a Breast Pump

Hospital-Grade Rental Electric Breast Pumps. Generally the most efficient, comfortable, and convenient breast pumps are the hospital-grade electric pumps that cycle automatically and mimic the suckling action of a vigorous newborn. Most of these pumps have a special feature that allows you to select both the speed at which the pump cycles and the amount of vacuum generated to achieve maximum comfort and efficiency. Many women find their milk flows more readily at a specific cycle rate and vacuum setting. I strongly recommend obtaining such a hospital-grade rental electric pump if you will be solely dependent upon pumping to bring in and maintain your milk supply while you are separated from your infant. You can probably count on the hospital having one or more of these pumps for use in the postpartum period and when you come to visit your baby. However, once you are discharged from the hospital, you will need to have your own pump for optimal ease and efficiency of milk expression when you are at home. Hospital-grade electric pumps can be rented from lactation consultants, private rental stations, hospitals, home health supply stores, and pharmacies. To locate a pump-rental station near you, call the pump manufacturers listed on page 446.

Originally, hospital-grade rental electric pumps were equipped with single collection containers that were used to express milk from one breast at a time. Today, double collection systems are almost universally available and should be considered the preferred method of pumping. A double collection system allows you to simultaneously pump both breasts, thereby collecting your milk in half the time. Also, since milk lets-down in both breasts at once, it makes good sense to empty both breasts simultaneously. A number of years ago, a colleague and I conducted a small study which demonstrated that double pumping generated a higher blood prolactin level than single pumping. Higher prolactin levels may increase a mother's milk supply.

Hospital-grade electric pumps include heavier classic models, as well as lightweight, highly portable pumps. Generally, daily rental fees are higher than monthly or long-term rates. Most rental stations will require a security deposit that is reimbursed when you return the pump. You also need to purchase a personal-use double collection kit. Before you protest that you can't afford this expense, consider the long-term benefits of providing your own milk to your baby and of being able to nurse your little one after she comes home. Friends and relatives who want to give you a baby gift can contribute toward the pump-rental expense. Call your insurance company to inquire whether your particular policy will cover the cost of renting an electric breast pump to obtain milk for feeding a high-risk infant. You may need to ask your baby's neonatologist to write a letter to your insurance company explaining that breast milk is an essential part of your baby's medical care and that the hospital-grade rental electric pump is medically necessary for your baby's optimal health.

Getting Started Pumping. A hospital nurse or lactation consultant should demonstrate the proper use of your electric pump. I also urge you to take the time to read the manufacturer's instructions that accompany the pump. Most new mothers are so tired and distracted when pumping is first demonstrated that they do not remember everything that was told to them. Don't hesitate to request additional assistance if necessary. Most hospitals provide mothers of high-risk infants with written guidelines that can be reviewed to refresh your memory about specific protocols for collecting expressed breast milk.

Most women prefer to start pumping at the lowest vacuum setting. Pumping will be more comfortable if you are careful to center each nipple in the opening on the breast shield before you turn the pump on. Once you are accustomed to the pumping cycle, you can gradually adjust the vacuum control level from minimum to normal suction. Using a normal vacuum level for pumping should be comfortable and usually will extract more milk than a lower vacuum setting. Pumping seldom causes sore nipples unless damage to the nipple skin occurs due to overpumping during breast engorgement (see page 226). Some women who develop sore nipples cannot tolerate the normal level of pump suction. These women need to select the most tolerable vacuum setting and cycle rate that generates milk flow.

If desired, you can apply a thin coating of USP modified anhydrous lanolin (medical grade) to your nipples prior to pumping. This serves as a lubricant between the skin and the breast shield and can make pumping more comfortable. Use only ultrapure medical-grade lanolin.

Other Options for Pumping. I find it difficult to generalize about the effectiveness of other methods of milk expression, including smaller electric, battery-operated, and manual pumps or hand expression. Women's response to these pumping options varies widely. A particular pump may work well for one woman and be ineffective for another. In my experience, only the hospital-grade rental electric pumps prove comfortable and highly effective for the vast majority of women.

Hand expression. I was fortunate in being able to obtain milk easily using hand expression, but I found the method tiring and certainly more time-consuming than today's option of double pumping. Occasionally, I encounter a woman whose breasts respond best to the human touch and who prefers hand expression over a fancy pump. Certainly, women in underdeveloped countries all over the world rely solely on hand expression to obtain milk for feeding their high-risk infants. Hand expression is free and always available (for example, if your pump malfunctions in the middle of the night). Some women find that hand expression is an excellent way to stimulate their let-down reflex. By manually compressing the storage areas, or lactiferous sinuses, located under the areola, they can initiate milk flow. However, hand expression does not generate any suction to help with milk extraction. For some reason, few women in America seem able to preserve a long-term generous milk supply while using only hand expression. Nevertheless, I think every nursing mother should be taught the technique for those times she needs to express her milk without her baby's help or the availability of a mechanical pump (see chapter 5, pages 162–163).

Essential Hygiene. When you pump your milk, you are preparing your baby's meal. Proper hygiene practices are essential to protect your vulnerable baby from becoming infected with any germs that might contaminate your milk. It's not realistic to expect your expressed milk to be sterile. The process of pumping almost always causes harmless skin bacteria to be present in expressed breast milk, and this is not cause for worry. Concern arises, however, when the bacterial counts in milk are excessively high or when disease-causing germs get introduced into your milk. Each hospital adheres to specific policies and procedures to help assure the hygienic collection and storage of breast milk. Ask the nurse or lactation consultant who helps you get started pumping to clarify these guidelines.

The most important measure you can take is to *meticulously wash your hands each time you express milk for your baby*. While you are pumping, take extra care to keep your hands clean. For example, don't wipe your toddler's nose or run your fingers through your hair. In addition, you need to wash all the breast pump parts that come into contact with your milk with hot soapy water after each use. Cover the washed parts with a clean, light towel, and leave them to air dry until the next pumping session. As long as your baby is hospitalized, you should also sanitize these pump parts at least once each day by boiling them for twenty minutes. Other necessary hygiene measures include taking a daily shower and wearing a clean nursing bra each day, since your bra is easily soiled with leaking milk.

Pumping Routines

The following guidelines will clarify for you how often and how long you should pump and how much milk you can expect to obtain. Nearly half of the women who want to breastfeed their high-risk infants give up before their baby goes home. Establishing a successful pumping routine that maintains a generous milk supply is one of the best ways to assure your success.

When to Begin Pumping. Ideally, you should begin pumping as soon after delivery as you feel up to it and can get access to the necessary equipment. Getting started soon after giving birth will help familiarize you with expected pumping routines before your milk is being produced in abundance. Although pumping early and often may bring your milk in a few hours sooner, no real harm will be done if you must delay pumping for a day or two. Many women with a C-section delivery or a medical problem aren't able to pump on the first day. However, as soon as your milk starts to increase on the second or third day, you should be pumping faithfully, *at least* every three hours. If you don't start removing milk regularly once abundant milk production begins, you may not establish a generous milk supply. Remember, the pressure of unrelieved breast engorgement and chemical inhibitors in residual milk have a powerful negative influence on milk production. But even if you get a late start pumping, don't give up. Any milk you obtain for your baby will be a big help to her, and by frequently expressing your milk, you may be able to build an adequate supply.

Frequency of Pumping. In my experience, a plentiful milk supply can usually be established and maintained if a woman pumps her breasts at an interval of at least every two and a half to three hours from the beginning of one pumping session to the beginning of the next. Especially during the first two weeks, you should try to pump eight or more times each twenty-four hours to assure that an excellent milk supply is established. During this time, you can allow one longer interval of four to five hours at night without pumping. Beginning around two to three weeks, you can expect to maintain your milk supply by pumping at least seven times a day. By this time, you can let five to six hours pass once during the night between pumping sessions. I must warn you that a longer interval without breast emptying is likely to cause your milk supply to decrease. Examine your daily routine and outline a realistic pumping schedule that will enable you to empty your breasts *at least seven times in each twenty-four-hour period*, allowing no more than a *single five- to six-hour interval at night* without pumping.

Sample Pumping Schedule by Three Weeks Postpartum
(Minimum of Seven Times in Twenty-four Hours)

7:00 A.M.	7:00 P.M.
10:00 A.M.	10:00 P.M.
1:00 P.M.	4:00 A.M.
4:00 P.M.	

I realize that adhering to the ideal frequency of pumping is very difficult for mothers of high-risk infants. Not only are you worried and overwhelmed about your baby's condition, but you may be commuting back and forth to the hospital while juggling the demands of other children. You may have health problems of your own related to premature delivery (e.g., high blood pressure or an infection). Finding time to pump regularly amid so many competing priorities can be a real challenge. It's not surprising that some women who were told to pump *every three hours* later say they thought they were instructed to pump *three times a day*. These women wonder why their milk supply is discouragingly low. The surest way to bring in and preserve a generous milk supply is to pump faithfully *at least eight times in twenty-four hours the first couple of weeks, and at least seven times in twenty-four hours thereafter*. Avoid excessive or prolonged breast fullness. Many breastfeeding counselors reassure women that they can build up a low milk supply later, after their baby starts nursing or goes home. My own experience working with many hundreds of mothers of premature infants is that it is *far easier to bring in and keep producing a bountiful milk supply than it is to increase a low supply later on*.

It is tempting for women who must express their milk for many weeks to postpone pumpings until their breasts are uncomfortably full. The problem with this practice is that excessive pressure and residual milk send a strong message to the breasts to make less milk. Soon, a woman will notice that it takes longer for her breasts to feel full, as her milk supply declines.

Duration of Pumping. Generally, I advise women to pump their breasts for approximately ten to fifteen minutes each time they express milk. One reason the double collection system is so desirable is that it can save over an hour and a half of pumping time each day. A common mistake is to pump only until milk flow tapers off and the breasts feel soft. If the milk supply is low, the breasts may well be drained after only five minutes. To stimulate extra milk production, it's important to continue pumping for a total of at least ten minutes. If your milk is still flowing well after ten minutes and your breasts still feel full, then continue another five minutes or until milk flow tapers. Few women need to pump longer than fifteen minutes, and more prolonged pumping is seldom advisable because it can cause sore nipples.

Volume of Pumped Milk. On the day of delivery, you may obtain only a few drops of clear or yellowish colostrum each time you pump. It is the rare woman who can express a measurable volume of colostrum with a pump on the first day. Pumping is still worthwhile, however, as it stimulates release of the hormone prolactin and starts colostrum flowing through the milk ducts. As milk starts to come in abundantly—usually on the second, third, or fourth day postpartum—the quantity of milk obtained will rise dramatically. By the fourth day you will probably obtain at least an ounce from each breast at a pumping session. At first milk may flow in rapid drops. As you get accustomed to the pump and as your let-down reflex becomes conditioned, your milk will probably start to spray in several jet streams while you pump.

The milk volume increases dramatically each day during the first week, and continues to climb steadily for several weeks. By two or three weeks postpartum, a simple rule of thumb for milk production is about one ounce per hour. Thus, if you pumped after a five- to six-hour interval at night, you should expect to obtain five to six ounces. If you pumped after only a two-hour interval, you would expect to obtain about two ounces. Women usually have more milk in the mornings than later in the day, but overall you should be getting twenty to twenty-four ounces each day. Mothers of multiple infants should expect to obtain more milk.

Remember, your goal is to produce a *full* milk supply as if you were feeding a full-term, healthy baby. Many mothers of high-risk infants mistakenly believe that all they need to produce is sufficient milk to feed their tiny, sick baby. If you focus on bringing in and preserving a milk supply that is adequate for a full-term baby, then you can be certain you will have enough milk to meet your baby's rapidly changing needs. If you produce a little less, don't be dismayed. You will probably have plenty for your baby's present needs, and you can work on increasing your milk supply later if necessary (see pages 380–382). Fortunately, by bringing in a generous milk supply at first, most mothers still have enough milk for their baby even if their production dwindles after weeks of pumping.

Keeping a Pumping Diary. I strongly recommend that you keep a record of your pumped milk volumes so you can monitor your milk supply. A pumping diary is easy to maintain and provides a daily record of your pumping routines and milk production. Using a separate sheet for each day, jot down the times and duration that you pump and the amount of milk obtained from each breast. Note any fluctuations in your milk production throughout the day and any volume discrepancies between your breasts. Slight differences in milk production between the left and right breast are not uncommon, but a marked or consistent difference might place you at risk for insufficient milk. When the two sides are very different, it usually means the low one is not producing enough milk. The other breast may not be able to compensate for the underproducing side.

Every twenty-four hours, calculate and record on your pumping diary the *total* milk volume you expressed that day. This amount should increase daily for the first several weeks and then remain fairly steady at twenty ounces or more per day. If your total daily volume is decreasing, you will want to explore why and reverse this trend as soon as possible. Reviewing your pumping diary periodically will help you detect downward trends in milk production, excessively long intervals without milk expression, or specific pumping sessions that don't go well for you. Documenting your pumping routines proves more useful than relying on your memory. A sample recording form of your pumping diary is provided for your use on page 369.

Facilitating Milk Flow. Some women find their milk sprays easily when using a pump, while others have trouble getting milk to flow. Initially, you may feel awkward, embarrassed, or uncomfortable about using a mechanical breast pump to substitute for a cuddly baby at your breast. Because some women consider pumping to be a nuisance or an inconvenience, they may not use the pump consistently. A few view the pump as a painful symbol

PREEMIE PUMPING LOG

Today's Date / / **Baby's Age Today** ____ **Days**

Time Interval	Actual Time	Pumped Volume (ml)		Comments
		Left	Right	
12–1 am				
1–2 am				
2–3 am				
3–4 am				
4–5 am				
5–6 am				
6–7 am				
7–8 am				
8–9 am				
9–10 am				
10–11 am				
11–12 noon				
12–1 pm				
1–2 pm				
2–3 pm				
3–4 pm				
4–5 pm				
5–6 pm				
6–7 pm				
7–8 pm				
8–9 pm				
9–10 pm				
10–11 pm				
11–12 mdnt				
24-Hour Total				
Total Pumped Volume (left breast + right breast)				

of their separation from their baby. All of these negative feelings can inhibit a woman's milk ejection reflex and interfere with milk flow during pumping. I urge you to try to view the pump as your friend, a helpful tool to bring you closer to your ultimate goal of successfully breastfeeding your baby. I recall one good-natured woman who gave her pump a pet name and called it her "mechanical baby." Another mother sheepishly admitted that she became so "bonded" to her pump after "all they had been through together" that she actually felt a sense of loss when it came time to return it.

Most women find that milk flow is enhanced by gentle breast massage prior to pumping. Begin at the outer margin of your breast and gently massage in a circular motion as you progress toward the nipple. You also can stroke your breasts lightly with your fingers, going from the chest wall toward your nipple and moving in a circle around your breast. These maneuvers help you relax and make your let-down reflex more effective. Looking at a picture of your baby and drinking a beverage can also help trigger milk let-down. For more strategies to condition your milk ejection reflex, see Inhibited Milk Ejection Reflex, pages 313–314.

Where to Pump. Try to pump in familiar, pleasant surroundings whenever possible. Most nurseries now have designated pumping lounges for mothers of sick or premature infants to make pumping in the hospital as convenient as possible. Many of these rooms are relaxing, homelike, and comfortable, and are equipped with necessary supplies, including a sink, music, telephone, reading materials, and rocking chairs. Unfortunately, some hospitals have no private place to pump or highly unsatisfactory facilities. One woman reported difficulty in getting her milk to let-down because the pump room was located next to the circumcision room! I don't have to explain how discomfiting it was to try to pump while a newborn was being circumcised nearby.

Some women find they obtain more milk after visiting their infant. A breastfeeding nurse specialist at a prestigious NICU encourages mothers to use the hospital's electric breast pumps right at their babies' bedsides. This nurse has observed that women not only obtain more milk by expressing in the presence of their babies but also are willing to pump more often when they don't have to be absent from their infants to do so. Other women may have difficulty relaxing at the hospital and find they obtain more milk in the familiarity of their own home. Chances are you will need to become comfortable pumping in a variety of settings since you probably will be spending considerable time at the hospital with your baby, may visit relatives' homes, or even return to work. (Many employed mothers of high-risk infants elect to return to work relatively early, while their baby is hospitalized, and then take their maternity leave when their baby comes home.)

The Collection and Storage of Expressed Breast Milk

Storage Containers. You might be surprised to learn that no universally recommended, safe, hygienic, and cost-effective container exists for collecting and storing expressed breast milk. A variety of glass and plastic containers are used for this purpose, and each nursery has its preferred method of storing expressed breast milk. Your baby's nurse or the hospital's breastfeeding specialist can advise you about the procedures used in your nursery. Some hospitals provide sterile containers to mothers of prematures. Commonly used containers include glass bottles with caps; plastic specimen cups with lids; or small, hard plastic calibrated bottles with caps. A few nurseries like to have mothers use plastic bottle bags because these containers are readily available, inexpensive, and compact. Others do not feel that bottle liners are suitable for storing milk for premature infants, as they rupture easily and are difficult to seal tightly. Double lining the bags (placing one bag inside another) helps protect them from tearing. You can also place several filled bags into a larger ziplock storage bag to prevent them from sticking to the freezer shelf. I prefer using clean, packaged rubber bands to close bottle bags because they form a tighter seal than twist ties or masking tape. The manufacturers (Ameda/Egnell and Medela) of electric breast pumps make a higher-quality calibrated storage bag with a suitable sealing mechanism. Although these products cost more than the bottle bags found in your supermarket, they better protect the nutritional and immune properties of expressed breast milk, which is especially important for high-risk infants.

Most nurseries prefer that you store the milk you obtain from one pumping session in a single container. Your baby's nurse can pour several feedings from the same container and return it to the refrigerator for up to twenty-four to forty-eight hours. This method works especially well when babies receive mostly fresh (not frozen) breast milk. Even if your pumped volumes are small, it is best not to combine milk from multiple pumping sessions into one container, unless you are instructed to do so by your baby's nurse.

Nurseries that use predominantly frozen milk may choose to have you store it in volumes close to the amount your baby takes at a feeding. If your baby is receiving very small quantities at each feeding, this might necessitate pouring your expressed milk from one pumping session into several containers. Ask your baby's nurse or the hospital lactation consultant how much milk to put in each container.

Labeling of Containers. Each individual container of milk should be labeled with your baby's name and the date and time you expressed the milk. Attach an adhesive label to each container or write on the container's labeling area. Sometimes two babies in the nursery have the same last name, so it's a good idea to write your baby's whole name or include your own name on the label. You should also add other relevant notations, such as any medications you are taking. Dating the milk allows the nurses to feed the earliest colostrum first, and then progress to more mature milk in the order that your body produced it for your baby.

Storing Expressed Milk. Your expressed milk might be fed to your baby immediately or stored for later use. Although each nursery has its own guidelines for storing milk, in general, expressed milk for premature infant feeding can be safely refrigerated for twenty-four to forty-eight hours or frozen for up to several months. Under most circumstances, feeding fresh or refrigerated milk is preferable, since all the immune properties are preserved. However, some of your milk inevitably will need to be frozen for later use because you undoubtedly will produce more milk than your baby takes at first. Although freezing destroys the living white blood cells in milk, most of the nutrients and immune properties are not altered. You will want to stay in close communication with your baby's nurse about whether to freeze or refrigerate the milk you pump at home. When you pump at the hospital, ask if your expressed milk can be fed to your baby fresh.

Your expressed milk can be stored for three months in a separate freezer unit of a refrigerator. Milk can be kept even longer in a deep freezer that maintains temperature at −20 degrees C. or

0 degrees F. or below. Place milk toward the back of your refrigerator or freezer, not in the door where the temperature is less stable. Some mothers accumulate so much pumped milk that they need to temporarily borrow freezer space from a relative. Don't worry about having lots of surplus milk. Once your baby starts consuming larger quantities of milk, your stockpiles will diminish rapidly. Don't decrease your pumping schedule because you have run out of freezer space. Your supply could decline drastically and remain low.

Transporting Milk to the Nursery. Always transport your milk on ice when bringing it from home to the nursery. Use an insulated cooler and refreezable ice packs to prevent frozen milk from thawing en route to the hospital.

Thawing and Warming Frozen Milk. As long as your baby is hospitalized, her nurses will be responsible for thawing and/or warming your milk for her feedings. Frozen milk should be quick-thawed under tepid running water or in a warm-water bath, or thawed slowly in the refrigerator over many hours. It should *not* be left out for several hours to thaw at room temperature. Authorities recommend *against* using a microwave to either thaw or warm expressed milk. Inadvertent overheating of milk occurs easily in a microwave, and infants have accidentally been burned. Furthermore, many of the immune properties of human milk are heat sensitive and can be destroyed by overheating.

Feeding Your Expressed Milk to Your Baby

At first, your premature baby will probably receive your expressed milk by gavage—through a feeding tube that is passed into her stomach. The early colostrum you produce makes an ideal first feeding. Not only is it easily digested, but it contains special growth factors to help your baby's intestinal tract mature and absorb nutrients.

Fortifying Expressed Milk. Many neonatologists feed premature infants only their mother's milk until the baby's feedings are progressively increased to a maximum volume. At this point, it is generally accepted that a mother's own milk needs to be fortified with additional nutrients (especially protein, minerals, and calo-ries) in order to meet the rapid growth requirements of babies with very low birth weights. The neonatologists caring for your baby may decide to either mix your milk with premature infant formula (a practical option when your own milk volumes are low) or add powdered fortifier to your milk (a nice choice when you have abundant supplies) to increase the nutrients your baby receives when your milk is fed to your infant. The extra nutrients are added to your milk during your baby's rapid growth phase and are discontinued around thirty-four to thirty-six weeks gestation.

Unfortunately, the frequent need to enrich expressed breast milk for feeding premature infants can cause women to view their milk as less than adequate. The problem is not with your milk; it is that tiny preemies have exceptional nutrient requirements. Doesn't it make more sense to add extra nutrients to your own milk than to enrich cow's milk to create premature infant formula?

Feeding Hindmilk. You will recall that the fat content of your milk rises as a feeding progresses or as you continue pumping (see chapter 3, pages 81–82). The fat and calorie content of the milk you obtain in the latter minutes of pumping is higher than the fat content of the first milk you collect. Your hindmilk is also more concentrated in calories and fat than the milk from a full pumping. Some neonatologists ask mothers to switch collection containers midway through their pumping session in order to separate the calorie-rich hindmilk from the lower-fat foremilk. Premature babies have been shown to gain weight more rapidly when they are fed hindmilk. Ask your baby's nurse or doctor about this practice.

Screened, Processed Donor Milk. Women who produce insuf-ficient milk to meet their babies' nutritional needs should be aware that approximately six distributing donor milk banks are opera-tional in North America. Premature and sick newborns are among the most common recipients of donor human milk. The Human Milk Banking Association of North America can help you locate the milk bank nearest your community or one that can ship milk out of state (see page 451). Donors are healthy, lactating women who undergo the same laboratory screening tests performed on blood donors. These volunteers hygienically collect their surplus milk, which is processed and pasteurized at a milk bank before being dis-tributed by physician prescription to infants in need of human milk.

The Denver Mothers' Milk Bank is the largest distributing milk bank in North America, so we are privileged to have donor milk as an option for certain at-risk infants whose mothers cannot provide sufficient milk. Some neonatologists will prescribe screened, pasteurized donor milk from a mothers' milk bank when a baby has a special need for human milk and his own mother's milk is not available. Insurance usually covers the milk processing fee, since donor milk, a precious commodity, is only prescribed when medically necessary.

Communication with Your Baby's Nurses. Make it a habit to communicate closely with your baby's nurses about your milk stores and your visits. Because your baby may be cared for at a regional center some distance from your home, it might not be feasible for you to be present in the nursery on a daily basis. Stay in close touch with your baby's nurses to make sure your breast milk is being fed to your baby. Inquire often about your frozen milk stores in the nursery and replenish them as needed. When you know you will be visiting, ask in advance whether you can pump prior to a feeding and provide fresh milk for your infant.

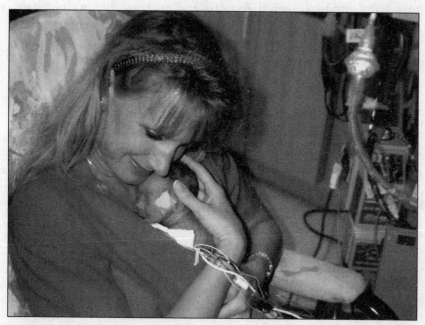

Kangaroo care of premature infants provides essential comfort and skin-to-skin contact.

Kangaroo Care. Many nurseries practice "kangaroo care" as a convenient way to provide premature infants with skin-to-skin contact with their parents. Similar to the concept of a kangaroo's pouch, a mother is helped to cuddle her premature infant against her body. Clad only in a diaper, your baby can be placed against your bare chest between your breasts and covered with a loose blouse and a blanket. Your baby stays warm held against your body and is kept completely covered. Babies who receive kangaroo care tend to cry less, sleep more soundly, and start breastfeeding earlier. Mothers who practice kangaroo care are said to breastfeed longer and more often, and the skin-to-skin contact may increase their milk production. As soon as your baby's condition is stable, ask his nurse if you can hold your baby skin to skin.

Nonnutritive Sucking at Your Empty Breast. Sometimes babies will suck on a pacifier while they are being tube-fed. Although pacifiers are not recommended for full-term newborns until breastfeeding is well established, sucking on a pacifier during tube feeding may be beneficial for a premature infant. This type of nonnutritive sucking has been shown to calm and soothe a premature baby, improve her digestion, and increase her weight gain. Some nurseries allow babies to suck at their mother's empty breast instead of using a pacifier during gavage feedings. Ask your baby's nurse whether you can pump your breasts immediately prior to your baby's feeding so that your infant can use your nearly empty breast as a pacifier while being tube-fed. This is an excellent way to familiarize your baby with your breast and practice correct latch-on before she is ready for actual breastfeeding. Nonnutritive sucking at your breast is also likely to raise your blood prolactin level and boost your milk supply.

Your Personal Care

See also chapter 6, Daily Life While Breastfeeding.

Nursing Bra and Pads. You will want to wear a properly fitting nursing bra to provide adequate support for your lactating breasts. Washable, reusable cotton or disposable nursing pads can be worn inside your nursing bra to collect any leaking milk and to prevent soiling your outer clothing. Be sure to change the pads often, how-

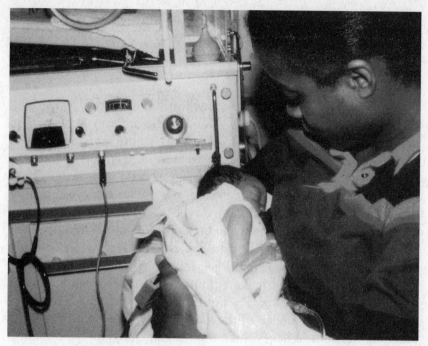

A premature infant can nuzzle and practice at the empty breast
in preparation for learning to breastfeed.

ever, since chronic moisture can make your nipples sore, and the
moist pads can harbor germs.

Rest. You will need all the rest you can get, since you are
pumping regularly, visiting your baby at the nursery, possibly
caring for older children, recovering from labor and delivery, and
experiencing the emotional highs and lows of having a baby in a
neonatal intensive care unit. Try to take a nap each day and graciously accept all the household help you can get.

Diet. Although your appetite may vary and you may be tempted
to skip meals, it is important that you eat regularly in order to produce ample milk. You will need approximately five hundred additional calories each day to support lactation. Your doctor will
probably advise you to continue taking your prenatal vitamins as
long as you are breastfeeding. Eat a variety of foods in as natural a
form as possible. You will also need extra fluids and should drink
whenever you are thirsty. Pour yourself a nutritious beverage or a

glass of water each time you nurse or pump. Limit your intake of caffeinated beverages to two each day. There are no particular foods that must automatically be restricted from a nursing mother's diet.

Medications. Almost every medication a mother takes will enter her milk to some degree. Usually, the amount appearing in milk is too small to be of any consequence to the infant. However, a sick newborn or small preemie is more susceptible to adverse drug effects. Furthermore, some drugs should not be given to infants in any amount, so it is important to notify your baby's doctor about any medication that you take. Occasional alcohol consumption is permissible while breastfeeding a full-term, healthy infant, but I advise against drinking *any* alcohol while you are pumping milk for your high-risk infant. If you do ever drink alcohol, you should "pump and dump" your milk for a period of at least two hours per drink. Do not breastfeed or save any milk for your baby until all effects of the alcohol are gone—plus one more pumping session. When you resume saving milk for your baby's feedings, indicate the date, time, and amount of alcohol you drank. Using any recreational drugs while breastfeeding poses a serious threat to your infant. **Illicit drug use is incompatible with breastfeeding** (see chapter 6, pages 187–188).

Common Problems When Mothers Must Maintain a Milk Supply by Pumping

Breast Engorgement

Engorgement is the breast swelling and firmness that occurs when your milk first comes in abundantly or when a long interval has elapsed without nursing or pumping. Breast engorgement is usually most severe around the third to fifth days postpartum, but it can recur anytime your breasts go too long without milk being removed. The pressure of unrelieved engorgement can damage some of the milk-producing glands, and a chemical inhibitor in residual milk decreases milk production. Thus, unrelieved breast engorgement can rapidly diminish your milk supply. You should avoid letting your breasts get hard and lumpy by pumping faithfully about every two to three hours from the start of one pumping session to the start of the next. It is especially important to keep milk flowing well once your production starts to increase dramatically around the third postpartum day.

Gentle breast massage, applying moist heat to the breasts shortly before pumping, or taking a warm shower may help start milk flowing. Cold packs applied between pumpings will help decrease swelling and discomfort. Try pumping one breast at a time, while massaging with the other hand. Go back and forth from one breast to another every few minutes. Sometimes a clogged duct can cause localized breast engorgement; pumping while gently massaging the clogged area usually will bring relief. For additional strategies to relieve breast engorgement, see chapter 7, pages 225–233.

Inhibited Milk Ejection Reflex

Few women feel very maternal toward their mechanical pump, making the let-down reflex harder to trigger with a pump than with a nursing baby. In addition, nipple pain, anxiety, fear, stress, and other negative influences can inhibit milk let-down, causing incomplete emptying of the breasts and a decrease in your milk supply. To enhance your milk ejection reflex, try to get comfortable and to pump in pleasant surroundings. For example, one woman found she expressed little milk when she set up her pump in the laundry room, but she obtained abundant milk when she expressed in her baby's furnished nursery. Allow yourself sufficient time at each pumping session, and try to relax. Bring something light to read or perhaps a tape of relaxing music. Establish a routine around your pumping, such as pouring a glass of juice or water, sitting in familiar surroundings, or calling the nursery first to check on your baby. Many women have found innovative ways to facilitate their let-down, such as viewing pictures of their babies before pumping, taping pictures of their babies to the pump, playing a tape recording of their babies' cry, performing relaxation exercises, or having their husbands give them a backrub. Synthetic oxytocin nasal spray can be effective in helping to condition the milk ejection reflex. (For information on how to obtain this medication, see chapter 7, page 231.) An additional strategy is to make an effort to pump whenever your milk lets down spontaneously. This will help condition your milk ejection reflex to respond more readily to pumping.

Low Milk Supply

Diminished milk supply is probably the most common problem encountered by lactating mothers who are separated from their babies and must pump their breasts. Your milk seems so abundant when your production surges several days after giving birth that you can scarcely imagine not producing enough. Initially, your baby seems to need so little milk, as feedings are introduced and slowly advanced. Within several weeks, however, your baby may be consuming steadily increasing volumes of milk, while your own supply slowly dwindles and eventually may fall short of your baby's need.

The main reason mothers of sick newborns gradually lose their milk is that they seldom are able to pump their breasts as often as they would have nursed their babies. This is especially true if a woman has returned to work, has other children to care for, or has a long commute to the hospital to visit her baby. Also, many women simply do not obtain as much milk by pumping as they would by feeding a healthy baby directly at their breast. Little is known about prolactin response to pumping compared to direct breastfeeding. For many women, the extreme stress and worry associated with having a high-risk newborn impairs their milk supply despite frequent pumping. Skipping meals and being exhausted will also affect a woman's milk production. Women with hypertension, chronic medical problems, or a postpartum infection may produce insufficient milk. Often several of these factors combine to gradually diminish a mother's milk through no fault of her own. Declining milk production will be of less significance for those mothers who are able to establish a generous supply at the outset.

Strategies for Preserving a Generous Milk Supply with Long-Term Pumping.

- Use a hospital-grade electric breast pump with a double collection system.
- Begin regular milk expression no later than forty-eight to seventy-two hours postpartum.
- Don't go longer than five to six hours at night without pumping.
- Pump at least seven times each twenty-four hours (approximately every three hours with a single longer interval at night).

- Pump for a minimum of ten minutes at each pumping session.
- Use techniques to trigger your milk ejection reflex so your breasts get drained well.
- Eat an adequate diet, drink plenty of fluids, and get sufficient rest.

If your milk supply does become low, look for ways to minimize stress, such as improving your nutrition, getting more rest, or enlisting more help from others. Review your pumping routines to see what might be improved, such as the type of pump you are using, the frequency of milk expression, the effectiveness of your milk ejection reflex, or the environment where you are pumping. Finally, remain optimistic that you might produce more milk once your baby is able to nurse directly at your breast. Your infant will benefit from whatever volume of milk you produce, and you can still nurse your baby long-term whether or not you need to supplement with formula.

Galactogogues. Galactogogues are special food supplements or medicines that are believed to increase milk production in breastfeeding women (see chapter 9, pages 338–341). Because declining milk supply is such a widespread problem among mothers of high-risk infants who must use a pump long-term, numerous strategies have been attempted to raise milk production in these women. Ask your baby's doctor and your own physician about trying one or more of these possible galactogogues if your milk supply is low.

Fenugreek. Fenugreek is an annual herb that has been used for centuries as a cooking spice and as a folk remedy for a variety of ailments. It is a legume, in the same plant class as soybeans, peas, peanuts, and garbanzos. Extracts of fenugreek seeds are used to flavor maple syrup substitutes and curry. Fenugreek, which is rich in protein and fiber, has been used in India as a galactogogue, and many positive testimonials exist among breastfeeding women in the United States who have taken fenugreek to raise a low milk supply. Ground fenugreek seeds in capsule form can be obtained from a health food store. The reported effective dosage ranges from one to five capsules taken three times a day, or three to fifteen capsules daily. Women are said to notice increased milk production within two days of starting this food supplement. When taken in a large enough dose, fenugreek causes your perspiration and urine to smell like maple syrup. While those who prescribe fenugreek insist that it is harmless, no scientific research has investigated its effects on lactating women and breastfed infants. Fenugreek has been shown to lower blood sugar and blood lipids. It should not be taken by pregnant women, as it can cause contractions. Severe allergic reactions to fenugreek have been reported, and women with known allergies to other leguminous plants (chickpea, peanut, soybean, green pea) are at greater risk of reacting to it. I must insist that you get permission from your baby's doctor before trying fenugreek, since it probably will appear in your milk, and a premature or sick newborn could be more susceptible to any potential adverse effects (also see Fenugreek, pages 339–340).

Metoclopramide. Metoclopramide (brand name Reglan) is a prescription medication that is sometimes used to try to increase a low milk supply in breastfeeding women, including mothers of premature infants. The medication, commonly used to treat heartburn and nausea, happens to raise the blood level of prolactin, the milk-making hormone, as a side effect. This observation prompted some practitioners to consider whether the drug might work to increase milk production in lactating women with a low supply. In fact, several studies have been conducted that show metoclopramide is effective in raising prolactin and milk production after a week or so of treatment. Unfortunately, milk production often declines to former levels after metoclopramide is stopped. Some doctors taper the dosage slowly to try to prevent this from happening. The drug can have side effects, including fatigue, headache, and depression. Women with a history of depression should not take the medication. You will need a prescription from your doctor if you decide to try metoclopramide, and you should discuss the matter with your baby's physician before you take the drug, as some of it will appear in your milk.

Human growth hormone (hGH). Some promising new research has shown that human growth hormone (hGH) can improve milk production in breastfeeding women with a low milk supply. A recent study with mothers of premature infants found a 31 percent increase in milk volume on average after seven days of treatment. However, hGH must be given by a daily injection and it is very expensive. It is not being used to treat low milk except in research protocols. Nevertheless, within the near future, successful hGH therapies for low milk supply may become a reality.

Sore Nipples

Most women experience transient, mild nipple tenderness during the early days of breastfeeding. Nipple pain is usually less severe with breast pumping than early breastfeeding, but discomfort still may occur. Damage to the nipples can result from using excessive suction or pumping for a prolonged duration when the breasts are engorged and the nipple skin is most sensitive. The risk of nipple trauma in the early days of pumping can be minimized by using a hospital-grade electric pump and techniques to help trigger the let-down reflex. Sore nipples also can be due to a yeast infection (see chapter 7, pages 243–247). A premature infant who receives antibiotics may develop a yeast infection in his mouth, which can be passed to the mother's nipple during breastfeeding attempts. Abrupt onset of nipple pain after pumping had been comfortable can be an early sign of a breast infection.

Some women find that using USP Modified Lanolin (medical grade) on their nipples as a lubricant makes pumping more comfortable. Other techniques to prevent sore nipples include starting pumping at the minimum vacuum setting and increasing the suction very gradually; using the most comfortable vacuum setting and pump cycle rate that permit good milk flow; pumping for ten minutes every few hours, rather than pumping for longer periods at less-frequent intervals; removing surface moisture from your nipples after pumping. Fortunately, regular pumping soon conditions your nipples for nursing so that you are unlikely to experience any discomfort with actual breastfeeding, provided your baby latches on correctly.

Mastitis

Occasionally, a woman who is nursing or pumping her breasts will get a painful breast infection known as mastitis (see chapter 7, pages 254–260). Mastitis is more likely to occur when (1) the breasts are not emptied well; (2) a cracked nipple is present; (3) a woman massages her breasts too vigorously or the pump creates too great a vacuum; (4) a woman becomes physically exhausted; (5) a woman engages in vigorous upper-body activity that jostles her breasts, such as aerobics. Symptoms of mastitis include a "flu-like" or achy feeling, chills and fever, and pain, redness, and warmth in the affected breast. Because breast inflammation impairs milk flow, women with mastitis may obtain less milk from the infected breast. Ineffective removal of milk can cause a mother's supply to decline.

Whenever mastitis is suspected, it is important to promptly start treatment with antibiotics. Delays in treatment can place a woman at risk for a breast abscess—a painful pocket of pus that must be drained. Therapy should be continued for at least ten days, even though you usually feel much improved within twenty-four to forty-eight hours after beginning antibiotics. Be sure your baby's doctor knows about your breast infection and the name of the medication that is prescribed for you. When a woman nursing her healthy baby at home develops mastitis, she usually can continue to breastfeed during her illness. However, if a woman gets mastitis while pumping milk for her hospitalized newborn, she should discard the milk expressed from the infected breast, and save only the milk expressed from the healthy side. Disease-causing bacteria may be present in the milk from her infected breast and could pose a risk to her premature or sick newborn. Once all her symptoms have resolved, she can ask her baby's doctor if she can resume saving milk from the breast that was infected.

Since mastitis can be very uncomfortable, pain medication is often prescribed for the first day or two. Applying hot or cold compresses to the breast usually offers additional relief. Because milk flows less readily with mastitis, you may need to pump more often to empty your breast well. Try pumping the "good" side first with a single collection container to trigger your milk ejection reflex. Then switch to the infected side when your milk starts dripping. Extra rest is very important in the treatment of mastitis.

Beginning Breastfeeding in the Hospital

Your baby's nurse will help decide when he is ready to begin breastfeeding. There is no specific age or weight at which premature infants can start to nurse. It depends on your baby's general condition and his ability to coordinate sucking, swallowing, and breathing. Most prematures are able to begin breastfeeding by thirty-four weeks gestation, and some will be ready earlier. Each baby shows signs of readiness to take oral feedings at their own individual pace.

In the past, we delayed breastfeeding of premature infants until they first were able to bottle-feed well. We now are finding that breastfeeding is less stressful on a premature infant than previously believed. Premature babies take less milk during their first attempts at breastfeeding compared to bottle-feeding. The slower flow of milk typical of early breastfeeding attempts makes it easier for a baby to coordinate sucking and swallowing at the breast. If at all possible, try to arrange with your baby's nurse to have his first "nipple" feeding be at your breast instead of by bottle. Successful breastfeeding is promoted when your infant is given the opportunity to learn correct latch-on and milk extraction techniques required for breastfeeding *before* being fed by bottle. Hopefully, your baby already will have had numerous "practice sessions" latching on to your empty breast during tube feedings.

As you begin breastfeeding, it will help if you can be available in the nursery for several hours each day. This will allow you to initiate breastfeeding sessions when your baby is in an optimal alert, responsive state. When your availability is very limited, you may be disappointed to find that your baby is sleepy and disinterested in feeding at the time you were expecting to be able to nurse. Think of your first attempts as learning sessions that are not meant to provide much, if any, nutrition. The emphasis will be on helping you become comfortable and confident with breastfeeding, while assuring that your baby's condition remains stable as he learns to coordinate sucking and swallowing. At first, your baby will breastfeed only once a day and continue to receive feedings by tube. Your baby's nurse will help you judge when he is ready to increase the number of daily breastfeedings. Communicate closely with her to work out a plan that permits you to breastfeed as often as possible.

Breastfeeding Technique

As you prepare to nurse your baby, try to arrange as much privacy as possible, even if it is only a screen in the nursery. Take your time. While an inappropriately lengthy nursing attempt can stress your infant, it is unrealistic to expect to adhere to strict time constraints. Get comfortable, preferably in a chair with both back and arm support. Place a pillow on your lap and another under your arm, and use a footstool to decrease the distance between your lap and your breast. If your infant has an IV or is receiving supplemental oxygen, ask his nurse to assist you in positioning him with all his "lines."

You can expect to need expert assistance from your baby's

nurse or a lactation consultant to help you position your baby correctly to nurse. Correct positioning will greatly facilitate your
baby's breastfeeding efforts.

Review the information about correct positioning and latch-on
that is covered in chapter 4. A premature baby will need extra support for his heavy head, since his neck muscles are relatively weak.
The positions that work best for most premature infants are the
football hold and the cross-cradle hold. Both of these positions
provide good support for the baby's head and a clear view of his
mouth on your breast. Take care to keep your baby's head, shoulders, and hips in a straight line when you support his body as you
position him to nurse.

The small size of your baby's mouth may make it difficult for
him to place his lips and gums over the dilated milk sinuses located
under your areola. His weak muscle tone makes it harder for him
to keep your breast in his mouth. Tickle his lower lip with your
nipple and wait until he opens WIDE before pulling him onto your
breast. If necessary, the nurse assisting you can help your baby

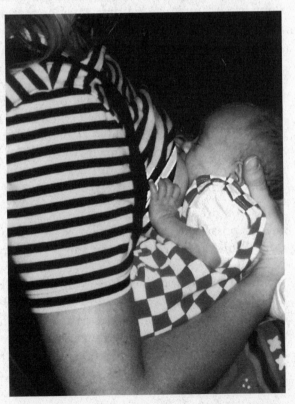

The football hold
works well for
breastfeeding a
premature infant
because it provides
good support for
the baby's head and
a clear view of his
mouth on your
nipple.

open wide by gently pulling down on his chin. Gentle steady pressure on the back of your baby's head will help him stay latched on.

If your baby has trouble learning to latch on to your breast, try pumping just before nursing to help pull your nipple out and to start some milk flowing. At your first breastfeeding sessions, the pump may be more effective than your baby in triggering your milk ejection reflex. Your let-down may have become well conditioned to the pump after many weeks of expressing milk. Another strategy to enhance infant latch-on is to wear breast shells (see page 224) for about thirty minutes before feedings to help make your nipples more protractile.

If your baby is unable to grasp your breast correctly after repeated attempts, ask his nurse or the hospital lactation consultant about using a silicone nipple shield to help your infant latch on. In the past, nipple shields were considered ineffective, and their use was widely discouraged. More recent experience with newly designed silicone nipple shields has established their clear value in helping to solve persistent latch-on problems. A nipple shield should be used only with the supervision of a lactation consultant or breastfeeding specialist. With the silicone shield placed over your nipple, your baby may latch on more readily, since the artificial nipple is more protuberant and firm than your own. As your baby nurses with the use of the nipple shield, your own nipple will be drawn into it. If he nurses effectively, he will receive your milk through the nipple shield. Partway through the feeding, you should try to remove the nipple shield and offer your breast directly. The shield should be used only as a temporary solution to help your baby eventually learn to grasp your breast directly.

Alternative Methods for Providing Your Expressed Milk

Realistically, it is unlikely that you can be present for every feeding. And even when you do breastfeed your baby, additional milk may need to be provided afterward, if the volume your infant obtained from the breast was not adequate. In U.S. nurseries, virtually every baby takes some feedings by bottle. To minimize the chances that bottle-feeding will interfere with your baby learning to nurse well, make every effort to introduce breastfeeding prior to bottle-feeding. It also will help if you can be present daily to give your baby regular opportunities to breastfeed. Under these circumstances, premature babies usually manage to go back and forth between feeding methods quite readily.

Cup Feeding. In many parts of the world, hospitalized newborns are fed by cup instead of bottle when breastfeeding isn't possible. Cup feeding of infants is practiced in some Western nurseries, including a few in the United States. Small plastic medicine cups are commonly used (see illustration, page 115). The idea is to avoid bottle-feeding when possible while infants are learning to nurse. You might discuss this option with your baby's doctor or nurse, although routine bottle-feeding of premature infants in U.S. hospitals remains a widespread practice. If your infant seems to be doing fine with breastfeeding, receiving additional nutrition by bottle is probably not a valid concern. *Cup feeding of premature infants should be performed only by a health professional experienced with this feeding method and with the care of high-risk infants.*

Using the Supplemental Nursing System (SNS). If your milk supply is low or your baby latches on correctly but does not suck long enough to obtain milk, the Supplemental Nursing System can be helpful in teaching your baby to nurse effectively. This unique device enables your baby to obtain supplemental milk while learning to nurse at your breast (see the illustration on page 348). The baby grasps both your nipple and a thin soft tube that is laid next to it. The tubing is attached to a plastic bottle containing formula or expressed breast milk that is suspended around your neck. The infant's nursing attempts promptly are rewarded with milk from the tube, even if your own milk supply is low. In this way, the baby is "trained" to nurse correctly at your breast, while receiving necessary supplement. Although detailed instructions for its use and cleaning accompany the device, it is still important to have a health professional thoroughly familiar with its use provide hands-on guidance before trying the SNS with your baby (see chapter 4, page 114, chapter 9, pages 347–349, and Resource List, page 450).

Pumping After Nursings. Because your baby's early breastfeeding attempts will be largely nonnutritive, it remains essential that you pump after each nursing to drain your breasts well. If you don't pump after nursing, you can expect your milk supply to decline. Remember, it is your generous supply that will help your baby learn to take adequate milk with breastfeeding. Mothers of prematures often are mistakenly advised that either pumping *or* nursing their baby will empty their breasts adequately. But the two are not equivalent. While your baby is hospitalized and for the first several weeks at home, the pump is almost certain to provide more effective breast stimulation and emptying than your baby. Don't let all your hard work be jeopardized now by cutting back on pumping.

Measuring Your Baby's Milk Intake. Many nurseries have begun using accurate measures to tell how much milk babies take when they breastfeed. In the past, nurses tried to guess the quality of a breastfeeding by observing how well the baby sucked or how often he swallowed. Today, we realize that such "guesstimates" are highly inaccurate and they don't provide the information we need to give babies the best care. Test weighing is a simple and accurate method of measuring the amount of milk a baby drinks while breastfeeding (see chapter 9, pages 333–335). The baby is weighed (with the same clothes) before and after breastfeeding. The difference in his weight equals the amount of milk he drank. One gram of weight equals one milliliter (ml) of milk. There are 30 ml in an ounce. Thus, if your baby gained 30 grams (one ounce) after the feeding, you can assume he drank one ounce or 30 ml of your milk. It is important not to change your baby's diaper while performing the test-weighing procedure. Test weights can help you follow your baby's progress in learning to obtain milk with breastfeeding. The results help you know whether or not your baby needs to be supplemented after nursing. Don't be alarmed if test weights show that your baby has taken negligible milk with his first breastfeeding attempts. This is entirely normal for premature infants who are just learning to nurse effectively. With practice, breastfeeding sessions become more nutritive.

Going Home

As your baby's discharge date approaches, you will probably be breastfeeding several times daily. Most mothers, however, will take their babies home before their infants have progressed to full breastfeeding. Often, an infant is both being breastfed and receiving expressed milk by bottle. One of the most difficult transitions involved in breastfeeding a high-risk infant is taking your baby home and deciding how often and how long to nurse, whether and how much to supplement, when to stop pumping, and how closely to follow your baby's weight. While you have long awaited this moment—to nurse your baby in your own home—you may find that you are anxious not knowing how much milk your baby is getting at the breast.

Today, mothers can rent accurate, user-friendly, electronic infant scales (see Resource List, page 451) and perform test weights and daily infant weights right in their home. I highly recommend that you rent such a scale for the early weeks at home if at all possible. Being able to tell how much milk your baby takes while nursing and following your baby's weight gain each day can give you peace of mind. In-home weighing of your infant can provide essential information to enable you to make feeding modifications that meet your baby's needs. I also advise you to seek ongoing assistance and follow-up from a lactation consultant experienced in the care of premature infants. Meanwhile, the following suggestions will help you make the transition to full breastfeeding after you go home:

• Prior to your baby's discharge, you should meet with her neonatologist and find out how many ounces of milk your baby requires on a daily basis. The test weights performed in the hospital can provide a realistic estimate of how much milk your baby can be expected to take by direct breastfeeding. Additional expressed milk (or formula) will need to be fed to make up the balance of her daily requirement. Usually, this milk is given by bottle after some or all nursings.

• If your twenty-four-hour pumped milk volume is less than your baby's daily milk requirement, you can assume that formula supplement will be necessary for your baby's adequate growth. If your milk supply with pumping exceeds the amount your baby needs each day, you can expect to provide all your baby's nutrition yourself. However, you can't automatically assume that your infant will obtain sufficient milk with breastfeeding during the early days home from the hospital. She will probably need to drink additional expressed milk after some nursings.

• During the first weeks at home, you can expect your premature infant to continue to show some immature feeding behaviors, like not waking to feed, difficulty latching on, falling asleep early in the feeding, and irregular sleep patterns. Breastfeeding will continue to require extra effort and patience. Gradually, as your baby matures and gains weight, she will learn to nurse more efficiently, but it will take additional time before she obtains all her nutrition from breastfeeding. It might be several weeks after discharge, and maybe longer, before you can discontinue your breastfeeding "props"—pump, scale, special nursing techniques, and very close follow-up.

• Your baby will need to feed at least eight times each twenty-four hours. Don't expect her to nurse at exactly three-hour intervals, however. She may sleep four to five hours one time at night and feed every one and a half to three hours during the day. She should have a wet diaper with every feeding and at least one bowel movement each day (3–4 each day if less than one month).

• Your baby will probably obtain more milk nursing from both breasts at a feeding than from one, even if the total sucking time is the same. However, you will want to be sure she has nursed at the first side long enough to obtain the rich hindmilk. If your let-down isn't delayed and your baby doesn't fall asleep, ten minutes should be long enough on the first breast. She can nurse as long as she desires on the second side. Some babies do better nursing from a single breast at each feeding, however.

• Don't let your infant waste valuable energy by frequently sucking a pacifier until you are confident that she is obtaining sufficient nutrition by nursing. Until she is gaining weight well with exclusive breastfeeding, it's best to avoid nonnutritive sucking on a pacifier that could limit the time she spends at your breast.

• Ideally you will have a generous milk supply and be producing at least 50 percent more milk than your baby needs to take each day. This surplus will help your baby obtain milk more easily when she nurses. Although you will be anxious to discontinue the hassle of pumping, it is *crucial* that you keep pumping after most nursings when you take your baby home. The hospital-grade electric pump will remove milk from your breasts more effectively than your premature baby. If your breasts don't get well drained on a regular basis, your milk supply will diminish and your baby will have to work harder to obtain milk. Keep pumping any residual milk after feedings until it is clear that your baby is nursing effectively and gaining adequate weight with breastfeeding alone. Then you can gradually taper your pumping.

Follow-up at the Pediatrician's Office. You will need to stay in close contact with your baby's doctor as you make the transition from partial to full breastfeeding in the first weeks after discharge. Even if you are using an electronic scale at home, *it is essential to have your baby followed closely by her physician.* In-home weighing cannot substitute for regular medical check-ups. Prior to your baby's discharge, you should make your pediatrician aware of your breastfeeding plans and arrange to stop at his or her office on the way home from the hospital to obtain a baseline weight on the office scale. This is the weight that will be compared with subsequent infant weights at follow-up visits. Your baby should be seen and weighed again at the physician's office within a few days of discharge and at weekly intervals as long as you are making feeding changes. In the first several months, infants gain about an ounce per day if they are receiving adequate nutrition. Your pediatrician will guide you in determining how often your baby should be weighed and examined.

The experience of pumping milk for a hospitalized infant is unique for each mother. Milk production is not always related to the effort expended or a mother's motivation, and success is defined in different terms by different women. No matter how long or short a period of time you are able to provide milk for your high-risk infant, you are to be commended for your efforts and congratulated for your commitment. A mother who has contributed to her baby's care in this special way has provided a very precious gift to her infant. I hope you enjoy a sense of accomplishment and reward for your selfless efforts. And I hope you enjoy many months of breastfeeding your baby after the two of you are reunited at home.

Chapter 11

Breastfeeding in Unique Situations

Perhaps you are contemplating breastfeeding, but feel your personal circumstances are unlike those of most other women. You've learned about routine breastfeeding, but still harbor reservations about whether nursing can work for women like yourself who face unique challenges. The truth is that motivated women have succeeded in breastfeeding despite all kinds of obstacles and unknowns. Whatever your specific situation, you may be surprised to find that breastfeeding, whether partial or exclusive, is probably feasible.

Breastfeeding Twins and Higher Multiples

Nursing twins is certainly possible and can be very rewarding. Breastfeeding triplets also can be accomplished, and a few women have nursed higher multiples, usually partially. To succeed in breastfeeding more than one baby, a mother needs to be highly motivated and have abundant support, since one of the greatest obstacles in the early weeks is sheer fatigue. Advance knowledge and intense commitment can be major strengths. Before you embark on breastfeeding multiple-birth babies, consider the following unique challenges presented by your special circumstances.

Initial Adjustment

Fatigue. No matter how thrilled you may be with the prospect of raising twins, the stark reality of having more than one baby to feed, diaper, bathe, comfort, love, and play with proves overwhelming for many parents. Instead of feeling as lucky as the whole world says you should, profound exhaustion can rob new parents of their rightful joy at the birth of multiples. Few well-wishers can really appreciate the magnitude of the emotional and physical strain of those first early weeks at home taking responsibility for more than one infant. Furthermore, mothers of multiples are more likely to have had a cesarean delivery, adding postpartum discomfort to their fatigue.

Mixed Emotions. Don't be surprised if you find yourself emotionally vulnerable around the arrival of twins. Most parents initially will feel a mixture of contrasting emotions—pride, joy, relief, anticipation, self-doubt, fear, and even anger. Such ambivalent feelings are natural, and it will help to express them to a supportive listener whom you can count on to accept your conflicting feelings without judging you.

Be aware that older siblings can also have mixed emotions when twins arrive. The presence of a new baby is threatening enough to an older sibling, but the excessive attention typically lavished on twins can leave an older child feeling insignificant. Even though you have more than enough to do already, you can help ease the adjustment of your older child by showing special attention to and spending some one-on-one time with him.

Attachment. The human parent is best suited to deal with and form an attachment to one infant at a time. With twins, there is a tendency to bond to the twin set, rather than forming a unique attachment to each baby. There are many things you can do to help develop an effective, individual attachment to each infant. Start by visualizing two different babies during your pregnancy. Immediately after giving birth, begin spending time with each baby, holding them both together and separately. Focus on the differences in the infants' appearance and behavior to help foster separate and unique identities.

In raising twins, it is important to help the children see themselves as two distinct individuals, rather than as a set. Each baby develops two strong early attachments—one to its mother and another to its twin. As the twins grow, they must learn to see themselves as separate, not only from their mother, but from their twin as well.

While parents of twins struggle to give the babies separate identities, well-meaning family and friends often thwart their efforts by treating twins as a unit and focusing on their sameness. Expect to hear remarks that treat the two babies as if they were a single person: "How are the twins today?" or "I just can't tell them apart!" To counter society's tendency to unitize all twins, you'll have to make a conscious effort to avoid blending your babies' identities. Refer to each one by name, avoid dressing them alike, and allow them to spend time alone with you and with older siblings.

Direct Help and Support. Caring for more than one baby requires physical help and emotional support from others. No matter how much you wish you could cope alone without outside help, there simply is too much to do at first and you need to accept the reality of your temporary dependency on others. It is possible to maintain the control you desire while delegating responsibility to others. Arrange for help with daily household chores to allow you to focus your attention and energy on the physical care and feeding of your babies. Despite your best efforts, there simply aren't enough hours in a day to allow you to give each baby the care and attention you would afford a single infant. Being forced to choose between the needs of two babies at once is sure to leave you feeling inadequate at times.

The National Organization of Mothers of Twins Clubs, Inc. (see Resource List, page 449) can refer you to a local support group for mothers of multiples. Such clubs are an excellent source of emotional support and information about twin care and adjustment at home. These groups also provide access to twin equipment and literature and an opportunity to meet other parents who have dealt successfully with multiples. To help relieve the inevitable marital strain that results from the monumental demands of twin infant care, make it a priority to schedule some time alone with your partner each week.

Breastfeeding Multiple Babies

Infant feeding is indisputably the most basic, time-consuming, and anxiety-provoking activity of new parents. There's no doubt that feeding is far more stressful for mothers of twins and higher multiples than for mothers of single infants. In the long run, breastfeeding can be more convenient than bottle-feeding because the babies can be fed simultaneously without any preparation and with minimal disruption at night. Getting off to a successful start is no easy matter, however. We do a disservice to mothers of twins by implying that nursing multiples is a simple feat when, in fact, it is far more difficult than breastfeeding one baby. Statistics show that mothers of twins are less likely either to start or to continue nursing their babies when compared with other mothers.

Obstacles to Breastfeeding Success. Numerous circumstances make breastfeeding multiples more difficult than nursing a single infant. For one thing, there is an increased risk that the babies will be born smaller than normal size and earlier than full-term. (See chapter 10 for information about breastfeeding premature or sick newborns.) Often delivery occurs before a mother has attended a prenatal class on breastfeeding, so she may lack knowledge about even routine aspects of breastfeeding. The mother of twins is more likely to have a cesarean birth or to experience complications of labor and delivery. Her infants have an increased risk of respiratory distress or other medical problems, causing a delay in starting breastfeeding. Her babies may require supplemental feedings in the nursery and may need extra help learning to nurse effectively.

Even some healthy, full-term babies have difficulty latching on to their mother's breast and sucking correctly. With two infants who are likely to be born too small or too soon the chance of early feeding difficulties is even greater. Extra help will be required in guiding each baby to learn to nurse correctly. If one or both infants do not nurse vigorously and regularly, you may not establish a milk supply sufficient to nourish both babies.

Few women have a realistic understanding of how time-consuming breastfeeding can be during the early weeks when the babies are learning to nurse effectively and may need to be fed individually. Although helpers can bring the babies to the mother and assist with positioning, burping, and changing, the mother who has chosen to nurse exclusively must do all the feedings herself. The intense time commitment required to successfully establish breast-feeding with twins leaves many exhausted women with the perception "all I do is nurse." One determined mother later recalled that she hadn't buttoned her blouse during her babies' entire first month!

Maximizing Milk Supply. Under the best of circumstances, it is well known that the breast is capable of producing sufficient milk to nourish two, and even three, infants. However, the fact that some women can produce extremely high volumes of milk does not guarantee that every mother who attempts to nurse multiples will have sufficient milk. Yet, many professional and lay publications insist that insufficient milk is not a problem for mothers of multiples. Twin mothers typically are reassured that adequate milk production automatically follows the law of supply and demand—"the more you nurse, the more milk you produce." In my experience, however, breastfeeding mothers of twins definitely are at increased risk for inadequate breast milk. To prevent this frustrating problem, every effort should be made in the early days after delivery to maximize milk supply.

I have repeatedly emphasized that low milk supply usually results from ineffective milk removal, especially in the first days after milk comes in abundantly. Milk production declines rapidly if milk is not removed from the breasts regularly and effectively. If accumulated milk in the breasts is not drained at frequent intervals, a chemical inhibitor in residual milk causes further production to be suppressed. These principles apply to all mothers, but they are especially important for mothers of twins. If one or both babies have trouble latching on or sucking effectively, the mother's milk supply is likely to decline.

Whenever any doubt exists about either twin's ability to nurse well, I recommend that you obtain a hospital-grade electric breast pump and use it to express remaining milk after nursing the babies. If deemed necessary by the babies' doctor, your expressed milk can be used to supplement your infants until they are nursing well. The goal is to establish and preserve a generous milk supply from the start, even if the babies don't yet nurse effectively or take all the milk available. As the babies grow, mature, and obtain more milk with nursing, you can gradually taper your use of the breast pump until you no longer need to express residual milk. Your pumping regimen should be supervised by a lactation consultant who can tailor your breastfeeding plan to meet your babies' unique needs.

Techniques for Breastfeeding Twins. Just as for singletons, successful breastfeeding of twins is promoted by starting breast-feeding early, nursing on demand, rooming-in with your babies, and avoiding unnecessary supplements. Because twin infants usually nurse from a single breast at each feeding, twins can be expected to breastfeed at closer intervals than single babies (at least nine times daily).

When first learning to nurse your twins, you will probably need several pillows to make yourself comfortable and to bring your babies into proper position. A well-cushioned sofa, wide over-stuffed chair, or bed will allow you ample room to practice different holds. Several pillows specially designed for nursing twins are commercially available.

Simultaneous vs. separate nursing. Twins may be breastfed simultaneously, separately on an individual demand schedule, or separately on a modified demand schedule. In the beginning, you'll probably find that it takes both hands just to get one twin latched on correctly. Without help from another person, it is initially almost impossible to handle and position two infants in order to nurse them both at once. As soon as both babies are breastfeeding well, twin moms inevitably will nurse the infants simultaneously at times, either out of necessity or convenience. One mother explained that she strived to nurse each baby separately during the day but resorted to simultaneous nursing to save time at night.

Individual demand feedings. Nursing each twin individually when he or she displays feeding cues has the important advantage of allowing you to give each baby your full attention during feedings. Besides, a baby who is demanding can be expected to nurse better than one who has been awakened to feed. In addition, you have both hands free to position the baby and can focus on the unique personality and feeding style of one infant at a time. Although individual demand feedings are extremely time-consuming and tiring, feeding each baby separately is an excellent way to form a unique attachment with each infant.

Modified demand feedings. For many mothers, the most sensible way to feed their twins is a modified demand schedule. Whichever baby awakens first is fed on demand, then the second twin is gently awakened to nurse so that you will have a reasonable interval until the next feeding. The main drawback to the modified demand schedule is that the awakened baby may be difficult to arouse and may not nurse well.

Simultaneous nursing. Simultaneous nursing has the important advantage of being time-efficient and allowing the more vigorous baby to stimulate the let-down reflex for a smaller twin. Some research also suggests that nursing twins simultaneously actually generates a higher prolactin level, which might stimulate increased milk production. On the other hand, it is hard to simultaneously nurse both babies discreetly in public. And some mothers will

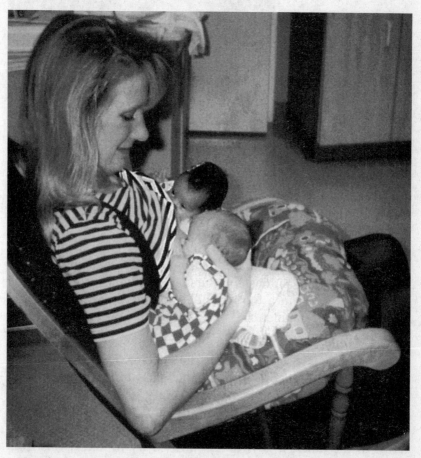

Simultaneous breastfeeding of premature twins using football holds.

Simultaneous breastfeeding of older twins using cradle holds.

decide that simultaneous nursing does not permit the individual-ized attention to and socialization with each child during feedings that they desire.

With simultaneous nursing, the hungrier baby sets the pace. The second twin is awakened to feed when one baby demands. You can try a variety of positions for nursing simultaneously, including holding each baby in a football hold, each in a cradle hold, or a football-cradle combination.

Alternating breasts vs. same breast. It has been suggested that mothers of twins assign each baby the same breast at each feeding. Indeed, babies often develop a preference for one side, either because of the shape of the mother's nipple, the rate of milk flow, or the sound of the mother's heartbeat. Although same-breast nursing theoretically might reduce the risk of one infant spreading germs to the other, it is virtually futile to try to keep twins from sharing the same germs.

Actually, it is advantageous to alternate breasts when nursing twins to assure that each breast receives balanced stimulation from the two babies. If one infant nurses less effectively than the other, it is especially important for the vigorous baby to suckle both sides to keep the milk supply generous.

Techniques for Breastfeeding More than Two Infants. Although it is far more difficult than breastfeeding twins, some women have successfully nursed triplets, and a few have produced enough milk to nourish four or more babies for several months. In addition to the obvious challenges of near-continuous feedings and phenomenal milk requirements, breastfeeding of higher multiples is further complicated by the fact that the babies are usually born prematurely and are hospitalized with special health needs. Mothers of triplets can nurse two babies simultaneously, then allow the third baby to breastfeed from both sides. The baby who nurses last should be rotated at each feeding. In reality, most mothers of three or more infants end up working out a combination of breast- and bottle-feeding. For triplets, a mother might simultaneously nurse two infants, while another caretaker feeds the third baby by bottle. For quadruplets, two infants can be bottle-fed while another two are nursed at each feeding. The infant(s) who receive bottles are rotated, so each baby receives the same number of daily breastfeedings. Other mothers of multiples simply breastfeed as often as they are able and bottle-feed as often as necessary. Mothers who use a breast pump to empty any remaining milk after nursings can use the expressed milk for some of the bottle feedings.

Summary. Breastfeeding more than one baby requires a huge commitment, especially in the early weeks. One mother of twins acknowledged that she never got out of her pajamas for several weeks. Another described the experience as "totally consuming" and explained that there "never seemed to be enough of me to go around." Within three to four weeks, however, you'll probably find the initial crisis is over as some degree of routine begins to emerge. One of the most helpful ideas I ever heard came from the close friend of an overwhelmed mother of twins. This considerate and enterprising friend boldly called everyone the new mom even remotely knew and scheduled them to bring dinner after the babies were born. That first month went a lot smoother, because along with the nourishing meal that appeared each evening came the comforting knowledge that an entire community of support had been mobilized to uplift and encourage a new breastfeeding family.

Breastfeeding Through a Pregnancy and Tandem Nursing

Now that most women start breastfeeding and many are successful nursing for the long term, more women are still breastfeeding when they discover that they are pregnant again. Although breastfeeding offers some protection against conceiving, especially during the first six months postpartum, it certainly is possible to become pregnant while nursing. Breastfeeding women who learn they are pregnant usually voice many concerns: Is it necessary to wean because of the pregnancy? Are there any harmful effects of continued nursing on the developing fetus? Are there any negative effects of pregnancy on lactation? Can breastfeeding during pregnancy cause premature labor? If I decide to nurse through my pregnancy, will my new baby obtain colostrum? Is it possible to continue nursing my older baby even after my new infant is born?

Milk Production During Pregnancy. Probably the first concern to be raised has to do with the nutritional risks involved in nursing through a pregnancy. Those who counsel pregnant women usually doubt that a pregnant nursing mother simultaneously can meet the enormous nutrient demands of a growing fetus and a nursing infant. Although some women who nurse through a pregnancy state that their milk supply does not change, it has been my observation that a woman's milk supply rapidly and drastically decreases within weeks or months of conception. Presumably, it is the pregnancy hormones that cause the volume of milk to decrease. The scantier milk produced also returns to a more colostrum-like composition. This decrease in milk production may be Mother Nature's way of making it clear that the nutrient requirements of the developing fetus rank higher than those of the nursing infant.

If a mother is breastfeeding a toddler when she becomes pregnant, the baby is already receiving other sources of nutrition. Obtaining less milk from nursing will probably not place her youngster at significant risk. On the other hand, if a mother conceives when her nursing baby is two months old and being exclusively breastfed, the infant could fail to thrive as a result of the mother's diminishing milk supply unless the baby receives supplemental formula. Many women report that their older baby loses interest in nursing shortly after the mother finds out she is pregnant. The decline in milk volume and change in milk taste probably cause many babies to wean. One frustrated toddler, confused as to why his pregnant mother's milk supply had drastically diminished, announced to all within earshot, "Milky all gone."

Oxytocin Release During Breastfeeding. Oxytocin, the hormone that causes milk to let-down during breastfeeding, is also the hormone that causes contractions of the uterus during labor. Thus, it is not surprising that questions should arise about whether premature labor could be triggered by nursing through a pregnancy. Actually, in the early months of pregnancy, the uterus does not react to oxytocin, but by midpregnancy, oxytocin causes uterine contractions. This makes it theoretically possible that breastfeeding throughout a pregnancy could provoke premature labor due to frequent oxytocin release. This possibility would be of particular concern for women with high-risk pregnancies, such as a mother who has had a previous premature birth or is carrying multiples. Although I am not aware of any formal studies that have confirmed a link between nursing through a pregnancy and premature labor, I would discourage the practice for at-risk women.

Breast Changes. Women who nurse through a pregnancy report that their milk comes in again after delivery just as it does in women who haven't been nursing. Thus, it would seem that the newborn still receives the special benefits of colostrum even when a sibling has breastfed through the pregnancy.

Women who become pregnant while breastfeeding often report that their nipples, previously accustomed to nursing, become extremely sensitive for no apparent reason. This new onset of nipple tenderness is believed to be due to pregnancy hormones. Some women describe nursing during pregnancy as being somewhat unpleasant, aversive, or off-putting. As pregnancy progresses, finding a comfortable nursing position also can be difficult. These physical challenges prompt many women to wean their older baby during their pregnancy. Weaning is usually not difficult, as the baby's interest in nursing often wanes as the mother's milk production gradually diminishes.

Tandem Nursing. Despite these changes and challenges, some women continue to nurse through their entire pregnancy because they feel it is in their older baby's best interest. Many of these mothers go on to nurse both babies after delivery. Breastfeeding two siblings who are not twins is known as tandem nursing. It requires a great deal of understanding and patience on the part of the mother to meet the unique needs of two nursing babies at different developmental stages. For example, an older baby may be jealous of the new infant and compete for nursing privileges. On the other hand, while care must be taken to assure that the younger baby has first access to the milk supply, a vigorously nursing older sibling can prove very helpful in stimulating generous milk production.

Relactation and Induced Lactation

The breasts are ideally primed to produce milk immediately after giving birth. The complex hormone influences of pregnancy stimulate growth of the milk ducts and glands, and further hormone shifts after delivery cause a woman's milk to come in abundantly. It is at this point that the milk glands and ducts, the hormones, and the blood supply to the breasts are all perfectly suited to producing and releasing milk. Certainly, the vast majority of women begin breastfeeding shortly after delivery.

Yet, amazing reports confirm that some women are able to start producing milk again long after having weaned their previous child. Reestablishing breastfeeding after an interruption is known as *relactation*. In underdeveloped societies, one hears reports of postmenopausal grandmothers who were able to nurse a grandchild after the infant's mother died in childbirth. I am also aware of numerous accounts of women who have been able to start producing milk again for an adopted infant, sometimes months or years after having breastfed a biologic child.

Mothers have attempted to relactate for a variety of reasons. Some women who experience breastfeeding problems may wean before they had originally planned. They may regret their decision or find their baby doesn't tolerate formula and attempt to "get their milk back." Occasionally, sudden separation of mother and infant through hospitalization of either may cause the milk supply to decline drastically, making relactation necessary when the two are reunited. Or, the mother of a hospitalized premature infant may find her milk supply has dwindled following weeks of pumping. By the time her baby is able to nurse at her breast, her supply may fall very short of the infant's nutritional needs. Some of these women have been able to successfully relactate and produce a full milk supply once again.

The production of breast milk by a woman who has never been pregnant or has never previously nursed a baby is called *induced lactation*. Today, many adoptive mothers have heard about induced lactation and ask whether they can produce milk and nurse a baby without having been pregnant.

Although relactation and induced lactation are no doubt *possible* for certain women in certain circumstances, neither should be considered *probable* for an individual woman. Based on my professional experience, I have drawn the following conclusions about relactation and induced lactation:

1. Relactation attempts generally result in more milk production than efforts to induce lactation. Without ever having a biologic pregnancy, a woman is unlikely to produce a significant volume of milk, despite heroic efforts. Women whose breasts have experienced the hormonal influences of pregnancy, and particularly women who have previously breastfed, can expect to produce more milk if they try to relactate than women who attempt to induce lactation.

2. When a mother desires to nurse an adopted infant, the main focus should be on experiencing the nursing relationship. Any milk produced should be viewed as a bonus. Unsubstantiated and exaggerated reports about milk production in adoptive mothers can create unrealistic expectations that leave a mother feeling inadequate and disappointed. Even when a woman has breastfed previously, it is unlikely that she will produce a full or near-full milk supply for an adopted infant. For a woman who has never been pregnant, such a goal is highly unrealistic.

3. Relactation is more likely to be successful if a woman is still nursing or has recently weaned than if she hasn't breastfed for years. The closer a woman is to delivery and the shorter duration that her milk supply has been low, the more likely her efforts to relactate will be successful.

Techniques to Induce Milk Production. Although various drugs have been tried to stimulate milk production, the most important requirement for relactation or induced lactation is an effective, regular suckling stimulus. For adoptive mothers, breast stimulation can be provided by using a hospital-grade rental electric breast pump for ten to fifteen minutes approximately every four hours for many weeks before the baby arrives. Once the baby is available to nurse, enticing the infant to suckle usually is more effective and rewarding for the mother than a mechanical pump because of the emotional reaction to having your baby at your breast. However, an adoptive infant probably will have little interest pursuing breastfeeding unless the baby's efforts are rewarded by a flow of milk. An ideal way to encourage a baby to suckle the breast when little milk is produced is to use the Supplemental Nursing System (see the illustration on page 348 and the discussion on pages 347–349). This device allows an infant to simultaneously receive supplemental formula while breastfeeding.

No drugs are presently FDA-approved for the specific purpose of promoting relactation or inducing lactation, but several medications have been found to have the side effect of raising prolactin levels. Some of these drugs have been prescribed, with variable success, to increase a mother's milk supply. The most commonly used medication to aid with relactation or induced lactation is metoclopramide (Reglan), a drug commonly prescribed to treat heartburn or to combat nausea (see chapter 9, page 340, and chapter 10, page 382). Several studies have shown that metoclopramide raises prolactin levels and can increase milk production. Although the drug is relatively safe, some patients experience adverse side effects, including drowsiness and fatigue, depression, restlessness, headache, dizziness, and abnormal body movements.

Because so many adoptive mothers long to be able to breastfeed, some physicians will prescribe metoclopramide for them to try to stimulate milk production. Some prospective adoptive women take the medication for weeks or months before adoption is anticipated. During this time, the woman also is advised to pump her breasts four or more times a day in an attempt to start some milk production. A few physicians have also temporarily prescribed estrogen and progesterone to prospective mothers before their adoptive baby arrives to stimulate development of the milk glands and ducts in hopes of producing milk. However, no research confirms the safety and effectiveness of hormonal therapies to try to induce milk production. When the adopted baby arrives, the estrogen and progesterone are stopped to mimic the sudden withdrawal of pregnancy hormones after delivery. Meanwhile, the woman may continue to pump and take metoclopramide for a number of weeks, while the baby nurses at the breast using the SNS device.

Milk production varies widely among mothers who have tried relactation or induced lactation. Women who have never been pregnant may produce only drops, while women who have nursed in the recent past are more likely to produce larger quantities of milk. Even under the best of circumstances, a woman trying to relactate should expect her baby to require supplemental formula in addition to the milk she produces. It goes without saying that any woman attempting to induce lactation or relactate should be under the care of her own physician and remain in close contact with the baby's physician. Infants have failed to thrive when well-intentioned mothers overestimated their milk production and did not give their babies adequate quantities of supplemental formula. Regardless of the quantity of milk produced, most adoptive mothers who have breastfed rightly emphasize the quality of the mother-infant relationship as the most rewarding aspect of their breastfeeding endeavor.

Breastfeeding After Breast Surgery

Few would argue that our society places excessive emphasis on physical appearance and outward beauty. No wonder so many men and women today decide to have some type of cosmetic surgery to enhance their appearance. Women may choose cosmetic breast surgery to enlarge or reduce their breast size, correct sagging breasts, or otherwise create shaplier breasts. At the time such breast surgery is performed, women may be giving little thought to having and feeding babies in the distant future. Years later, they might have concerns about the possible impact of breast surgery on their ability to breastfeed.

Breast Augmentation

Modern silicone gel breast implants were first developed in the early 1960s. During the next three decades, between one and two million American women received breast implants. Most of these women obtained implants because of dissatisfaction with their existing breast size or shape, while a smaller percentage had breast reconstruction following mastectomy for breast cancer.

More than thirty years after silicone breast implants first appeared on the market, questions remain unanswered about their safety and effectiveness. In early 1992, speculation about possible health hazards of silicone gel implants led to widespread consumer alarm. As a result of the ensuing public outrage, the Food and Drug Administration decided in April 1992 to impose voluntary restrictions on the use of silicone gel implants until controlled research studies provide answers about their safety. In the meantime, augmentations continue to be performed using implants filled with saline (salt water).

Health Risks of Silicone Implants. Today, the health risks to women who have silicone gel implants are still unknown. Some evidence suggests that the implants might increase a woman's chances of autoimmune diseases such as rheumatoid arthritis, lupus, or scleroderma. Other research has failed to confirm that such a linkage exists; thus, the risks to women remain inconclusive. Meanwhile, recent questions have been raised about potential risks to infants who breastfeed from mothers who have silicone implants. Silicone, the second most common element in the earth's crust, is widely present in our daily lives. Infants are regularly exposed to silicone in baby bottle nipples and pacifiers and in medicines as a food additive. Hundreds of thousands of babies have been born to women with silicone breast implants over the past thirty years, and still no conclusive evidence suggests that these women should not breastfeed. Without more convincing data, many experts agree that mothers with silicone implants should continue to breastfeed their babies because of the compelling health benefits of breast milk. At the time of this writing, I agree with those who believe that women who have had silicone implants should not be discouraged from breastfeeding.

Impact of Breast Implants on Breastfeeding. Little research has been conducted to examine the impact of implant surgery on breastfeeding success. Generally, women who receive breast implants are advised that the surgery will not affect their ability to breastfeed. Patient-education materials that discuss augmentation often make no mention of subsequent breastfeeding or claim that breastfeeding should not be affected by the procedure. However, shortly after I started helping women with breastfeeding difficulties, I began to suspect that cosmetic breast surgery, including augmentation procedures, might have an adverse effect on breast-feeding success. At the Lactation Program in Denver, my colleagues and I have encountered many women, some of whom previously have breastfed successfully, who have experienced insufficient milk when breastfeeding after augmentation surgery. It seems reasonable to question whether performing an operation on the breast might affect how it functioned afterward. I certainly don't dispute the fact that many women appear to breastfeed successfully after augmentation surgery. I just don't think we can accept the common assumption that such surgery never causes a problem.

In fact, research evidence now exists to link augmentation with breastfeeding difficulties. A recent study has found a significantly greater risk of insufficient milk in breastfeeding women with breast implants compared with women who have not had implant surgery. Continuing to gather data about women's breastfeeding experience after breast augmentation is the only sure way to confirm the impact of the procedure on breastfeeding success.

Below I outline the ways that augmentation surgery might adversely impact breastfeeding. These explanations are based on the personal stories and in-depth evaluations of scores of women with breast implants seen at the Lactation Program.

Disruption of milk ducts. Breast augmentation can be performed through several types of surgical incisions. The most common sites are slightly above the crease where the breast attaches to the chest wall; along the margin of the areola (the brown part surrounding the nipple); and in the armpit. The location of the incision is usually based on the surgeon's preference and experience, as well as the woman's desires. During the operation, the surgeon attempts to avoid injury to the milk ducts, but when the incision is made at the border of the areola, damage to the ducts sometimes occurs. Cutting or damaging milk ducts can interfere with successful breastfeeding by preventing milk flow from certain lobes of the breast. A few days after giving birth, all functioning glands of a woman's breasts will fill with milk. However, continued milk production will occur only in the lobes of the breast that drain well. Milk cannot flow from lobes whose milk ducts have been cut. Within a matter of days, the unrelieved pressure and accumulated milk in the lobes that cannot drain results in cessation of further milk production in those areas. This will decrease a woman's chances of providing a full milk supply to her infant.

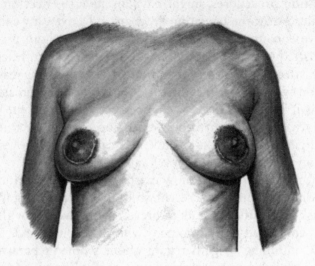

Milk ducts may be cut or damaged when implant surgery is performed with incisions at the margin of the areola.

Nerve damage. The nerve supply to the nipple not only allows normal sensation to the nipple area, but it plays an important role in triggering the normal hormone responses involved in breastfeeding. When the nipple is stimulated by suckling, nerves carry a message to the brain, which results in the release of the hormones prolactin and oxytocin into the bloodstream. You will recall that prolactin and oxytocin are important for milk production and release (see chapter 3, pages 75–78). It is not uncommon for women to notice altered nipple sensation following breast augmentation surgery. Women may have diminished or absent nipple sensitivity, and in some cases the nipples are overly sensitive. Changes in nipple sensation following surgery suggest that the nerve supply to the nipple has been damaged. However, it is not known to what degree such nerve damage interferes with the normal prolactin and oxytocin responses. Although regrowth of nerves can occur, the process may be slow, and sometimes causes uncomfortable hypersensitivity of the nipples. I have encountered several women whose nipples were so exquisitely sensitive following augmentation that breastfeeding was intolerable, even though the mother used proper nursing technique.

Exaggerated postpartum breast engorgement. Exaggerated postpartum breast engorgement sometimes occurs in women with breast implants. Extreme breast discomfort and generalized swelling and firmness make it difficult for the infant to latch on correctly to nurse. These factors combine to impede normal milk flow, causing residual milk to accumulate in the glands. If not remedied quickly, diminished milk production can result. The presence of implants can cause increased breast "tightness" when milk comes in abundantly and an exaggeration of the normal engorgement symptoms. Applying hot packs to the breasts before nursings and cold packs between feedings and the use of synthetic oxytocin nasal spray, cabbage leaf compresses, or gentle breast massage may help improve milk flow and provide some relief (see chapter 7, pages 225–232). I have found that early, regular use of a hospital-grade electric breast pump to express some milk remaining after breastfeedings is particularly helpful in successfully establishing milk flow, softening the breasts, and maximizing the milk supply. Once excessive pressure is reduced and engorgement subsides, the infant is usually able to remove milk efficiently by breastfeeding. Pumping after nursings can be gradually discontinued over a week or so.

Can the use of a hospital-grade electric breast pump cause an implant to rupture? I have never observed or heard about such an occurrence, and plastic surgeons with whom I have consulted do not feel that a hospital-grade electric breast pump posed such a risk, especially if the implant is placed behind the chest muscle. Furthermore, the negative pressure generated by a hospital-grade electric pump should not exceed the vacuum created by a normal nursing baby. Nevertheless, it makes good sense to begin using the pump on the lowest setting, to increase the suction level gradually, and to use the pump only as prescribed, usually about ten minutes every three hours.

Tubular Hypoplastic Breasts. Sometimes women choose to have breast augmentation surgery because of a problem with breast development. Perhaps one breast is underdeveloped and much smaller than the other, making it difficult for a woman to find clothing that fits well. Other women might choose surgery to correct a breast deformity known as tubular breasts. Tubular breasts lack normal fullness and have an elongated shape. They may also have fewer milk glands, which are concentrated beneath the nipple and areola, creating a bulbous appearance at the tip of the breast (see the illustration on page 54). I have encountered many women with underdeveloped or tubular breasts who have had difficulty producing sufficient milk for their babies. Before attributing breast-feeding problems to breast implant surgery, it is important to distinguish whether breast augmentation was performed to enhance normal breasts or to correct an abnormality that might have interfered with breastfeeding anyway.

Breast Reduction Surgery

Excessively large, heavy breasts can be physically and psychologically disabling for a woman. The condition tends to run in families, with rapid breast growth often beginning during the teenage years. Disproportionately large breasts can cause a woman to feel self-conscious, limit her physical activity or athletic participation, and make it difficult to find clothing that fits well. In addition, huge breasts often cause physical complaints, such as muscle strain and neck or upper-back pain, bra strap pressure marks, breast pain, and irritation of the skin where the lower breast attaches to the chest.

No wonder many women whose excessively large breasts cause chronic discomfort or embarrassment decide to have a breast reduction procedure to achieve smaller, more comfortable, shaplier breasts that are more proportionate to the rest of their body. During the surgery, excessive breast tissue and skin are removed, the breasts are reshaped, and the nipples are repositioned at a higher level. Sometimes the nipples are removed and reattached during the procedure, while in other instances they can be repositioned without being removed. Breast reduction surgery is more disruptive than augmentation procedures and carries an increased likelihood of nerve or duct damage. The result may be absent or diminished nipple sensation and some degree of impaired milk flow that often prevents full breastfeeding. Even so, I have found that when women have been well informed in the preoperative period about their realistic chances of breastfeeding in the future, they usually report that their improved lifestyle, appearance, and comfort are sufficient compensation for their inability to breastfeed exclusively.

Previous Breast Biopsy

Breast biopsy of suspicious lumps detected by breast self-exam, medical exams, or mammograms has been performed in numerous women of childbearing age to allow for early detection of breast cancer. On first consideration, a simple breast biopsy may not seem likely to have an effect on breastfeeding. However, a biopsy incision that is made in the vicinity of the areola may jeopardize breastfeeding ability by cutting milk ducts and preventing proper milk drainage. If this occurs, a woman's milk still comes in abundantly after delivery, but normal milk flow may not occur from the biopsied breast. If the milk volume from the biopsied breast is very low, the mother may not be able to provide sufficient milk to meet her baby's nutritional requirements. Other times, generous milk production from the other breast is able to compensate for diminished milk on the biopsied side. Fortunately, modern breast biopsy no longer requires surgery, as newer needle biopsy techniques have beome available.

Breast Surgery During Lactation

Sometimes a breast biopsy or other breast surgery needs to be performed while a woman is still breastfeeding. This is increasingly true as more older women conceive, give birth, and breastfeed their babies. Because there is so much additional blood flow to the breast during pregnancy and lactation, surgeons consider operating on the breast to be more difficult during those times. Some physicians will ask a woman to wean her infant if breast surgery is needed. However, many women are reluctant to discontinue breastfeeding before they had planned unless it is absolutely necessary. Postponing required surgery until a woman has weaned is not an acceptable option, as prompt diagnosis and treatment of breast problems is essential, whether or not a woman is breastfeeding. Fortunately, more surgeons are gaining experience operating on the breast during lactation, usually with good results.

Many physicians and parents do not realize that it is possible to wean from one breast while continuing to nurse on the other side. This option is especially attractive if the mother is reluctant to give up breastfeeding but must wean from one breast for medical reasons, such as an abscess, chronic infections, or debilitating pain. Sometimes the "problem breast" produces much less milk than the healthy one, so weaning on that side has little impact on a baby's breast-milk intake. Once suckling is discontinued on one breast, the unemptied breast will begin drying up and gradually will stop lactating, even though the woman continues to nurse from the other side. The length of time before milk production ceases can vary, depending on the milk supply and the age of the infant. Usually within a week, the unsuckled breast will be producing little or no milk.

Breastfeeding After Breast Cancer

While not common, pregnancy and parenthood can occur after treatment for breast cancer. Many women who choose lumpectomy and radiation therapy for breast cancer are in their childbearing years. Some of these women later become pregnant and wonder whether breastfeeding is possible for them. We now know that radiation therapy for breast cancer causes radiation damage to the milk glands and ducts, preventing full lactation from the breast that received radiation exposure. If a woman conceives after receiving radiation therapy, the treated breast does not experience normal pregnancy changes (see pages 52 and 72–73) and milk does not come in abundantly on that side after delivery. Typically, only a few drops of milk are produced from the radiated breast, and the baby quickly loses interest in nursing from that side. However, breastfeeding from the breast that was not treated with radiation is still possible. In some cases, the baby may receive ample milk by nursing exclusively from the untreated side. Even if some formula supplement is required, partial breastfeeding can be highly satisfying to a mother and beneficial to her infant.

Breastfeeding and Illness in the Infant or Mother

Because routine breastfeeding can span many months, and even years, you can expect that you and your infant will have one or more illnesses while you are breastfeeding. Fortunately, most of these will be minor inconveniences that should cause no disruption of nursing. In some cases, however, a mother or infant may have a serious infection or chronic medical problem that calls for special breastfeeding management. Rarely, a mother's or baby's condition is incompatible with breastfeeding. In all cases of significant illness in yourself or your infant, it is imperative that your own and your baby's physicians are aware of the problem and collaborate about medical decisions and breastfeeding recommendations. You may also want to seek input from a lactation consultant or breastfeeding specialist who has counseled women under similar circumstances. In some instances, expert advice can be obtained by contacting individual medical specialists, the La Leche League International Center for Breastfeeding Information, the University of Rochester Lactation Study Center, or the Centers for Disease Control and Prevention in Atlanta (see Resource List, pages 447–448).

Illness in the Breastfeeding Mother

Minor Illnesses. Common illnesses like colds, sore throats, sinus infections, diarrhea, or urinary tract infections are not valid reasons to wean. In most cases, by the time the mother develops symptoms, her infant has already been exposed to the infectious cause of her illness. Interrupting breastfeeding at this point is counterproductive. Antibodies to the germs causing the mother's illness will appear in her milk and help protect the infant from getting sick. Localized infections, like urinary tract or uterine infections, are not spread directly from one person to another. With any illness, make it a practice to wash your hands thoroughly before handling your breasts or your baby. If you take any prescribed or over-the-counter medications to treat your illness, be sure to check with your doctor about their passage into breast milk and whether they pose any risk to your nursing baby (see chapter 7, pages 265–269).

A nursing mother who isn't feeling well should get extra rest and drink plenty of liquids, especially when her fluid requirements are increased due to fever, diarrhea, vomiting, or heavy nose secretions. For a few days, make your top priorities breastfeeding and resting; other chores can wait until you are feeling better. Although your milk supply might temporarily decline, it should climb again once you recover.

Serious Infectious Diseases. Occasionally, an infection in the breastfeeding mother poses a serious threat to her nursing infant. In some cases, such as HIV infection, the infecting organism is present in breast milk and can be passed to the baby through breastfeeding. In other instances, such as active tuberculosis, infection is spread by close physical contact between mother and baby, and not by breast milk. Unfortunately, health professionals often have insufficient information about the transmission of infections by breastfeeding. Well-meaning doctors may prohibit nursing when they aren't sure about the safety of breastfeeding. The American

Academy of Pediatrics Committee on Infectious Diseases publishes and updates an important reference book, a red paperback volume known as the *Red Book*. This valuable resource for physicians answers many questions about more than one hundred infectious diseases and often includes information about whether breast-feeding is permissible. Another excellent source of up-to-date information about the risk of transmitting infectious diseases by breastfeeding is a local children's hospital. Ask your baby's doctor to speak with an infectious disease specialist at the nearest children's hospital if additional information is needed about the advisability of breastfeeding with your particular illness. Meanwhile, a few infections that raise immediate concerns about breastfeeding are addressed below.

Human immunodeficiency virus. The most serious and well-publicized infection in mothers that poses a risk to nursing infants is human immunodeficiency virus (HIV). HIV has been detected in the breast milk of infected mothers, and cases have been documented throughout the world in which HIV has been transmitted from mother to baby through breastfeeding. In certain parts of the developing world, the risk of infant death from malnutrition and infectious diseases as a result of not breastfeeding may outweigh the possible risk of acquiring HIV infection by breastfeeding. In these locations, breastfeeding by an HIV-infected mother is still currently recommended by the World Health Organization and UNICEF. In the United States, however, infectious diseases and malnutrition are not major causes of infant deaths, and safe alternatives to breastfeeding are easily available. Thus, the American Academy of Pediatrics and the Centers for Disease Control and Prevention recommend that women in the United States who are infected with HIV should NOT breastfeed or provide expressed milk for their infants. Voluntary, confidential testing of pregnant women is urged so each woman will know her HIV status and receive counseling about whether to breastfeed and about methods to prevent acquiring and transmitting HIV. A pregnant woman who tests positive for HIV can receive new treatments that greatly reduce the risk of transmitting the infection to her baby and that will help her stay healthier longer.

Tuberculosis. Tuberculosis (TB) is a chronic bacterial infection that usually affects the lungs. It has been on the rise in the United States during the past decade. Women with active TB are highly contagious to their babies. Although the disease is passed by respiratory droplets and not by breast milk, infected mothers should not breastfeed (or even be in the presence of their infants) until they have been treated and are no longer contagious (usually a few weeks after treatment is started). Meanwhile, an infected mother can pump and collect her milk for her baby until she can safely start nursing. The drugs used to treat TB are excreted into breast milk, but most are compatible with breastfeeding. Babies of infected mothers also need treatment. Breastfeeding is permissible for women with a previously positive TB skin test but no evidence of disease. If a woman has a recent conversion to a positive skin test, she should be evaluated for active disease before breastfeeding begins or continues.

Hepatitis. Hepatitis is a viral infection of the liver that can cause fever, jaundice, loss of appetite, nausea, and fatigue. The three major types of hepatitis are known as hepatitis A virus (HAV), hepatitis B virus (HBV), and hepatitis C virus (HCV). The baby's physician always should be informed when a mother has been diagnosed with acute hepatitis or is a carrier of chronic hepatitis. However, breastfeeding is permissible in most cases.

Hepatitis A usually causes a mild, self-limited illness and does not become chronic. Human feces are commonly infected with the virus, which is easily passed from person to person due to poor handwashing habits. Food-borne and water-borne epidemics occur commonly, and the disease spreads easily in child care centers, especially when diapered children are present. When a mother with hepatitis A has been given gamma globulin, breastfeeding is permitted.

Hepatitis B can cause illness ranging from minimal symptoms to death or chronic liver disease. It is passed through blood or body fluids, for example by sexual activity or a contaminated needle. Transmission by a blood transfusion is now rare in the United States due to current screening and handling procedures. Although HBV has been found in breast milk, infants born to mothers with HBV are permitted to breastfeed so long as the following precautions are taken. *All infants born to mothers with HBV should receive hepatitis B–specific immune globulin and their first vaccination against HBV immediately after birth.* Two additional vaccine doses (at one to two months and six months) are necessary to complete the vaccine series and protect the infant.

Hepatitis C tends to cause mild disease, but persistent infection is common, with up to half of patients developing chronic liver disease. Liver cancer can later develop in patients who have had HCV. The virus is passed by blood, and transmission by sexual activity is suspected, but has not been proved. Little data is available on which to base a recommendation about breastfeeding when a mother has HCV. At this writing, breast milk has not been proven to transmit HCV, and according to current U.S. Public Health Service guidelines, HCV infection of the mother is not a contraindication to breastfeeding. However, some physicians advise against breastfeeding because, while the risks may be small, the stakes are high. The decision whether to breastfeed should be individualized after discussing the matter with your doctor and your baby's pediatrician.

Herpes virus infection. Herpes simplex virus causes oral (cold sores) and genital herpes infections. Women with active herpes infections, either oral or genital, can pass the herpes virus to their infant by close contact. Young infants can become very seriously ill from herpes infections, and even fatal illness can develop. Thorough handwashing before and after caring for the infant is important to help reduce the risk of transmission of disease. Breastfeeding is believed to be safe if there are no herpes sores on the mother's breasts and if sores elsewhere on the body are covered. Mothers and other infant caretakers with active oral cold sores must wear disposable surgical masks when touching newborns and refrain from kissing or nuzzling babies until their lesions are crusted and dried. Women with herpes sores on their breasts should not breastfeed until the infection has cleared completely.

Chronic Illness of the Mother. Many women with chronic illnesses want to know if breastfeeding will affect their disease or place their baby at risk. In the past, women with chronic medical problems typically were discouraged from breastfeeding because little information was available. The prevailing attitude was "if we don't know, it's best not to breastfeed." As breastfeeding rates have increased in recent decades, more women with chronic problems have sought information and expertise to enable them to breastfeed. Today, many women with chronic illnesses breastfeed successfully with close monitoring by their physician. In most instances, women with an underlying chronic illness make milk of normal composition and adequate amount. Women have successfully breastfed despite a wide variety of medical diagnoses, including blindness, deafness, paraplegia and other physical limitations, diabetes, kidney transplant, heart disease, epilepsy, cystic fibrosis, inflammatory bowel disease, arthritis, lupus, multiple sclerosis, and asthma.

In each instance, special guidance may be necessary to accommodate breastfeeding, such as a review of the mother's medications, appropriate dietary changes, practical advice about breastfeeding issues, or assistance with nursing technique. For example, a diabetic mother may have a decreased insulin requirement and increased need for calories while she is lactating. An infant born to a diabetic mother may have newborn complications and low blood sugar that lead to early separation of mother and baby after birth. Breastfeeding may be delayed and supplemental formula temporarily required. Since diabetics are generally more prone to infections, including yeast infection, a breastfeeding woman with diabetes may be more likely to experience yeast infection of the nipples (see chapter 7, pages 243–247).

Women with cystic fibrosis produce milk of normal composition, but their milk production may be low if they have very little body fat. A few chronic illnesses may be aggravated by the metabolic burden of lactation, and occasionally breastfeeding is not possible due to life-threatening illness, such as severe heart failure. Rarely, the medications required to treat a mother's chronic illness are not compatible with breastfeeding, such as chemotherapy for cancer. If you have a chronic medical problem, chances are that breastfeeding will still be possible. However, you should discuss your breastfeeding plans with your obstetrician and the other physicians, including the specialists, who care for you.

Psychiatric Illness. Women who suffer from mental health problems, such as depression, anxiety, bipolar illness, eating disorders, and schizophrenia, are often able to breastfeed successfully. Of course, such women should be under the care of a psychiatrist or other mental health worker. Major depression is the most common psychiatric illness in new mothers. Depressed women are often socially isolated and unsupported and have more difficulty with breastfeeding and infant care. They are less able to read their babies' cues and interpret their babies' needs. Infants of depressed mothers may have delayed development, poor growth, and flat emotions.

Unfortunately, little information is available about the safety of commonly prescribed antidepressants and other psychiatric medications for nursing mothers. It is possible that daily exposure to these drugs might affect newborn behavior and development. Although the effects of psychiatric drugs on nursing infants are largely unknown, they are considered to be of concern. Some women refuse medication because they are unwilling to discontinue breastfeeding and worry about the safety of the medications. However, symptoms are likely to worsen when mothers with depression or other mental illness are not treated. Many psychiatrists advocate making medication decisions on a case-by-case basis, weighing the theoretical risks of the drug against the convincing benefits of breastfeeding. Although I can't guarantee that an antidepressant or other psychiatric drug is completely risk-free for a nursing baby, several published reports provide reassuring data for a number of psychiatric drugs that appear to have no adverse effects on breastfeeding infants. Treating the mother with the minimum effective dose while closely monitoring the infant seems to be a prudent approach until more experience and data can be accumulated.

Maternal Hospitalization. Occasionally a nursing mother needs to be hospitalized, whether for a medical problem, elective or emergency surgery, or as the result of an automobile accident. In addition to the usual stress associated with a major medical problem, a nursing mother admitted to the hospital inevitably will worry about the welfare of her breastfeeding infant. However grave her own health concerns, she may be preoccupied or anxious about how her baby is being fed and consoled in her absence and the need to relieve uncomfortable breast engorgement and to collect and store her milk. If a hospitalized woman does not have to be separated from her nursing infant, her reduced anxiety may contribute to a speedier recovery. Many hospitals will allow nursing infants to stay in the mother's hospital room so long as an adult family member or support person remains with the infant at all times to attend to the baby's needs. If you must be hospitalized, ask your own and your baby's doctors jointly to support your request to have your baby welcome in your room and to review any medications you must take to assure their safety for your infant.

When your baby is not available to nurse directly, ideally you should use a hospital-grade electric breast pump to empty your breasts in order to maintain your milk production and save milk

for your baby's feedings. Have your doctor write an order out-
lining the necessary frequency of pumping and requesting that the
staff nurses assist you with pumping and storing your milk. Most
hospitals that deliver babies have one or more electric pumps on
site for use by nursing mothers. If no pump is available, ask a
family member to rent a hospital-grade electric breast pump for
you and bring it to the hospital (see Resource List, page 447). Your
breasts need to be emptied with the pump as often as your baby
would normally nurse.

Women who have a scheduled elective hospital admission can
begin days or weeks in advance to express and store their surplus
milk in order to collect a sufficient stockpile of milk before they
enter the hospital. This option gives the most peace of mind
because it assures your baby will have an ample supply of your
milk even if you must take a medication that temporarily prevents
you from breastfeeding. If you are able to pump in advance, begin
expressing and storing some of the milk that remains after feedings.
Women usually have more residual milk after the morning nursings
than later in the day (see chapter 8, pages 291–292). Another
advantage of a scheduled elective admission is that it allows the
opportunity to introduce your baby to bottle-feeding. Some exclusively breastfed babies do not readily accept other feeding alternatives. Trying to give a bottle to an upset breastfed baby whose
mother has been suddenly hospitalized can be a frustrating experience. If the admission is anticipated, the baby can be familiar-
ized with bottle- or cup-feeding in advance so that necessary
feedings away from the mother don't have to represent a crisis (see
pages 292–294 and 349).

Breastfeeding and Illness in the Infant

Minor Illnesses. Although it is well known that breastfed
infants enjoy some protection against many illnesses, your nursing
baby may still suffer from occasional colds, ear infections, diarrhea, vomiting, and other minor illnesses. Breast milk is an ideal
food for a sick baby, providing essential fluids and easily digested
nourishment. In addition, the breastfeeding relationship will be
an invaluable source of comfort and solace for a sick, uncomfortable baby.

In the past, doctors commonly recommended discontinuing milk
feedings and giving babies only clear liquids during bouts of

vomiting and diarrhea. Today, mothers of infants with stomach or intestinal illness are encouraged to continue breastfeeding because breast milk is well absorbed and does not aggravate diarrhea. Furthermore, frequent breastfeeding consoles an irritable infant and helps preserve the milk supply when the baby may be nursing less effectively than usual. If oral rehydration solutions are required to treat infant dehydration, they can be fed in addition to nursing.

A baby's normal breastfeeding routines may be disrupted during a minor illness. For example, an infant may nurse more often than usual, preferring to be comforted at the breast for prolonged periods. Or, a fussy baby with an ear infection may nurse less vigorously than normal. If you suspect that your baby is not draining your milk well, you would be wise to hand express or use a breast pump to remove milk remaining after nursing in order to prevent breast engorgement and a decline in your milk supply.

Infant Illnesses for Which Breast Milk or Breastfeeding Is Problematic. Although breast milk is ideal infant nutrition for almost every baby, breastfeeding is contraindicated for a few rare infant conditions. One of the illnesses for which breastfeeding is not allowed is the inherited metabolic disorder known as galactosemia. Lactose, the milk sugar present in breast milk and other animal milks, breaks down to glucose and galactose. Babies born with the rare condition galactosemia cannot break down galactose, which accumulates in the liver, brain, and kidneys. Untreated, the disorder can quickly be fatal or lead to permanent brain damage. Fortunately, galactosemia can be detected by routine newborn screening performed in most states. Treatment is a galactose-free diet that makes breastfeeding impossible.

Another inherited metabolic disorder that poses a problem for breastfed infants is phenylketonuria (PKU). Babies born with this condition cannot break down the amino acid phenylalanine, which causes excessive amounts to accumulate in the blood. Left untreated, PKU leads to severe mental retardation. The disorder can be detected with newborn screening programs for metabolic diseases and is treated with a low-phenylalanine diet. Since some phenylalanine is essential in the diet of all infants, treatment involves limiting a child's intake of phenylalanine to amounts that permit normal growth and development without allowing excessive quantities to accumulate. Infants can breastfeed to a limited degree and receive the remainder of their milk as a special phenylalanine-free infant formula. The ideal balance of breast milk and special formula must be figured for each infant. Babies with PKU require expert care and close monitoring by a metabolic disease expert who can assure that phenylalanine levels remain in the normal range. If necessary, the mother can use an accurate electronic infant scale to perform test weights in her home to monitor the infant's precise daily intake of breast milk.

Chronic Medical Problems Impacting Breastfeeding Effectiveness. A few infants have medical conditions that keep them from nursing effectively. If such infants are allowed to breastfeed without special guidance and close monitoring, they may suffer malnutrition due to inadequate milk intake.

Cleft Lip and Palate. Cleft lip and palate are common birth defects that can cause multiple complications, including feeding difficulties, ear infections, dental abnormalities, and speech and language problems. Cleft lip and cleft palate can occur separately or in combination and can be present on one or both sides. The defect can range from a tiny separation of the lip on one side to a complete bilateral gap that extends from the base of the nose, through the lip and gum, and along the entire length of the roof of the mouth. Children with cleft palate require an extensive program of care involving many specialists who need to work together as a team. A cleft palate support group can be the source of enormous information and support (see Resource List, page 449).

The most immediate problem posed by cleft defects is that of feeding the infant. An infant with an isolated cleft lip may be able to nurse effectively since the soft breast tissue may fill the defect and allow the baby to create a seal with his mouth. However, infants with cleft palate are usually unable to nurse directly at the breast because they cannot compress the breast against the roof of the mouth or create an adequate seal. A plastic palatal obturator, also called a plate, is a made-to-fit oral prosthesis for infants with cleft palate that separates the baby's mouth from the nose passages. With the palatal obturator in place, feeding is made much easier for a baby with cleft palate, and effective breastfeeding may be possible. However, the plate must be changed often and adjusted as the baby grows, and some centers do not routinely make palatal obturators.

Without an oral prosthesis, infants with cleft palate may

attempt to breastfeed, but are at very high risk for obtaining little milk. I have encountered several infants with cleft palate who suffered severe malnutrition due to ineffective breastfeeding that wasn't recognized. Early "practice sessions" at the breast provide important comfort and skin-to-skin contact and may help your baby eventually learn to nurse effectively. However, you cannot assume that your baby is obtaining milk during breastfeeding attempts without confirming this with infant-feeding test weights (see chapter 9, pages 333–334). I strongly recommend that you obtain early and ongoing help from a lactation consultant or other breastfeeding specialist who has experience feeding infants with cleft palate. Several special techniques are available to help such a baby nurse more effectively, and alternative feeding methods can be used to supplement the infant's intake by breastfeeding, which often is minimal. *Under no circumstances should a baby with a cleft defect be assumed to nurse well without confirming actual milk intake.* Renting an electronic infant scale to perform in-home test weights and to monitor daily weights would prove very beneficial to your baby's care (see Resource List, page 450).

Because direct breastfeeding is unlikely to be effective at first, the mother of an infant with a cleft lip or palate should be shown how to use a hospital-grade electric breast pump to establish and maintain an abundant milk supply. Initially, your focus should be on establishing a generous milk supply and assuring that your baby consumes sufficient milk for proper growth. Feeding expressed breast milk to a baby with a cleft palate will help protect the infant from chronic ear infections that often plague infants with this defect. With an abundant milk supply and a thriving baby, you can further explore techniques for helping your infant learn to take milk by direct nursing. Corrective surgery is usually performed within weeks for cleft lip and by nine to twelve months for cleft palate. The commitment to express milk represents a true labor of love on the part of the mother who may not be able to nurse effectively for many months, if ever. I recall one mother who stored so much milk during the nine months she pumped that her baby was able to be fed breast milk for over a year.

If you are pregnant when the diagnosis is made, use the prenatal period to seek a surgeon who is supportive of your breastfeeding efforts and a lactation consultant with experience assisting other mothers of infants with clefts. I fondly recall a dedicated mom whose baby's cleft lip and palate were detected on prenatal ultrasound. After dealing with the initial shock of learning that her baby had a birth defect, this determined mother began interviewing plastic surgeons until she found one whose skill, demeanor, and philosophy impressed her most. She explored the option of a palatal prosthesis and contacted a local support group. She also met with breastfeeding specialists, rented an electric breast pump, and learned about alternative feeding methods and test weights. I was left feeling certain that never had a baby with a problem had a mom so prepared to cope with it.

Heart and lung disease. Other medical problems, such as a heart defect, chronic lung disease, Down syndrome, or low birth weight, can affect a baby's nursing effectiveness and make it difficult for the infant to obtain sufficient nutrition for adequate growth through breastfeeding alone. Infants with these medical problems fatigue easily, making it difficult for them to obtain enough milk during feedings, and they actually have increased nutrient needs compared with those of healthy babies. Because such infants may be unable to extract sufficient milk or stimulate an abundant milk supply by their own nursing efforts, their mothers should obtain a hospital-grade electric breast pump and express residual milk after most feedings. Pumping provides extra breast stimulation and emptying that can help preserve an abundant milk supply. It may be necessary to supplement some breastfeedings with expressed milk to ensure that an infant with a heart or lung condition receives adequate nutrition. The expressed milk can be fortified with extra nutrients if prescribed by the baby's doctor. Meanwhile, keeping your milk supply generous will help your baby obtain maximum volumes of milk during nursing sessions. I also highly recommend renting an accurate electronic infant scale for home use (see Resource List, page 450). Using such a scale allows parents to monitor their infant's weight closely and to perform periodic test weights to evaluate the baby's progress with breastfeeding.

Infant Hospitalization. Nursing infants may require hospitalization for a variety of reasons, such as serious infections, accidents, minor or major surgery, or cancer treatment. Fortunately, most pediatric wards allow parents to remain with their children at all times. Rooms may have couches or pull-down beds to accommodate parents overnight. Continued breastfeeding not only provides your baby with easily digested nutrients but also serves to calm and comfort your baby after necessary procedures and provides a sense of security and reassurance in unfamiliar surroundings. Make sure your baby's doctors and nurses know you are breastfeeding and try to convey to them the importance of the nursing relationship to your infant.

If your baby's intake of fluids must be monitored, offer to weigh your baby (identically clothed) before and after nursing sessions to document milk intake. Performing infant-feeding test weights might be a new concept for your doctor (see pages 333–334). The method is highly accurate if a reliable scale is used and the procedure is performed correctly. If your baby's oral intake is restricted for some reason, you might ask whether you could "comfort nurse" your baby after first expressing your milk with a breast pump to empty your breasts. Your baby will likely get only a trickle of milk when nursing after you have pumped. If your baby is having surgery, find out when you need to discontinue breastfeeding prior to surgery and how soon your baby can go to breast afterward. Whenever your infant isn't able to breastfeed on schedule or doesn't suckle vigorously, plan to use an effective breast pump to express your milk and maintain a generous supply.

Don't skip meals or neglect your fluid intake while you stay with your baby. Ask the nurses if you can arrange to receive meal trays, fruit juice, or snacks. Sometimes families have access to a communal refrigerator or microwave on the ward where you can store and prepare some convenience foods. If you periodically must go home to get some much-needed rest yourself, try to arrange for another familiar caretaker to remain with your baby if possible. You can leave your expressed milk to feed your infant in your absence. Don't forget to pump if you are gone more than a few hours. One of the most distressing aspects of your baby's hospitalization is the uncomfortable sense of near-total dependence on the care and expertise of others. Being able to nourish and comfort your baby by breastfeeding allows you to provide for your infant in a way no nurse or doctor possibly can. It helps restore a measure of control to a frightening situation by giving you something essential to do to benefit your baby.

Chapter 12

Nursing Your Older Baby and Weaning

For many women, weaning their breastfed infant represents the first among a host of developmental transitions that characterize childhood. The long journey involved in transforming a totally dependent newborn into a fully responsible, contributing adult is charted by a progressive series of transitional milestones, including weaning, becoming toilet-trained, starting kindergarten, entering puberty, or going off to college. It is our job as parents to serve as guides to see our child safely through the course, helping her at each junction to let go of old, familiar patterns and embrace new opportunities. In some instances, when circumstances magnify the sense of loss about what is being given up, negotiating life transitions can be uncomfortable, even painful, for both parents and children. On the other hand, when parents and children successfully move from one milestone to another with a sense of accomplishment and expectation, they emerge better equipped to navigate the next transition in a satisfying manner. For more than half of all infants in the United States, the process of weaning from the breast is one of their first significant transitions, making the topic worthy of an in-depth discussion.

What Is Weaning?

Few terms convey such broad connotations as the diverse meanings that can be expressed by the word "weaning." A single word hardly seems adequate to describe all of the following: breastfeeding that could stop at either three weeks or three years; the prolonged, gradual discontinuation of nursing and the abrupt termination of breastfeeding; a process that is initiated by the mother's desires and one that is guided by the baby's needs. Obviously, weaning can refer to diverse situations.

In the broadest sense, weaning begins as soon as an infant starts consuming any foods in addition to breast milk. Thus, the two-week-old baby who is given a daily bottle of formula has already begun the weaning process. An exclusively breastfed infant may not start to wean until solids are introduced at six months of age. Babies who enjoy the full natural course of breastfeeding, extending into the second or even third year, eventually spend more time weaning than breastfeeding exclusively.

Although weaning was meant to be a gradual process, sometimes abrupt termination of breastfeeding becomes necessary. This is especially difficult on mother and baby when an exclusively breastfed infant must be weaned suddenly.

Mother-Led Weaning

In our society, weaning is commonly structured around the mother's plans and desires. For example, many American women wean their babies prior to returning to work because they doubt they can combine breastfeeding and employment (see chapter 8). Women may commit to breastfeeding for an arbitrary length of time, such as six months, and then stop nursing when they reach their predetermined goal. Unfortunately, countless women who originally intended to nurse longer resign themselves to weaning early due to unresolved lactation difficulties that place a damper on their breastfeeding experience. Some women say they feel tied down by breastfeeding, especially when their babies refuse to accept nutrition by any other means. They may decide to wean in order to share responsibility for feedings with their partners. Other common mother-led reasons for weaning include to go on a strict weight-reduction diet, to resume alcohol consumption, to participate in certain athletic activities, or to go on a vacation with their partner. Probably the most frivolous explanation I've ever heard for early weaning was to be able to wear a particular gown to a formal affair!

Sometimes mother-led weaning occurs for more valid reasons. For example, I have known some older women who, having started their families late, decided to wean in order to increase their chances of conceiving another child. I also have encountered a number of women whose breastfed babies displayed severe allergic reactions to numerous foods in the mothers' diets. These dedicated women had restricted their own diets while breastfeeding, sometimes to a drastic degree. Once their babies were old enough to drink cow's milk, some of these women were anxious to wean in order to be able to eat a more varied diet.

A few women must wean their babies due to compelling health issues that leave them no choice. For example, a young mother with cystic fibrosis chose to wean her three-month-old infant because her lung function had deteriorated so rapidly while breast-feeding and she had lost excessive weight. In another heart-wrenching case, a woman was diagnosed with extensive breast cancer while exclusively breastfeeding her six-month-old baby. With her very survival at stake, the mother was forced to wean abruptly, much to her own and her baby's distress. Within a matter of days, she underwent a mastectomy and began a course of chemotherapy. I can't imagine the turmoil of emotions with which she must have wrestled as she reluctantly weaned her confused infant in the battle for her own health. Happily, this exceptional woman is alive and well, free of cancer, more than fifteen years later.

While most babies handle weaning without permanent trauma, sometimes a mother's decision to wean conflicts with a baby's health or emotional needs. I recall an infant with severe, chronic liver disease whose mother had managed to breastfeed her through multiple hospitalizations. After many months of nursing and providing specialized care for an extremely ill infant, the weary mother expressed her desire to wean. While I applauded this woman's remarkable efforts to that point and empathized with her wish for more control over her life, my compassion for her critically ill little girl was even greater. Breastfeeding clearly served as the principal source of consolation and pacification for this unfortunate, and often miserable, baby. Her tired mother wistfully imagined that weaning would bring respite from the near-constant care required by her chronically ill infant. In actuality, it was more probable that the sudden withdrawal of this child's emotional anchor would create more problems than it would solve. After a candid discussion, we attempted to balance the needs of both parties by validating the mother's weariness, providing her with regular breaks and sufficient opportunity to attend to her own needs, while allowing her sick infant to continue to nurse.

Whether the decision is based on a trivial want or a pressing need, the fact is that mothers often determine when breastfeeding stops. As a family advocate, I view my principal role in this matter as providing accurate information to enable parents to make the best possible decision given their unique circumstances. Then I commit to supporting parents, especially mothers, in the achievement of their goals. I know many well-meaning breastfeeding advocates whose mission is to prolong the duration of breastfeeding at any cost. However, coercing mothers to nurse or inflicting guilt when they decline to breastfeed does not serve families well. Many of the reasons for weaning that I cited above might be considered invalid by you or me. But I believe we must honor, and not judge, another woman's decision based on her circumstances and values. Whenever weaning occurs and whatever the reason, I believe emphasis should be given to validating the breastfeeding that was accomplished, rather than focusing on the breastfeeding that might have been.

Baby-Led Weaning

In cultures where unrestricted breastfeeding is the norm, weaning is a slow, baby-led process, geared to the baby's developmental needs. Among dozens of societies and cultures studied, breastfeeding extends into the third year, with the average age of weaning being around two and a half. The Bible contains references to weaning at age three, while the Koran calls for nursing until two years. In many cultures, breastfeeding continues to four years of age.

The gradual nature of the weaning process is captured by the expression "You never know when the last nursing has occurred." Toward the end of the transition, days or even weeks may elapse between nursings. Obviously, by this stage, the volume of milk is usually inconsequential. A nursing may last only a moment, as a

Nursing into toddlerhood is part of the natural course of breastfeeding.

youngster reassures himself of his mother's presence and love. What starts out as principally a method of feeding a newborn gradually evolves into principally a method of comforting and reassuring an increasingly independent toddler or preschooler. Baby-led weaning guarantees that the process is paced according to the child's unique dependency needs rather than society's expectations or the mother's preference. The chief advocate of child-led weaning in the United States is La Leche League. Bolstered by the support and example of like-minded peers, League members often nurse into their baby's third year or longer.

Late Nursing in the United States

Certainly, contemporary American patterns of breastfeeding are extremely abbreviated by worldwide standards. In the United States, only about 25 percent of babies are still being breastfed at six months of age and about 15 percent at one year. The result is pervasive unfamiliarity with the image of the older breastfed baby and inadequate social supports for achieving the full, normal course of breastfeeding. All too often, what is *uncommon* translates into what is *unacceptable*. Instead of commending those few American women who manage to breastfeed the full course, we are quick to pass judgment. "Are you *still* nursing?" "Don't you think she's too old for that?"

A number of years ago, a new intern at a teaching hospital was performing a two-year checkup on a little boy when the anxious toddler became upset, lifted his mother's blouse, and petitioned, "Nursy, nursy." The stunned intern had not even considered the possibility of breastfeeding at this age, and it never would have occurred to him to even ask about it. Now he wondered whether the child was developmentally appropriate. He made an excuse to slip out of the exam room so he could ask the attending physician in the clinic whether breastfeeding at this late age was normal and what he should do about it.

This encounter prompted the faculty member to schedule a teaching conference to discuss late nursing, and I was invited to serve as a consultant at the seminar. After hearing the brief case presentation, I decided to pose a few more questions before making my comments. "How often does the youngster nurse?" I inquired. After a brief pause, the puzzled intern hesitantly replied, "I suppose with his meals."

This story serves as a reminder of how ill-informed and unfamiliar our society is about late nursing. Few Americans have any appreciation for the full natural course of breastfeeding and the way a baby moves from depending on the breast as the sole source of food to relying on the breast for comfort and reassurance. The same intern who doubted the normalcy of a two-year-old requesting to nurse would have been unaffected if a three-year-old asked for his pacifier or began sucking his thumb.

It's little wonder that many American women resort to "closet nursing" their older babies to avoid incurring the hostile comments of an uninformed public. Some have their toddlers use code words for nursing to avoid exposing their secret, such as the woman who taught her twenty-month-old to announce, "I want a snack," when she wished to nurse. Intuitive toddlers soon learn not to ask for "milky" in certain settings, but to save their request until they arrive home. Not only is late nursing uncommon, but when it does occur, it is largely hidden from public view.

Unfortunately, the tendency for late nursing to be masked in the United States only serves to perpetuate the problem of lack of familiarity with breastfeeding older babies. Rather than succumbing to societal pressure to disguise the practice, the relatively few women who manage to achieve the full natural course of breastfeeding should be encouraged to talk about their experience with confidence. Publicizing the normalcy of late nursing is the only way to make Americans more comfortable with the image of the older nursing baby. Rather than hiding it, we need to implement de-sensitization strategies to increase Americans' exposure to late nursing.

Several years ago, I observed one such desensitization opportunity when I had the privilege of being a guest on the *Leeza Show*. The entire hour was devoted to various aspects of breastfeeding. Early in the show, a woman guest who was breastfeeding her newborn admitted that she had nursed her first son, Philip, until he was four years old. Philip, now seven, was seated in the audience next to his grandmother. He was a darling child—engaging, confident, and apparently quite normal. Leeza approached the youngster, mike in hand, and asked him if he remembered breastfeeding and what it was like. The boy, speaking softly and articulately, explained with great precision that breastfeeding was "warm . . . and sweet . . . and nice for babies." In this brief moment, Philip became an effective spokesperson for late nursing by demystifying and normalizing it.

Deciding When to Wean

My best advice about deciding when to wean is *not* to decide in advance. Instead, keep your options open. After all, how can you know before giving birth what the breastfeeding relationship will mean to you or your baby or just how intertwined feeding, comforting, and mothering can become? Just take one day at a time. And don't insist, "I could *never* nurse past a year." I don't know many new mothers who specifically plan to still be nursing two years later. These things just happen as successful breastfeeding takes its natural course. So stop worrying about *when* to wean and savor your breastfeeding experience. It's such a short and precious time out of your life. The American Academy of Pediatrics recommends that breastfeeding continue for *at least twelve months, and thereafter for as long as mutually desired.*

Common Myths About Weaning

Myth: *My baby weaned himself at an early age.*

Fact: The full natural course of breastfeeding was designed to continue a year or more. Yet, it's not uncommon for a woman to report that her baby "weaned himself" at four months or at seven months, for no apparent reason. Although these mothers might have liked to nurse longer, their babies just didn't cooperate. I am convinced that the usual common denominator in these cases of early weaning is insufficient milk and the regular use of formula supplements. When the production of breast milk diminishes and formula is readily available by bottle, many babies will develop a preference for bottle-feeding and progressively lose interest in nursing. I believe that few babies naturally wean before nine to twelve months if they are nursed at will, consume most or all of their milk from breastfeeding, and if the mother's milk supply is adequate. We may hear, "My baby just lost interest in breastfeeding and weaned himself before six months," but all too often excessive use of bottles and low milk production turn out to be the culprits behind premature weaning. The best prevention is unrestricted breastfeeding.

Myth: *Babies can't breastfeed once they have teeth.*

Fact: I once conducted a survey among about 250 newly delivered adolescent mothers who planned to breastfeed. In response to a question about how long they intended to nurse their babies, the most frequent reply was "until he gets teeth." The common assumption prevails that teeth make it impossible, even hazardous to the mother, for an infant to breastfeed. While a teething infant certainly can bite her mother's nipple, most breastfed infants quickly learn not to bite (see Biting, chapter 6, pages 210–211). Even babies with all twenty primary teeth can nurse without causing their mothers discomfort.

MYTH: *He's too old to still be nursing.*

FACT: Most Americans have acquired a certain comfort level with the image of the tiny, helpless newborn taking her life-sustaining nutrition at her mother's breast. As stated earlier, it's an entirely different matter when an active toddler scrambles onto his mother's lap, pulls at her buttons or lifts her blouse, and announces insistently, "Nummie, nummie." Women who nurse older babies often encounter rebuke and criticism: "I can't believe you're still doing *that*." "Do you plan to have him come home from kindergarten to nurse every day?" If you are the recipient of such barbs, please ignore them, trust your own heart, and know that you are doing the right thing for your baby when you allow her to wean at her own pace. Insist that you are following the doctor's advice (mine) and inform your critics that the American Academy of Pediatrics endorses nursing beyond a year. Believe that by meeting your child's dependency needs now, you will foster even greater independence later.

MYTH: *Everything will be better when you wean.*

FACT: Having a baby changes your life dramatically. Your commitments and priorities change. Your body changes. Sleep deprivation sometimes leaves you tired and discouraged. Your relationship with your spouse is renegotiated. Breastfeeding may bring temporary physical complaints like nipple soreness and breast tenderness. Perhaps as a result of the highly visible changes that accompany lactation and the intimacy of the nursing dyad, breastfeeding sometimes takes the rap for more than its share of the disruptions and adjustments that accompany the arrival of a new baby in the family.

Women with a wide-ranging spectrum of postpartum complaints for which medicine has no easy answers have been advised to wean, as if breastfeeding were the sole explanation for a new mother feeling fatigued, or a new father feeling left out, or a newborn being fussy. Weaning has been recommended to countless women, not only as the solution to frustrating lactation difficulties like cracked nipples or a breast infection, but as the answer to such divergent complaints as exhaustion, depression, marital conflict, sibling jealousy, illness in the mother, and even a painful episiotomy! After such ill-advised weaning, mothers discover the reality that babies still need to be fed and cared for, new fathers and siblings still feel displaced at times, fatigue and exhaustion still accompany sleep deprivation, young babies still fuss, and other parts of your body still ache from time to time. I urge you not to view weaning as a cure-all for the common ailments and discouragements of new parenthood. What you just might find out is that relinquishing the joy of breastfeeding gains you nothing, while adding resentment to your list of complaints.

Myth: *My husband/partner wants me to wean.*

Fact: Unfortunately, it is not uncommon for fathers and mothers to differ in their commitment to breastfeeding. When such differences exist, typically it is the mother who wants to continue nursing and the father who is pressuring her to wean (although, occasionally, it can be the other way around). All too often, a couple's overt disagreement over weaning is just one manifestation of broader conflict in the parental relationship. The way parents resolve their differing opinions about weaning usually reflects the way they handle other potential areas of conflict. Do they mutually encourage the expression of each other's feelings in a safe, accepting, and nonjudgmental atmosphere? Are they willing to compromise and negotiate mutually acceptable solutions? Or does one member dominate the relationship and impose his or her will on the other?

In my experience, when women give in to their husbands' demands about weaning, inevitable lingering resentment can further erode their relationship. Instead of passively submitting to a partner's demands, I would urge breastfeeding women to explore other possible motives their partners may have for advocating weaning. Maybe he feels the breasts are off-limits sexually as long as the mother is lactating. Perhaps he is jealous of the intimate bond between a nursing mother and baby. Maybe he is not sure what role he can play in the breastfeeding relationship. Often the husband's desire to see the baby weaned is simply a misdirected attempt to gain more of his partner's time and attention.

I recall a nurse who returned to work at the hospital while still breastfeeding her four-month-old baby. Juggling new parenthood, full-time employment, and breastfeeding left her little time or energy for nurturing her relationship with her husband. One day, she confided in me that her husband was pressuring her to wean the baby. After talking with her further, I began to suspect that the real issue behind her husband's demand was not whether she should continue breastfeeding. Rather, the conflict was about how they could renegotiate their marital relationship in the face of recent childbirth and dual-career parenting. This insight spurred the nurse to make some essential alterations in her schedule and to redirect some of her limited energies into her husband and her marriage. With a little extra attention from his wife, the husband stopped mentioning breastfeeding and no longer blamed it for making his partner unavailable to him. Once she began acknowledging him more, the husband became more willing to help his wife in practical ways that left her more energy for him. If breastfeeding seems to be impacting your marital relationship adversely, I urge you to review the section on the role of the father in the breastfeeding family (see chapter 6, pages 214–218).

Please also bear in mind that babies are extremely perceptive little beings who can detect divergent parental attitudes about nursing. I have observed older babies who seemed acutely aware of their father's resentment toward breastfeeding. This caused anxiety for the youngsters whenever they needed to nurse in their fathers' presence.

Ambivalence About Weaning

I find that most women acknowledge some ambivalence about discontinuing breastfeeding. Ambivalence is a good word to describe weaning because it evokes simultaneous feelings of attraction and repulsion. Along with the increased freedom that can accompany weaning comes the termination of one of the most unique, intimate, reciprocal relationships found in nature. One minute a nursing mother may complain of being tied down and wonder when her body will be her own again. A short while later, she may be tempted to awaken her child and offer her breast, finding nothing so dear as the comfort of a nursling. This natural ambivalence contributes to the indecisiveness that often surrounds weaning. Not only is some ambivalence perfectly normal, but it might be a clue to a woman's innermost feelings. Strong ambivalence suggests that you should examine more carefully whether this really is the right time to wean.

On the other hand, I must caution that a few women have such difficulty relinquishing the intimate breastfeeding relationship that they unwittingly allow their own need to continue the nursing relationship supersede their babies' need to wean. While it is highly appropriate to awaken a newborn baby to nurse if too much time has elapsed between feedings, toddlers should signal their need to nurse rather than having the breast offered to them. A helpful guideline suggested by La Leche League is "don't offer; don't refuse." If you find yourself regularly offering your breast to keep your older child nursing, chances are that your own ambivalence is getting in the way of letting your baby move on developmentally. In that case, you would be wise to acknowledge your pain and ambivalence, and then honor your baby's developmental timetable.

Recently, I dreamed that I gave birth to another baby, and was basking in the magnificent glow of new motherhood, with a warm, naked infant nestled contentedly at my breast. I awoke to the realization that all my children are grown, and I will never again relish the experience of breastfeeding. If I still miss breastfeeding twenty years after weaning my last child, is it any wonder that women express mixed emotions as they face this transition?

Suggestions for Structured Weaning

Despite the merits of baby-led weaning, many parents seek some structure in facilitating the weaning process. They may request help for introducing bottle-feedings to a baby whose mother is returning to work. Or, they may wish to implement guided weaning for their three-year-old.

Children vary widely in how they tolerate the weaning process. Some seem to adjust smoothly to decreasing breastfeeding, while others protest vehemently. What works for one baby may not for another. Babies over seven months of age may be able to wean directly to cup feedings, while younger infants usually will substitute a bottle for missed breastfeedings.

The most important principles of weaning are to have great empathy for your baby, to keep her needs foremost, and to proceed gradually, positively, and with love. Focus on substituting other

Drying Up

If the weaning process is kept gradual, your milk will taper slowly, and you shouldn't experience uncomfortable breast engorgement. The younger your baby is when you wean and the more abruptly you do it, the more likely it is that your breasts will become painfully full when your baby stops nursing. Abrupt weaning is uncomfortable, and it could predispose you to a breast infection. If you must stop nursing suddenly for some reason, you should use a breast pump to taper your milk production gradually. Wearing a good support bra, applying cold compresses to your breasts, and taking ibuprofen as directed also will help relieve breast discomfort due to rapid weaning.

When the milk supply drops markedly, the sodium content increases and milk tastes more salty. This phenomenon actually helps babies give up nursing when the supply becomes very low. A small amount of milk may continue to be produced for many months after weaning. It is not uncommon for a woman who has breastfed to be able to express a few drops of milk even a year or more later. Frequent attempts to check if milk is still present and lovemaking involving nipple stimulation may contribute to its continued production. Consult your doctor if you leak milk spontaneously or produce more than a few drops six months after weaning.

Your breasts should return to your prepregnancy size several months after weaning. Any droopiness or sagging that might be present is more related to having been pregnant and the skin elasticity you inherited than the fact that you breastfed.

Untimely Weaning

Untimely weaning refers to the discontinuation of breastfeeding before a mother had wanted to stop nursing. It is difficult for someone who has not breastfed her own baby to appreciate fully the enormous sense of disappointment that can accompany a woman's loss of her anticipated breastfeeding experience. Well-meaning physicians and others often underestimate what breastfeeding means to women and may exclaim with all sincerity, "I don't understand why you're so upset. Your baby will

forms of intimacy for the close nursing relationship that your baby is being asked to relinquish.

- **Consider the timing of weaning.** Try to structure weaning when your baby is losing interest in breastfeeding anyway. Some babies are easily distracted from nursing by nine months of age. If you haven't weaned by twelve to fifteen months, be aware that toddlers can become very attached to the breast as a security object, making weaning harder than it would have been earlier. Avoid weaning during times of family stress or turmoil in a baby's life, such as a divorce, move, hospitalization, or starting day care.

- **Whenever possible, plan to wean gradually rather than abruptly.** Gradual weaning is easier on both mother and baby. Requiring an infant to abruptly relinquish both his method of feeding and his principal source of comfort and security can be emotionally distressing. Furthermore, you won't want to stop nursing completely and drastically decrease your milk production until you are confident that your baby tolerates formula well. For younger infants, plan to eliminate one nursing at first, substituting formula for the skipped breastfeeding. Several days to a week later (depending on how rapidly you want to wean), you can replace a second nursing with a feeding of formula. Gradually tapering your breastfeeding also helps prevent your breasts from becoming uncomfortably engorged.

- **Eliminate first those nursings that hold the least interest for your child.** Certain nursings have special significance for a baby, who is sure to protest if you stop these breastfeeding sessions before she is ready. Perhaps you've been bringing your baby into your bed first thing in the morning and the two of you start the day with a leisurely nursing. Consider how special those times are for your little one. Or maybe you always nurse your baby to sleep for naps or at bedtime. Think about what you can substitute for the comfort, security, and intimacy of nursing.

It might help to keep a diary for a few days to note when, why, and how long your baby nurses. Try first to eliminate one of the midday nursings, or one when your baby typically stays at the breast for only a few minutes. Or, you might choose to omit an evening nursing, especially if your milk supply is noticeably lower in the evenings or if a substitute caretaker is available to take over.

- **Substitute other intimate activities.** Breastfeeding is such a highly effective method of soothing and quieting an upset child that it's easy to rely solely on nursing when other comforting measures might be equally effective. Consider whether there are times when you offer your breast to your child simply because it seems easier at the moment to restore calm. Or there may be times when your child nurses simply out of boredom. Children may resist weaning if nursing is the principal form of one-on-one attention they receive. Be creative as you taper nursing, and make sure you offer your child ample opportunities for comforting and interesting stimulation. When several children in the family compete for Mom's attention, the youngest may use nursing as a surefire way to get Mom all to himself. No wonder the last child often breastfeeds the longest! Try substituting rocking, cuddling, stroking, singing, reading a story, making a puzzle, or playing a game.

• **Wear inaccessible clothing.** A nursing toddler soon learns to pull at her mother's blouse buttons and lift her mother's shirt to nurse. Seeing the exposed breasts—for example, as you change clothes or emerge from the shower—will trigger the desire to nurse. When you are structuring weaning, try wearing clothing that is inaccessible for nursing, such as a one-piece dress that pulls over your head or zips up the back. Explain in a matter-of-fact tone that you simply aren't able to nurse right now because of what you are wearing. Although toddlers and preschoolers have a limited capacity to reason, your explanation may postpone their desire to nurse for a while, especially if you can distract your child with an interesting activity or offer some cuddling and extra hugs.

• **Change your routine and avoid situations where you normally would nurse.** If you had a favorite rocker where you often nursed, move it into the garage for a while. If you normally nursed while on the phone, keep calls short and remain standing while you talk. If you often nursed in front of the TV, don't watch any programming while your child is awake. If you want to eliminate the early-morning or bedtime nursing, ask Daddy to help out by being the one to get your child up or tuck her in at night.

• **Use a timer to limit the duration of nursings.** In addition to eliminating the number of breastfeedings, you can also structure the weaning process by limiting the length of nursings. If you try to end a nursing before your youngster is ready, it can feel like rejection to her. Instead, use a timer to monitor the length of some nursings. Explain to your child that when the sand is gone or the timer buzzes, you will have to stop nursing. Whereas a parent's limits might easily evoke an emotional response in a child, a neutral instrument like a timer can serve as an objective way to limit nursing.

• **Focus on your child's increasing independence.** Emphasize what a big girl she is becoming and the new privileges she enjoys, like going to preschool, becoming potty-trained, and staying overnight at Grandma's house. You can acknowledge how special nursing is for little babies and reminisce about her babyhood.

• **Enlist the help of other caretakers.** Encourage Daddy, grandparents, and baby-sitters to lavish extra love and affection on your child during the time she is tapering her nursing. They can help distract and entertain her and keep her preoccupied, especially at former nursing times. Their close involvement will remind your child that other loving adults can be effective sources of comfort and love.

• **Let your child know you have needs too.** One woman put Band-aids over her nipples and explained to her three-year-old that she had "owies" on her breasts and wouldn't be able to nurse anymore. Her cooperative and considerate child agreed to wean. Another mother told her child that her breasts were getting tired of making milk and wanted to rest now. When your child requests to nurse while you are doing something else, ask her to wait a few minutes until you are done.

• **Keep your sense of humor.** On those days when you wonder whether your breasts will ever belong to you again, remember that a sense of humor can help you maintain your perspective and a positive outlook. Every child does wean eventually, and late nursers are sure to leave their moms with some funny anecdotes. For example, I recall a woman whose recently weaned four-year-old gazed at her breasts in the bathtub and remarked, "Those used to be mine, but they're no use to me now." Another preschooler reluctantly weaned after announcing that his mother's breasts were "broken," since her milk flow had slowed to a trickle.

• **Don't put noxious substances on your nipples.** Although countless stories are told of women who have put foul-tasting substances on their nipples to dissuade a baby from nursing, I have never recommended this method. I must emphasize that nothing ever should be applied to the nipples that could prove to be toxic to a baby. Cases have been documented where babies were harmed by ingesting a potentially dangerous substance that was topically applied to the mother's nipples. Besides, don't you want your child to end your nursing relationship with positive memories and complete trust in you?

forms of intimacy for the close nursing relationship that your baby is being asked to relinquish.

• **Consider the timing of weaning.** Try to structure weaning when your baby is losing interest in breastfeeding anyway. Some babies are easily distracted from nursing by nine months of age. If you haven't weaned by twelve to fifteen months, be aware that toddlers can become very attached to the breast as a security object, making weaning harder than it would have been earlier. Avoid weaning during times of family stress or turmoil in a baby's life, such as a divorce, move, hospitalization, or starting day care.

• **Whenever possible, plan to wean gradually rather than abruptly.** Gradual weaning is easier on both mother and baby. Requiring an infant to abruptly relinquish both his method of feeding and his principal source of comfort and security can be emotionally distressing. Furthermore, you won't want to stop nursing completely and drastically decrease your milk production until you are confident that your baby tolerates formula well. For younger infants, plan to eliminate one nursing at first, substituting formula for the skipped breastfeeding. Several days to a week later (depending on how rapidly you want to wean), you can replace a second nursing with a feeding of formula. Gradually tapering your breastfeeding also helps prevent your breasts from becoming uncomfortably engorged.

• **Eliminate first those nursings that hold the least interest for your child.** Certain nursings have special significance for a baby, who is sure to protest if you stop these breastfeeding sessions before she is ready. Perhaps you've been bringing your baby into your bed first thing in the morning and the two of you start the day with a leisurely nursing. Consider how special those times are for your little one. Or maybe you always nurse your baby to sleep for naps or at bedtime. Think about what you can substitute for the comfort, security, and intimacy of nursing.

It might help to keep a diary for a few days to note when, why, and how long your baby nurses. Try first to eliminate one of the midday nursings, or one when your baby typically stays at the breast for only a few minutes. Or, you might choose to omit an evening nursing, especially if your milk supply is noticeably lower in the evenings or if a substitute caretaker is available to take over.

• **Substitute other intimate activities.** Breastfeeding is such a highly effective method of soothing and quieting an upset child that it's easy to rely solely on nursing when other comforting measures might be equally effective. Consider whether there are times when you offer your breast to your child simply because it seems easier at the moment to restore calm. Or there may be times when your child nurses simply out of boredom. Children may resist weaning if nursing is the principal form of one-on-one attention they receive. Be creative as you taper nursing, and make sure you offer your child ample opportunities for comforting and interesting stimulation. When several children in the family compete for Mom's attention, the youngest may use nursing as a surefire way to get Mom all to himself. No wonder the last child often breastfeeds the longest! Try substituting rocking, cuddling, stroking, singing, reading a story, making a puzzle, or playing a game.

• **Wear inaccessible clothing.** A nursing toddler soon learns to pull at her mother's blouse buttons and lift her mother's shirt to nurse. Seeing the exposed breasts—for example, as you change clothes or emerge from the shower—will trigger the desire to nurse. When you are structuring weaning, try wearing clothing that is inaccessible for nursing, such as a one-piece dress that pulls over your head or zips up the back. Explain in a matter-of-fact tone that you simply aren't able to nurse right now because of what you are wearing. Although toddlers and preschoolers have a limited capacity to reason, your explanation may postpone their desire to nurse for a while, especially if you can distract your child with an interesting activity or offer some cuddling and extra hugs.

• **Change your routine and avoid situations where you normally would nurse.** If you had a favorite rocker where you often nursed, move it into the garage for a while. If you normally nursed while on the phone, keep calls short and remain standing while you talk. If you often nursed in front of the TV, don't watch any programming while your child is awake. If you want to eliminate the early-morning or bedtime nursing, ask Daddy to help out by being the one to get your child up or tuck her in at night.

• **Use a timer to limit the duration of nursings.** In addition to eliminating the number of breastfeedings, you can also structure the weaning process by limiting the length of nursings. If you try to end a nursing before your youngster is ready, it can feel like rejection to her. Instead, use a timer to monitor the length of some nursings. Explain to your child that when the sand is gone or the timer buzzes, you will have to stop nursing. Whereas a parent's limits might easily evoke an emotional response in a child, a neutral instrument like a timer can serve as an objective way to limit nursing.

• **Focus on your child's increasing independence.** Emphasize what a big girl she is becoming and the new privileges she enjoys, like going to preschool, becoming potty-trained, and staying overnight at Grandma's house. You can acknowledge how special nursing is for little babies and reminisce about her babyhood.

• **Enlist the help of other caretakers.** Encourage Daddy, grandparents, and baby-sitters to lavish extra love and affection on your child during the time she is tapering her nursing. They can help distract and entertain her and keep her preoccupied, especially at former nursing times. Their close involvement will remind your child that other loving adults can be effective sources of comfort and love.

• **Let your child know you have needs too.** One woman put Band-aids over her nipples and explained to her three-year-old that she had "owies" on her breasts and wouldn't be able to nurse anymore. Her cooperative and considerate child agreed to wean. Another mother told her child that her breasts were getting tired of making milk and wanted to rest now. When your child requests to nurse while you are doing something else, ask her to wait a few minutes until you are done.

• **Keep your sense of humor.** On those days when you wonder whether your breasts will ever belong to you again, remember that a sense of humor can help you maintain your perspective and a positive outlook. Every child does wean eventually, and late nursers are sure to leave their moms with some funny anecdotes. For example, I recall a woman whose recently weaned four-year-old gazed at her breasts in the bathtub and remarked, "Those used to be mine, but they're no use to me now." Another preschooler reluctantly weaned after announcing that his mother's breasts were "broken," since her milk flow had slowed to a trickle.

• **Don't put noxious substances on your nipples.** Although countless stories are told of women who have put foul-tasting substances on their nipples to dissuade a baby from nursing, I have never recommended this method. I must emphasize that nothing ever should be applied to the nipples that could prove to be toxic to a baby. Cases have been documented where babies were harmed by ingesting a potentially dangerous substance that was topically applied to the mother's nipples. Besides, don't you want your child to end your nursing relationship with positive memories and complete trust in you?

Drying Up

If the weaning process is kept gradual, your milk will taper slowly, and you shouldn't experience uncomfortable breast engorgement. The younger your baby is when you wean and the more abruptly you do it, the more likely it is that your breasts will become painfully full when your baby stops nursing. Abrupt weaning is uncomfortable, and it could predispose you to a breast infection. If you must stop nursing suddenly for some reason, you should use a breast pump to taper your milk production gradually. Wearing a good support bra, applying cold compresses to your breasts, and taking ibuprofen as directed also will help relieve breast discomfort due to rapid weaning.

When the milk supply drops markedly, the sodium content increases and milk tastes more salty. This phenomenon actually helps babies give up nursing when the supply becomes very low. A small amount of milk may continue to be produced for many months after weaning. It is not uncommon for a woman who has breastfed to be able to express a few drops of milk even a year or more later. Frequent attempts to check if milk is still present and lovemaking involving nipple stimulation may contribute to its continued production. Consult your doctor if you leak milk spontaneously or produce more than a few drops six months after weaning.

Your breasts should return to your prepregnancy size several months after weaning. Any droopiness or sagging that might be present is more related to having been pregnant and the skin elasticity you inherited than the fact that you breastfed.

Untimely Weaning

Untimely weaning refers to the discontinuation of breastfeeding before a mother had wanted to stop nursing. It is difficult for someone who has not breastfed her own baby to appreciate fully the enormous sense of disappointment that can accompany a woman's loss of her anticipated breastfeeding experience. Well-meaning physicians and others often underestimate what breastfeeding means to women and may exclaim with all sincerity, "I don't understand why you're so upset. Your baby will